A SHORT HISTORY OF
SCOTLAND

A SHORT HISTORY OF SCOTLAND

R. L. MACKIE

Edited by
GORDON DONALDSON

FREDERICK A. PRAEGER, *Publisher*
NEW YORK

BOOKS THAT MATTER

Published in the United States of America in 1963
by Frederick A. Praeger, Inc., Publisher
64 University Place, New York 3, N.Y.

Library of Congress Catalog Card Number: 63-15343

Printed in Great Britain

PREFACE TO REVISED EDITION

THE late Dr Mackie's *Short History of Scotland* won a well-deserved reputation as a work which was at once lucid, readable and accurate. When the author wrote, he took account of what were then the latest findings of historical research, but the further work done in the past generation has made some revision of the text necessary. Besides, the changing emphasis of historical studies has made it desirable that more extended treatment should be given to the history of Scotland since the Union of 1707. In this new edition, the pre-history has been omitted, the section on Roman Scotland re-written, and new chapters added on the history of the past two and a half centuries. On the other hand, a certain amount of detail which seemed irrelevant to the needs of the modern reader has been excised. Even in the re-written and new chapters, however, it has been found possible to incorporate some of Dr Mackie's phraseology and thought, and throughout the entire book his wide sympathies and his feeling for the whole of Scotland's heritage are still reflected.

I owe a great deal to consultation with my colleague Dr Ranald Nicholson, who read the entire text in proof.

GORDON DONALDSON

Edinburgh, 1961

ACKNOWLEDGMENTS

PLATES

1 (upper) Reproduced by permission of the Committee for Aerial Photography, University of Cambridge.

1 (lower), 4, 18, 46, 47, 58: Photographs by Scottish National Museum of Antiquities, Queen Street, Edinburgh.

2, 5, 6, 14, 25: Reproduced by permission of the Clarendon Press, Oxford, and the Exclusive News Agency.

3, 60 Photographs by Valentine, Dundee.

7, 19, 20, 31, 34, 35, 39, 40, 51, 56, 69, 72: Photographs by Scotsman Publications.

8 Reproduced by courtesy of the University Court of the University of Aberdeen from A. C. O'Dell, *St. Ninian's Isle Treasure*, Oliver and Boyd, 1960.

9, 12, 22, 24, 45 (lower): Reproduced by courtesy of The Keeper of the Records of Scotland, H.M. Register House, Edinburgh.

10 Reproduced from Brøgger and Shetelig: *The Viking Ships*.

11 Reproduced from a print of the old tapestry.

13, 17, 28 Crown copyright reserved: reproduced by permission of H.M. Ministry of Works.

15 Reproduced by permission from W. P. Simpson: *The Castle of Bergen and the Bishop's Palace at Kirkwall*, Oliver and Boyd, 1961.

16 Photograph by Douglas Scott.

21 Reproduced by courtesy of the Dean and Chapter of Westminster.

23, 41, 45 (upper), 55: Reproduced by courtesy of The Librarian, The National Library of Scotland.

23 (lower) Reproduced by permission: Archives der Haustestadt, Lübeck.

26 Reproduced by permission of W. F. Mansell, Red Lion Court, London.

27 Reproduced by permission from Sir F. C. Mears: *Edinburgh, 1329–1929*, Oliver and Boyd, 1929.

29, 37, 71 Photographs by Robert M. Adam.

30, 43 Reproduced by gracious permission of H.M. the Queen.

32 Photograph by G. M. Cowie, St. Andrews.

33 Reproduced from R. Billings, *Baronial Antiquities of Scotland*.

36 (upper) Reproduced by courtesy of the Scottish National Museum of Antiquities, Queen Street, Edinburgh (original coin in the British Museum).

36 (lower) Reproduced from a Glasgow university student's notebook. The original is in the National Library of Scotland.

38 Reproduced by permission of the Chatsworth Estates Co.

42 Reproduced by courtesy of Bibliothèque Nationale, Paris.

ACKNOWLEDGMENTS

Plates	
44	Reproduced from State Papers by permission of The Public Record Office, London.
48	Reproduced by permission of the Trustees of the National Maritime Museum, London.
49	Reproduced by permission of W. and R. Chambers Ltd., from their *Shrines and Homes of Scotland.*
50	Reproduced by permission from M. R. Kelsall and S. Harris: *A Future for the Past*, Oliver and Boyd, 1961.
52	Reproduced from Hogenberg's print which was first published in 1582.
53, 64	Reproduced by courtesy of Edinburgh Corporation: Public Libraries.
54	Photograph by Francis Caird Inglis, Edinburgh.
57	Crown copyright reserved: reproduced by permission from *The Official Guide* to the Historical Museum of the Scottish Record Office, H.M. Stationery Office.
59	Reproduced from the original by Sir Henry Raeburn, photograph by T. and R. Annan, Glasgow.
61	Reproduced by permission from G. Hay: *The Architecture of Scottish Post-Reformation Churches,* Clarendon Press, Oxford.
62	Photograph by Alinari, Rome.
63	Photograph by *The Daily Mail.*
65	Reproduced from D. O. Hill's Views of the Opening of the . . . Railway (1832).
66	Reproduced from photograph supplied by British Railways, Waterloo Place, Edinburgh.
67	Reproduced by courtesy of Captain Wm. Reid, Master of Trinity House, Leith. This illustration was selected from his fine collection of prints and photographs of nineteenth century " Clippers ".
68	Photograph by John Brown and Co., Clydebank.
70	Photograph by E. W. Tattersall.
73	Crown copyright reserved: reproduced by permission of The Controller of H.M. Stationery Office, London.

CONTENTS

CONTENTS

ILLUSTRATIONS

LIST OF ILLUSTRATIONS

LIST OF ILLUSTRATIONS

Plate 1 Roman Remains

Site of Roman Fort at Birrens, Dumfriesshire.

Stone erected at the east end of the Antonine Wall, near Bo'ness, commemorating the completion of the first stretch of the wall by the Second Legion.

CHAPTER 1

THE BEGINNINGS OF SCOTTISH HISTORY

FROM the middle of the first Christian century until the beginning of the fifth, there was a province of the Roman empire known as "Britain," but it never included the whole island, and the Roman power only occasionally, and for brief periods, extended into even the southern parts of what is now Scotland. Scotland, or most of it, had little to attract the conqueror, and what interest the Romans had in it was incidental to their concern in maintaining their hold, in peace and security, on southern Britain.

A generation after the beginning of the Roman conquest in 43 A.D., the Roman power had been consolidated in southern and central England, and it became necessary to settle, in one way or another, Rome's relations with the western and northern areas. One of the tribes of northern England, the Brigantes, extended across the Cheviots into south-western Scotland, and it is likely that as a result of operations against them a Roman force penetrated into Annandale between 71 and 74.

In the year 80, Julius Agricola, who had come to Britain as governor two years earlier and had made it his first task to subdue North Wales, moved against Scotland. The account of his invasion, written by his son-in-law, Tacitus, is not easy to follow in detail, but it seems clear that in a series of campaigns Agricola advanced into Scotland by a western route from Carlisle through Annandale and upper Clydesdale and also by an eastern route over the Cheviots to Newstead, near Melrose, and that he even conducted operations along the north coast of the Solway and probably in Ayrshire as well.

His two routes northwards converged at Inveresk or at Cramond, on the Firth of Forth, and he then built a chain of forts or military posts across to the Firth of Clyde. After thus securing southern Scotland, Agricola advanced, probably in 83, by a route from Stirling on towards Perth. He did his work thoroughly, for he did not believe in showy victories followed by undignified retreats: his fort at Ardoch, between Stirling and Perth, was defended by seven ditches, and at Roughcastle, on the Forth-Clyde isthmus, rows of pits were dug and pointed stakes concealed in them. A fleet cruised off the east coast, to show the might of Rome and to bring supplies to the camps which Agricola so often formed near navigable rivers and estuaries.

At Inchtuthil, at the entrance to Strathmore, the Romans built a great fortified camp as a base for future operations, and from it in 84 a farther advance was made which brought Agricola face to face with a large native force, formed through the union of several tribes in the face of common danger. The site of the battle which followed has never been determined: some would place it in the north-eastern part of Strathmore, near Forfar or Brechin, others farther north still, near Stonehaven, and it has even been argued that it was as far north as Banffshire. At any rate, somewhere in the region between the Firth of Tay and the Moray Firth, on the slopes of a great hill called Mons Graupius, the Britons or Caledonians were waiting for Agricola. They were commanded by the chieftain Calgacus, the first native of Scotland whose name has been handed down to us. The battle, though not a complete route of the tribesmen, was a Roman victory which enabled Agricola to march through the territories of some of the native peoples and receive hostages from them, while his fleet cruised northwards to, and beyond, the farthest extremity of the coast, so demonstrating that Britain was an island.

In the year after Mons Graupius, Agricola was recalled; about the same time one of the four legions that formed the backbone of the Roman army in Britain was transferred to Germany. The successors of Agricola contented themselves with defending as much as they could of the territory which Agricola had gained. About 115, however, the tribes in Scotland and the north of England turned upon the Roman garrisons; fort after fort was assailed and captured; the luckless Ninth Legion marched northward to the relief of the beleaguered garrisons and was never heard of again. So serious did the situation become that in the year 122 the Emperor Hadrian himself came to Britain to restore order. He succeeded, but he decided that Scotland was not worth the trouble which it had given him, and that a line of stone forts between the Tyne and the Solway should become the northern boundary of the province of Britain. A deep ditch, stretching from sea to sea, marked the exact position of the northern limit of empire; within a few years the distinction between the peaceful south and the unconquered north was emphasised still further by a great wall of stone.

But it seemed to the Roman commanders that something more was needed, some kind of breakwater or outpost line away to the north, where troops could be stationed to check a southward movement of the tribes before it had well begun. So in the reign of the Emperor Antoninus Pius, about the year 140, the legions, with Lollius Urbicus, the governor of the province, at their head, took the road once more. They were making for the line of deserted forts that Agricola had built across the isthmus of the Forth and Clyde. Along this line they now built a rampart of earth, ten feet high and six feet broad at the top, which stretched without a break for thirty-nine miles, from Carriden on the south side of the Firth of Forth to Old Kilpatrick on the north side of the Firth of Clyde. Nineteen forts abutted on the wall, and its flanks were protected by outlying forts on the Forth and Clyde estuaries.

About 154, when a rebellion was raging farther south, the Britons broke through and forced the Romans to abandon the line of the Forth and Clyde. The rebellion was suppressed; the Romans came back, repaired the damaged forts, and waited. Again the Britons broke through; again some of the forts were lost and recovered.

In the confusion of another rebellion, about 185, the wall of Lollius Urbicus was abandoned, but not till the barracks had been set on fire and the boundary slabs, set up proudly by the legionaries forty years before, removed from their places and laid face downwards upon the ground. The same thing happened at Newstead and the other southern forts; altars were buried to save them from desecration, and everything that would burn was set on fire. Soon the last soldier disappeared over the slopes of the Cheviots, leaving behind him as memorials of the ineffectual might of Rome the smoking ruins of the forts and the long empty road.

The Romans did return to Scotland, however. In 208 the stout-hearted old Emperor, Septimius Severus, sailed into the Forth at the head of a fleet, seized on the deserted harbour of

Cramond, and used it as a base whence he launched an attack on Fife and north-eastern Scotland. He did succeed in forcing a way through the marshes and forests of this unexplored country, and bringing many of the Caledonians to surrender. He returned south to make plans for the conquest of what he knew was a still unconquered country, but after his death in 211 all these plans were abandoned. Yet for a century or so after the campaign of Severus, although Hadrian's Wall remained the Roman frontier, there was no serious fighting with the tribes, and the inhabitants of Scotland had much peaceful intercourse with the Roman province to the south.

Even of the Romans we know little enough, for the scanty scraps of information they have left us have to be eked out with other scraps gained from a careful examination of their forts and settlements. The inscribed slabs fixed at intervals along the Antonine Wall, for example, let us know that it was built by men of the Second, Sixth, and Twentieth Legions, and altars found within the forts give us the names of the cohorts that garrisoned the Wall after it was completed.

But the natives have left neither histories nor inscriptions to help us. Still, one or two things are certain; they were not savages, nor were they forever fighting against the Romans. Some of them at any rate dwelt in little towns, collections of wattled huts arranged in regular rows on some level hill-top. They tilled the soil, cut the grain with bronze or iron sickles, and carried the sheaves to their hill-towns in carts drawn by horses. They seem to have spoken a language very closely akin to, though not exactly the same as, that spoken by the Britons south of the Tweed. Probably, like the Gauls, they wore tunics and breeches of brightly coloured cloth, but not a shred of these garments is left, though many spindle-whorls—perforated stones which they used when they spun the thread—and loom-weights of clay have been picked up. Some of these spindle-whorls are not stone at all, but pieces of glazed red pottery—Samian ware it was called—from the Roman potteries in Gaul. Hundreds of other fragments, both of Samian ware and of other kinds of Roman pottery, have been picked up on the sites of the dwellings of those early inhabitants of Scotland.

The natives evidently preferred the beautiful glass and earthenware vessels that the Romans made to the clumsy products of their

A ROMAN WARSHIP, MANNED BY LEGIONARY SOLDIERS
From a marble bas-relief.

Plate 3

The Broch of Mousa, Shetland

own potteries, and this trade went on after the Antonine Wall had been abandoned. From Roman traders the natives learned the use of coins as a medium of exchange, and so Roman coins found their way into the remotest corners of Scotland, into regions that neither Agricola nor Severus had ever seen. As with the coins, so with the fragments of Samian ware; we find them in dwellings that no Roman ever built, in the "crannogs" for example, in the "weems" or earth-houses, and in the "brochs" that dot the shores of northern Scotland and rise beside the voes and flows of Orkney and Shetland.

The crannogs were artificial islands or natural islands which had been enlarged with stones, earth and wooden piles. The inhabitants crossed to and from the mainland by causeways of stone or wood an inch or two beneath the surface of the water.

A weem was a long narrow tunnel, anything from fifty to a hundred and ninety feet long, made by digging a trench, about six feet deep, and roofing it over either with branches or with large stone slabs, on the top of which earth was piled. In some earth-houses the tunnel was approached by a flight of well-hewn stone steps, and it usually bulged out after a certain distance to form a fairly commodious chamber. Even should an enemy discover the weem, the occupants had little to fear, for a too bold pursuer would probably trip over the slab set on end across the tunnel and be dispatched before he could rise; if he escaped that danger he might be stabbed as he tried to squeeze past the stone pillar set in the middle of the passage, or take the wrong turning in the darkness, and meet the dagger of his foe as he blundered back.

Far more imposing structures were the brochs—massive round towers sometimes as much as sixty feet high and sixty feet in diameter. Their enormously thick walls, built of unmortared stone, rose unbroken on the outside by any window opening. The wall was hollow: it contained stairways and galleries, lighted by openings on the inner side of the wall. The circular space enclosed by the wall was presumably covered with a roof of stone slabs or of timber, little more than six feet high, and above this the interior of the tower was open to the air. An enemy would find the broch as difficult to tackle as the earth-house. There were no windows on the outside through which he could send an arrow; he could gain the interior of the broch only by squeezing himself through a low and narrow doorway, and crouching almost double in a long, low passage. He would be lucky if he got to the end of the passage, for over the passage was a guard-room with a hole in the floor, through which a sword or a spear could easily be thrust into a stooping back.

While excavations can reveal so much to us about the homes of the people north of the Roman wall, and about their way of life, a great deal happened among them that we cannot understand. From the end of the third century, tribes that had remained quiet for generations were seized with a strange restlessness. It may be that the long years of peace had allowed their numbers to increase but had not brought a corresponding increase in the supply of food. It may be that the people of the brochs were pressing southward and spreading confusion among the more civilised Britons immediately to the north of the Wall; and that the confusion was increased by the Scots from the north of Ireland, who in the fourth century began to harry the west coast of Britain, as well as by Saxon pirates from the continent who had begun to plunder the eastern shores.

The fall of the Roman province was due only partly to attacks from outside. It was due partly to internal weaknesses in the Empire. Time and again the imperial throne was vacant and might be the prize of any soldier bold enough to seize it. The generals in Britain were determined not to be left out of the scramble, and repeatedly one of them took his troops off to the continent in an attempt to make himself master of Rome, leaving Britain stripped of the forces which should have been defending it. This had happened for the first time at the end of the second century, and the consequence had been furious incursions from the north, remedied by the work of Severus. It happened again almost exactly a century later, and this time the province was assailed by Scots on the west and by Picts, as the inhabitants of Scotland were now called, on the east. Thereafter attacks went on intermittently.

In 367 it seemed as if the province of Britain were to be lost to the Empire: the invaders swept right through the Midlands and got within a few miles of the walls of London; bands of them even appeared in Kent. But the inevitable collapse was delayed for another half-century; in 368 the Roman general Theodosius crossed to Britain at the head of a large army, swept the invaders back over the Wall, recaptured the forts that they had taken, and repaired their broken ramparts. But when Theodosius departed, back they came—Pict, Scot, and Saxon. If the Roman regular troops had stood by them, if the Roman commanders had been faithful to their trust, the Romanised Britons of the south might have beaten off these northern kinsfolk of theirs that they had come to regard as barbarians. But once again a Roman commander was turned from his duty by the lure of the imperial throne. The Spaniard Magnus Maximus in 383 proclaimed himself emperor, and squandered part of the precious garrison of Britain in an attempt to make himself master of Rome.

The attenuated garrisons of the province were reinforced after the death of Maximus, but the Roman counter-attacks weakened as Rome herself fell under the hammer of barbarian onslaughts, and could spare no forces for Britain. And the town-dwelling Latin-speaking Britons of the south could not defend themselves by their own exertions.

Farther and yet farther did the raiders penetrate into the country, away into peaceful regions of meadows and cornlands, of stone-built villas rising white among blossoming orchards, regions where there were no fortresses, where troops had not been seen for hundreds of years. Places like these were a tempting and easy prey.

Of Scotland in these dark years we know next to nothing. Yet it does seem that down to the very last days of the Roman province, and even beyond them, there were Romanised or partially Romanised Britons in southern Scotland, maintaining what they could of an organised civilisation despite the constant threat and the frequent attacks of Scot, Pict and Saxon.

CHAPTER 2

NINIAN AND COLUMBA

THOUGH Christianity reached southern Britain during the Roman occupation, we look in vain for any sign of church or altar in the Roman forts north of Hadrian's Wall. Altars have been found in plenty, but they are dedicated to Mars, to Mercury, to Fortune, to the Emperor, to the strange gods of the Britons, or to the gods whom the soldiers believed to watch over their own distant homes.

Some sculptured stones found in a remote corner of southern Scotland tell another story. Three of them come from the old churchyard of Kirkmadrine, in Wigtownshire. On each appears the same design—a circle surrounding an equal-armed cross, one arm of which forms the Greek letter *P*. The equal-armed cross itself stood for the Greek letter *X*, equivalent to English *Ch*, and, along with the *P*, equivalent to English *R*, it represented the first letters of *Χριστός* or Christ. All three crosses bear Latin inscriptions, one of which may be translated as "Here lie the holy and renowned priests Viventius and Mavorius." A fourth slab, with the same symbol upon it, was found at Whithorn, a few miles farther east.

What is the meaning of these Roman names and this Christian symbol—a symbol that began to be used on the Continent about the end of the fourth century? The strange answer is that at the very time when Roman Britain was distracted by the onslaughts of Picts, Saxons, and Scots, a Romanised Briton settled in the country to the north of the Wall, and tried to convert the Picts to Christianity. His name was Ninian, he is said to have visited Rome itself, to have talked with the great St. Martin of Tours and to have brought with him from St. Martin's monastic settlement at Tours men skilled in the building of churches. With these followers he made his way westward to the secluded peninsula of Whithorn. Here, on the shore of Wigtown Bay, he began, possibly in 397, to build Candida Casa—"the white house"—the first Christian church to be built in Scotland.

Ninian may not have been content, as people once believed, with the evangelisation of one little corner of Scotland; he may have gone on missionary journeys that took him farther and farther afield, as far as the great mountain mass which stretches inland from Aberdeen.

Meantime much was happening in other parts of the island. Early in the fifth century the Saxon pirates began to make permanent settlements on the southern shores of the province, which they had plundered and rendered desolate. Adventurers of a kindred race, the Angles, planted themselves on the east coast, and about the middle of the sixth century began to raid Lothian, the name given in early times to the whole of the region between the Forth and the Tweed. That region became part of the Anglian kingdom of Northumbria.

This barbarian conquest of Britain proceeded slowly, and with many long pauses, for the Britons resisted stubbornly, but at length they had to fall back into the barren and mountainous west, leaving the fertile plain of the midlands and south to the invader. Some of them took refuge in Wales and Cornwall, others made their way across the ruined and deserted Wall into south-western Scotland. It was on these rolling moorlands that the British hero, Arthur, fought some of his battles against the encroaching heathen, and, according to the old Border tradition, it is in a great cavern under the Eildons that he lies entranced, with all his knights about him.

Thus there were Britons in south-western Scotland. The sea-rovers from the north of Ireland, too, had begun to make settlements in Kintyre and by the shores of the sea-lochs in Argyll; in 501 Fergus, son of Erc, a Scot from Ireland, became the first king of this new Scottish kingdom of Dalriada. The Scots spoke a Celtic language, which, however, differed so much from the speech of the Picts and Britons as to be all but unintelligible to them. It is from this language that modern Irish and modern Scottish Gaelic are descended. The Scots had some tincture of Christianity: before the middle of the fifth century Patrick, a Briton, had brought the Gospel to Ireland, and so, when the churches in the parts of Britain overrun by the pagans lay empty and silent, the sound of the bell calling to prayer could be heard from many a green Irish valley.

In the middle of the sixth century Scotland was only a

name. In fact, it was not even that: not till the tenth century was the name "Scotland" applied to the country north of the Cheviots. It seemed hopeless to expect that out of this medley of races a single nation, subject to one king, obeying one code of laws, could ever be evolved. There was one king in Dalriada and others in Pictland. How could these two hostile kingdoms ever be united? And even if they were united, what of the lands south of the Forth? There seemed no possibility of Lothian escaping the clutches of the Northumbrian kings; on the other hand it seemed highly probable that the Angles, after possessing themselves of Lothian, would add Fife and Angus to their other conquests. Likewise the country between the Clyde and the Solway formed part of a great British kingdom, which, even after the victory of the Angles at Chester in 613 cut it off from Wales, still stretched south as far as the Cheshire Dee.

Meantime it fared ill with the Scots: in the year 559 they were defeated in battle by the Pictish king, Brude mac Maelchon. It seemed as if they must come under the yoke of the Picts, but four years later a strange ally appeared. They called him Columba, "the dove," but it would have been hard to see anything dove-like in this loud-voiced, aggressive Irish ecclesiastic. Enraged by the insistence of the Irish king Diarmit that he should give up a copy he had secretly made of another priest's psalter, Columba stirred up his friends, and in 560 defeated Diarmit at the battle of Cuildremne. But his triumph turned to bitterness; people shrank from the turbulent priest whose obstinacy had cost the lives of so many men. According to an old story, he was ordered to go into exile, and forbidden to return to Ireland, or even to come within sight of it, until the number of souls he saved equalled the number of those that he had caused to perish in battle. Be that as it may, he had made Ireland, for the time, too hot for him. He landed on Iona, off the west coast of Scotland, in 563, with twelve companions, and proceeded to build a little monastery, after the pattern of the ecclesiastical settlements that were familiar to him in Ireland.

As all the Irish clergy were monks, they did not live among ordinary people, but lived apart in self-contained communities. Within an enclosure the most important building was the church, a building so small that priest and worshippers often stayed outside while the psalms were being sung and the gospel read. At first the church was only a hut of clay and wattles, but after a time logs of pine and oak were floated over from the mainland, and a more substantial building erected. At a little distance from the church stood the huts of the monks, for, unlike the monks of the later Middle Ages, they did not share the same dormitory, but each had his beehive-shaped hut of wattle and daub, or of unmortared stones. There were other buildings: a guest-house, a granary, cattle-sheds, and stables. Two huts were set apart for Columba: one, which was floored with planks of wood, was his study and contained the library of the monastery; in the other, where there was no floor but the bare earth, he lay at night, with his head resting upon a pillow of stone.

Though Columba became gentler, more considerate of others, his fierce, unsleeping spirit would not let him rest. He would study and write all day, and stay awake half the night chanting the psalms in the black darkness of the little church or under the stars on the seashore. But there were times when this seemed inglorious ease, when he would order a boat to be manned and set out with one or two companions on a long and perilous journey. The first and most famous of the journeys, made soon after he settled in Iona, took him to the stronghold of the Pictish king, on the banks of the River Ness. For Columba was a statesman as well as a missionary; before he left Ireland he knew that his kinsmen the Scots were in danger of being overwhelmed altogether by the Picts, and he seems to have resolved to plead their cause before the victorious King Brude.

When he came to the King's stronghold he found that the gates had been barred against him. He touched the ponderous timbers with the cross that he carried, whereupon the bolts clattered back and the doors swung open. It seemed to his simple-minded followers that the saint had worked a miracle, and their belief was confirmed when the King himself stepped forward to greet the saint.

The King promised to stay his hand against the Scots and to refrain from hindering Columba in his missionary work. But the priests of the old religion who frequented the palace looked on the stranger with no friendly eye; a few days later they came up to Columba and his companions as they were singing psalms outside the green ramparts of Brude's stronghold and tried to interrupt the service by shouting some heathen chant of their own. But lo! another miracle. The saint sang the forty-fifth psalm so lustily that the heathen could not make themselves heard, and shrank away defeated. Again, when the missionaries were delayed by contrary winds on their homeward journey down Loch Ness, they were convinced that the revengeful pagans had raised a magic gale, and when the saint uttered a prayer and the wind died away, they believed that he had wrought still another miracle. We may smile at these "miracles"; we must not smile at the courage and devotion that made Columba brave not only the imaginary dangers from wizards and demons and water-kelpies, but the very real dangers from wind-swept seas, flooded rivers, and barbarous men.

Many marvelled at his gentleness and humility. It seemed strange to them that a man who was master of a great ecclesiastical organisation should wash the feet of the brethren, or carry sacks of corn to the mill. They told how, when a robber who had, time and again, killed seals belonging to the monastery was brought before him, Columba simply inquired why he had not asked for food instead of stealing it and told him that he would get all that he required in future. But there were times when the saint hurled the most terrible curses at the heads of people who had thwarted him, or prophesied horrible deaths for his enemies. On the other hand, we are told that when, a few days before his death, the white horse that drew the monastery milk-cart came up to him and nuzzled into his bosom, he forbade his servant to drive it away, and gave the affectionate beast his blessing. And his last utterance to his monks was a prayer that they would live together in unfeigned charity and peace.

Columba died in 597, but his influence grew and spread far beyond the bounds of Dalriada. A few days before his death he had climbed to the little hill that overlooks the monastery and, looking down on it, had blessed it. "Upon this place," he declared, "small and mean though it be, not only kings of the Scots and their peoples, but even rulers over strange and barbarous nations, with the peoples subject to them, will bestow great and especial honour."

In the half-century following his death his prophecy came near to fulfilment. But there were other workers in the field, for instance Moluag, whom Columba is said to have cursed bitterly because he occupied the island of Lismore, which

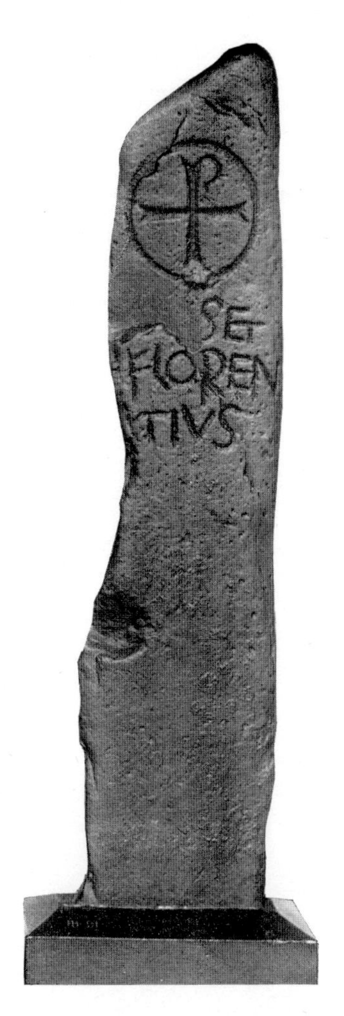

THE KIRKMADRINE STONES

Two of the early Christian monuments, probably of the fifth century.

PLATE 5

A PAGE FROM THE LINDISFARNE GOSPELS

First page of St. John's Gospel written (in Latin) about A.D. 700. The book is a landmark in decorative history, for the English monks writing in Northumberland developed a new style, based on Celtic, Anglo-Saxon and Continental ornamentation, which was followed also in Irish and no doubt in Scottish monasteries.

Columba coveted. The dwellers in the Clyde valley, again, heard the Gospel, not from Columba or any of his followers, but from Kentigern the Briton, whose empty shrine can still be seen in the crypt of Glasgow Cathedral. In 597, too, St. Augustine and monks from Rome landed in Kent, and began their work of converting England to the Christian faith.

For a time, however, it seemed as if the churches in the north of England were to be ruled, not from Canterbury or Rome, but from Iona. In 634 a sudden twist of fortune's wheel placed upon the throne of Northumbria the exiled prince Oswald, who had spent his youth in the monastery of Iona. No sooner did he become king than he sent a request to the community at Iona for some one to preach the new faith to his people. One of the monks was accordingly dispatched to Northumbria, but he returned in a short time to confess that his preaching had been a failure because the Northumbrians were "intractable men, and of a hard and barbarous disposition." One monk, Aidan by name, hinted very gently that the hardness and obstinacy might not have been confined to the hearers. The shot went home; the assembly promptly decided that Aidan must go south in place of his crabbed comrade. He succeeded; noble and peasant alike came under the spell of one who was completely free from all self-seeking, all priestly arrogance. They felt that there must be something in the religion of one who might have been rich and yet chose to remain poor, who gave away the costliest gifts as soon as the donor's back was turned, whose episcopal palace was only a rickety lean-to propped against the buttress of a church, and who, in spite of his austere manner of life, did not become soured or self-righteous, but remained courteous and cheerful.

On the island of Lindisfarne he erected his cathedral, a structure with oaken walls and a thatched roof. All over Northumbria similar churches sprang up, ministered to by Celtic clerics from Iona.

But the stories of Aidan and of Cuthbert, the border shepherd-boy in whose honour the great cathedral of Durham was erected, belong to English rather than to Scottish history. For Iona was not destined to become the ecclesiastical capital of northern England. The Celtic churches in Ireland and Scotland had been founded at a time when Rome had ceased to exercise any control over her distant province; the result was that for two and a half centuries they had existed and developed in complete isolation from the rest of Christendom. But now, at the court of the Northumbrian king, Romish priests from Canterbury or York met Celtic priests from Iona. Though their religious beliefs were the same, the southern priest recoiled in horror from the Scottish monk, for he noticed that his head was shaven across from ear to ear. A priest must shave his head, he believed, but why should he refuse to shave it at the proper place, which was the crown? He was confirmed in his belief that his Scottish rival was an impious heretic when he learned that the Celtic method of computing the date of Easter differed from the Roman one, so that Easter might fall in March at Canterbury, and in April at Lindisfarne and Iona.

The controversy about these differences was allowed to sleep while Aidan was alive, but after his death in 651 it raged fiercely, till in 663 King Oswiu of Northumbria grew alarmed, and summoned the Romish and the Celtic champions to meet in his presence at Whitby. Colman, the Celtic bishop of Lindisfarne, buttressed his arguments with the authority of St. Columba; the arrogant Wilfrid of York boldly claimed that he had on his side St. Peter, the keeper of the keys of Heaven. "Has a similar power been conferred on your Columba?" the King asked Colman. The bishop admitted that he could not honestly make such a claim. "Then," said the King, "this is the doorkeeper whom I am loath to contradict, lest haply when I arrive at the doors of the Kingdom there shall be none to open them unto me." So the decision went against Colman, and he and the other Celtic monks who refused to conform to the Roman usage returned sorrowfully whence they had come.

The controversy spread to Scotland. In 710 King Nechtan became seriously concerned about the two questions, and asked Ceolfrith, the Abbot of Jarrow, for his opinion on the dispute and also for architects who would show him how to erect a church of stone. Ceolfrith responded to the appeal, and in a short time Nechtan compelled all the clergy in his realm to choose between shaving their crowns and observing Easter at the orthodox time or being driven out. Six years later Iona and the churches under its jurisdiction conformed to the Roman usage.

But the Scottish churches still kept apart from the church

in England. Though Whithorn became the seat of an English bishop, and though the surrounding district became part of the ecclesiastical province of York, the rest of Scotland owed no allegiance to either York or Canterbury.

"But what of St. Andrew?" you ask. "Why have the Scots chosen him, rather than Ninian or Columba, as their patron saint?" It is true that St. Andrew never set foot on Scottish soil, but in the reign of Angus, King Nechtan's successor, a stranger appeared bearing with him some bones which he said were the veritable bones of the Apostle. The King believed his story, and allowed him to build a church to enshrine the relics at Kilrymont on the Fifeshire coast. Later a great cathedral, the finest in Scotland, took the place of the older church, and people came from far and near to St. Andrews, as Kilrymont was now called, to gaze on the shrine of the Apostle. So the patron saint of the greatest church in Scotland came, in the course of time, to be regarded as the patron saint of Scotland itself. In the later Middle Ages the banner of St. Andrew, the white cross placed diagonally on a blue background, became the national flag of Scotland; and to this day it can be seen, combined with the red and white banners of St. George and St. Patrick, in the Union Jack.

CHAPTER 3

THE BUILDING UP OF SCOTLAND

After the death of Columba more than four centuries had to elapse before Scotland was united under the rule of a single king. The obstacles to unification were many. He who aspired to rule the whole of Scotland must break three rival kings in battle, or march into their kingdoms when they were attacked by other enemies, or take advantage of a disputed succession to snatch the coveted crown, or establish a claim through marriage and descent. Even if he succeeded, he had no guarantee that his new-made kingdom would not crumble to pieces in his hands. How could you build up a nation when the very idea of nationality did not exist, when no inhabitant of

Scotland thought of himself as a Scotsman, when the Pict regarded the Scot as an alien, speaking a barbarous jargon, ruling his life by unfamiliar laws and customs? Even Pictland itself was not always a single kingdom, for there were often two kings, one ruling over Moray in the north and the other over Fortriu in the south.

To these invisible barriers of race, language, and custom must be added certain visible, tangible barriers—the great marshes that stretched where now one sees only fertile cornland, the virgin forests that still clothed many of the valleys in central and southern Scotland, the trackless moorlands, and the unbridged rivers. There could be little trade, little peaceful intercourse of any kind between one part of Scotland and another, and so unfamiliarity bred suspicion and fear. Moreover, these natural barriers made effective government almost impossible. How was the King to make his authority felt in every part of his kingdom?

For a time it seemed as if the whole of Scotland might be merged in the English kingdom of Northumbria. That kingdom already included Lothian, and in the middle of the seventh century the Northumbrian king forced the rulers of Pictland and Strathclyde to acknowledge him as their overlord. When a more vigorous Pictish king challenged the Northumbrian power, King Ecgfrith of Northumbria invaded Pictland. The crafty old Pict lured his enemy on, beyond the Forth, beyond the Tay, till at Nechtansmere, among the lonely marshes and moors north of the Sidlaws, he turned upon the invader. The Northumbrian army was cut to pieces; King Ecgfrith was among the slain.

The Picts, freed from the Northumbrian menace, resumed vigorous warfare against the kings of Dalriada, and before the middle of the eighth century, in the reign of King Angus, Dalriada had become, to all intents and purposes, a Pictish province. But at the same time the conquered were invading the territory of the conquerors: bands of Scots, tired of the hopeless fight for a livelihood in the rain-washed, rocky west, drifted eastward into more fertile lands. So Gaelic began to be spoken in places where hitherto only the ancient Pictish speech had been heard, and so some of the Picts began to use the language of their new neighbours.

THE ABERLEMNO CROSS-SLAB

Pictish work, probably of the eighth century, inspired by the art seen earlier in the Lindisfarne Gospels. The back of the slab shows a battle scene.

PLATE 7

IONA

It seemed, then, that Picts and Scots were to be united under the rule of a Pictish king. But at the end of the eighth century a new element appeared in Scotland, with the arrival of raiders from the west and south-west of Norway. They came in vessels of a new fashion: long, narrow boats of wood, with a single mast and a single square sail. Along the bulwarks were hung the shields of the warriors who crowded the vessel, and on either side oars flashed in the water.

The Celtic monasteries, planted as they often were on lonely islands or by the shores of some secluded inlet, were peculiarly exposed to the attentions of these visitants. But what could robbers find worthy of notice in these insignificant little stone churches, no bigger and no more imposing than the cottage of a present-day ploughman, and the still more insignificant huts clustered about them? Bread that they had not baked, and ale that they had not brewed—and much more.

These Celtic monks, though they could not rear beautiful buildings, were lovers and makers of beautiful things. If one of them set himself to copy a manuscript of the Gospels, he filled the margin of his parchment with a maze of intricate designs and made the initial letter of each chapter gorgeous with colour. If only he had put in pictures we should know much more than we do about the appearance of the people of these far-off times; but the Celtic artist preferred patterns to pictures; if he had to bring in a living creature he chose the serpent because he could twist and stretch its body into so many interesting shapes. But the heathen Norsemen were more interested in the cover than in the book, for many of these beautiful manuscripts were enclosed in cases that were even more beautiful—caskets of silver and gold, covered with the same intricate patterns and studded with precious stones. Similar caskets of gold or silver were made to contain the little hand-bells used by the saints of an earlier day, and the plain oaken staff of the founder of the monastery was usually transformed by the monkish craftsman into a glittering silver crosier, twinkling with gems. Even on brooches and other trifles there was lavished the same fastidious workmanship.

So there was enough plunder even in the barren Hebrides to lure the Norsemen back again and again. And they soon discovered that the Hebrides formed only the fringe of Scotland;

they descended on the mainland and showed the luckless natives that no ruler—Scot, Pict, Briton, or Angle—was strong enough to keep them out if they chose to come. Nor, if they plundered a place once, did it follow that they would leave it alone ever after. In 795, for example, they sacked Iona, in 802 they burned the monastery, in 806 they killed all the monks. Then they left it alone for almost twenty years, and a new monastery rose on the ruins of the old, but in 825 this in its turn was sacked and the monks slaughtered. The relics of Columba had been concealed, but, as no one could be sure that the monastery might not be raided again, the relics were now divided, and removed, some of them to Kells, in Ireland, and the remainder to Dunkeld. With the bones of Columba the mother church at Iona lost the supremacy which it had enjoyed over the churches of Ireland and Dalriada; for half a century Dunkeld remained the ecclesiastical capital of Scotland, till, at the beginning of the tenth century, it was overshadowed by a newer foundation at St. Andrews. But, though St. Andrews had now become the Canterbury of Scotland, a special sanctity attached to Iona: hither for another two hundred years the bodies of the Scottish kings were brought for their burial.

It was not only Iona and the other Western Isles that attracted these Scandinavian pirates; some held on past Kintyre till they reached Ireland, others—from Denmark as well as Norway—sailed straight across the North Sea and descended on the unprotected English coasts; others again sailed right up the Seine and threatened Paris itself. Wherever they went it was the same story, first plundering raids on the coast that were over in a few weeks, then prolonged campaigns carried out by larger forces, then a permanent occupation of the country. For long they seemed invincible: their shields of linden wood and shirts of mail could stop any ordinary blow, their ships could out-distance anything else that sailed, and when they left their ships behind they seized the first horses they came across, and changed from sailors into swift-moving, hard-fighting cavalry. Then we must remember that, for all their ferocity and barbarian ignorance, they were men who knew how to "live dangerously".

When England, France and Ireland were assailed, Scotland could not hope to escape. Again and again the Picts strove to beat back the invaders, but they were hampered by a rebellion of the Scots under Alpin, a descendant of the old kings of Dalriada. In 839 disaster overwhelmed the Picts; their king with a great multitude of his followers was slain by the Norsemen, and though the rebel Alpin was slain soon after, his son Kenneth possessed himself of the stronghold of the Pictish kings at Forteviot and became king of both Picts and Scots. Kenneth's accession marks the end of the first stage in the unification of Scotland.

But he would have been bold indeed who would have prophesied that this new kingdom of Alba would not crumble as quickly as it had been built. The Norsemen had unwittingly helped Kenneth to his kingdom, and the Norsemen were no more friendly to the supplanters of the Pictish kings than they had been to the Picts themselves. In fact, the Norsemen were becoming more dangerous: about 872 Harald Harfagr made himself master of the whole of Norway, and so Scotland was now harassed both by rebel chieftains who settled there to be safe from Harald, and by loyal chieftains whom he sent there to act as his lieutenants. Harald reduced Orkney and Shetland and handed them over to Earl Sigurd; a little later he despatched Ketil Flatnose to the Hebrides to enforce his authority there; towards the end of the century Sigurd, along with Thorstein, the grandson of Ketil, crossed to the mainland of Scotland and conquered Caithness, Sutherland, Ross, and Moray. Three kings of Alba perished fighting against the Norsemen—Constantine I in 877, Donald II in 900 and Indulf in 962.

Farther south, as the Britons of Strathclyde knew to their cost, the Norse made their power felt. In 870 they captured Dumbarton, the fortress which guarded the northern frontier of the British kingdom, and overran the valley of the Clyde. On the Solway coast, too, the invaders came to raid and to settle.

About the end of the ninth century the Danes and Norsemen seemed to become less dangerous. Alfred of England set a definite limit to their advance, and in the first half of the tenth century Alfred's vigorous successors freed northern England from their control. But this English advance brought a new anxiety to the kings of Alba. Might not some southern monarch follow up his successes in northern England by an attack on Scotland?

This question agitated the mind of Constantine II, the shrewd and ambitious prince who became King of Alba in 900. In the early part of his reign the Norsemen penetrated almost to the heart of his realm and plundered Dunkeld, but Constantine soon began to look on the Norsemen as less dangerous neighbours than the all-conquering English. In 921, along with the Danish rulers of Northumbria, he did homage to Edward of England. Five years later the Danish Earl of Northumbria died, whereupon Athelstan, the new King of England, drove out his two sons. As Constantine befriended the exiles, Athelstan retaliated by harrying Constantine's kingdom, and so drove the wavering Scot into the arms of the Norsemen. In 937 Athelstan learned that Constantine, with a great host of Scots, Norsemen, and Britons of Strathclyde, was hovering on the northern borders of his realm. It seemed for a time as if the newly fashioned kingdom of England would be shattered to pieces, but Athelstan defeated his enemies in a battle best known as Brunanburh. The site has never been identified, but some believe it to have been the lofty, flat-topped hill of Birrenswark, some ten miles north of the Solway. Constantine had to humble himself before Athelstan, and become a vassal once more. A year or two later he gave up the unequal struggle, resigned his crown to his kinsman Malcolm, and sought peace in a monastery at St. Andrews.

King Malcolm, Constantine's successor, received an unexpected gift of territory. Edmund of England discovered that he could never hold Northumbria as long as the Norsemen settled in Ireland could sail over unchecked to the Cumbrian coast and wander at will across the British kingdom of Strathclyde. To drive the Norsemen out of Cumbria was easy enough—Edmund succeeded in doing it in 945—to keep them out was a different matter. Edmund got over the difficulty by presenting Strathclyde to Malcolm of Scotland on condition that Malcolm promised to be his helper and to defend his new province. Malcolm, like many of his successors, saw no objection to becoming a vassal of the King of England if something substantial was to be gained by the transaction, and so Cumbria was added to the territory controlled by the Kings of Alba.

Malcolm discovered, too, that Norse pirates and English kings were not his most dangerous enemies. His stronghold at Forteviot and his newer palace at Scone commanded the fertile and populous plains of Strathmore, Strathearn, and Gowrie, but the Grampians formed a barrier between the central part of his realm and the northern province of Moray. Further, while the Kings of Alba believed Moray to be part of their kingdom, their belief was not shared by the rulers and people of Moray. On the other hand, by 962 Lothian north of the Pentlands and Lammermoors had passed into the hands of the Scots.

In addition to the ever-present danger from the men of Moray, Alba was distracted at the end of the tenth century by a dispute about the succession. Before the time of Kenneth II, who reigned from 971 to 995, a king was succeeded not by his eldest son but by the eldest of his near male relatives. King Kenneth, however, decided to set aside the claims of the other branches of the royal family and make his son Malcolm heir to the kingdom. Kenneth himself died suddenly and mysteriously—his disaffected kinsmen had a hand in the matter—and the claim of Malcolm was brushed aside. First Constantine the Bald and then Giric seized the crown. But the reigns of these disaffected kinsmen were short and troubled; each of them was slain by the son of the man whose death he had compassed, and in 1005 Malcolm II became King of Alba.

CHAPTER 4

THE ELEVENTH CENTURY

MALCOLM II, like all the kings who preceded him, is little more than a name to us. We know that he became king in 1005, that he died in 1034, and that he was succeeded by his grandson Duncan, but we do not know the man himself. No portrait of him has survived, no fragment of his conversation, no tell-tale anecdote. Yet we would gladly know more about him, for ever since his time Scotland has included the land between the Forth and the Cheviots and he has some claim to be thought of as the first king of Scotland, and not merely of Alba.

Though in the early part of his reign he dealt out sharp punishment to any marauding Norseman who dared to invade his kingdom, he succeeded in winning the friendship of Sigurd, the Norse Earl of Orkney, who, as we saw, had become the master of a great part of northern Scotland. For one thing, Sigurd had become a Christian; for another, he did not relish the manner of his conversion: his over-lord, King Olaf of Norway, had threatened to kill him and harry his lands if he remained a heathen. So Sigurd married the daughter of King Malcolm, and when in 1014 Sigurd set off on an expedition to Ireland, he left his young son Thorfinn not with his elder brothers in Orkney, but with the King of Scots. Sigurd never returned from Ireland; his dead body was found on the fatal field of Clontarf, wrapped in the enchanted raven banner that was supposed to bring victory to the soldiers who marched behind it. When the news of his death reached Scotland, King Malcolm bestowed Caithness and Sutherland upon the young Thorfinn, who succeeded also to Orkney and Shetland. Moray reverted to Findlaech, the representative of the old mormaers or rulers of Moray.

Malcolm's attempt to push his frontiers southward at first met with no success: though in 1006 he advanced far into England, he was driven back from the walls of Durham by Utred, the son of the aged Earl of Northumbria, and fled to Scotland with only a remnant of his army. As a reward for Utred's valour King Ethelred of England bestowed his father's earldom upon him.

Utred had soon to reckon with a more formidable adversary than Malcolm. Though the hold of the Norsemen on Scotland had relaxed, the Danes had come back to England; in 1013 their random plundering raids developed into a war of conquest, and in 1016 Cnut, the Danish king, seized the crown of England. Utred, after fighting against him for a time, surrendered, only to be treacherously murdered, and his brother, Eadulf Cudel, succeeded to his earldom. But the new earl was a timorous soul: fearing that Malcolm might try to avenge his ten-years-old defeat, he bought him off by surrendering to him the whole of Lothian. Thus, without a battle, the frontiers of Scotland were advanced to the Cheviots and the Tweed.

But Cnut had no share in this transaction, nor did he mean to let Lothian slip out of his grasp; in 1018 an army went northwards to do battle with the Scots. It was not for nothing, the superstitious said, that a comet had flamed for thirty nights in the heavens: at Carham, on the Tweed, the southern army was cut to pieces by the Scots and the Britons of Cumbria. Cnut

Plate 8

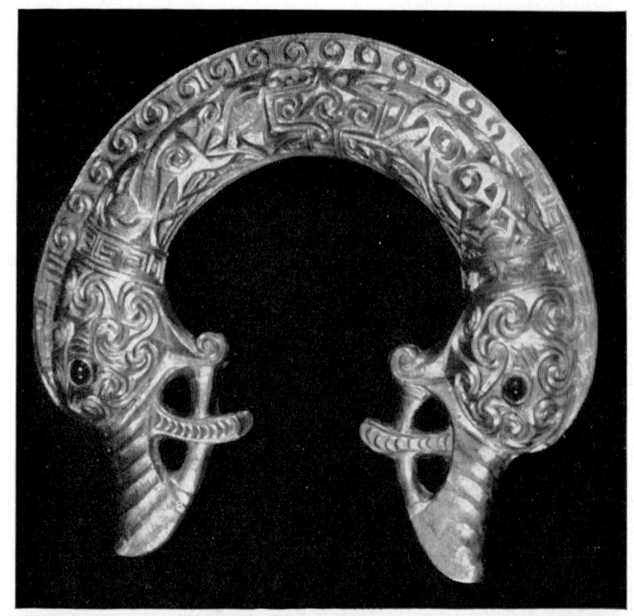

Chapes in Gilt from The St. Ninian's Isle Treasure

This 'Treasure' was found at the presumed site of an early religious establishment on St. Ninian's Isle, Shetland.

next tried negotiations, but though he got some sort of submission from the Scot, he had to leave Malcolm in possession of Lothian.

In the same year the bond that united Cumbria or Strathclyde to Malcolm's other possessions was tightened. Up to this time Cumbria had had its own line of kings, although they had long been kinsmen of the kings of Alba. When in 1018 Owen the Bald, the last of his line, died, he was succeeded by Duncan, the grandson of King Malcolm and the heir to the Scottish crown.

So in the year 1018 the boundaries of Scotland became pretty much what they are at the present day. There were two important differences: the southern boundary line dipped much farther down than it does now, for Strathclyde included not only the basin of the Clyde, but Cumberland, Westmorland, and part of Lancashire, and the western boundary line kept close to the mainland, for though the Norsemen in the Hebrides seldom obeyed the King of Norway, they never obeyed the King of Scots.

But though Malcolm had gathered the stones, he had not built the house. Six years after his death the fires that had smouldered in the north burst into flame; in 1040 Macbeth, the mormaer of Moray, slew King Duncan, the grandson of Malcolm II, and ruled in his stead.

Here at last we seem to encounter a king of Scotland who is something more than an empty name. Shakespeare has made us familiar with the great soldier who is led astray by his ambition and murders his royal guest. We see him tortured by remorse, haunted by the ghost of the "blood-boltered Banquo", hemmed in by Duncan's avengers, yet meeting them with a courage in which hope has no part. Yet as we gaze back through the centuries at the figure of Macbeth, his features become less precise; he becomes as colourless and shadowy as the Kenneths and Malcolms whose crown he had usurped. Shakespeare's Macbeth was not the real Macbeth; of this we are sure, but what the real Macbeth was like we do not know. We do know, however, that the slaying of Duncan was not quite so black a business as Shakespeare made it out to be: Duncan was not a frail old man, but a monarch in the prime of life; both Macbeth and his wife were of royal descent, and Macbeth probably considered that, according to the old rules of succession, he had as good a right to the throne as Duncan himself. His rule seems to have been acceptable to the people, and he was able to leave his kingdom in peace while he went as a pilgrim to Rome and there "scattered money among the poor like seed".

Duncan's two sons had escaped at the time of their father's death, and the elder, Malcolm, called Canmore—Big Head or Chief—had found a refuge in England. Edward the Confessor supported the cause of the exiled prince, and in 1054 sent Siward, Earl of Northumbria, into Scotland with an army. Macbeth was defeated, and Malcolm may at this stage have become ruler of southern Scotland. Malcolm carried on the war, drove Macbeth far away from Birnam Wood and Dunsinane Hill, and in 1057 slew him in battle somewhere in Aberdeenshire. Even then the men of Moray would not yield to Malcolm; they took Macbeth's stepson, Lulach, as their king. Only after Lulach had been slain in 1058 did Malcolm III sit securely upon the throne of Scotland.

Eight years later something happened which changed the whole course of Scottish history: William, Duke of Normandy, made himself master of England. We are apt to look on the Norman Conquest as something that affected England alone; as a matter of fact, it wrought almost as big a change on Scotland. There was a Norman Conquest of Scotland, carried out by kings of Scottish descent with southern help.

The first sign of the coming change was in language. The Scottish kings had been Gaelic speakers; Gaelic had ousted the ancient Pictish tongue in the east and was ousting Norse among Scandinavian settlers in the Hebrides. In Strathclyde a language akin to Welsh was spoken, though Gaelic had lately been gaining ground there at the expense of this older British speech. But the rulers of Northumbria had also been the rulers of Lothian, some English-speaking settlers had made their homes north of the Tweed, and now the Conquest sent fugitives from north-eastern England into south-eastern Scotland. These refugees spoke English, but an English that differed in many respects from the English of London and the Midlands, which is the ancestor of modern English speech, and this northern or Northumbrian English became in time the speech of the whole Scottish lowlands. So modern Scots is really an importation from the north of England; in fact, all through the Middle Ages the Lowland Scot called his speech not "Scots" but "English"; "Scots" to him always meant Gaelic.

Among these refugees came, in 1070, a prince and princess of the house of Alfred, Edgar Atheling and his sister Margaret. Their father was the English prince Edward, who, after the death of his father, Edmund Ironside, had been banished by Cnut to Hungary. In 1057 he had returned to England with his children, but died soon after. With the seizure of the English throne by William the Conqueror, these representatives of the old royal house were in exile again. Soon after they arrived in Scotland, King Malcolm determined to marry Margaret. At first the lady refused; she wanted to be a nun, not a queen, she said, but she yielded at length to the prayers of Malcolm and her brother.

Her longing for the quiet of the convent was not a weak shrinking from the turmoil of the everyday world. Margaret possessed an indomitable will, a restless conscience, and clear-cut and definite ideas of what was right and wrong. Even the King was moved by this passionate piety, which he did not quite understand: the grim warrior who had slain Macbeth and who tried to defy the Conqueror himself, would kneel beside the Queen to wash the grimy feet of some old beggar-man, or help her to distribute food to the three hundred poor folks who were her guests in Advent and in Lent. Sometimes, as Margaret's English chaplain tells us, he would take up one of the Queen's books of devotion, gaze at the unintelligible Latin, and then put his lips to the parchment; sometimes he would remove it altogether, and return it a few days later in a cover of gold and precious stones. Some of the King's gifts, however, were involuntary; he would find that a costly ornament or a handful of gold coins had disappeared, and would learn later that the Queen had bestowed his property upon some "gangrel body" whose tale of woe she had been unable to resist. Margaret would see nothing ridiculous, or even unusual, in an action like this. She had no sense of humour and no sense of proportion.

This was plainly revealed in her dealings with the Scottish clergy. There was much in the state of the churches in Scotland to perplex and worry her. In the eleventh century a new religious zeal had shown itself in the churches on the Continent in all sorts of ways: in the building of larger and more beautiful churches, in the founding of new monasteries, and in a general tightening up of church organisation and discipline. Even the secular priest, who was not a member of a monastic community and who lived in his own house, found that certain things permitted to his predecessors were forbidden to him. He was not allowed to marry, for example. He found, too, that his bishop visited the parish more frequently and asked some very searching questions about the spiritual welfare of his parishioners. And there was many a man who felt that the secular priest was too much exposed to temptation, who did not feel safe till he had entered a monastery to spend the remainder of his life with men of the same mind as himself. He was left with nothing of his own, for he surrendered all his belongings to the monastery when he put on the plain black or white robes of a monk; he had not even a room of his own; he slept in the common dormitory and had his meals in the common refectory or dining-room. Even his will he surrendered: he had taken the vow of obedience, and must now regulate his life by the "rule" of the monastery to which he belonged.

Of all this stir of life on the Continent the Scottish clergy knew little. There had been at St. Andrews ever since the beginning of the tenth century "head bishops" of Alba, and other bishops had seats elsewhere, but there was no systematic organisation of the church under their jurisdiction. And though the Scottish church had monks, they were somewhat different from the monks that Queen Margaret had seen in England and on the Continent. They did not take the vow of poverty, and each had his own little house within the monastery grounds. Many of the monks, too, were married; in fact, in most of the monasteries the office of abbot had become hereditary. In effect, the monasteries had become exclusive communities of hereditary landowners, who had often ceased to be clerics even in name.

In all this there was much that required to be changed, and much that Queen Margaret wanted to change. Some things, however, the Queen did not attempt to meddle with: she could not, or would not, diminish the number of lay proprietors of church lands. Nor did she try to reform the organisation of the church, and though her own chaplain was an Englishman, she made no attempt to replace the easy-going Celtic clerics by the more enthusiastic and austere English and Normans. But the example of her life of alms-giving and prayer had its effect

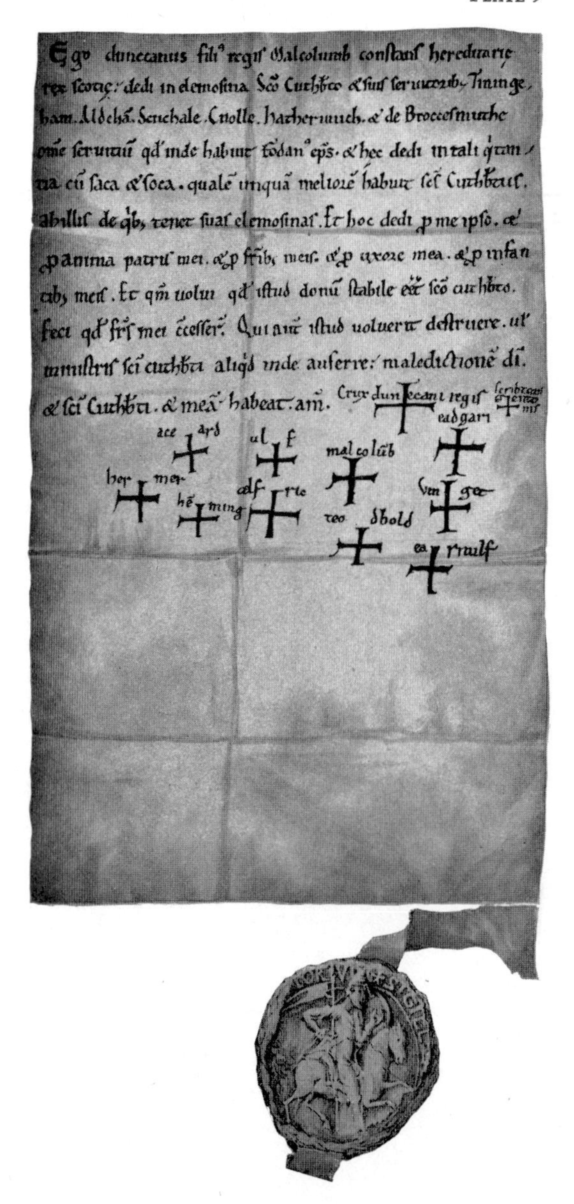

Ego dunecanus fili' regis Malcolumb constans hereditarie
rex scotię: dedi in elemosina Sco Cuthberto & suis seruitorib, Tininge
ham. Aldehã. Scuchale. Cnolle. hatheruuich. & de Broccesmuthe
omne seruitiũ qd inde habuit Fodan' eps. & hec dedi in tali quitan
tia cũ saca & soca. quale unquã meliorẽ habuit scs Cuthbertus.
ab illis de qb; tenet suas elemosinas. Et hoc dedi p me ipso. &
p anima patris mei. & p frib; meis. & p uxore mea. & p infan
tib; meis. Et qm uolui qd istud donũ stabile eet sco cuthbto.
feci qd frs mei cocesser. Qui autẽ istud uoluerit destruere. ul
ministris sci cuthbti aliqd inde auferre: maledictionẽ di.
& sci Cuthbti. & meã habeat. am.

Crux dunecani regis + eadgari + acceard + ulf + malcolũb + hermer + hemming + aelfric + uengeot + teodbold + earnulf

CHARTER OF DUNCAN II, 1094

By this document, which is the earliest extant Scottish charter, King Duncan granted Tynninghame, Auldhame and other lands in East Lothian to the monks of Durham.

on both clerics and ordinary people. She visited religious communities, too, and talked to their occupants; from some she came away, not censorious but full of humility. For not all communities were like those we have described; in some, occupied by men called Culdees, the life was as hard, the fire of religious enthusiasm as pure and keen, as in any of the new monasteries on the Continent. But even in these Culdee communities she saw something to grieve her. Why did the Scottish clergy begin Lent not on Ash Wednesday but on the Monday following? Why did they not insist that the people should receive Communion at Easter? Why did they allow people to work on Sunday just as if it were an ordinary day? Why had certain unusual practices become interwoven with the ritual of the Mass?

In the end she summoned an assembly of the clergy and tried to argue them out of their old customs, and into conformity with the practice of the rest of Christendom. The clerics at last admitted that they were beaten, and agreed to abandon the practices to which she objected. Perhaps they were moved less by the arguments of Margaret than by the frowns of the grim warrior her husband, for Malcolm, who knew both English and Gaelic, attended as Margaret's interpreter.

Saint though she was, Margaret did not despise pomp and display. Not only did she wear beautiful and costly raiment herself, she ordered her subjects to do the same. Rich hangings now brightened the bare walls of the King's palace, gold and silver plate glittered on his table; his meat was seasoned with spices brought from the ends of the earth; the liquor that sparkled in his cup was not home-brewed ale, but wine from France. So the little communities of fishers and farmers along the east coast—hardly deserving as yet the name of towns—became familiar with the Flemish and Frisian merchants who imported these new and strange wares, and some of the merchants in their turn found it profitable to act on the Queen's advice, and make their homes among the people with whom they traded. It was at the Queen's wish, too, that the King never stirred without an imposing escort of well-disciplined troops, for she knew that people are impressed by the outward shows of kingly power.

But though Margaret brought English fashions and customs into Scotland, though she encouraged English refugees to settle there, her coming involved King Malcolm in a quarrel with the Norman King of England. It was only natural that Malcolm should take up the quarrel of Margaret's kinsfolk and invade England on their behalf, but he burned his fingers badly in the process: in 1072 William penetrated into the heart of Scotland, and forced Malcolm to do homage to him at Abernethy.

Worse followed in the reign of the Conqueror's successor: in 1092 William Rufus occupied Carlisle; the whole of Cumbria south of the Solway was at this one blow lost to Scotland. A year later Malcolm invaded England, but he was slain in battle near Alnwick. His son Edgar went back to Edinburgh, heavy at heart, to break the news to the Queen. He found his mother lying stricken with a mortal sickness, with just enough strength to ask him how her husband fared. "He is well," the prince answered, but she would not let herself be deceived. "I know, my son, I know," she sighed; "but tell me what you know to be the truth." He stammered out the miserable story. Not a word of complaint did she utter, only a prayer of thanksgiving that this grief should have been sent her at the very end of her life to purify her soul from the last stains of sin.

Donald Bane, the brother of the dead King, put himself at the head of those who disliked English innovations and half-English princes, and besieged the castle. Not till a thick mist descended were the Queen's attendants able to steal out with the body and ferry it over the Forth, to lay it in the new church that she had built at Dunfermline. It seemed for the moment as if her work had been undone. Donald Bane made good his claim to the crown, and though in 1094 he was deposed by Duncan, the son of Malcolm III by his first wife Ingibiorg, the murder of Duncan a few months later put him again in possession. But William Rufus, who had helped Duncan to his temporary success, was equally ready, and for the same reason, to support the sons of Margaret. He suggested to Edgar Atheling, who had now become his very dutiful subject, that he should lead an army into Scotland and put his nephew Edgar on the throne. For once Edgar Atheling acted with promptitude; Donald Bane's army retired before his force of English and Norman adventurers; the usurper himself was captured, and so, in 1097, Edgar, the eldest surviving son of Malcolm and Margaret, became King of Scotland.

CHAPTER 5

THE SONS OF MALCOLM AND MARGARET

THE time was to come when in Scotland the phrase "the Auld Enemy" would have only one meaning—England; when men, looking back on two hundred years and more of open war or of brief truces, made only to be broken, would find it impossible to imagine that England and Scotland could ever be other than mortal foes. But the two and a half centuries of open warfare were preceded by two centuries of almost unbroken peace, during which Scotland—lowland Scotland, at any rate—was fashioned into the likeness of the southern kingdom. The merchant who went from Newcastle to Dundee in the twelfth century found himself in a town governed exactly as Newcastle was governed, among merchants who dressed exactly as he did, and who spoke the same dialect of the same language. The English lady who became the wife of a Scottish baron found that her new home was built on the same plan as the Norman castle she had left, and that her husband spoke Norman-French by preference. The large and beautiful monasteries that arose in the twelfth and thirteenth centuries were little more than copies of the larger and more beautiful monasteries of England and northern France, and their inmates, to begin with at least, were usually Englishmen or Normans. So the Lowland Scots—and among them we count the dwellers on the east coast as far north as the Moray Firth—were not simply abstaining from war with their English neighbours; they were, more or less willingly, copying English speech and learning English ways.

Why did they do it? Partly because England was their nearest neighbour, and, as Henry VII sagely remarked, "the greater will always draw the less"; partly because the Scottish kings deliberately set themselves to make Scotland another England. This is not to be wondered at: they were as much English as Scots, and they were closely connected with the royal house of England. In 1100, for example, Henry I married Edgar's sister, Matilda. Edgar's youngest brother, David, spent much of his time at the English court, and by marriage he became an English baron, lord of the two counties of Huntingdon and Northampton, full ten years before he became King of Scotland.

The anglicisation of the Lowlands was helped, too, by the fact that the English kings showed no desire to unite Scotland by force to their own realm. They were wise enough to let well alone, to be content with the homage of the King of Scots without asking what precisely it was that he rendered homage for, and though the long period of peace was thrice interrupted by war, it was the ambition of the King of Scots, not the ambition of the King of England, that caused the breach.

In fact, danger threatened the Scottish kingdom not from the south, but from the north and the west. The Western Isles were still under the rule of Norse or half-Norse chieftains, who, however, showed little more deference to the King of Norway than they did to the King of Scots. In 1098 Magnus Barelegs, King of Norway, harried the Hebrides far and wide, and forced a reluctant acknowledgement of his supremacy from their inhabitants. Not content with this, he threatened to invade Scotland itself, and forced Edgar to buy him off. It was arranged that Magnus was to have all the Western Isles: however near the island might be to the mainland it was to be his, provided that he could go between it and the mainland in a boat with rudder in position. But Magnus succeeded in getting the peninsula of Kintyre as well; when he approached Tarbert he ordered his men to beach the boat, without unshipping the rudder, and drag it across the isthmus. Such at least is the story in the saga of King Magnus; but, although the Norse had settled in Kintyre in earlier times, there is no evidence that they possessed it after this date. In any event, Edgar had simply given up what neither he nor Magnus could control; though the Hebrides nominally belonged to the King of Norway, from the middle of the twelfth century their real rulers were the half Celtic, half Norse Kings of the Isles.

When Edgar died in 1107 he was succeeded by his brother Alexander, who, however, entrusted to Prince David the rule over southern Scotland. Neither of these princes trusted their Celtic subjects overmuch, and when David became King of Scotland in 1124 he began what we may call a peaceful Norman

Conquest of Scotland. Knights whom he had met at the court of Henry I he invited to settle beyond the Cheviots, and so, many an ambitious younger son who had despaired of ever becoming a great baron in England found himself enrolled among the Scottish nobility. Such was Walter, son of the Breton Alan Fitz-Flaad, whom David made Steward of Scotland; such, too, was Robert de Brus, an English baron whose father had come from Normandy with the Conqueror, upon whom David bestowed great estates in Annandale. The son of the Breton was the ancestor of the royal house of Stewart; from the Norman adventurer the patriot king, Robert the Bruce, was descended.

Sometimes the new-comers were given lands that had been forfeited by their Celtic lords; sometimes they gained their new estates by marrying Celtic heiresses, but though they held the same territories, the relation in which they stood to the land and its inhabitants was different. The Celtic mormaer, like the old Scottish king, was looked on not so much as a landowner but as the ruler, judge, and leader of the people inhabiting a certain area. His privileges and duties were determined, too, not by any written agreement between him and the King, but by immemorial custom; thus his people paid him "cain"—gave him a pig or a few hens or a bushel or two of oats—because their grandfathers had rendered the same tribute to his grandfather.

But the new Norman lord usually held his land by virtue of a written charter granted him by the King, specifying the exact extent of his estate, the privileges which he enjoyed as lord of that estate, and the conditions on which he held it. The most important condition was usually military service: the landowner was expected to follow the King to war with a specified number of knights for a period of forty days. When a baron died he was succeeded by his eldest son, or by his daughters if he had no son. Even if the son or daughter was an infant, the claims of the defunct baron's brothers or cousins were set aside, and the King became guardian both of the child and of the estates. Should the child be a girl, he might reward some faithful follower by bestowing her upon him as a bride. Even when the child was a boy, the King drew the revenues of his estates till he came of age, and even then the heir could not enter into possession of his estates till he had paid into the royal treasury a sum equal to the yearly revenue which he would derive from them.

So in a sense the baron was only joint owner of the land with the King: on the other hand the dwellers on the land were the baron's men rather than the King's. Only in exceptional cases did the King's justiciars and sheriffs interfere with the administration of justice within the lands of a baron, and there was no penalty which the baron could not inflict. Ordinary offenders he would thrust into his own private "pit" or prison; criminals who had committed really serious offences, such as stealing more than one sheep, would be strung up on his private gallows.

Just as the King would deal out land to one of these Norman adventurers on certain conditions, so his new tenant, after reserving a portion of the land as his demesne or private estate, would divide the remainder among his followers on similar conditions. Just as the baron followed the King, so they had to follow their lord to battle; just as he had to attend the King's Council along with the other great barons, so they had to be present in the baron's court whenever he dealt out justice to malefactors. Some of the original Celtic occupants of the land remained free tenants, paying their "cain and conveth" [1] to a Norman as they had done aforetime to a Celtic lord; others became serfs, compelled to work on their lord's demesne without money payment, forbidden to leave the place where they had been born, forbidden even to allow their daughters to marry without their lord's consent.

These Norman knights and men-at-arms were evidently meant to be a garrison, a bulwark against invasion from the north. Mounted on horseback, protected by a conical steel helmet and coat of mail, equipped with shield and lance, they were more than a match in hand-to-hand fighting for the Celtic warrior, who despised armour, and rushed into battle protected only by a helmet and a light shield of leather.

Besides, as soon as the Norman baron entered his new territories, he set about building a castle. He chose, if he could, a hillock near a river; if a loop of the river almost enclosed the site of his castle, so much the better. Where a natural hillock was not available, he got his men to raise a great mound of earth surrounded by a deep trench; the top of the mound, or

[1] Contributions of food-stuffs.

A VIKING SHIP
The Oseberg ship, built *c.* 800.

Plate 11

Bayeux Tapestry

This section shows work in progress on the building of the castle at Hastings.

motte, as it was called, he encircled with a stout palisade; the trench he flooded with water from the river. Within the palisade he erected a stout tower of timber, daubed with clay. There was usually an exterior set of defences as well: in most castles the motte was set at one corner of a large rectangular or oval enclosure, a little above the level of the surrounding ground, from which it was separated by a palisade and a ditch. Within the bailey, as this enclosure was called, were other wooden buildings, stables, workshops, and stores. Most of the occupants of the castle, however, took their meals and slept, not in any of these outhouses, but in the great hall on the first floor of the tower, which they approached by a drawbridge spanning the inner ditch. Here the lord of the castle dined at a trestle-table, which was piled up against the wall when the meal was over; here he sat in the dark nights of winter, before the fire that burned in the middle of the earthen floor, while the wind blew through the chinks in the timber and sent the smoke eddying round the room, sometimes listening to some old story of Arthur or Gawain. For a carpet underfoot he had rushes, for pictures a yard or two of tapestry stretched on the wall behind him; there was no room to which he could withdraw with his friends, for in addition to the great hall the tower contained only one or two tiny bedrooms.

One would expect him to be dissatisfied with such quarters, but if he objected to them at all, it was not because they were uncomfortable—he did not know that they were uncomfortable—but because they were not absolutely secure. A stone castle, like those which were being raised in England, could not be set on fire by the enemy; still, a castle of earth and timber could be rushed up in a week or two at very little expense, and would defy any force not provided with siege engines. So these palisades and wooden towers were the rule in twelfth and thirteenth century Scotland.

But Alexander I and David encouraged an invader of another type: along with the Norman noble came the Norman bishop and the Norman abbot. The Celtic bishops of St. Andrews, Dunkeld, Moray, Aberdeen and Ross were succeeded, when they died, by English or Norman bishops, and David revived old, or founded new, bishoprics in Glasgow, Galloway, Brechin, Dunblane, and Caithness.

There had been bishops in the ancient Celtic church, but while everyone believed that there were certain functions, such as ordaining a priest, which only a bishop could perform, a great deal of the authority and jurisdiction over the priests had been in the hands of abbots, who might or might not be bishops. Under David this confusion came to an end. Each bishop had his own special bishopric or diocese allotted to him; the district controlled by the Bishop of St. Andrews, for example, stretched from the Dee to the Tweed, and the diocese of Glasgow extended from the head of Loch Lomond to the Solway. And just as the whole country was divided into dioceses, so each diocese was subdivided into parishes, in each of which one found a parish church and the adjoining parsonage, where the parish priest dwelt. In districts where an old Celtic church already existed, the new Norman lord waited till a suitable opportunity arose. When the old Gaelic-speaking priest died, he put an Englishman or a Norman in his place; when the little old church fell into disrepair, he pulled it down and substituted a larger and more beautiful building, with massive walls, small, round-headed windows filled with stained glass, and doorways framed by twin clusters of pillars, supporting a round stone arch. The church was maintained and the parish priest supported by the parishioners, who were required to pay him every year a tenth or tithe of the produce of their fields. These tenths were known in Scotland as "teinds."

The parish priest was not a law to himself. At intervals his bishop would descend upon him and ask him a multitude of inconvenient questions. Did he hold divine service regularly? Did his parishioners attend regularly, and how did they behave when they were persuaded to come to church? Did they gossip or laugh at the most solemn parts of the service, as was the habit in some churches? If they did, whose fault was it? Had they been sufficiently instructed by their priest? Did he make them confess their sins to him regularly, and were the penances that he laid upon them sufficiently severe? And if the bishop did not come in person, he sent his deputy, the archdeacon, sometimes known as the eye, the arm, or the tongue of the bishop.

In the intervals of rest from his travels among the country clergy, the bishop lived in his castle or palace in the cathedral town. For in every bishopric there was one church, conspicuous by its size and beauty, which was regarded as the principal church of the diocese. Here, not far from the high altar, stood the "cathedra," or bishop's chair, which gave its name to the building. Here the newly consecrated bishop was installed, here he officiated in person at the high festivals of the church, and here, under the flagstones of the choir, his bones were laid when in his turn he had to make way for a new bishop.

The services in the cathedral were conducted by a fairly large body of canons or cathedral clergy, under a dean. In most Scottish cathedrals the canons were secular priests, living in separate houses in the cathedral close or chanonry; in St. Andrews and Whithorn, however, they were canons regular, living together in the priory, a group of buildings that differed in no important respect from the great monasteries that were springing up in southern Scotland.

For King David was a builder of monasteries as well as of cathedrals, monasteries which he manned with English or French-speaking monks of the new, strictly disciplined orders. It was he who founded Holyrood, where he enshrined a piece of wood that Queen Margaret had believed to be a fragment of the true Cross or "holy rood"; it was he who reared the "antique pillars massy-proof" that loom through the darkness of the nave in Dunfermline Abbey; it was he who brought the white-robed Cistercians to Melrose, where the loveliest abbey in all Scotland—lovely still in its ruin—rises by the placid waters of the Tweed.

A few miles below Melrose the River Tweed in its winding course almost encircles the ruins of Dryburgh Abbey, another monastery founded in David's reign, though not by David himself. Very little is left of the church, but to the other monastic buildings time and the spoiler have been unusually merciful; as we stand on the smooth turf of the cloister garth and look around, it is comparatively easy for us to imagine what the monastery was like seven hundred years ago, when the great church stood entire and complete.

The chief purpose for which a monastery existed was the daily performance of the services of the church. Seven times daily the appointed prayers had to be said, and the appointed psalms and hymns sung. For this solemn and beautiful ceremonial a solemn and beautiful background had to be provided—a great church, cross-shaped in plan, the lofty roof of which was supported by a double row of stone pillars. The head of the cross always pointed to the east, the shaft to the west. The western half of the church was called the nave: here ordinary folk might come and go freely, but the rood-screen, a decorated partition of wood or stone, surmounted by a great cross, shut them off from the choir in the eastern half, which only the monks could enter. If the nave served as a parish church, Mass was said there for the people, while the monks' services were held in the choir. The other buildings of the monastery were usually erected to the south of the church; they were always arranged in the form of a square, the northern side of which was formed by the south wall of the nave. On the eastern side came the south transept, or arm, of the church, and then a long building, containing, first, the sacristy, where the costly vestments and other articles of value were kept, then the chapter-house, where the monks met in council, and where the abbot dealt out admonitions and penances to careless brethren, and, adjoining the chapter-house, the parlour, where the monks could gossip in winter over one of the few fires in the monastery. Above these rooms was the dormitory, where the monks slept in the same coarse robes that they had worn all day. It was with good reason that they went to bed fully dressed, for soon after midnight the great bell of the church would begin to ring, and they had to rise, shuffle along a draughty corridor, past the room of the wakeful abbot, and down a flight of chilly stone stairs into the cold blackness of the great church.

The southern side of the square was occupied by the refectory or dining-hall, a more stately apartment than the hall in the king's palace. Little of it is left at Dryburgh, but we can still see the remains of the kitchens, wine-cellars, and store rooms that filled up the basement below. On the west side of the square stood buildings that were probably occupied by the lay-brethren, these members of the community who were not actually monks.

Round the four sides of this quadrangle ran a covered walk or cloister, where the monks spent most of their leisure in milder weather, some of them sitting near the big stone bookcase that we can still see, reading some legend of the saints full of the most incredible miracles and adventures—the nearest thing to a novel that the monastery possessed.

But some of the monks had duties that took them away from the church and the cloister. One of the brethren had to distribute

SEALS OF THE ARCHBISHOP AND CHAPTER OF ST. ANDREWS

The Chapter seal (on the right) shows the earliest cathedral, the building including St. Rule's Tower.

PLATE 13 DUNBLANE CATHEDRAL

The lower portion of the tower is of date not later than the early twelfth century. The remainder of the building is thirteenth century and later.

food to the crowds of poor people who pressed round the monastery gate every morning; others had to see that the uninvited guests of the monastery were properly lodged. For the monks looked upon hospitality as one of their chief duties; every monastery contained a hostel or guest-house, where travellers were accommodated according to their rank. We must remember that in those days inns were few and bad, and that to the wandering packman or minstrel, journeying through the Forest of Ettrick, and listening to the howl of the wolves reverberating from the sides of the Eildons, the sound of the bell of Melrose or Dryburgh must have come with a peculiar sweetness. Even kings and barons did not disdain to become guests of the monastery; after all, bare and chilly as they seem to us, the rooms in the monastery were more comfortable than those in the king's castle.

Similarly, the monks set an example to the ordinary farmer: the cold stone buildings of the monastery were soon embowered in orchards and gardens; the monasteries introduced improved methods of farming and were good landlords to their tenants; in some places, especially in the Borders, they concentrated on sheep-farming; elsewhere they turned readily to the utilisation of some of Scotland's other natural resources and were pioneers in the mining of coal and the manufacture of salt by distillation from sea-water.

But the monks did not depend for a livelihood on the produce of the fields and orchards round about the monastery; they had estates in every part of Scotland, occupied by their tenants or vassals, who made to them, just as they would have done to an ordinary landlord, regular payments in money or, more usually, in food-stuffs. In addition, every monastery had certain parish churches which belonged to it, from which it collected the bulk of the tithes, leaving only a pittance for the parish priest. So the monk whose business it was to collect these revenues would have very little time for the seven daily services in the monastery church; would be in danger, to tell the truth, of forgetting that he was a monk, and of looking on himself as a business man, one, too, who handled far larger sums of money than the ordinary merchant. The time was to come, in fact, when men would ask if David's zeal for the church had been altogether wise, if the great monasteries which he had endowed did not take far more from the community than they gave back to it. But in the twelfth century that time was far away.

CHAPTER 6

SCOTLAND, ENGLAND, AND NORWAY

THERE were limits to the English enthusiasms of these half-English Kings of Scotland: none of them, for example, wanted the remodelled Scottish Church to be brought into subjection to the English Church. Though Alexander I brought an English monk, Eadmer, from Canterbury to be Bishop of St. Andrews, Eadmer found, when he proposed to be consecrated by the Archbishop of Canterbury, that the King was justly named Alexander the Fierce, and both Alexander and his brother David turned a deaf ear to the remonstrances of the Pope himself, when he tried to insist on the consecration of Scottish bishops by the Archbishop of York.

The dispute smouldered on for half a century, to flare up again in the reign of David's grandson, William the Lion. This time, however, more was at stake than the independence of the Scottish Church: the cathedral clergy of St. Andrews had elected a certain John Scot to be their bishop, as they were entitled to do; the King declared the election void, which he was not entitled to do, and tried to force the canons to accept his own chaplain instead. This high-handed action brought him into conflict with the Pope, who excommunicated him and laid his land under an interdict. But the trouble blew over: in 1188 the King's candidate, Hugh, died; John declared himself willing to accept the inferior bishopric of Dunkeld rather than brave the King's wrath; the canons, summoned to Perth to choose a bishop in the presence of the King and his barons, accepted William's suggestion that they should choose his cousin, Roger de Beaumont, Chancellor of Scotland; and, finally, in 1192 Pope Celestine III announced that he had taken the Scottish Church under his special protection. The Scottish Church, as the "special daughter" of the Roman See, was to be subject to the Pope but to no archbishop.

The King's defeat was more apparent than real: though in theory the chapter—the cathedral clergy—elected a new bishop, in practice they could not proceed to an election without the

King's permission, and they seldom dared to vote against a candidate whom the King favoured. The election had to be confirmed by the Pope, it is true, but if the King anticipated opposition, he sent ambassadors to Rome armed with copious explanations and ample sums of money, and the Pope's objections almost always disappeared.

It was not mere caprice that made the King interfere with his cathedral chapters; he required judges, ambassadors, auditors, and other officials, but as few of his barons and knights had more than a smattering of letters, he had to recruit his civil servants from the ranks of the clergy, and as he could not pay them out of his own pocket, he secured handsome incomes for the most efficient of them by making them bishops. And the bishops repaid their debt; they were consistent supporters of the King and opposed any attempt to increase the political influence of the English King in Scotland, for they feared that if the Scottish King became the vassal of the King of England, they would become the humble servants of the Archbishops of York and Canterbury.

Such fears would have seemed foolish in David's reign. In 1135 the death of Henry I plunged England into anarchy: one set of barons bestowed the crown on Stephen of Blois; another set supported the claim of Henry's daughter, Matilda. David, who was Earl of Huntingdon as well as King of Scotland, had vowed to Henry that he would support his daughter's cause, so no one was surprised when, in 1136, he crossed the border at the head of an army, seized Carlisle and Newcastle, and marched on Durham. But his action was not quite as chivalrous as it seemed: he was more anxious to gain territory in England than to help his niece to the crown; when Stephen hurried north with his barons he found that David was willing to refrain from further fighting if the three northern counties of England were bestowed upon his son Henry. Stephen let Prince Henry have Carlisle and the surrounding district, and with this David appeared to be satisfied. Two years later, however, he invaded England at the head of a great army, drawn from every part of his realm. He advanced to the borders of Yorkshire without meeting any serious opposition, nor did he expect any, for he knew that Stephen was fully occupied elsewhere. But David reckoned without the stout-hearted Thurstan, Archbishop of York, who summoned noble and peasant alike to meet the invader. His appeal was answered; from every village the country folk came tramping in to the rendezvous, with their parish priest at their head, bearing aloft a sacred banner. They knew their duty to fight against the invaders. But some of the great northern nobles were not in such a happy position. What of Robert de Brus, Lord of Annandale in Scotland, and master of wide estates in Yorkshire? Should he fight for David or for Stephen? One thing he did know was that if he sided with the English and the Scots were victorious, he would lose his Scottish estates; if he sided with the Scots and the English were victorious, he would lose his English estates. In vain he pointed out to the King of Scots that he himself was really more a Norman than a Scot; David refused to be turned from his course. De Brus thereupon renounced his fealty and went over to the English; he left one of his sons, however, in the Scottish camp, and made over his Scottish estates to him before he went away. He was now fortified against every risk, even against bodily hurt in the battle, for it had been arranged that if success seemed to incline to the Scots, the son should make the father a prisoner, while if the day went in favour of the English, the father was to capture the son.

The prudence of de Brus was justified when the two armies met at Northallerton. David found it difficult to maintain order in his motley host; the undisciplined men of Galloway got out of hand altogether on the southward march, and they now insisted that they, and not the mail-clad cavalry, should lead the attack upon the English position. The English were ready for them: alternating groups of archers and of spearmen and dismounted knights had been arranged in a compact body round a great ship-mast, from which floated the sacred banners of St. Peter, St. John, and St. Wilfrid. Few of the Galwegians crossed spears with their opponents, for as soon as they got within range the pitiless hail of arrows descended. "Like a hedgehog with quills," says an old writer, "so would you see a Galwegian bristling all round with arrows, and none the less brandishing his sword, and in blind madness rushing forward now smite a foe, now lash the air with useless strokes." Those who did reach the English ranks had the shafts of their spears broken in two, and were slain while they fumbled with their swords.

The gallant Prince Henry, seeing the Galwegians waver,

called up his mail-clad cavalry, hurled himself at another part of the English line, broke it "like a spider's web," and fell upon the guards who had been left with the horses of the dismounted knights. For a moment it seemed as if the English were to be seized with panic, but they rallied when some one held up a dead man's head, and shouted that the King of Scots had been slain. The Galwegians fell back in confusion, their exultation of a few minutes before changed to terror; a chance shot killed the leader of the men of Lothian and created a panic among them, a panic which spread to the reserve division, commanded by the King. Even when David saw the remnants of his army streaming past him in wild disorder, he refused to flee, "thinking that he was bound by his promise to conquer or die." His knights, however, compelled him to mount his horse, and, forming a close body about his standard, they escorted him from the field.

The Scottish army, though defeated, was not destroyed, and in 1139 Stephen, moved by the prayers of his Queen, who was a niece of King David, granted the earldom of Northumberland to Prince Henry. This transaction did not hinder David from taking up arms again for Matilda when she landed in England, but Stephen could not take back his gift by force of arms, and David remained master of the three northern counties of England. When in 1149 young Henry of Anjou, Matilda's son, came to England, it was David who knighted him in Carlisle, which for the time had become a Scottish town. Henry promised in return that when he became King of England he would confirm the King of Scots in his possession of the northern counties and of Huntingdon.

In 1152 Prince Henry of Scotland died, and next year David followed him to the grave. He was succeeded by his grandson Malcolm, a boy of twelve. In 1157 Henry of Anjou, who since 1154 had been King of England, invited the youngster to Chester, made him do homage, though for what he did not specify, and wheedled him out of the three northern counties. He was generous enough, however, to take Huntingdon from Malcolm's younger brother William and bestow it upon Malcolm.

Malcolm did not re-open the question, but after his death in 1165 his more ambitious and energetic brother William followed King Henry to France and asked that the three counties should be restored. William was sent away ill content, but he was afraid to risk a war with Henry as long as Henry had the united strength of England behind him. In 1173, however, it seemed that William's chance had come. Henry's sons had risen in rebellion against their father, and England and Normandy were distracted by civil war. William promptly sided with the rebel princes, on the understanding that he was to have Northumberland for his pains, and led his army over the border, under a golden-yellow flag blazoned with a crimson lion. He was forced to retreat, but in the summer of 1174 William "the Lion," as he was called from his lion standard, returned with a larger army.

Northern England lay at his feet, for Henry was far away, at Canterbury, kneeling in an agony of remorse and wounded pride before the shrine of Thomas Becket, to whose murder his own rash words had led. But William's over-confidence was his ruin: he allowed the bulk of his army to scatter far and wide in search of plunder, while he remained near the castle of Alnwick with a bodyguard of sixty knights. A mist rolled over the level ground on which he was encamped, and when he caught sight of the figures of horses and their riders looming through the fog he thought them some of his own cavalry, returning from a foray. Only when they were a few yards away did he see that they were English. "Now will it appear who knows how to be a knight," he shouted, as he drove the spurs into his horse and charged. He did not go far; his horse was slain and he himself made prisoner. Henry shipped his captive overseas to his castle of Falaise in Normandy, and refused to release him till he had become his vassal.

Other Scottish kings had done homage to Henry's predecessors, just as Henry's predecessors had done homage to the kings of France for their duchy of Normandy. But in the second half of the twelfth century no one knew what precisely the kings of Scotland did homage for. It might be for their estates in England; it might be for Lothian, or for Lothian and Strathclyde together; the one thing of which they were certain was that they did not do homage for the whole of Scotland. Besides, the English kings did not dream of treating the kings of Scots as they treated their English vassals; they did not, for example, listen to complaints by Scottish barons about the quality of the justice dealt out to them in the Scottish courts. But there was to be no ambiguity about the position now: William had to do homage to Henry for the whole of his possessions; his barons had to follow his example and take the oath of fealty to the English King, while the castles of Edinburgh and Stirling and three border fortresses were to open their gates to receive English garrisons.

William made no attempt to free himself from the yoke of his vassalage during Henry's lifetime. But with the accession of Richard Cœur de Lion in 1189 deliverance came: Richard was so eager to go on a crusade to the Holy Land that he allowed William to buy back for ten thousand marks all that Henry had taken from him.

In 1215 the wheel had come full circle: William the Lion, grown cautious, and even timid with old age, had died in 1214, and an ambitious young monarch, his son Alexander II, now sat on the throne of Scotland. Civil war had again broken out in England, this time between King John and his barons; again the King of Scots joined the rebels that he might gain possession of the northern counties, and invaded England. But, like his father, Alexander burned his fingers badly: when King John died in 1216 he joined the English barons who supported the French Prince Louis against the young Henry III, and so drew down a Papal interdict upon his country. The reconciliation of Henry and Louis, in 1217, left him with no choice but to abandon his conquests in the north of England and do homage to Henry for his English estates.

Twenty years later the question that had caused so much heart-burning and bloodshed was finally settled: Alexander agreed to drop his claim to the three northern counties in return for certain estates in the north of England, worth £200 a year.

These "alarums and excursions" in 1138, 1174, and 1216 must not blind us to the fact that during the greater part of the period between the death of Malcolm III in 1093 and the death of Alexander III in 1286 the two countries were at peace. Strange as it may seem, the kings of Scotland waged war against their own subjects far more often than against the kings of England, and on one or two occasions they actually got troops from England to help them to subdue the northern rebels. In 1130, for example, while King David was at the English court, a rebellion broke out in Moray. Troops were hurried north from

England by one of David's English cousins, the rebels were completely defeated, and Angus their ruler was slain.

Trouble threatened in the west as well: when in 1153 David was succeeded by Malcolm IV, Somerled, the half-Norse ruler of Argyll, threw off his lightly-worn allegiance to the King of Scots, and began to plunder the rich and peaceful country in the neighbourhood of Glasgow. But Somerled tried to raid Glasgow once too often; when he came in 1164 he found himself opposed at Renfrew by a determined little army, "very bold, like dragons or lions," headed by the bishop. Somerled was laid low by a spear before the battle had well begun. Bereft of their leader, the invaders surged back in confusion.

The men of Moray were not so easily daunted. Although the last descendant of Lulach had perished, they had found another prince of the blood royal to lead them to battle, Donald Ban MacWilliam, the grandson of Duncan, the eldest son of Malcolm Canmore. In 1179 and again in 1187 William "the Lion" had to lead an army into Moray against the rebels. Though on the second occasion the rebel army was defeated and its leader slain, three other rebellions followed within little more than forty years.

Further north still, in Caithness, there was trouble of a different kind. Adam, the bishop, had had a dispute with the people of his diocese about the payment of teinds. They refused to pay, and when he still insisted they attacked him in his own episcopal palace, wounded him with a battle-axe, dragged him into his kitchen, stoned him till he dropped exhausted, then set fire to the building and let him burn to death. A swift vengeance overtook the murderers; the King hurried north, arrested ninety suspects, and ordered their hands and feet to be cut off.

No sooner was the north pacified than trouble began in the south-west. Galloway had been subjugated by Malcolm IV in 1160, after three hard-fought campaigns, and the Celtic lords of Galloway had lived in amity with their half-Norman kings. But Alan, Lord of Galloway, died, leaving three daughters and one illegitimate son, Thomas. Alexander II divided the province into three parts and gave one third to each daughter. The Galwegians, disliking this division of their land, declared for Thomas and, in 1234, rose in rebellion. In the following summer the King's forces appeared in Galloway, the rebels broke

DUNFERMLINE ABBEY: THE NAVE

The Church of Queen Margaret's time is represented only by foundations beneath the later floor-level. The nave dates from David I's reign.

PLATE 15

HAAKONSHALLEN

The palace of King Haakon at Bergen

and fled and a few weeks later Thomas gave himself up to the King. The land was apportioned as the King had desired, and each of the three heiresses married the inevitable Norman baron. One of them, Devorgilla, married Sir John de Balliol, a name with which we shall soon be more familiar.

Alexander might well have rested content. The men of Moray had now no descendant of Lulach or Duncan for whom to fight, and the Norman baron had at last got a footing in the most Celtic part of southern Scotland. But the King's eyes were turned westwards, to the islands which had once been part of the heritage of the Kings of Scots. For a century and a half they had belonged to the King of Norway, but as Norway was far away they had come under the control of the descendants of Somerled, who were known as the Kings of the Isles.

Alexander first tried what money could do: in 1243 he sent two bishops to the court of King Hakon to offer to buy back the lands. "I am aware of no such urgent need of money that I need to sell the lands," answered the Norse King dryly. Other ambassadors received no more polite a reply, and in 1249 Alexander resolved to attempt the conquest of the Hebrides. At the head of a fleet he sailed down the Firth of Clyde, round the Mull of Kintyre, and northwards into the Firth of Lorne. But while his ship lay in Kerrera Sound he was stricken with a fever and died.

It seemed that with the death of Alexander II more than the Hebrides would be lost to Scotland. His successor was a boy of eight, and ten years passed before he was master in his own house. In the year 1263 a fear that had been dead for centuries suddenly came to life again: news arrived that King Hakon, with the greatest fleet that had ever left the shores of Norway, was making for the west coast of Scotland. The old King, fearing that the Hebrides were slipping out of his grasp, had come to frighten the Islesmen back to their allegiance. Southward through the Hebrides the great fleet sailed, round the Mull of Kintyre and up the Firth of Clyde till it anchored off the island of Arran.

King Alexander knew that the summer was waning, and that if Hakon lingered much longer he ran a serious risk of being overwhelmed by the equinoctial gales. So he sent ambassadors to the fleet, apparently to negotiate a treaty of peace, but really to waste Hakon's time. At the end of September Alexander broke off the negotiations, whereupon Hakon led his great fleet farther up the Firth, and anchored under the shelter of the Cumbraes. At the beginning of October, a great storm rolled up from the west. Eight anchors could not keep the King's flagship from drifting, and the other ships fared worse; ten of them, including a merchant ship stuffed with provisions, were driven ashore at Largs. Nor was that all; as the crews of the stranded vessels tried to push off and get into deep water again, they heard arrows whistle past their ears, and saw that the Scots were assembling on the beach. But Hakon, taking advantage of a lull in the tempest, sent ashore a strong landing-party, which succeeded in driving back the Scots. On the following day King Alexander brought up mail-clad cavalry and launched an attack on the Norsemen on the beach. The latter succeeded in holding on till evening, when the Scots withdrew; then they suddenly delivered a counter-attack, drove the Scots back, and ere they could recover, returned to the beach and pushed off. Thus ended the famous battle of Largs, an indecisive skirmish that brought little glory to either side. Though a few ships had been lost, Hakon still had a mighty armada, but he had to withdraw and he died in Kirkwall a few months later. When Alexander learned of the death of Hakon, he opened negotiations with the new King of Norway, Magnus; again the offer of money was made, and this time it was accepted. In 1266, by the Treaty of Perth, Magnus agreed to surrender Man and the Hebrides for 4,000 marks down, and an annual payment of 100 marks.

So the Hebrides at last formed part of the kingdom of Scotland. It made very little difference to the Islesmen: hitherto they had disobeyed the King of Norway; now they disobeyed the King of Scots.

CHAPTER 7

SCOTLAND IN THE TIME OF ALEXANDER III

When Alexander our King was dead
That Scotland led in love and le,[1]
Away was sons [2] of ale and bread,
Of wine and wax, of game and glee:
Our gold was changed into lead,
Christ, born into Virginity,
Succour Scotland and remede [3]
That stad [4] is in perplexity.

So sang a forgotten Scottish poet. For the quarter century between the battle of Largs and the death of King Alexander was indeed a golden age. Nevermore would a threat to Scotland from Norway be serious, for in 1281 Eric, the young King of Norway, had taken the Princess Margaret, the daughter of the King of Scots, to be his bride. As for a war with England, that had become, to all appearance, quite impossible. Had not the King married a sister of Edward I of England? After the death of his wife,[5] it was to his brother-in-law that Alexander turned for comfort, in that black hour when he saw his son, the Prince of Scotland, follow his daughter to the grave. Then there had been no serious rebellion either in the north or in the south-west for many years, partly because the remoter regions were now very effectively bridled with castles of timber or of stone, partly because Galwegian and Highlander alike no longer regarded the King and his barons as aliens and intruders.

For in the thirteenth century a curious change came over Scotland: the Norman baron, the bishop who knew more Latin and French than English, the English-speaking traders and farmers of Fife and Lothian, the Gaelic-speaking herdsmen from the hills, all began to look on themselves as Scotsmen, as people bound together by some mysterious tie, like, but not quite the same as, the tie of kinship. In other words, they were no longer a collection of different races; they had become a nation. Something

[1] loyalty. [2] abundance. [3] remedy. [4] placed.

[5] Alexander's first wife, Margaret, daughter of Henry III of England, died in 1275. In 1285 he married Yolande, or Joleta, daughter of the French Count of Dreux.

very like national pride in the independence of the Scottish kingdom was expressed by the monk of Melrose who made this comment on the transaction by which William the Lion was released from feudal servitude: "And so, by God's assistance, he worthily and honourably removed a heavy yoke of domination and servitude from the kingdom of the Scots." But this sense of national solidarity, this belief in the kinship of all who lived between the Cheviots and the Pentland Firth, was still very vague; it was something that seemed as if it might be lost far more easily than it had been won. For it could not be denied that the Scottish baron had really more in common with the English baron than with the Scottish peasant at his castle gate, and that the douce burgess of Edinburgh or Berwick would feel more at ease in the company of a merchant or master-mariner from Newcastle than in that of a wild, shock-headed Highlander speaking a language that to him was incomprehensible.

Though the Scotland of Alexander's time was in after years regarded as an earthly paradise, to us it would seem bleak and comfortless enough. It is true that the King and some of his great barons had begun to make extensive alterations to their older castles of timber and earth. Sometimes they replaced the wooden palisades by walls of stone, which might be no less than ten feet thick and twenty-five feet high; sometimes, in addition, a massive stone tower or donjon took the place of the old wooden tower. But even in the newest castles many of the interior buildings were still made of wood, or of wood and clay, and always the main consideration was not comfort, but security.

None of the castles of that period stands unaltered today, and most of them were demolished and rebuilt during the English wars, but it is not difficult to imagine what one of them, say Bothwell Castle on the River Clyde, was like at the end of the thirteenth century. Its very position shows how anxious its builder had been to make it secure: on the south and west it was protected by the river; on the north and east by a great ditch. The bailey or courtyard was enclosed by a lofty and massive stone wall or "curtain." Along the top of this ran a walk protected by a battlemented parapet, from the cover of which the archers could take leisurely aim at the besiegers below. At four of the five angles of the curtain stood a great flanking tower, from the loop-holes

Plate 16 Bothwell Castle

PLATE 17

KILDRUMMY CASTLE

of which arrows could be directed against any of the besiegers who attempted to undermine the curtain with pick and crowbar. At the fifth angle stood the gatehouse, where the great gateway of the castle was almost lost to view between two projecting towers. It was approached by a drawbridge, very tempting to a bold besieger. But he would be well advised to give it a wide berth, for if he set foot on it one end would sink beneath him, and deposit him in a deep pit, while the other would tilt up, and block the gateway completely. Should he be lucky enough to get over the drawbridge before the bolts holding it in position had been removed, he would probably be crushed beneath the portcullis, a heavy wooden gate shod with iron spikes, which slid down from a chamber above the gateway; if he slipped past he had still to grope along a long, dark passage, and batter in a massive wooden door. Even when the besiegers reached the courtyard they could not call themselves masters of the castle, for each of the four towers was really a miniature fortress, capable of being defended by a few resolute men.

The change from wood to stone made no difference to the comfort of the castle: the gales of winter still blew through the unglazed windows, the acrid wood smoke still eddied round the room, and the dogs still fought for bones and scraps of meat among the rushes that carpeted the floor. But it was luxurious in comparison with the huts that clustered not far from its gates, huts walled and roofed with turf, without windows, without chimneys, with no door but a curtain of hide. Here the peasant —serf, or free tenant—slept under the same roof as his cattle, as people did in some parts of the Hebrides until very recently.

Though the Scottish village changed little in five hundred years—when the poet Gray visited Forfarshire in 1765 he noticed "just above ground, the huts . . . built of and covered with turf"—in the Scottish town changes came more rapidly. We can only guess how the older Scottish towns came into existence. No single explanation will fit all of them; some, like St. Andrews and Glasgow, obviously grew up round a great religious establishment; others, like Edinburgh and Stirling, plainly owe their origin to the presence of a fortress. They were almost always situated beside some good natural harbour; even Stirling and Perth could be reached by a medieval ship of ordinary size. Their position attracted foreign traders, who brought into port goods far in excess of what the inhabitants required for their own use. The wealthier inhabitants deliberately bought more than they required, and sold the surplus at a profit after the traders had departed. In this way a merchant class came into existence. Nor were these merchants all Scottish: Queen Margaret and her successors encouraged foreign traders to settle in Scotland; in Berwick, for example, there was a large colony of Flemings. On the other hand, all the goods that were sold in a Scottish town were not imported from overseas; some were made by the local craftsmen. They too made more than their fellow-townsmen required, in the hope that, sooner or later, the surplus would be bought by people from the rural districts nearby.

A burgh was more than a collection of houses, it was a trading community enjoying certain definite rights or "liberties," granted to it by the King or by some great lord, and embodied in a written "charter." The members of such a privileged community were allowed to manage their own affairs, or rather to elect officials who would direct the policy of the burgh, make special laws, settle disputes between one burgess and another, and punish evil-doers. In addition, the burgh was given a monopoly of the trade of the district in which it was situated; for example, every foreign ship that entered the Firth of Tay was expected to put in first of all at the port of Dundee. Only after the wares that it carried had been displayed in the market-place, only after the Dundee merchants had chosen what they wanted, was it allowed to proceed up-stream to the rival burgh of Perth. Nor was that all: within the sheriffdom of Forfar no one who was not a burgess of Dundee was allowed to buy wool and hides, the only Scottish commodities, with the exception of salt fish, that the foreign merchants were eager to take home with them. So the foreign merchant could buy wool only from a burgess. Further, the weekly market and annual fair were taken under the King's protection: to assault or rob any one coming from or going to a fair or market was looked on as an offence against the King himself, to be dealt with, not by the burgh officials, but by the sheriff or some other representative of the sovereign.

The burgesses had to give something in return; for the land which he held within the burgh, every burgess had to pay an annual rent of seven pence to the King's Chamberlain. It seems a paltry sum, but the thirteenth-century master craftsman never dreamed of paying more to his journeyman for a week's work.

The burgh, as we have seen, was self-governing. The King or his Chamberlain appointed the magistrates to begin with, but in later times the provost, bailies and other officials were appointed by the burgh council, which in its turn was elected by the whole body of the burgesses. Not all the Scottish burghs were royal burghs; in some, like St. Andrews and Glasgow, the burgesses were vassals of the bishop; in others, of some great earl or baron.

Though none of the burgesses was very rich, and none very poor, a thirteenth-century trading community was not exactly a band of brothers. They might present a united front to outsiders, but they were divided themselves: the merchants were in general more wealthy than the craftsmen; they knew that without trade the prosperity of the burgh would disappear, and so they began to look on themselves as more important than they really were. They strengthened their position by organising themselves into a Merchant Gild, from which all craftsmen, however wealthy, were excluded. The gild controlled the wholesale and the external trade of the burgh; if a strange merchant came to town, he had to display his wares first of all to the members of the gild, and similarly no burgess who was not a member of the gild could put his goods on a ship bound for a foreign port. And just because the gild included the majority of the wealthiest and most influential burgesses, it came in many places to control the government of the burgh; the members of the burgh council were most of them gild brethren, and the gild hall was used indifferently for meetings of the council and of the gild.

We have seen what a twelfth-century monastery and a thirteenth-century castle looked like; can we form any very clear idea of the appearance of a thirteenth-century burgh? It will be all but impossible, for though the castle and the church have sometimes survived, the dwellings of the thirteenth-century merchants and craftsmen have long since disappeared. But suppose we take a modern industrial town, Dundee, for example, and try to see it as it was in the year before the death of Alexander III.

We see only a little cluster of houses, strung along the two sides of a single broad street. Behind the lines of houses long, narrow gardens stretch north and south, for every town then was a garden city. Beyond the gardens on the landward side is a broad stretch of cornland, and beyond that again rough pasture covered with whin and broom, for many of the burgesses are also farmers, grazing their sheep and cattle on the common pasture, growing wheat and oats in their holdings in the burgh fields, and taking their corn to be ground in the burgh mill. Town wall there was none, though the east and west ends of the solitary street are protected by a substantial gate-house or "port," and the burgh was enclosed after a fashion by the "head dykes" at the end of the gardens behind the houses.

You hurry through the East Port, and find yourself in the one main street, Market Street or "Mercat Gait," as it is called. You notice few houses of any size; even the provost is content with a squat little wooden structure, roofed with thatch. There are one or two more imposing buildings, however; the east end of the burgh is dominated by the castle, perched on an eminence that rises sheer from the water's edge; at the west end rises the parish church. About half-way between them another of the rare stone buildings catches the eye; the pillar on the stone pedestal in front of it tells you what it is: it is the gild hall, and the pillar is the market cross. The market cross, you may say, is the very heart of the burgh. It is here that strange merchants have to display their goods to the burgesses; it is at the tron, a great balance a yard or two away, that their goods have to be weighed; it is from the steps of the pedestal that the town-crier announces any new regulation made by the rulers of the burgh; it is from these steps that the royal herald announces the forthcoming visit of the King, the Justiciar or the Chamberlain. Another group of stone buildings stands beyond the gardens to the north of the town. It is occupied by Franciscan or Grey Friars, members of one of the new religious orders that came to Scotland about the middle of the thirteenth century. Like their rivals, the Dominicans, or Black Friars, they considered that their duty was not to shut themselves up away from the world, but to go out into the world and do the work that the parish priest often left half done. They knew how to preach, but though their audiences were thrilled by their eloquence, they were moved even more by their devotion to a life of poverty and good works.

As you move along the street you see nothing that you can

Chessmen Carved from Walrus Ivory

Found in the Isle of Lewis, they were probably carved in the early thirteenth century.

PLATE 19

recognise as a shop. Shops there are indeed, but they have no windows by which you can identify them, and they are few in number. For the average household is practically self-supporting; the housewife and her daughters bake bread, brew ale—there is no coffee or tea—spin and weave, and make the cloth into garments. People's wants are few: a furniture shop would not thrive in a town where the best room in the provost's house is furnished with a trestle table, one solitary chair, and a few stools and benches.

Most of such buying and selling as there is takes place at the weekly market, when people come in from the neighbouring districts to buy what their own villages cannot produce. Then you will see stalls set up in the middle of the street and surrounded by a motley throng, in which the herdsman from the Sidlaws, as shaggy and tousled as his own cattle, rubs shoulders with the merchant, very stately in his long robe, with the hood flung over his shoulder, or the merchant's wife, whom you would mistake for a nun, if you judged her by the cut, and not by the gay colour, of her raiment.

On the fifteenth of August the stalls are more numerous and the crowd about them far larger; it is the first day of the Lady Mary Fair, the great annual fair which lasts for a week. The people of Dundee, like the people of other Scottish burghs, have found that their community cannot be absolutely self-contained and self-supporting. The bailie's wife would fain rustle in silks, but only coarse homespun can be obtained in Dundee; she wants pungent spices to disguise the taste of the salt meat that must be her diet for almost six months of the year, but cinnamon, ginger, cloves, and nutmeg do not grow in Scotland; she has seen a panel of tapestry in the provost's house, and is determined to have one like it, but no Dundee webster would attempt to weave these gay, pictured cloths. The bailie would like something better than home-brewed ale to set before the provost or the dean of the gild; his business has prospered and he wants to invest his money in jewellery for his wife, and in two or three pieces of silver plate; but wine and wine-cups must alike be brought from over the sea. In the fair week, however, silks and spices, wines and silver plate, may be obtained by all who can pay for them, for merchants from England, France, and Flanders have set up stalls in the Mercat Gait on which these costly wares are displayed.

Hovering on the verge of the crowd you may notice a mail-clad knight with a party of spearmen. He is the Constable or Keeper of the Castle, the King's special representative in these parts. Usually he does not interfere if any disorder breaks out in the town—that is the bailies' business, not his—but in the fair week it is different: a breach of the peace is a breach of the King's peace, and the offender must be haled off to the castle, to hear his sentence from the mouth of the constable.

For though the burgh, like the baron's estate, was almost a kingdom within a kingdom, the burgh was not absolutely independent and self-contained, nor was the baron's will always law, even on his own estate. Certain crimes, like murder, were deemed too serious to be dealt with by an ordinary court; persons suspected of these crimes had to be handed over to the sheriff of the county, who either pronounced sentence himself, or waited till the royal Justiciar or the King appeared to relieve him of the responsibility. The King usually had two justiciars: one, the Justiciar of Scotland, toured through the northern half of the kingdom at regular intervals; the other, the Justiciar of Lothian, perambulated the country south of the Forth. A conscientious king like Alexander III was not content with this; he knew that a justiciar might become slack, or a sheriff allow himself to be browbeaten by a powerful baron, so with his great officers of state he travelled from one county town to another, pronouncing sentence at each on such criminals as the sheriff brought before him, or dealing with complaints from people to whom the sheriff had failed to do justice.

Most people preferred King's justice to baron's justice, but both were equally rough and ready. If a man accused of a felony could produce twenty-four people willing to swear that he was innocent he was acquitted. If he failed to produce the required number, or if his accuser arrived with another twenty-four, various things might happen, but no one would dream of cross-questioning the twenty-four "witnesses," and asking them if they really knew anything about the crime. The accused might be required to fight his accuser, or to grasp a bar of red-hot iron. "God will not allow the innocent to be hurt," argued the pious but indolent judge. Or he might be flung into a pool of water; it made little difference what happened then, for only if he sank was he pronounced to be innocent. Imprisonment was not a popular penalty with the judge; how liberally he dealt out the sentence of death we can estimate from the humane statute which recommended that no man should be hanged for theft unless he had stolen at least two sheep. Sometimes, however, the penalty fitted the crime; if a man drew a knife and threatened to strike, that same knife was driven through his own hand; if he struck and drew blood, his hand was cut off.

But wild justice, as the people of Scotland were soon to learn, was better than no justice at all. On the 19th of March, 1286, a tempest of wind and rain swept over Scotland as King Alexander sat in Edinburgh Castle, discussing affairs of state with his Chancellor and the two dozen prelates and great barons who made up his council. Afternoon was darkening into evening when the King horrified his lords by announcing that he intended to cross the Forth that very night and ride to Kinghorn, where Queen Yolande was living. They tried to dissuade him, but the King would listen to no entreaties; with three followers he rode off through the driving rain to cross the Firth at South Queensferry. He reached Inverkeithing in safety, and, after obtaining two guides, set off on the last stage of his journey. But the tempest raged more furiously than ever, and in the pitch-black night the King became separated from his companions. They shouted, but no answer came except the wild, melancholy shriek of the wind; he had vanished into the darkness.

Next morning the mystery was solved; the King's dead body was found on the beach, bruised and broken as if by a fall from his horse.

CHAPTER 8

THE WAR OF INDEPENDENCE: FIRST PHASE

THOUGH Alexander III was not an old man, he had outlived all his children; his sole living descendant was a little girl of three, the only child of his daughter Margaret, who had married King Eric of Norway. A few weeks after the King's death the Scottish nobles and prelates appointed six Guardians to rule the country in the name of the young Queen.

Meanwhile the very shrewd and ambitious King Edward I of England had been watching the turn that affairs were taking in Scotland. It seemed absurd to him that the island of Britain should be divided into three separate countries, each with its own ruler and its own separate laws. A few years before he had succeeded in making himself master of Wales; he would not see anything wrong in making himself master of Scotland if the opportunity should occur. The Scots would be no worse off under him, and, besides, their kings had often done homage to English kings in the past. If an eleventh-century King of Scots had acknowledged that he was the King of England's "man," then the thirteenth-century King of England must be the lawful master of the realm of Scotland.

Edward was right up to a certain point: an enduring friendship between the two countries could bring nothing but gain to both. And up to a certain point his conduct was wise and tactful; he secured the consent of the Scottish nobles to the marriage of their young Queen to his son, Edward of Carnarvon, afterwards the luckless Edward II. But the death of the Maid in 1290 brought this scheme to naught.

Disputes among the Scots soon gave Edward another opportunity. The old Lord of Annandale, Robert de Brus, who had been acknowledged heir to the throne almost half a century before, at a time when Alexander II thought that he was destined to die childless, had come to Perth with a formidable company; it was plain that, in spite of the opposition of the Guardians, he meant to be crowned King of Scotland; it was plain, too, that if he did succeed in his attempt, he would be attacked at once by one of the other nobles who asserted that their claim to the crown was better than his. But they were in no stronger position than de Brus; not one of them could be sure of the undivided support of his countrymen. Civil war was inevitable, unless the Scots could find someone in whose wisdom and impartiality they had absolute confidence, whom they could ask to decide the dispute about the succession.

Such a disinterested judge they seemed to have in the person of the King of England. Moreover, Edward eagerly proffered his services as arbiter, and in 1291 he met the nobles and prelates of Scotland at Norham on the Tweed. The opportunity had presented itself at last, and he yielded to the temptation; it was announced that no candidate would be considered who did not acknowledge Edward as his overlord, and promise to do homage to him for the whole of Scotland, should he be lucky enough to be awarded the crown. The Scottish nobles yielded to the temptation too; if the price of a crown was dependence on Edward, they were quite willing to pay the price. After all, the leading claimants were already vassals of Edward in respect of their English estates, and it would make little difference to their relationship if they were to hold Scotland of him as well.

It was soon discovered by those to whom Edward remitted the case that the claims of only two of the thirteen competitors required to be seriously discussed. One was the old Lord of Annandale, the son of the second daughter of David, Earl of Huntingdon, the younger brother of William the Lion; the other was John de Balliol, a grandson of the eldest daughter of Earl David. The auditors were hopelessly perplexed; if Scotland had been a private estate they might have divided it into three, and assigned the parts to Brus, Balliol, and John de Hastings, the grandson of Earl David's third daughter. But Scotland was not an ordinary estate, and the ordinary rules of succession might not hold. Towards the end of 1292 they referred the matter back to Edward, who decided in favour of Balliol, and at Christmas the new King went to Newcastle and did homage to Edward for his kingdom.

Edward's conscience was absolutely clear. He had kept to the letter of the law; he had given the crown of Scotland to the man who had the best claim to it. And he intended to keep to the letter of the law in future; he would let Balliol see that his homage was not an empty form. He would impose one or two tests, then, if Balliol proved docile, Edward would know that he had conquered Scotland without striking a blow; if Balliol resented his overlord's interference, Edward would treat him as any contumacious vassal ought to be treated and deprive him of his kingdom. So Edward let no chance slip of reminding Balliol that he was not master in his own house; he displayed a remarkable degree of sympathy with any one who complained that he had not obtained justice in the Scottish courts. When one of Edward's Gascon subjects complained that he had dunned Balliol in vain for the sum of £2,000 in payment of wine consumed by his predecessor Alexander, Edward summoned the King of Scots to appear at Westminster and explain why he had not paid his wine merchant's bill. Complaints from King John's own subjects received the same over-scrupulous attention, till at length the docile and long-suffering Balliol began to understand that the real King of Scotland was not himself, but Edward Plantagenet.

There seemed to be only one way out of this intolerable position. Balliol knew that Edward had quarrelled with the King of France and was meditating an invasion of his country, so when he received orders to follow Edward across the Channel he flatly refused, and in the autumn of 1295 he entered into an alliance with Philip of France.

Edward was furious when he learned that the worm had turned at last. In the spring of 1296 he crossed the Tweed at Coldstream and suddenly appeared outside Berwick, which, like most Scottish towns, was unwalled, with no defences except a shallow ditch and a hastily constructed palisade. The burgesses were full of confidence and when the English soldiers rushed across the ditch, swarmed over the palisade "as if it were a thing of naught," and fell upon them, they were so stupefied with astonishment and fear that they stood like men in a trance, not offering to raise a sword or bend a bow. In a few minutes the town was in Edward's hands. Only at two points was any resistance offered—at the Red Hall, the hostel occupied by the Flemish merchants who traded in the burgh, and at the castle. The castle surrendered before nightfall; the thirty gallant Flemings, however, defended their hall even after it had been set on fire, and to a man perished in the flames.

Edward determined to teach a lesson to Berwick and to the whole of Scotland; all day he let his soldiers roam through the streets at will, killing and plundering. Only when the King saw an infant crying and clinging to its dead mother did he turn away in horror from what after all was his own handiwork, and cry "Laissez! laissez!"

While Edward stayed behind in Berwick superintending the building of stouter fortifications, his lieutenant, the Earl de Warenne, hurried forward to besiege the powerful castle of Dunbar. But the defenders sent an appeal for help to Balliol, and when a powerful relieving army appeared they waved flags from the battlements and shouted insults to the besiegers, calling them long-tailed curs, and threatening to kill them and cut off their tails. For the more ignorant Scots believed then, and long afterwards, that the English did actually have tails. The besiegers, leaving a small force to watch the castle, advanced in good order to meet the relieving army, but fell into some confusion as they crossed a ravine that separated them from the Scots. Again the shout of exultation arose, mingled this time with the blast of horns "terrible enough to reach to the uttermost depths of hell." But the shouting died away when the English ranks closed, and the phalanx of mail-clad men-at-arms loomed up only a few yards away. The miserable story of Berwick was repeated and the English walked into the castle of Dunbar unopposed.

The news of these two disasters paralysed nobles and people alike. They seemed to look on Edward as invincible. The defenders of the powerful border castle of Roxburgh surrendered the moment they were asked to do so; Edinburgh Castle held out for eight days; the garrison of Stirling prudently cleared out as soon as word was brought of Edward's approach. Finally, when Edward reached Perth, three months after he had first crossed the Tweed, he received a letter from Balliol praying for peace "not according to his own deserts, but according to the King's loving kindness." A fortnight later, Balliol, who had already repudiated his alliance with France, formally surrendered his kingdom to Edward and so earned the name of "Toom Tabard" or "empty cloak."

The remainder of Edward's first Scottish campaign was simply a triumphal procession; he marched northward unopposed as far as Elgin, halted at the Abbey of Scone on his way south to remove the Stone of Destiny on which the Kings of Scots from time immemorial had been crowned, and returned to Berwick, to hold a Parliament at which practically every man of note in Scotland did homage to him.

So in the autumn of 1296 King Edward crossed the Tweed well content; it had taken him ten years to subdue the little country of Wales; he had conquered Scotland in half as many months.

But the campaign of 1296 had not been a fight to a finish, and the Scots, after they had gained some experience of the ways of English officials and English garrisons, began to wish that they had fought a little harder. But where were they to find a leader? Balliol had proved himself to be incompetent and weak; old de Brus was dead and his son had supported Edward in the vain hope that Edward would hand over the kingdom to him after he had defeated Balliol. His grandson, the young Earl of Carrick, had ambition and ability, but he could not be trusted to run straight; he did not want to see Edward King of Scotland, but still less did he want to see the feckless Balliol back again, and least of all did he want to do anything that would set Balliol's kinsman John Comyn, Lord of Badenoch, on the throne. So he pursued a zigzag course, appearing now as a Scottish patriot, now as Edward's ally.

Salvation came, not from any of the noble or semi-royal families of Scotland, but from a simple country gentleman. In the early summer of 1297 William Wallace slew the English Sheriff of Lanark; then with a band of determined men which grew in numbers daily he advanced into the north of Scotland, and set about capturing the castles that had been manned by English troops. Castle after castle fell into his hands, but while he was besieging the castle of Dundee, news was brought to him that the Guardian of Scotland, old Earl de Warenne, had shaken off his lethargy and was advancing on Stirling. Wallace hurried southward and posted his army at the northern end of the narrow wooden bridge that spanned the Forth.

To Wallace it must have seemed a desperate gamble. He was outnumbered; he had no heavy cavalry—and in those days battles were decided by the heavy cavalry—and his position was not so strong as it looked. Though the bridge was so narrow that horsemen had to cross it two abreast, there was a ford not far away where sixty horsemen could cross at once. But the English leadership at Stirling was as bad as the Scottish leadership had been at Dunbar. The commander was old and sleepy, and his second in command, Hugh de Cressingham, the Treasurer of Scotland, was a fat and conceited churchman who had turned amateur soldier. So it came about that a large body of English troops actually crossed the river before the Scots were ready for them, and, after waiting in vain for orders from their slumbering commander, retreated to their own side of the stream. So it came about that, after precious hours had been wasted, De Warenne refused to let the troops cross by the ford, and Cressingham bullied them into crossing by the bridge. No one molested them, the King's standard-bearer, the handsome and insolent

PLATE 20 THE WALLACE MONUMENT, STIRLINGSHIRE
On the Abbey Craig, overlooking the site of the Battle of Stirling Bridge

THE CORONATION CHAIR IN WESTMINSTER ABBEY

The chair was made to incorporate the Coronation Stone removed from Scone by Edward I.

Treasurer, the long line of knights in their glittering mail, the dark, squat bowmen from Wales, all passed undisturbed.

But Wallace knew what he was about; his men, lying almost invisible on the hill-side, only waited the word to charge. When barely half the hostile army had crossed, the word was given; the Scots rushed pell-mell down the slope, and while one party made straight for the bridge, cutting the English army in two, the remainder hurled themselves upon the distracted vanguard. On the bridge itself confusion reigned; of the mob of armed men that surged to and fro many were swept off and drowned. Meanwhile De Warenne could do nothing but gaze helplessly at his vanguard being cut to pieces; then after ordering the bridge to be broken down and burned, he returned to Berwick with more alacrity than one would have expected from one of his years. Cressingham's dead body remained on the field of battle.

The victory of Stirling Bridge made Wallace master of southern Scotland. Nor was he content to remain on the defensive; before the end of the year he had raided the northern counties of England.

But though by his prowess in the field Wallace had won the title of Guardian of Scotland, his position in 1298 was really a precarious one. An unknown knight could not command the allegiance of the great Scottish nobles; gallant soldier as he was he could not hope to be a match for one of the most skilful generals in Europe, for it was with Edward himself that he had now to deal. So when on a summer morning he stood on a moor beside Falkirk and compared the proud squadrons of mail-clad knights with his own little army—some cavalry whom he did not trust, four circles or "schiltrons" of spearmen joined up by lines of archers in loose formation—he can have had little doubt of the result. Yet for a time it seemed as if the day might go in his favour. The foremost division of English cavalry charged straight down on the enemy, and plunged into a marsh which guarded the front of the Scottish line. The second division, headed by the warlike Bishop of Durham, made a detour to the east, and arrived without mishap on the left flank of the Scots. The bishop signalled to them to halt till the third line came up, but in vain. "Leave soldiering alone, Bishop, and get on with your Mass," shouted the young knights as they galloped down upon the Scots. The Scottish cavalry fled almost without striking a blow; but though the English horsemen easily overwhelmed the lightly-armed archers they recoiled baffled from the impenetrable hedge of spears. Again and again they charged, but if a front rank man fell a rear rank man stepped into his place; the circle remained unbroken.

The end was not far off. Edward's archers picked their way forward to the edge of the marsh, and drawing the cords of their great long bows back to their shoulders, they loosed flight after flight of arrows into the serried ranks of the spearmen. It was more than flesh and blood could stand; one after another the circles were broken, and as the gaps appeared the English cavalry swept forward and completed what the archers had begun.

If Edward thought that his triumph at Falkirk would reconcile the Scots to his rule, he was mistaken. They never seemed to know when they were beaten; they would be hopelessly smashed in the autumn, mope all winter, and then rebel again the following spring. Twice did Edward spend Christmas in Scotland and, contrary to the medieval practice, carry on war all through the winter. At last, in 1304, he began to see something definite result from his labours. One after another, the more obstinate patriots surrendered to him; in February his most dangerous opponent next to Wallace, John Comyn, Lord of Badenoch, went over to his side; in July Stirling Castle, the last Scottish fortress to hold out against him, was battered to pieces by his great new engine, the "War Wolf."

Only Wallace remained at large, and Wallace was now a hunted outlaw, powerless for good or ill. Then in 1305 Wallace himself was captured, and brought to Westminster Hall to stand his trial for treason. He proudly declared that he was no traitor, for he had never taken the oath of allegiance to an alien monarch, and so could never have broken it. This defence availed nothing; he was found guilty and dragged to the gallows at Tyburn, there to die the unspeakably horrible death that in those days was reserved for traitors of whatever rank.

CHAPTER 9

THE WAR OF INDEPENDENCE: SECOND PHASE

Among his Scottish supporters there were few whom Edward trusted more than the younger Robert de Brus, Earl of Carrick. It is true that he had taken up arms against Edward in 1297, but he had laid them down again before the battle of Stirling Bridge. It is true that after the eclipse of Wallace at Falkirk he figured for a short time as Guardian of Scotland, but he went over to Edward's side in 1302, taking all his own vassals with him, followed him to Scotland in his last campaign, served as commander of the English garrison at Ayr, and supplied him with engines for the siege of Stirling Castle. Edward did not suspect that Bruce might have sided with him partly out of regard for the safety of his cautious, time-serving father, and partly through jealousy of his rival, John Comyn; he did not guess the effect that the surrender of Comyn and the death of the elder Bruce in 1304 would have on a mind as keen and ambitious as his own, nor did he know that at the very time when Bruce did homage to him for his father's English estates, he was actually negotiating with the Bishop of St. Andrews for his support in an attempt on the Scottish crown.

Bruce gained Bishop Lamberton's support easily enough—the Scottish clergy feared that the rule of an English archbishop would be the necessary consequence of the rule of an English king—but he found it more difficult to get the support of the powerful Lord of Badenoch. Early in 1306 Bruce invited Comyn to come to the Church of the Greyfriars in Dumfries and there discuss the business, but though Comyn came, he flatly refused to co-operate with Bruce. A blind fury overcame Bruce; he drew his dagger and plunged it into Comyn's body. The friars bore the wounded man from the cloister to the church, and laid him before the high altar, but they were interrupted by Bruce's followers, who rushed in and killed him before the eyes of the terrified clerics.

It was a black and horrible story, and it lost nothing in the telling. Everybody in England believed that Bruce had lured the "Red Comyn" to Dumfries and deliberately picked a quarrel with him so that he might remove his only possible rival from his path. The best that can be said of it is that it was a ghastly blunder. It drew down on Bruce's head the undying hatred of Comyn's kinsmen and friends, men like the Earl of Buchan, Alexander of Argyll and his son, John of Lorne, and the MacDowalls of Galloway. So he had to fight with England and half Scotland as well. Worst of all, he had to face the wrath of the Church; as soon as the Pope was informed that Bruce had slain Comyn in a consecrated building, he pronounced on him the dread sentence of excommunication.

When a few weeks later the slayer of Comyn was hastily crowned king at Scone, his wife said to him, "It seems to me that we are but a summer King and Queen, whom the children crown with flowers in their sports." There was no need for King Edward to come north; Aymer de Valence, his lieutenant, came upon Bruce's army at Methven all unprepared, with no outposts or sentinels, surprised and scattered it, and almost succeeded in capturing Bruce himself.

At the head of a few hundred followers Bruce retreated westward, to the seeming security of the hills and moorlands, only to suffer another crushing defeat at the hands of Alexander of Argyll. The game was played out; in the late autumn of 1306, after dispatching his Queen and his young brother Nigel to the strong castle of Kildrummy, he left Scotland altogether. His next movements are mysterious: he may have been in the island of Rathlin, off the north coast of Ireland; he may have been in Orkney, then a dependency of Norway.

A weakling would have been broken altogether by these trials, but adversity developed qualities in Bruce that hitherto he had not seemed to possess. He learned to school his temper, to be cheerful and good-humoured whether things went well or ill, to be courteous to friend and foe alike. Best of all, the self-seeking adventurer who would not fight for Scotland if Scotland was not to be his, learned that a great leader, a man who is a king in the fullest sense, must be willing to spend himself in the service of his followers, must do work which is too hard for them, and encounter dangers which they dare not face. Long afterwards did those who had been fugitives from that disastrous battle in the west tell how the King deliberately placed himself in the rear of the retreating army, and how he did not flinch when three Highlanders rushed at him, but waited for them and slew them single-handed.

With the return of spring the King's hopes revived and, accompanied by his brother Edward and his lieutenant Sir James of Douglas, he crossed the sea to his own country of Carrick. News of disaster met him: Kildrummy Castle had been taken, his brother Nigel had died on the scaffold, and the Queen and her ladies were prisoners in the hands of the English. For the high-spirited Countess of Buchan, who had placed the crown on the King's head, Edward reserved a peculiar punishment; he shut her up in a wooden cage within the castle of Berwick.

The King's own prospects were black enough. Fear of the English garrisons kept his Ayrshire vassals from joining him; the armies of John of Lorne and Aymer de Valence were closing in on him from the north and the east; though the hills of Galloway seemed to promise safety, he knew that there lurked the armed forces of the MacDowalls. With his small, badly-equipped force he could not risk a battle; if an enemy came in sight he could only order his men to scatter and vanish. Then, separated from his companions, with at most one attendant, he was dependent for his safety on his quick wit and his skill as a swordsman.

Once, for example, John of Lorne almost succeeded in rounding up his little army. The King discovered his danger in time and ordered his men to scatter. His brother Edward went off with one small party, Douglas with another, and he himself with a third. To his astonishment the pursuers did not hesitate, but made straight for the party which he commanded. Again Bruce gave the order; again some strange instinct seemed to tell the Highlanders which knot of fugitives he was with. Even when his following was reduced to one man the whole of John of Lorne's army kept steadily on his track.

The explanation was a simple one: John of Lorne had with him an innocent traitor, a hunting dog that had belonged to the King, and now was eager to rejoin his master. At a word from John of Lorne five fleet-footed Highlanders now sped after the two fugitives; they overtook Bruce and his companion, but in the wild struggle that followed all five perished, four by the terrible sword of Bruce. The two weary men made their way through a wood to the side of a stream and sank down exhausted, but they had not thrown off their pursuers; a minute or two later the baying of a dog echoed through the trees. For a moment Bruce thought of giving up the struggle, then, followed by his companion, he stepped into the water and, after wading down the stream for some distance, scrambled ashore on the other side. He listened; the disappointed yelping of the dog soon told him that his plan had succeeded.

Gradually more men came to his standard; he defeated various small hostile forces, and in the early summer of 1307 he felt strong enough to accept Aymer de Valence's challenge to do battle with him in the open. The two armies met at Loudon Hill. Every one except Bruce thought that de Valence's squadrons of heavy cavalry would make short work of the scanty band of spearmen opposed to them. But the hidden trenches that Bruce had dug in front of his position flung the dense masses of horsemen into hopeless confusion, and the impetuous charge of the Scottish infantry drove them headlong from the field.

All through the winter of 1306-7 King Edward had been lying in the grip of a mortal sickness at the Priory of Lanercost, near Carlisle. The news of the defeat at Loudon Hill fanned his dwindling energy into a flame. Again he put himself at the head of his army, though he had to be carried in a litter, but, before he had gone more than a few miles towards Scotland, the flame flickered down, and he knew that his end had come. Even in that awful hour his conscience seems to have been untroubled; his only regret was that he would not live to complete the conquest of Scotland. He resolved that if he could not lead the victorious army living he would lead it after he was dead; he gave orders that after his death the northward march was to be resumed, and that his bones were to be carried in a leathern sack at the head of the invading army.

His successor paid no heed to his request. For Edward II was a king of a different stamp, fonder of enjoying himself than of organising foreign conquests or attending to the routine business of government. As long as the English generals and garrison commanders in Scotland managed to hang on somehow or other, he did not worry over their complaints, or see that they were supplied with the reinforcements and provisions that they demanded.

And they did hang on for some time, for Bruce first gave all his attention to those Scots who were hostile to his cause. At the beginning of 1308 he devastated the district of Buchan, one of the strongholds of the Comyns, and in the summer of the same year he penetrated into Argyll and drove both John of Lorne and his father, Alexander of Argyll, from the kingdom.

The turn of the castles came at last. The walled town of Perth was the first to go. In 1312 some Scottish troops appeared before it, only to recoil in seeming dismay from the broad and deep moat by which it was surrounded. But Bruce had ordered soundings to be taken, and a fortnight later he returned at dead of night, led his men across the moat at the one place where it could be forded, over the walls, and into the sleeping town. The castles of Dundee and Dumfries soon followed; then in the early summer of 1313, Bruce dispatched his brother Edward to besiege the castle of Stirling, which, looking down as it did on Stirling Bridge, commanded the easiest route between northern and southern Scotland.

Edward Bruce had already distinguished himself by capturing thirteen castles in Galloway within a single year, but most of them were merely the old-fashioned timber blockhouses and palisades. The capture of the big stone castles, many of which had been rebuilt or strengthened by Edward's skilled engineers, was a much more difficult matter, especially to a besieging general unprovided with siege artillery and with only a handful of troops. He could do one of two things: he could capture the fortress by a trick, as the King had done at Perth, or he could cut off its supplies and starve it out, as he himself had done at Dundee. But the second method demanded patience, and excess of patience was not one of Edward Bruce's faults. As he looked at the frowning crags, topped by the massive walls of the fortress, he remembered that in 1304 King Edward's mangonels and trebuchets and "war wolf" had battered at it for three months before the garrison had seen fit to surrender. So when Sir Philip de Moubray, the Governor, offered to surrender the castle without any fighting if it was not relieved by the English King within a twelvemonth, Edward Bruce gladly consented.

The King did not share his delight with the bargain. He had taken risks in his time—no man more—but he fought for victory, not for fun, and if victory could be got without actual fighting, he preferred not to fight. In 1310, for example, he had baffled an attempt at invasion by laying waste the country through which the English army had to advance, and then retreating before them till they were exhausted by hunger and fatigue. But this agreement pinned him down to fighting on a definite spot at a definite time, against an army far superior to his own in numbers and equipment. For there was no doubt that King Edward would accept the challenge; the successful Scottish counter-raids of 1312 and 1313, following on his own unsuccessful invasion of 1310, made his northern subjects complain bitterly of his lethargy, and he knew that if he let Stirling Castle go without a fight, there was more than a chance that he would have to deal with a rebellion in his own kingdom.

Meantime the capture of the castles continued. Roxburgh fell on a night in the year 1314, when the hall of the castle was crowded with Shrovetide revellers. The sentinels had noticed what in the gathering dark seemed to be a herd of cattle grazing in the meadows, but naturally did not challenge them even when they came to the foot of the castle wall. It would have been well for them if they had given the alarm, for the horned beasts were none other than Douglas and his men. Edinburgh went a few weeks later. One dark night, while the main part of the besieging force thundered at the gatehouse of the castle, Thomas Randolph, the King's nephew, led a band of thirty men up the face of the castle rock, scrambled over the unguarded wall, and gained possession of the castle before the garrison knew what had happened.

But these exploits could not delay the inevitable approach of the English army. On the 23rd of June, 1314, from his position two miles to the south of Stirling, Bruce looked with feelings akin to those of Wallace before Falkirk at the squadrons of cavalry with dancing plumes and banners, and the companies of archers, which advanced in seemingly endless procession. He had an army of not more than six or seven thousand men—spearmen, with a handful of light cavalry—to oppose a force perhaps thrice as large. Still, he tried to make the best of a bad bargain. He posted his troops in the wooded New Park through which ran the main road to Stirling. Along his front flowed the Bannock Burn, on his right between low banks with firm, level ground on either side, then through a deep ravine, from which

Great Seal of John Balliol

Great Seal of Alexander II

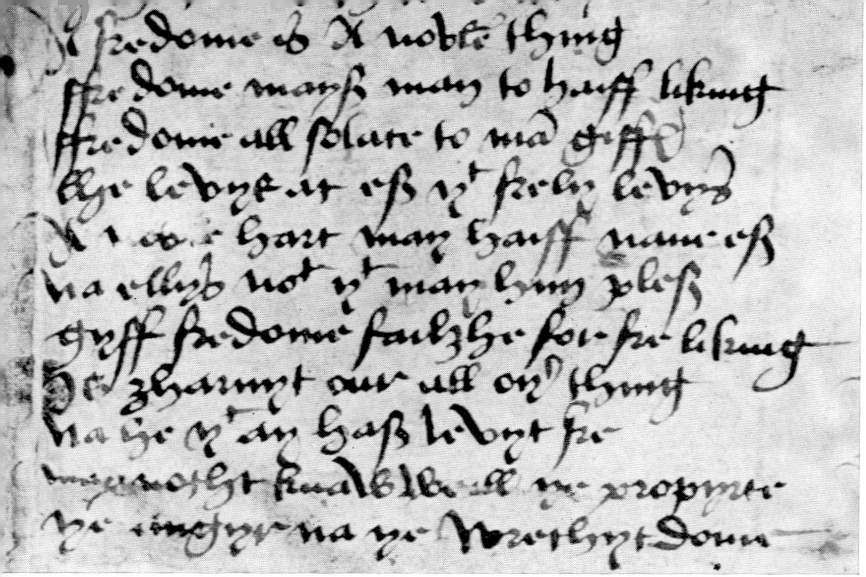

PLATE 23

'A fredome is a noble thing,
Fredome mayse man to haiff liking.
Fredome all solace to man giffis
He levys at ese that frely levys'

from the MS. of Barbour's *Bruce*, in the National Library of Scotland.

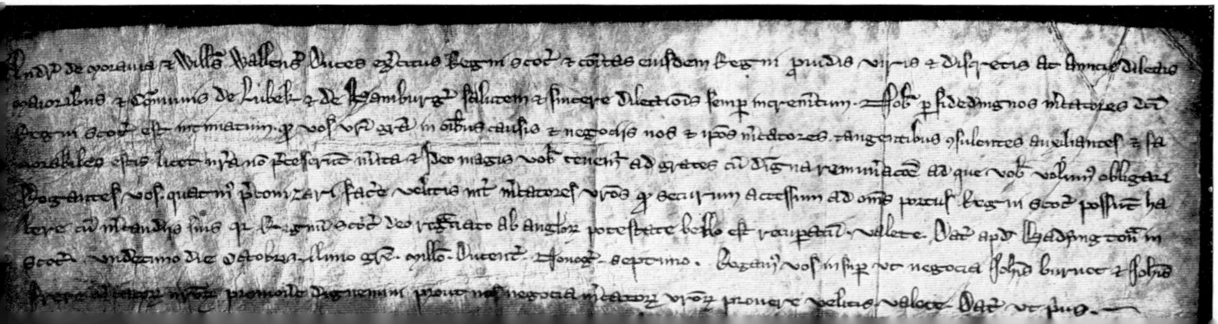

LETTER FROM ANDREW MURRAY AND WILLIAM WALLACE, COMMANDERS OF THE ARMY OF THE KINGDOM OF SCOTLAND, TO THE MAYORS AND COMMUNES OF LUBECK AND HAMBURG, 1297.

it emerged to meander through low-lying, marshy ground till it joined the Forth. He had strengthened his position, too, by constructing a multitude of concealed pits in the firm ground to the west of the ravine.

But things did not fall out exactly as the King had planned. A large body of English cavalry under Sir Robert de Clifford made a detour and succeeded in crossing the Bannock Burn unopposed and in getting almost half-way to Stirling unobserved by Randolph, who had been told to look out for such a movement. The King's eyes were quicker than those of his lieutenant; he rode up to Randolph and said, "Sir Thomas, a rose has fallen from your chaplet." Randolph took the hint, and at the head of his division of infantry set off in pursuit of the English horsemen. It seemed to be an utterly mad attempt, but it succeeded; the young knights in De Clifford's division, instead of holding on their course and setting the castle free, turned about and charged the marching infantry. At a word from Randolph the ranks closed. The English horsemen charged again and again, but they could not bend or break the ring of steel, and when they saw another body of Scots approaching they turned tail and rode off to the main army.

Meantime the Bannock Burn had been crossed nearer the Scottish position by another body of cavalry under the Earl of Gloucester. One of the English knights, Sir Henry de Bohun, who rode a little in advance of his comrades, attracted the attention of a horseman who had been riding slowly along the Scottish ranks. This horseman, though he bore no lance and was mounted on a light palfrey, turned and deliberately approached the venturesome knight. De Bohun clapped spurs to his steed, levelled his lance, and galloped down on the Scot, who waited calmly, then swerved quickly aside to avoid his impetuous rush, and, as he passed, cleft his skull with one mighty blow of his battle-axe.

As the victor rode back the English horsemen noticed that his helmet was encircled by a slender band of gold; they knew then that their comrade had been killed by the King of Scots himself. They charged, but they were repulsed.

Twice the English had tried to break through to Stirling and twice they had failed. But nothing was more certain than that a third attempt would be made. When darkness fell the English army began to straggle across the stream, and take up its position on ground between the Scottish camp and the lower reaches of the Bannock. This movement caused dismay among the Scottish leaders; their flank had been turned; the English were in communication with Stirling Castle and were threatening their rear. To slip out of this too tight corner seemed the only sensible course, and the King had actually decided to retreat, when a stranger was ushered into his presence. He was Sir Alexander de Setoun, a Scottish knight in the English service who had repented at the eleventh hour. He had come to tell the King that the English were depressed by their reverses and by the misery of their position on low-lying ground, which, although reasonably dry in mid-summer, was being churned into mud by the trampling of men and horses. There was a chance, Bruce saw, and the prize was enormous; he decided to attack when morning came.

When at sunrise on the twenty-fourth of June Edward looked westward and saw three bodies of Scottish spearmen advancing from the woods towards him he could think of only one explanation. His surmise seemed to be confirmed when the Scots halted and dropped on their knees. "Ha!" he said to a veteran knight who rode at his elbow, "they kneel to ask for mercy." "They do indeed ask for mercy," replied De Umfraville grimly, "but not of you. I tell you, these men will not flee for any fear of death."

There was method in Bruce's madness: he had no mind to stand on the defensive and see his closely packed schiltrons first riddled with arrows, and then ridden down by the English knights; he intended to launch his men on the English while they were hemmed in by streams and marshes, and so make their superior numbers of no avail. It all worked out as he had planned; the three clumps of spearmen advanced unmolested by the English archers, who had been pushed aside and ridden down by their own over-eager cavalry, and crashed one after another into the confused mass of mailclad horsemen. It seemed at first that they would be completely submerged, but they fought with a cold, silent fury, refusing to recoil when the crested and armoured knights swept down upon them, but keeping shoulder to shoulder, thrusting their spears into the bodies of the chargers, and so bringing horse and rider to the ground. But what Bruce had feared came to pass: the English archers at last struggled clear of the press of knights, took up their position on the flank of the

Scots, and sent volley after volley into their ranks. At a word from the King, however, a small body of cavalry which he had kept in reserve dashed among the archers and scattered them.

Bruce led up his own division to reinforce the other three, and the rout of the English was finally assured when, to the surprise of English and Scots alike, a host with banners displayed appeared a little to the rear of the Scottish position, and with wild shouts of "Slay! slay!" advanced to the help of their comrades. It was too much for the sorely pressed English, although this new army was composed of the ragtag and bobtail of Bruce's camp marching to battle under banners of sheets and blankets; at the next surge forward of the reinforced Scottish battalions the English recoiled, broke, and fled, or rather, tried to flee.

For they were trapped, pinned down to a narrow wedge of marshy land. Many tried to swim the Forth and were drowned, some flung themselves into the deep ravine to the south of the battlefield. Some, including King Edward himself, fled to the castle, but the Governor, faithful to his bargain, shut the doors against them, and the King had no alternative but to make his way to the castle of Dunbar with a handful of knights. Thence he escaped in a small boat.

The victory of the Scots was complete; in a few days all the remaining English strongholds in the south, with the exception of Berwick, fell into their hands. Still Bruce was not content; nothing would satisfy him short of Edward's definite recognition of him as the lawful king of an independent country, and he proceeded to pound at the northern counties of England. In 1318 he captured Berwick, and in the following year he countered Edward's attempt to recapture it by sending an army into the heart of Yorkshire. In vain the Archbishop of York, at the head of a hastily assembled force, tried to stop the invaders at Mitton; one yell from the Scots was enough to put the Archbishop's motley army to flight. Raid followed raid, till in many parts of Northumberland and Cumberland the inhabitants found it wise to make a separate peace with the Scots.

Yet the English government showed no signs of recognising the fact that Scotland was independent and that Bruce was its king. Not only so, but the Pope also declined to recognise "King Robert," although the Scottish bishops, or some of them, had done so long before. In 1320 the Scottish barons, assembled at Arbroath, wrote to the Pope in forthright terms, expressing their unwavering resolution to support Bruce or any other king who would resist England: "So long as a hundred of us remain alive we will never be subject to the English king. It is not for glory, riches or honours that we fight, but for liberty alone, which no worthy man will lay down save with his life." This letter is sometimes called the Scottish Declaration of Independence.

In 1322 Edward roused himself to attempt another invasion of Scotland, but, when he had advanced to within ten miles of Edinburgh through a country from which every living creature seemed to have vanished as if by magic, when all the food that his foraging companies could find was one solitary lame cow, he judged it wise to return. Bruce followed him up, came on part of his army near Rievaulx Abbey and scattered it, capturing the King's baggage and pay chests, and sending him flying headlong to York. Edward abandoned the struggle for the time, and in 1323 a truce of thirteen years was arranged.

The accession of the young Edward III in 1327 brought about a renewal of the war: Douglas and Randolph, with a swiftly moving force of mounted Scots, swept down upon the northern counties, played hide-and-seek for nearly a month with the great army which the young King led against them, and slipped away under cover of darkness after they seemed to be securely trapped. Negotiations were opened with King Robert's representatives, and in the spring of 1328 the Treaty of Northampton put an end to twenty-two years of strife. The independence of Scotland and the right of King Robert to the crown were fully recognised, a "perpetual peace" between the two countries was established, and, to cement this new friendship, a marriage between Prince David, the only son of the King of Scots, and Edward's sister Johanna was arranged.

But the great King had only a few months of life in front of him. He was not old in years, but prolonged hardship and exertion had sapped his strength and aged him before his time. And a more dreadful foe than the English attacked him; he was stricken with leprosy. Still, he required only one thing to make him content: the withdrawal of the sentence of excommunication. But it was not till 1329, only a few weeks before the King was laid to rest in Dunfermline Abbey, that the sentence was finally removed.

CHAPTER 10

"DARK AND DRUBLIE DAYS"

We look on the struggle for national independence as the most glorious chapter in the history of our country. Under the guidance of a leader of genius, himself transformed by some strange alchemy from a selfish adventurer into a statesman and hero, the Scottish people were lifted out of themselves, into forgetfulness of the differences that divided Highlander and Lowlander, baron and bondman, and became for a time a band of brothers, capable of facing the armed might of England with serene confidence in the result. But these few bright years were followed by a long period of gloom, when Scotland seemed destined to become one of the most miserable countries in Europe.

For these bright years were not as bright as they seemed; Scotland gained its independence at a very heavy cost. The loss in human life must have been enormous. Nor was it confined to the battle-field, for in those days, when doctors worked by magic and spells, slight wounds often gangrened and proved fatal; then in the wake of the armies followed famine and pestilence, to devour those whom the sword had spared. The country was much poorer, too; as the most fertile parts were precisely those that were most exposed to the inroads of the invaders, it is little wonder that cornland went out of cultivation and that flocks and herds diminished. And as wool and hides were almost the only commodities that Scotland exported, the Scottish merchants could offer little in exchange for the foreign products which their countrymen urgently needed, so that foreign trade dwindled. The loss was moral as well as material; people became restless and unsettled; the peasant could not be expected to take pains with the building of a farm-house which might be destroyed in the next English invasion; he would not toil at his own acres with over-much energy when a raid into England might furnish him with half a score of plump cattle.

Among the evils which followed these years of war, let us

chronicle one benefit. Sometime in the course of the fourteenth century, but when or how no one knows, villeinage disappeared from Scotland; the ordinary peasant was no longer a serf but a freeman. He was not emancipated altogether from his lord's control; he had still to appear at his court, render the old services to him at the appointed time, and take his corn to be ground at his lord's mill, but the bond, though sometimes vexatious, was no longer dishonourable and no longer tied the peasant to the estate.

Unfortunately, Scotland got no chance to recover from the strain of the thirty years of warfare; the "perpetual peace" established by the Treaty of Northampton lasted for only four years. To the ambitions of Edward III the treaty was only a flimsy barrier; he did not see why he should not repudiate a treaty which had been forced on him by his advisers; besides, he had a pretext in the complaints of certain barons who wanted to be reinstated in the possessions that they had formerly held in Scotland and of which they had been deprived by a Scottish Parliament held at Cambuskenneth Abbey after the victory of Bannockburn. He despatched those "disinherited" barons to Scotland with a force of a few hundred men, and sent with them no less a person than Edward Balliol, the son of the luckless King John. King Edward's plan was a simple one: if the expedition failed he would wash his hands of it; if it succeeded Balliol would be crowned King of Scotland and would straightway do homage to him for his kingdom.

It came very near to success. By an evil chance the Scots found themselves three years after the death of Bruce without a single one of the great soldiers who had led them to victory in the War of Independence. Edward Bruce had crossed to Ireland in 1315 to drive out the English there, had been accepted as King of Ireland by some of the Irish chieftains, and had fallen in battle three years later. In 1330 Douglas, in accordance with the last wishes of King Robert, set out to fight the enemies of Christendom, carrying with him his dead master's heart in a silver casket. He landed in Spain to help the King of Castile in his struggle with the Moors, and died gloriously in battle with the infidel. Randolph, who since King Robert's death had governed the kingdom on behalf of the child king David II, died suddenly while he was preparing to deal with the threatened invasion.

Balliol and his followers landed at Kinghorn in 1332, marched through Fife almost unopposed, and reached the banks of the Earn, beyond which, at Dupplin, the Scottish army was encamped. But the Earl of Mar, who had been hastily put in Randolph's place, was too young to have had experience in Bruce's campaigns. He had omitted to post guards by the river, with the result that Balliol's men forded it unopposed at night, and surprised and cut to pieces an isolated detachment of the Scottish army. At dawn, the Scottish vanguard hurried up, and threw itself upon the English, but Mar lost his head, and sent the main body of his men crashing into the rear of the vanguard. Jammed together in hopeless confusion, the Scots found it impossible to fight, and were slaughtered like sheep by the English archers. Balliol entered Perth, was crowned King of Scots, and set off on a triumphal tour of his newly won realm.

It came to an ignominious conclusion. At Annan a small party of Scots made a raid on his lodging by night, and he escaped only by rushing out with one boot off and one boot on and flinging himself on a horse that was neither saddled nor bridled.

He came back early in 1333, accompanied this time by Edward of England, who straightway laid siege to Berwick. A Scottish army, attempting to relieve it, came upon the English posted on Halidon Hill, but while the Scottish spearmen struggled across a marshy valley which divided them from their foes, the English archers shot them down. This disaster was followed immediately by the surrender of Berwick, which since that time, with one brief interval, has remained an English town.

The melancholy truth was that the Scots, unlike the English, had failed to profit by the lessons of the War of Independence. The Scots remembered only that spearmen fighting in mass formation had been successful against cavalry at Bannockburn; they forgot that spearmen in mass formation had been shot down wholesale by the English archers at Falkirk. The English generals had learned that to send cavalry against an unbroken body of spearmen was simply to ask for trouble; they also saw that a sudden cavalry charge, like the unexpected charge of the handful of Scottish cavalry at Bannockburn, might put their archers out of action, so when they drew up their troops in battle array, they made companies of archers alternate with companies of dismounted cavalry armed with lances. A rapidly moving force of hostile cavalry might elude the cloth-yard shafts of the bowmen, but they would be hurled back by the lances; the more slowly moving infantry would probably be shot down before they could come to close quarters. The Scottish leaders did not understand these tactics; time and again they sent spearmen against archers, and always with the same result.

But, as Edward was to find out in France a little later, it is one thing to win battles; it is a very different thing to hold down by force a kingdom that is determined not to submit to alien rule. Though he invaded Scotland in four successive years, though he received the homage of Edward Balliol, though he captured every castle in Scotland, he knew that he had not subjugated the country. The war had become a "war of attrition"; the Scots, under the direction of a new Guardian, Sir Andrew de Moray, deliberately avoided pitched battles and, by driving their cattle into the hills and letting their lands lie derelict, they tried to starve out the invaders—an attempt to save the country from conquest by making it not worth conquering.

At last the tide turned. Edward's enmity to Scotland became swallowed up in enmity to France—enmity that originated partly from his knowledge that the King of France had openly shown his sympathy with the Scots—and when in the summer of 1339 he began the Hundred Years' War by invading northern France, the pressure on Scotland had already diminished.

In the previous year the successful defence of the castle of Dunbar by the Countess of Dunbar, a daughter of the famous Randolph, had done much to restore the confidence of the Scots. When the stones from the mangonels sang through the air and crashed against the battlements, Black Agnes, as her admirers called her, infuriated the besiegers by sending a girl with a towel to wipe away the marks. Once the garrison was perturbed when a "sow," the medieval equivalent of a tank, a great wooden tower upon wheels, rolled up to the castle walls. Black Agnes called out to the English commander, "I sall gar thy sow farrow against her will." She gave the word to her engineers; at once the sow became a target for enormous stones shot from a mighty catapult which had been placed on the battlements; it crumpled up, and Black Agnes smiled grimly as she watched the miserable wretches crawling out from the ruins.

THE ARBROATH DECLARATION, 1320

This letter of the Scottish Barons was executed in duplicate. One copy was sent to the Pope at Avignon, the other (shown above) was retained in Scotland and is still to be seen in The Register House, Edinburgh.

Plate 25

A Tournament

One by one the English strongholds in Scotland were recaptured; in 1339 Sir William Douglas drained the water out of the moat that girdled the walls of Perth and led his troops over dryshod; two years later he captured Edinburgh Castle by an equally clever stratagem.

The long, grim struggle had come to an end at last; two centuries were to pass before an English King again attempted to convert Scotland into a province of England. But the evil effects remained: Scotland was even more impoverished in 1341 than it had been in 1328, and fifty years of warfare made hatred of England second nature to the Scots. The French, too, had learned what an English invasion meant, and so a common hatred drew Scotland and France more closely together; the treaties made by Balliol in 1295 and by King Robert in 1326 became the foundation of an alliance which endured down to the time of the Reformation—an alliance from which the smaller country did not always gain the greater profit. More than once, in obedience to a hint from a hard-pressed king of France, the Scots marched to disaster in northern England. In 1346, for example, while Edward III was absent in France, David II led a Scottish army southward, only to see it riddled with arrows at Neville's Cross, and to be himself led off captive to London.

The impoverished and disturbed state of Scotland in the fourteenth century was not altogether due to the after effects of the War of Independence; it is to be explained partly by the weakness of the Crown. In those days, when Parliament met only at long intervals to promulgate laws which few ever heard of, when there was no strong body of permanent officials to help the King to govern the country, the character and ability of the monarch counted for much more than they do to-day. With a weak king misgovernment inevitably followed, for the King had formidable rivals; every baron was an absolute monarch within his own territories, exercising the power of life and death over his vassals, who, however, regarded him not as a tyrant but as a protector. They knew well that if any outsider brought a complaint against them at their lord's court, he would have very little chance of obtaining a conviction. The complainant might lodge an appeal with the sheriff, but the sheriff was only human, he would hesitate to incur the wrath of a powerful baron by arresting his vassal. Every one remembered how in 1342 Sir

William Douglas had forced his way into the sheriff court at Hawick with a body of armed vassals, seized the sheriff of Teviotdale, Alexander Ramsay of Dalhousie, and carried him off to his castle of Hermitage to die of starvation, and how neither King nor Justiciar had lifted a finger. In addition, the sheriff was usually appointed, not because of his knowledge of the law or his zeal in dealing with law-breakers, but because his father had held the office before him. Then he might be bound to the neighbouring landowners by a definite treaty of friendship. For the baron claimed other kingly privileges in addition to the administration of justice—the right of levying war on any of his neighbours against whom he had a grudge, and that of entering into "bonds of manrent," agreements for mutual support, with those landowners who were inclined to be friendly to him. Thus a great earl who found himself in bad odour with the King could count on the support, not only of his own vassals, but of other landowners whom he had agreed to protect, and who, therefore, had to do their best to protect him. And these quarrels between one baron and another had a way of developing into hereditary feuds, which continued long after the original cause had been forgotten.

Even if the King had succeeded in imposing his will on the Lowlands, he would still have been confronted by the problem of the Highlands. The Highland chief was, if anything, more powerful than the Lowland baron: his rule over his clan was absolute and unquestioned; the clansmen did not regard him as a feudal superior but as a father, and he in his turn regarded them not as vassals, but as children to whom he was bound to give protection and support. Perhaps as a consequence of this, the feuds between chieftain and chieftain, between clan and clan, were even more fierce and obstinate than the feuds that distracted the south.

In general the King thought it wise not to meddle with the Highlands. But the Highlanders would not refrain from meddling with him, or rather, with his Lowland subjects. An invasion on a grand scale they seldom attempted, but they often swooped from their hungry moorlands into richer pastures and cornlands, to return in a few hours, or a few days, with a multitude of sheep and cattle.

Unfortunately for Scotland, a hundred years had to pass before a worthy successor sat on the throne of Bruce. It cost the Scots 100,000 marks to release David II from his captivity in England—an exceedingly bad bargain. When, after his return in 1357, his subjects crowded round him as he rode to a meeting of his Council, he damped their enthusiasm by snatching up a mace and shouting "Stand still, or the most forward of you shall get one with this mace on his head." Whatever his faults, David did not lack vigour, and that the times demanded of a King. But his relations with England were dubious, for he proposed that if he died without leaving a son, the crown should pass to one of the sons of Edward III, and was furious when his Parliament very properly refused its consent.

When David II died in 1371, leaving no children behind him, the crown was bestowed on Robert the Steward, the son of Walter the Steward, who had married Marjory Bruce, the daughter of the great King Robert. In his youth Robert II had been in the field as one of the opponents of Edward III, but advancing years had made him timid and unenterprising, and, conscious that the great nobles regarded him simply as one of themselves, he was more anxious to conciliate them than to contradict them. When in 1385 Jean de Vienne, Admiral of France, arrived at the head of a splendid army of about 2,000 knights and cross-bowmen to co-operate with the Scots in an invasion of England, he came at the invitation, not of the King of Scots, but of his nobles, and when he set out to raid the northern counties, it was not the King, but the Earl of Douglas, who drew up his plan of campaign.

Little good came of this expedition; the raid provoked a much more serious counter-invasion by John of Gaunt, in the course of which both Dundee and Perth were burned down. The French left soon afterwards, utterly disgusted with the poverty of the country and the independent spirit of the ordinary Scotsman. "Rude and worthless people," they called their allies, "like savages, who wish not to be acquainted with any one, and are too envious of the good fortune of others, and suspicious of losing anything themselves."

Another raid which Douglas made into England had a far different result. In the summer of 1388 he led an army up to the walls of Newcastle, within which Sir Henry Percy—Shakespeare's Hotspur—and other northern barons were assembled. Though no serious fighting followed, encounters took place between small bodies of English and Scottish knights, in the course of which Douglas gained possession of Percy's banner. After announcing that he meant to take it to Scotland, Douglas set off on his leisurely march home. But Hotspur had vowed that the banner should never reach Scotland; he followed hard on the track of the Scots, and two days later, as the sun was setting, he came on their camp at Otterburn. Both sides fought valiantly; not till the stars had faded away into the grey light of dawn did the English quit the field where they had so gallantly striven, leaving Hotspur and some hundreds of his men in the hands of the Scots. Only then did the Scots discover that their leader had been dead for hours. Soon after the fighting began, some of his knights, seeing him fall, had rushed up to ask how he fared. "Right evil," was his answer, "but thanked be God there hath been but a few of mine ancestors that have died in their beds." Then he charged them to say nothing of his plight to any one, but to bear his banner aloft confidently, and shout "Douglas." In this manner did "a dead man win a fight."

But the victory of Otterburn was only a transitory gleam in the darkness, a darkness that grew steadily deeper. In 1390 the old King died, to be succeeded by his son, Robert III, a prince whom ill-luck had pursued from his cradle. Even his name was not his own: he had been christened John, but before his coronation his advisers made him abandon the name of the unhappy Balliol. An injury received in a tournament had made him so lame that he could not bestride a horse, and so debarred him from commanding his army in the field, or journeying about his kingdom to administer justice. He was naturally inactive and timid, however; too ready to entrust the business of government to his more active brother the Duke of Albany, and to defer to over-powerful subjects, like Archibald the Grim, Earl of Douglas.

His timidity increased his troubles tenfold. The clans immediately to the north of the Highland line began to get out of hand, and to vary fierce fighting with frequent raids into the fertile plains of Strathmore. In 1396 it was arranged that the two clans which had caused most trouble by their perpetual feuds should each send thirty representatives to Perth to settle the business by a fight to the death. Barricades were erected on the North Inch to enclose a stretch of level turf, and thither, just as they come to-day to see a cricket match, the burgesses of Perth flocked to watch this grim entertainment. They had no need to be ashamed, for the King himself had come to see his subjects butcher one another. The sixty champions entered, armed with bow, sword, axe, and dagger, dashed together, and fought till only five were left alive on one side, and only two on the other. But the Highlands were not to be pacified as easily as all that.

The King's very anxiety not to offend his nobles offended them all the more. His elder son, David, Duke of Rothesay, had been betrothed to the daughter of the powerful Earl of March, whose castle of Dunbar guarded the eastern approach to Scotland, but when the Earl of Douglas demanded that his own daughter should be married to Rothesay, the King weakly gave way. The Earl of March was furious at the insult, and early in 1400 made his way to the court of Henry IV of England. The timid and well-meaning King of Scots had already offended Henry by affording shelter to a pretender who claimed to be Richard II, the rightful King of England. Henry could not strike hard, for he had a rebellious kingdom behind him, but in 1402 the Scots delivered themselves into his hands. Headed by the new Earl of Douglas, "Tineman"—the Loser—and Murdoch Stewart, the son of Albany, they advanced into Northumberland. Near Wooler they came in sight of an English army commanded by Hotspur, and, with an excess of prudence, formed up in dense masses on the slopes of Homildon Hill to await the English attack. Hotspur was for hurling his troops on the Scottish schiltrons at once, but the Earl of March, who was with him, advised him to send forward his archers only. A handful of the Scottish knights, after appealing in vain to Douglas to order a general attack, charged the English bowmen, but as Douglas remained passive on his hill and sent them no support, they failed to stop the archers, who, as soon as they got within range, sent volley after volley into the serried ranks of the Scots. Only when the schiltrons were riddled with arrows did Douglas order an advance. It was too late; his men were utterly broken, and like Murdoch Stewart he was forced to surrender to the English.

A blacker misfortune had already befallen the King. A few months earlier his elder son, the dissolute Duke of Rothesay, had died in the castle of Falkland, and it was whispered that he had been starved to death by order of his uncle Albany and his brother-in-law, Douglas.

The wretched monarch did not know which way to turn, or whom to trust, His Queen had died; men said that his brother had murdered his son. All that he had left in the world was his son James, a boy not yet in his teens. Not knowing what might happen to him, the King resolved at the beginning of 1406 to dispatch him to France, but the ship with the Prince on board was captured by an English vessel off Flamborough Head.

King Robert III died at almost the same time, so that the boy James became King of Scots while he was a prisoner in English hands.

Note.—The title of this chapter is taken from the first stanza of Dunbar's *Meditation in Winter*, which, in modern spelling, runs as follows:

Into these dark and drublie [dripping] days,
When sable all the heaven arrays,
With misty vapours, clouds, and skies,
Nature all courage [liking] me denies
Of songs, ballads, and of plays.

CHAPTER 11

JAMES I

THE death of the old King and the appointment of Albany as Guardian of the kingdom on behalf of the imprisoned James I made no difference to the country. Albany had already acted as Regent to the decrepit Robert II, and had been the virtual governor of the kingdom in the reign of Robert III. He seemed to cling to power, and yet to fear to use it; he did not exert himself to secure the release of the young King, though his own son Murdoch was liberated in 1415; on the other hand, he was ready to go to any length to secure the good-will of the great nobles. In 1409, for example, he pardoned the traitor Earl of March, and restored him to most of his estates.

But some of these petty kings were clearly becoming dangerous. In 1411 the great Celtic potentate, Donald, Lord of the Isles, gathered together an army of Highlanders and Islanders at Inverness and marched against Aberdeen. It was not a question of a mere cattle-raid this time. Donald wanted the earldom of Ross—his wife was the aunt of the rightful heiress—and he hoped by invading the Lowlands to terrify the Regent into letting him have his desire. When he reached Harlaw, however, only twenty miles from Aberdeen, he found his path barred. The opposing army was led by the Earl of Mar, himself a leader of Highland warriors, but it included also the burgesses of Aberdeen and all the available fighting men of the region between the Don and the Tay. Both armies fought gallantly, but the impetuous valour of the clansmen could not prevail against the grim determination of the Lowland spearmen, who refused to give way, though their losses were far heavier than those of their opponents. In the end Donald led off his men and withdrew baffled to the west.

A triumph of a different kind was celebrated in St. Andrews a little later. Hitherto the Scottish youth who wanted more learning than he could get at the burgh grammar school, where little more than Latin was taught, had to go to England or to the Continent. At Oxford he would find Balliol College, founded by the father and mother of King John Balliol, at Paris he would find a foundation for poor Scottish scholars, established by the bishop of Moray in 1326. But the wars between England and Scotland hindered the movements of students, and further difficulties arose with the Great Schism, when two, and later three, popes competed for the allegiance of western Europe: England and Scotland supported different popes, and after 1409 France also supported a different pope from Scotland, which meant that Scottish students were no longer welcome in France. In 1412, therefore, the Bishop of St. Andrews, Henry Wardlaw, granted a charter establishing a university at St. Andrews. The period was one in which the Church was disturbed not only by disputes over the Papacy but also by the radical teaching of Wyclif in England and Hus in Bohemia, and this movement affected Scotland, for a "Lollard," James Resby, was burned in 1407 and a follower of Hus, Paul Crawar, in 1433.

The old Duke of Albany died in 1420; his son Murdoch reigned in his stead; still King James remained a captive in England. But these were not wasted years. To the young prince's complaints that his imprisonment would interrupt his education, King Henry had replied that he knew French and would teach him all that he wanted. The King kept his promise; James grew up to be one of the most accomplished men of his age.

A little under medium height, thick-set, quick in his movements, he looked what he was, an expert at putting the weight and throwing the hammer. But one might be surprised to learn that this athlete was a musician and a really fine poet, and that his zeal for the arts was accompanied by an interest in artillery. What interested James most, however, was not the management of machines, but the management of men. He meant, if ever he returned to Scotland, to be a King in deed as well as in name, to be the mightiest man in his realm; to use his power, not for his own glory, but to make Scotland a safe place to live in. But how was he to make—in his own homely words—"the key keep the castle and the bracken bush the cow?"

Clearly the great noble with his private court of justice was the most formidable obstacle to the maintenance of law and order; clearly the policy of Robert II and his successors—bestowing estates and dignities on nobles who were already dangerously powerful, encouraging them to marry into the royal family, and avoiding a quarrel with them at all costs—had done the exact opposite of what it had been intended to do: it had diminished the authority of the Crown, and increased the power and arrogance of the nobles. So no more fair words! The great lord who would not bend to the King's will must be broken. James knew that he might himself be broken in the process, but it was a risk that he was quite prepared to run.

Though the King saw that over-much reliance on the nobles had proved disastrous to the Crown in the past, he recognised that he could not govern the country single-handed; he must have some body of men to advise and help him. Such a body, he knew, existed in England. Until the second half of the thirteenth century the English Parliament, like the Scottish Parliament, had been identical with the Great Council—an assembly of the great landowners, clerical and secular—but by Edward I's reign it usually included representatives of the towns and of the smaller landowners in the counties. Early in the fourteenth century the English Parliament divided into two bodies: the archbishops,

Aeneas Sylvius at the Court of James I

Aeneas Sylvius (afterwards Pope Pius II) visited James I in 1435. The above picture is an Italianate impression of his reception.

RECONSTRUCTED VIEW OF EDINBURGH, ABOUT 1450

To the right, adjacent to the Calton Hill, is Trinity College Church and at the other end of the Nor' Loch is St. Cuthbert's. On the left are the friaries of the Franciscans and Dominicans and the Kirk o' Field.

bishops, abbots, earls, and barons formed the House of Lords, and the "knights of the shire"—the county representatives—and the burgesses the House of Commons. This separation in the long run diminished the weight and influence of the great barons. Thrown together as they were with the merchants and craftsmen, the knights of the shire learned to look at questions of state from the point of view of their humbler comrades and the burgesses for their part were not afraid to oppose the Upper House, knowing that they would have the country gentlemen solid behind them. So it seemed to James that a Parliament after the English model, in which the smaller landowners and the burgesses acted as a counterpoise to the nobles, would solve the most difficult of his problems.

There was, indeed, a Parliament in Scotland, but it differed in some important respects from the English Parliament. Though the most important Scottish burghs had for long sent representatives to a little Parliament of their own, known first as the Court of the Four Burghs, and later as the Convention of Burghs, it was not till 1326, when a Parliament was held at Cambuskenneth, that burgesses appeared side by side with the bishops and the barons. The occasion was a special one; the damage done to the royal demesnes during the War of Independence had diminished the King's revenues, and had forced him to ask his subjects for money. For some time the burgesses attended Parliament only when they were specially summoned: not till the second half of the fourteenth century did they attend every session of Parliament as a matter of course. Of another class, the small landowners, Parliament often contained no representative at all. In theory every "tenant-in-chief," however small the parcel of land that he held directly of the Crown, was required to come to Parliament; in practice, only the greater landowners attended.

The Scottish Parliament never separated into Lords and Commons; the three "estates"—clergy, barons, and burgesses—sat together in the hall of some royal castle, for as yet there was no Parliament House, and the capital of the country was wherever the King happened to be. But there was a division of another kind: the Parliament of 1367 handed over its unfinished business to a commission of its own members, to allow the other members to go home for the harvest. In 1370 a more important change was made: at the beginning of the session Parliament appointed two committees, chosen from each of the three estates, one to draft new laws, the other to deal with lawsuits that had been referred to Parliament for decision. For the Scottish Parliament, like the English Parliament, was a law-court as well as an assembly for making laws. If, for example, a man thought that the sheriff had bestowed his inheritance upon the wrong person, his only remedy was an appeal to Parliament. Members who were not appointed to either committee were excused attendance till the end of the session, when they returned to hear what new laws had been proposed, and to give or withhold their consent.

This became the regular procedure. The legislative committee, known as the Committee of the Articles, and the judicial committee, known as the Committee of Causes and Complaints, were appointed at the beginning of every session. The scheme had serious faults: the Committee of Articles was at once too weak and too powerful; it was small enough to be controlled by one determined man, but in turn it controlled Parliament. But James saw that this might be to his advantage: only let him govern the Committee of Articles, and he could make Parliament play what tune he pleased.

At last he got an opportunity of translating his purposes into action. In 1424 he was released, after he had promised to pay 50,000 marks, the cost, he was informed, of board and lodging for eighteen years. He wasted no time: on the 5th of April he crossed the border with his bride, the Lady Joan Beaufort, a grand-daughter of John of Gaunt; on the 21st of May, Queen Joan and he were crowned at Perth, and before another five days had elapsed he had persuaded Parliament to pass a number of laws, in which his future policy was clearly defined. War between private persons was forbidden; rebels were reminded that they would lose not only their lives, but their goods; their property, in other words, would go, not to their families, but to the King; timid souls who might hesitate to help the King to suppress a rebellion were encouraged by the declaration that if they stood aside they would be treated as accomplices and punished with death and forfeiture of goods. Only men of property were to be allowed to be sheriffs, because only men of property could be heavily fined if they gave wrong decisions.

The hereditary sheriff whose legal skill was not above suspicion was allowed to retain his office only if he found a competent deputy, for whose actions, however, he had to take full responsibility. Unscrupulous barons who had been in the habit of helping themselves to the customs dues or to the "burgh mails" —the rents paid by the royal burghs to the King—were reminded that this money was the property of the Crown. The King suspected, too, that land which had once belonged to the Crown had often been grabbed by these same nobles; he ordered his sheriffs therefore to find out what land had belonged to the Crown within the last hundred years, and offended the great landowners by announcing that he meant to examine the charters by which they held their estates.

Within less than a year James held a second Parliament at Perth. Perth, he had decided, was to be his capital, and Parliament was now to meet regularly once every year. "Bonds of manrent" were forbidden by this Parliament, and those who offered hospitality to rebels were assured that they would be treated like rebels themselves.

But James knew that it was one thing to make laws, and another to see that they were obeyed; so he resolved to show evil-doers that he was in deadly earnest. He ordered his greatest subject, the Duke of Albany, to be arrested on a charge of high treason. He was tried by a tribunal of his fellow nobles, found guilty, and executed at the Heading Stone beside Stirling Castle. With him perished at the same time his two sons and the Earl of Lennox.

The Parliament which met in Perth in March 1426 had no such tragic interruption. It made one far-reaching change, however. It was evident that in the short time between the opening and the closing of Parliament the Committee of Causes could not deal with all the cases brought before it, so a similar Committee —known later as the "Session"—was ordered to meet three times a year when Parliament was not sitting.

But James was meditating a fresh stroke: he meant to give a warning to the turbulent Highland chiefs like that which he had already given to the Lowland barons; a few weeks later he held a Parliament at Inverness which most of them judged it wise to attend. As each chieftain entered the hall he was seized and thrust into a dungeon, while the King entertained the barons who stood about the throne by composing Latin verses, which may be translated thus:

To the dungeon strong
Hale the rogues along;
As in Christ's my hope,
Well they need the rope.

Of the less important captives some were hanged, some beheaded, and some banished. The Lord of the Isles fared better; the King, hoping to turn him from an enemy into an ally, made him a member of the royal household. But the young chieftain, chafing at what was really an honourable captivity, escaped and burned the town of Inverness. The King marched northwards and defeated his supporters, whereupon the young rebel judged it wise to surrender. He was kept a prisoner in Tantallon Castle till the King had reason to think that he had come to a better frame of mind, when he was summoned to Holyrood. There in the Abbey Church the great chieftain, clad only in his shirt and breeches, knelt before the high altar, surrendered his sword to the King, and humbly begged for pardon. Even with this humiliation James was not satisfied; not till the Queen herself had interceded for the captive was he set at liberty. The King's audacity had cowed the Highlands for a time, but more than audacity was needed for a permanent solution of the Highland problem.

James could now congratulate himself that he had succeeded in making the creaking machinery of Parliament work more smoothly; but he noticed that the poorer country lairds still regarded attendance at Parliament as a troublesome duty, to be dodged whenever it was possible. The King therefore proposed in 1428 that the much more convenient English system should be adopted: in future the great landowners were each to receive a special summons from the King forty days before the meeting of Parliament; other landowners were to be ordered by the sheriff of their county to assemble on a certain day and elect two of their number to represent them in Parliament. But the latter part of the scheme was wrecked through the apathy of the ordinary country laird, who still persisted in staying away from Parliament, unless the King, by making him a "Lord of Parliament," raised him above the level of a simple knight.

In truth the King's bright hopes were beginning to be dimmed.

He had undertaken a task too great for any single man, and he was left to grapple with it alone; there was no wise and wary counsellor at his elbow to tell him when to give soft words and when to strike hard; his bold policy had alienated the nobles without gaining for him the support of any other section of his people.

He had given the nobles ample cause to fear and hate him. In 1431 he had suddenly lodged the great Earl of Douglas in prison and as suddenly released him; in 1435 he stripped the Earl of March of his estates, for no better reason than that his father had gone over to the English more than thirty years before. If a great baron died without leaving a son, the King did not trouble over-much to discover the rightful heir, he calmly added the estate to his own royal demesnes. Nor could the nobles forget that many of their kinsfolk who had gone to England years ago as securities for the King's ransom had never returned: by leaving over four-fifths of the money unpaid James had condemned the hostages to perpetual banishment.

But James held on his course unafraid: in December 1436 he set off to celebrate Christmas at the Blackfriars' Monastery at Perth, not knowing that in his own household a plot against his life had already been hatched. The King's Chamberlain, Sir Robert Stewart, did not love the man who had allowed his father to die an exile in England; he believed, besides, that James's claim to the throne was invalid, and that the rightful king was no other than his own grandfather, the Earl of Atholl, who was a son of Robert II. He had entered into communication with Sir Robert Graham, a man who had long borne a grudge against the King because his nephew had been deprived of the earldom of Strathearn.

On the night of the 20th of February, 1437, everything was ready: Stewart had laid planks across the moat that surrounded the monastery and had removed the bolts from the doors. Still the King suspected no evil; at the moment when Graham and his accomplices were crossing the moat, he was talking gaily to the Queen and her ladies. Not till the clash of arms was heard, followed by a scream, did he suspect that anything was wrong. The conspirators had slain the page posted at the door of the King's apartment. Before they could reach the door itself, however, one of the Queen's ladies rushed up, thrust her arm through the staples, and kept the door shut till the King had time to wrench up a plank and leap into a vault below. But she could not keep them back for long; Graham and his accomplices forced open the door, breaking her arm as they did so, and rushed into the room, only to find that the King had vanished.

They retired disappointed, but a noise made them come back: the King, thinking the danger was past, was trying to climb back into the room. The conspirators leaped down upon him, but James, unarmed as he was, sprang at the foremost assassin, seized him by the throat, and trampled him underfoot. The second he served in the same way, but the struggle could have only one conclusion, and a few minutes later his dead body lay in the vault, pierced by twenty-eight wounds.

CHAPTER 12

STEWART AND DOUGLAS

THE savage tortures inflicted on the murderers of James I could not undo the evil they had wrought. They had destroyed more than the King; they had destroyed the law and order that the King had established. The new King, James II, was a boy of six, a mere prize to be contended for by the factions of ambitious nobles who would strive to rule the country in his name and in their own interest. Parliament was useless without the King; its small size and its practice of handing over all really important work to small committees made its control by a baronial clique or a single powerful baron a very easy business. This would not have mattered so much if any of the great barons had displayed the qualities of a real statesman, and used his authority to "prop the tottering throne," but every one of them thought only of increasing the wealth and influence of himself and of his house. The Earl of Crawford, for example, instead of suppressing theft, turned thief himself, and pocketed the customs duties levied at the port of Dundee, and though the

Earl of Douglas had been appointed Governor of the Kingdom, he stirred not a finger to end the dispute between two of the lesser barons, Sir William Crichton and Sir Alexander Livingston, for the possession of the King.

The death of Douglas in 1439 made Crichton and Livingston, reconciled for the time, the foremost persons in the kingdom. But they feared the rivalry of Douglas's successor, the young Earl William, and persuaded themselves that they should not be safe till the arrogant youth was removed and his fat, easy-going uncle, James the Gross, put in his place. They therefore inveigled the Earl and his brother to Edinburgh Castle, introduced them to the boy King, and entertained them to dinner in the great hall. After the usual courses of the meal were finished, the servants returned with what seemed to be another dish. It was a bull's head, which they placed on the table before the young earl. Douglas turned pale and started to his feet, for he knew what the bull's head meant—it was the sentence of death. He looked about wildly for some way of escape, but before he could leave his place, there was a movement behind the arras; the armed men who had been hidden there sprang forward and seized not only the Earl, but his brother and the gentleman who had accompanied him. The young King burst into tears when he saw the rough treatment meted out to his visitors, for he guessed what was to follow, but though he implored Crichton not to put them to death, Crichton answered rudely that Douglas deserved all he was going to get; he was a traitor, and as long as he remained alive the King would never be at peace. With that he gave orders for the Douglases to be taken to the highest part of the castle rock, where they were beheaded.

The sluggish James the Gross, as Crichton and Livingston had expected, continued to pocket the King's revenues, but made no effort to strengthen the King's authority. But when Earl James died in 1443 he was succeeded by a much more formidable person, William, the eighth Earl of Douglas. A fortunate marriage had increased Earl William's already vast possessions; he had estates in ten different counties, and the half-dozen castles which he owned included the powerful fortresses of Bothwell, Threave, and Abercorn. His brothers—Archibald, Earl of Moray, Hugh, Earl of Ormond, and John, Lord Balvenie—had great estates in the north of Scotland. That the young Earl could make himself master of Scotland, if he chose, Livingston understood full well; he therefore took the precaution of breaking with Crichton and making friends with Douglas. The King himself for a time came under the spell of the spirited, ambitious youth.

But in his castle on the brink of the sea at St. Andrews the sage and subtle Bishop Kennedy pondered long over the plight of his country. There was little to choose between Livingston and Crichton, he knew; but Livingston was Douglas's jackal, so he judged it prudent to make some sort of alliance with his rival. For Douglas was the real enemy, he considered. He distrusted him for his influence over the young King and for his friendship with the unscrupulous Earl of Crawford, and when in 1445 Crawford and Livingston invaded Fife and harried the lands of the bishopric, Kennedy was sure that Douglas had a hand in the business. As yet he could not strike back except with spiritual weapons; he excommunicated the spoilers, but though he repeated the curse again and again, nobody seemed a penny the worse. A twelvemonth and a day, however, after the curse had first been pronounced, the Earl of Crawford was mortally wounded in an encounter between the Lindsays and the Ogilvies at Arbroath. His own followers were terrified by this apparent judgement from heaven; when their master died they refused to bury him till they had received permission from the Bishop. The effect soon wore off, and in 1449 Scotland was again full of rumours of plots and rebellions.

But the King was no longer a child; long years spent in an atmosphere of plot and counter-plot had changed the tender-hearted boy who wept at the death of Douglas into a ruler with a fearlessness and a ruthless determination worthy of his father himself. Even his appearance was sinister and menacing: from birth one side of his face had been covered with a splash of scarlet, whence his subjects called him James of the Fiery Face.

As yet the King hesitated to strike at the Douglases, though in 1449 he clapped Livingston, with his sons and kinsmen, into prison. In 1450 the two sons of Livingston were executed on the castle hill, near the spot where the two Douglases had been beheaded; Livingston himself escaped only with the loss of all his possessions. Later in the year the King's chance came; while Douglas and his brothers were carrying themselves like great princes in Rome, attracting the attention of the Pope himself

MONS MEG, EDINBURGH CASTLE
Forged in Flanders and probably brought to Scotland in or about 1450.

Melrose Abbey

Roxburgh Castle and River Teviot

by the nobility of their bearing and the magnificence of their attire, James marched into Earl William's territories and captured some of his places of strength. Douglas hurried home, not to make war, but to surrender his estates to the King and to throw himself on the King's mercy. The device succeeded; the quick-tempered, impulsive Stewart gave him back the bulk of his possessions, and pardoned him for anything he had done amiss.

The King could not lay aside his suspicions altogether. There was trouble in the Highlands, where Livingston, lately escaped from prison, and his son-in-law, the young Lord of the Isles, were besieging and capturing the King's castles. Then somehow or other he learned that the Lord of the Isles had entered into an alliance with the Earl of Crawford and the Earl of Douglas.

James resolved that this coalition must be broken up at once. In February 1452, having first given him a letter assuring him that no harm should befall him, he persuaded Douglas to meet him in Stirling Castle. At first only pleasant words passed between the King and his guest, but after supper the King took him to an inner room, and told him plainly that he must at once break with Crawford and the Lord of the Isles. "I cannot, and will not," was Douglas's insolent reply. "False traitor, since you will not, I shall," cried the King, as, drawing a dagger, he stabbed the Earl in the throat. One of the courtiers at once smashed in his skull with a pole-axe, and the others who rushed up showed their approval of the King's deed by plunging their daggers into the dead body of his guest.

Crawford at once summoned his vassals to march against the King, and while James with a small force lay at Perth waiting for Huntly to join him, the Douglases, headed by the new Earl, dashed into Stirling. They displayed the King's letter to the astonished burgesses at the market cross, then nailed it to a board, which they fastened to a horse's tail and dragged through the streets, and departed, after they had plundered and burned the town.

For a moment the King lost heart; but for Bishop Kennedy's exhortations he would have abandoned the struggle altogether and taken refuge in France. Soon, however, he was rewarded with better news: Huntly, instead of marching to Perth, made for Brechin, where he came upon the Lindsays, the kinsmen and followers of Crawford, and completely defeated them.

Encouraged by this success the King harried the Douglas lands in southern Scotland, till Earl James judged it wise to submit to his brother's murderer.

Though Douglas had solemnly promised to lay aside all thoughts of revenge, though he was employed by James as an ambassador to England, he was still carefully watched by the King. In 1453, for no reason at all, it seemed, a horde of Islesmen sailed into the Firth of Clyde and plundered the villages that lay along the coast. James knew that Douglas had visited the Lord of the Isles, and he put two and two together. It seemed to be only goodness of heart that made Douglas negotiate for the release of a Scottish prisoner when he was an ambassador in England. But the prisoner was Malise Graham, nephew of Sir Robert Graham, who had murdered James I, and great-grandson of Robert II—a man whose title to the crown was supposed by some people to be better than that of the reigning King. Again the King put two and two together: the inevitable Douglas conspiracy must be faced once more.

According to an old story he went to St. Andrews and told Bishop Kennedy of his perplexity. The Bishop answered by laying before him a sheaf of arrows bound by a leathern thong. "Put the bundle across your knee and break it," he said. The King answered that it was impossible. "I will let you see that I can break it," replied the Bishop, as loosening the thong he drew out the arrows one by one and snapped them across till every one in the bundle was broken. The King understood: if he could detach the Earl's supporters from him by promises of pardon and rewards, he would find it a comparatively easy business to break the Earl.

In the early spring of 1455 the last act in the long drama of hatred began. The King suddenly appeared with an army before Douglas's castle of Inveravon and ordered the garrison to surrender. The garrison capitulated, and the castle was completely destroyed. From Inveravon the royal troops marched westward through the Douglas country, burning and plundering, and then, returning, invested the castle of Abercorn. The besiegers seemed destined to become the besieged; Douglas, with one of his most powerful supporters, Hamilton of Cadzow, hurried to the rescue of the garrison. But the thong which bound the arrows together had been loosened: Hamilton unexpectedly went over to the King's side, leaving Douglas with no alternative but to take refuge in England.

It was a fight to the death now. When Abercorn was captured at the end of May its defenders were executed. A few weeks later the Earl's brothers, who had been lurking on the other side of the border, made a last desperate raid into Scotland, but they were attacked and routed at Arkinholm by the Earl of Angus. Moray was slain, and his head brought to the King as a trophy. Ormond fared little better. He was captured, but not before he had been severely wounded. James kept him in prison till his wounds were healed, and then ordered him to be beheaded. The victory was followed by the capture of the Douglas strongholds, including (after a long siege) the castle of Threave. Parliament decreed the forfeiture of the vast Douglas territories and passed an Act of Annexation stating that certain properties were to remain with the crown and not be alienated to subjects in future except with the consent of Parliament.

For the next five years Scotland had peace; no other baron dared to bring on himself or his kinsfolk the fate that had overwhelmed the house of Douglas.

South of the border it was different: there a faction of the barons, led by Richard, Duke of York, in an attempt to dethrone the feeble Henry VI had plunged the country into civil war. In an unlucky hour for himself, James moved towards the border and laid siege to the castle of Roxburgh, which had been in English hands since the time of Edward Balliol. The King, who had inherited his father's interest in mechanical contrivances, often amused himself by working the great siege pieces with his own hands. His zeal made him share the fate of many medieval gunners: one of his own guns burst and a flying splinter killed him (3 August 1460). Roxburgh, however, surrendered two days later, and in the following year Henry VI handed over Berwick to the Scots.

The new King, James III, was a boy of only nine, but he had the sagacious Bishop Kennedy behind him, and for a time, except for the raids of the Lord of the Isles and his men, the country remained tranquil. But after Kennedy's death in 1465 the old scramble for the King's person and the royal revenues began. Lord Boyd, the head of a hitherto inconspicuous family, was successful in this dishonourable contest, and dealt out titles and honours to his sons and kinsfolk as Crichton and Livingston had done.

At first it seemed that the young King would surmount his troubles. The fall of the Boyds in 1469 was as sudden and dramatic as that of the Livingstons had been, and, in the same year, by marrying the Danish Princess Margaret, James put an end to the two-century-old dispute about the payment of tribute for the Hebrides, and gained possession of the Orkney and Shetland Islands as security for the payment of his bride's dowry. In 1474 he strengthened his position further by a treaty with Edward IV of England. That monarch had twelve years before made a treaty with the exiled Douglas and the Lord of the Isles, by which they agreed to assist Edward in the conquest of Scotland and to partition Scotland north of the Forth between them, while Edward was to annex the south. Now, however, there was to be peace between England and Scotland, and in 1476 James attacked the territory of the Lord of the Isles by land and sea, forced that turbulent chieftain to submit to him, and deprived him of the earldom of Ross.

But the great nobles could not understand the King. He was not one of themselves. He kept them at arm's length and spent most of his time in the company of men of low birth who were interested in the things that interested him—music and architecture, astrology and alchemy. He did not travel about his kingdom, but lived sequestered in the castle of Stirling planning new buildings with his architect Cochrane, or wearing out his eyes in a vain search for the philosopher's stone. For he was over-fond of money; stories ran through the realm of his mysterious black "kist" and the gold that was hoarded in it, and the issue from the mint of coins made of copper or billon[1] instead of the usual silver was looked on as a subtle device to enable the King to enrich himself at the expense of his subjects.

James, for his part, was jealous of his over-mighty subjects. Like most princes of his time, he wanted to be an absolute monarch, sharing the work of government with men of low degree, whom he had made and whom he could unmake, men chosen simply for their cleverness and their diligence in his service. To the Secret Council, the little committee chosen by

[1] An alloy of silver with copper or tin, in which the baser metal predominates.

JAMES III

One of the panels of the altar-piece of Trinity College Church in Edinburgh, founded by Mary of Gueldres. The figure behind the King is St. Andrew and the young Prince is probably one of the King's brothers.

PLATE 31

HERMITAGE CASTLE

himself which shaped and directed his policy, he invited busy clerics like Schevez, who had once helped to buy his clothes, and Elphinstone, whose only wealth was a subtle brain and a store of learning amassed in the colleges and law courts of Paris. He paid them by securing for them preferment in the church; Schevez, for example, through the King's influence became Archbishop of St. Andrews,[1] and Elphinstone Bishop of Aberdeen.

The great nobles liked the Council even less than they liked the King. It is true that the Council was no new invention: as the calling together of Parliament was a very slow business—forty day's notice had to be given to all who were invited to attend—the Scottish Kings had for centuries referred urgent business to a smaller body, consisting mainly of the great officers of state whose duties kept them near the King's person. But its power, or its pretensions, seemed to be increasing; it was a committee of the Council now, and not a committee of Parliament, that, under the name of the Session, met three times a year to settle disputes about property, and this same committee did not hesitate to overturn the decisions of the hereditary sheriffs, and even to inflict punishments on these amateur judges.

But the Council could not exercise to the full these powers with which the King was willing to entrust it: the great nobles had resolved that they would not be at the beck and call of a handful of upstarts, and spread all sorts of ridiculous stories about it. Its policy was supposed to be shaped and directed, not by Elphinstone, who was one of the greatest jurists and statesmen in Europe, but by Cochrane the architect—or mason, as they styled him—and the King's tailor, Hommyl, was reputed to be an influential member. So it is little wonder that the Council could not maintain order, and that civil wars on a small scale raged unchecked in various parts of the kingdom.

From murmuring against the Council the barons proceeded to murmur against the King, and to talk of replacing him on the throne by his brother Alexander, Duke of Albany. The King's suspicions were aroused; in 1479 he imprisoned Albany in Edinburgh Castle and his younger brother Mar in Craigmillar. Mar died suddenly, murdered by the King's orders, the nobles said; Albany slew his guards, clambered down the castle rock

[1] St. Andrews became an Archbishopric in 1472, Glasgow in 1492.

with the help of a rope that had been smuggled into his prison, and succeeded in making his way to France.

But the King's troubles were only beginning. War broke out with England, and in the summer of 1482 James set out for the borders. His brother Albany had already been a guest at the court of Edward IV, and at that very moment was marching northward with King Edward's brother, the Duke of Gloucester, resolved on the subjugation of Scotland. Meanwhile, the Scottish barons, ready to turn the occasion to their own advantage, were hurrying, at the head of their vassals, to join the King.

At Lauder they overtook him; then a sudden timidity seized them. They all wanted the King to surrender his power to them, but not one of them dared to face the angry monarch. Lord Gray, seeing them hesitate, told them the story of the cat and the mice. Still they hesitated, then the young Earl of Angus calmly remarked "I will bell the cat," and set off for the royal tent to demand the surrender of the detested councillors. He came back a few minutes later to their meeting-place in Lauder Kirk with the news that the King had flatly refused.

While they debated what their next step should be, a knock was heard, and the door opened to reveal a gorgeous figure—Cochrane, the most hated of all the King's low-born friends. The sight of the favourite, all gorgeous in black velvet and gold, with a chain of gold about his neck, and a horn tipped with gold at his side, was too much for the nobles. "A rope will suit you better," cried Angus, as he snatched the chain from his neck. "My lords, is this jest or earnest?" exclaimed Cochrane. "It is good earnest," was the ominous reply. The nobles rushed from the church to the royal quarters, seized every one of the favourites and hanged six of their captives, including the gorgeous Cochrane, over the bridge at Lauder. Cochrane died as he had lived, protesting that he should have been hanged in a silken cord, and not in "ane tow of hemp, like ane thief."

The King was escorted to Edinburgh and lodged in the Castle. The retreating armies were followed by Albany and Gloucester, who made their way into the capital unopposed. But Gloucester judged it prudent to leave his confederate to fight his own battle and returned to England, taking care to capture Berwick on his way south.

Now that the Scottish nobles had Albany they were not altogether satisfied with him. They did not like James, but they liked still less a prince who, as they suspected, was in the pay of King Edward, and who had let Berwick slip into English hands. For a short time Albany ruled as Regent, but he was forced to release the King and go through a form of reconciliation with him, and in 1483 he found his position so precarious that he fled to England.

He came back in 1484, accompanied by the long-banished Earl of Douglas. At the head of a company of horsemen they dashed into Lochmaben at fair time, but the burgesses resisted stoutly, till the local lairds, galloping in from the country with their tenants behind them, completed the rout of the raiders. Douglas was captured and brought before the King, but when he looked on the face of the monarch against whom he had hatched so many plots, he turned away his head and said not a word. Only when they told him that he was to be lodged in Lindores Abbey did he mutter "He that may no better be, must be a monk." Albany escaped, and made his way to France, where he was killed a year later in a tournament.

Gradually the King put together the ruins of his fallen authority; Elphinstone and the other low-born experts returned to the council-table, and as the hold of the King on his turbulent nobles grew tighter, the old murmurs against royal avarice and the arrogance of the upstart Council began to be heard. In 1488 the nobles again rose in rebellion, seized Prince James, the King's eldest son, proclaimed him Governor of the country, and marched with him in triumph through southern Scotland. The King, according to an old story, went to Lindores to ask the Earl of Douglas for his support. "Sir, you have kept me and your black coffer in Stirling too long," was the bitter reply. "Neither of us can do you any good."

The King made his way to Aberdeen, rallied the northern earls to his support, then turned southwards and met the rebel lords near Blackness on the Forth. An agreement was patched up between the two armies, whereupon the King rashly disbanded his army and went to Edinburgh Castle. Almost immediately the nobles rose in rebellion again. The King hurried to Stirling and the armies met south of the village of Bannockburn.

In the Battle of Sauchieburn, as later generations called it, the rebels were victorious, but the victory saddened the young prince more than defeat would have done. His conscience already reproached him for his alliance with his father's enemies, and he tried to deaden it by giving strict orders that no one should lay hands on the King. The King's horse, however, bolted, and threw him when he was a few yards from the mill of Bannockburn, whereupon the miller and his wife rushed out and dragged him in. Knowing that he was badly hurt, he asked them to send for a priest. The miller asked who he was. "I was your King this day at morn," he sadly replied. On hearing these words the miller's wife ran out crying for a priest for the King. "Here am I, ane priest," said a man who was passing by. "Where is the King?" She took him into the mill and led him up to the wounded man, who implored the stranger to give him absolution. "That shall I do hastily," said the pretended priest, as he drew a sword and stabbed the King to the heart.

James IV could never rid himself of the idea that he was his father's murderer. One thing he resolved to do. Till the day of his death he would wear an iron chain round his body.

CHAPTER 13

SCOTLAND IN THE TIME OF JAMES IV

THE rebel lords soon found that they had not destroyed the monarchy when they killed James III; that, on the contrary, they had made it stronger than it had been since the time of Bruce. It is true that some of them, like Alexander Hume, who became Lord Chamberlain and Keeper of Stirling Castle, and his confederate Patrick Hepburn, who emerged from the scramble as Earl of Bothwell and High Admiral of Scotland, secured estates and offices of profit for themselves and for their kinsfolk, but they were plainly not in a position to govern—or to misgovern—Scotland according to their own devices. They had overreached themselves: the news of the King's death caused

Plate 32 Collegiate Church of St. Salvator, St. Andrews
Founded by Bishop Kennedy in 1450.

Plate 33 Borthwick Castle
Fireplace in the Great Hall.

a wave of horror and indignation to run through every town and village in Scotland, and made their own position very precarious. They could not afford to be vindictive, and though they banished some half-dozen of the King's associates, within a few weeks they were compelled to admit the chief of the late King's supporters, including his Chancellor, Bishop Elphinstone, to Parliament and to the Secret Council.

They had made another mistake: James IV was not altogether the thoughtless, pleasure-loving youngster that they had supposed him to be. It is true that he was an impulsive, high-spirited boy, bent on making full use of the opportunities for enjoying himself which his lofty position offered to him. His boyish restlessness, his insatiable curiosity, his zest for enjoyment never left him; dancers, jugglers, jesters, and story-tellers always found a ready welcome at the royal palaces, and never went empty away. He was a grown man when he sent a gipsy to the King of Denmark with a letter of introduction stating that the bearer was an Egyptian prince, and when he bestowed an abbacy upon a rascally Italian who professed to be able to fly from Scotland to France. Equipped with a pair of wings the adventurer attempted a flight from the walls of Stirling Castle, but he "crashed" and broke his leg; he disarmed the King, however, by explaining to him that he had made the mistake of putting some hens' feathers in his wings, and they had "drawn him to the midden and not to the skies."

James spent money profusely, for he liked to go richly attired and to be lodged in a palace that was worthy of a king. But his extravagance was more popular than his father's avarice. The unlettered, hard-riding nobles welcomed the change from the moody recluse to the gallant youth who shared their enthusiasm for hunting and jousting, who liked to have his new-built palaces crowded at Christmas and Easter with a gay company of revellers, and who did not seem to object to losing money to his dutiful subjects at the card-table. The burgesses liked to see him "come sounding through the toun" at the head of a glittering cavalcade, and noted with approval that the blind and the crippled, even the loathsome lepers clustered outside the burgh port, never asked him for an alms in vain.

But under the cloth of gold lay the iron belt; with all this avidity for pleasure went an extraordinarily keen sense of duty;

restless and changeable as he was, his determination to be master in his own house, to be a terror to evil-doers, never changed. He did not trust the rebel lords who had once made him their tool; he did not break with them, but he shaped his policy to please himself, and when he was in doubt he let himself be guided by the advice of Bishop Elphinstone, the wisest of his father's counsellors.

The administration of justice was tightened up. The justiciars, accompanied sometimes by the King in person, once more went on their rounds regularly from county town to county town, twice every year, to deal out punishments to malefactors. At last the average country laird began to understand that if he plundered the dwelling or drove off the cattle of a neighbour with whom he had quarrelled, he would be lucky if he got off with the payment of a heavy fine, and that an action before the Council could force him to disgorge the goods of which he had despoiled his victim.

But the King knew that there were great stretches of his land where his writ did not run, remote border valleys which no royal messenger dared to enter, islands in the west where the word of the Lord of the Isles, humbled though he had been in 1476, still counted for more than the word of James Stewart.

At the very beginning of James's reign the Islesmen invaded the mainland in an attempt to win back Ross for their master; the King retaliated by declaring that the whole of the vast territories of the Lord of the Isles was forfeit to the Crown, and followed up his declaration by taking a fleet to the Hebrides in the autumn of 1493. Though the Lord of the Isles surrendered a year later, it was not till the end of 1505, after James had invaded the Hebrides for the sixth time, that he could feel certain that the Islesmen would remain quiet.

Meantime James had achieved a triumph of a very different kind. Though it seemed at one time as if his chivalrous, impetuous character would make him reopen the old, bitter, fruitless struggle with England, though, by raiding the northern counties of England in 1496 on behalf of the impostor Perkin Warbeck he almost forced a war upon the unwilling Henry VII, in the following year he was persuaded by the Spanish ambassador, De Ayala, to agree to a truce with England. In spite of the truce the two countries were again brought to the brink of war a few months later over a scuffle between some Scottish youths and some of the garrison of Norham Castle. James began to ask himself if any good came of these age-long hatreds; if friendship with France must always exclude friendship with England. Even if he were to establish a friendship with England, how could he be certain that it would endure? More than one treaty of "perpetual peace" had already been signed and broken. But why should he not strengthen the fragile tie that bound the two countries together by marrying Margaret Tudor, the elder daughter of the English King?

Henry VII welcomed the proposal; he was not deterred even by the prospect of a Scottish king becoming King of England at some future date. Better that than the perpetual menace of war, he argued. Besides, as he pointed out to his Council, even if Scotland and England were united the greater would always draw the less, England would always be the predominant partner. So in 1502 another treaty of perpetual peace was signed, and in August 1503, before the high altar in the abbey church of Holyrood, the King of Scots was married to the young English princess.

The autumn was spent by James and his Queen in a triumphal progress through the southern half of his kingdom. He had reason to be pleased with what he saw; once more, over the greater part of the country, "the key kept the castle and the bracken bush the cow," and farmer and craftsman alike, freed from the fear of foreign invasion and of civil war, were giving their whole minds to the arts of peace. "There is as great a difference between the Scotland of old time and the Scotland of to-day," De Ayala had written six years before, "as there is between good and bad." But if we could transport ourselves back to Scotland as it was in the year 1503, we should be amused at De Ayala's raptures.

Progress was slow in this remote northern country; the rural districts especially had changed little since the time of Alexander III. South of the Grampians the country was still for the most part bare and treeless, undivided by hedgerow or by dry stone dyke; marshes and reed-fringed lochs that have long since disappeared still occupied the undrained river valleys. Though good stone was plentiful the country folk still dwelt in smoky, windowless huts of turf, and they tilled the ground in the old unthrifty way, ploughing the barren hill-sides, because the rich land beside the river was waterlogged, exhausting their best arable land by never letting it lie fallow, contenting themselves at harvest with plucking off the ears of the corn and leaving the straw to rot. On the "infield" near the dwelling-houses, crops of barley and oats, oats and barley, were grown every year without intermission; portions of the "outfield", the inferior land, would be cultivated for two or three years on end and then used as pasture for another two or three, but, unlike the infield, it was never manured. Like the husbandmen of Alexander's time, they used the clumsy wooden plough, dragged by a team of eight oxen, for though you might see hundreds of shaggy ponies at the fairs in Perth or Dundee, though you might buy one for a shilling or two, heavy draught horses were both scarce and expensive. Few countrymen had as many as eight oxen fit to pull the plough, for their farms were small—twenty-six Scottish acres[1] was quite an ordinary size—but their holdings were often arranged in groups of four, and four neighbours would arrange to make up a plough team among them. Still, they might have made more use of the little land they had, by manuring fields systematically, and their cottages might have been surrounded by gardens, and shadowed by orchard trees. But they refused to plan for the future. If you visited a cluster of Scottish farm-houses in the spring you would see a strange sight—three or four men tenderly leading out emaciated cattle from the low-roofed cottages, where they had spent the winter. The poor beasts were starved, for the problem of the winter-feeding of cattle was not solved until the eighteenth-century. Consequently, every year when Martinmas (11th November) came round, there was a great slaughter of "marts"—superfluous cattle—and the survivors had to exist as best they could on a meagre diet of poor hay and chopped straw. The carcasses of the marts were salted, and eaten during the winter.

It is true that the ordinary countryman was no longer bound to the soil as he had been in the thirteenth century; his complaint now was that the tie binding him to the soil was not strong enough. As his land was now leased to him for a period of not more than five years, he would be foolish if he wasted time and labour in building a comfortable house which he might not be

[1] About thirty-two modern acres.

allowed to occupy, or in planting an orchard from which he might not pluck a single apple. The King saw the injustice of this arrangement: in 1504, he announced that he meant to set his own lands in feu farm, and hinted that his barons should do the same with theirs. This meant that the land was granted, not for a short time, but in perpetuity; the landowner virtually surrendered the land to the occupier in return for a fixed annual rent, or feu-duty, and as long as this sum was paid the occupier could look on the ground as his own.

Though the township had changed little, a glance at the baron's castle would have convinced us that Scotland had become a wealthier country. It is true that the poorer laird was content to dwell in a single stone tower. The small barred windows set high up in the wall, the iron yett or grille protecting the entrance, which was usually on the first floor, the battlemented parapet which surmounted the tower, all showed that the place was built so that it could resist a sudden attack—a necessary precaution in the days when almost every respectable family boasted at least one hereditary feud.

But the wealthier baron refused to be content with these cramped quarters, he built additions to the single tower, till it became L-shaped or Z-shaped in plan, or expanded it to form a great hollow square, such as we may see at Crichton or Craigmillar, with a courtyard in the centre. The King set the example; at Holyrood, at Linlithgow, at Stirling, additions were made to the buildings.

The building of splendid churches, too, went on. Mary of Gueldres, the widow of James II, had endowed and started to build Trinity College Church in Edinburgh, and James III had developed the church of Restalrig as a royal foundation. Now, James IV gave lavish endowments to the Chapel Royal at Stirling. The nobles likewise were founding collegiate churches, where priests carried on the services with a dignity unknown in parish churches and said numerous Masses for the souls of the founders and their families. Some of these churches were very fine buildings—Rosslyn Chapel, for example, and Crichton and Dunglass.

In the towns the wealthy merchants followed where King and barons led; they pulled down the wooden structures that had satisfied their fathers, and built houses of stone, with vaulted basements and crow-stepped gables, often surrounding a courtyard. From the courtyard, which, like the courtyards of the great castles, was approached by a pend or covered passage, a flight of steps led to the first floor, where the principal rooms were situated. The burgesses spent a lot of money on their churches, too, and gave us splendid buildings like St. Michael's at Linlithgow, St. Mary's at Haddington, and the Holy Rude at Stirling.

Suppose then that we are in Edinburgh in the year 1503; suppose we enter the pend, cross the courtyard, and climb the stairs of the new house that some prosperous merchant has built for himself. If we swung back the heavy iron-studded door at the top of the outside stair, we should find ourselves in the hall, which in those days was not a mere vestibule, but the principal living-room in town house and palace alike. It is not too well lighted, for only the upper halves of the windows are glazed, the lower halves being obscured by wooden shutters, but as our eyes grow accustomed to the dim light we notice that the walls are hung with tapestry, and that the rafters in the low roof are picked out in gay colours. Carpets there are none; rushes or dried grass must serve instead even in the King's palaces. There is very little furniture; a trestle table covered with a green cloth, a counter or table with fixed legs, one chair, reserved for the master of the house, one or two benches or settles with loose cushions, a kist or chest, and an aumbry or cupboard would probably complete the list. Though the arch over the handsome stone fireplace might serve for a bishop's tomb there is no grate, the flaming logs are kept from rolling among the rushes only by metal fire-dogs.

In the profusion of handsome silver plate on the table and counter we notice neither forks nor knives, and only a very few spoons. As every one carried a knife on his person in those days it was not thought necessary to provide him with another for use only at meals. As for forks—the basin and towel placed in a conspicuous position on the table let us into the secret. As the diners held their meat with their fingers, they had to wash their hands immediately after every meal. We should notice other omissions: there is no glass or china; silver plates are used for occasions of state; for everyday use pewter or wood has to suffice. And the food would seem strange to us: we should weary of the salt beef and mutton which formed the staple fare throughout the winter, for it would be too "gamey" in flavour for the modern palate, even though smothered in mace and nutmeg and other eastern spices. Fish was usually eaten on Wednesday, Friday and Saturday throughout the year, as well as during the whole of Lent. White bread, too, we should find regarded as a luxury, for little wheat was grown in Scotland; barley bread, or oatcakes, baked on a "girdle" or on the hearth, were used on ordinary occasions.

The bed is the only feature of the bedroom that is worth mentioning—a noble structure, a great swelling feather-bed rising from a foundation of wooden boards and surmounted by a canopy, from which hang curtains of heavy cloth. For it was only at night, when he fastened the curtains at either side, and "kest on claithis threinfauld" that the medieval Scotsman could keep the airs of heaven at bay; even when he sat before the great fireplace the winds whistled through the holes in the shutter and waved the arras till the pictured shapes seemed to come to life.

To his distrust of fresh air—of which he got too much—the average Scotsman added a distrust of soap and water—of which he got too little. Soap was a costly commodity, imported from abroad in small quantities, and even the most comfort-loving merchant did not dream of fitting up a bath in his house. So you might see unwashed faces with jewels and costly raiment, for strangers thought the Scots inordinately fond of fine clothes. And the streets of Edinburgh, as of any other Scottish town, gave evidence of this same disregard of cleanliness.

To one who did not examine it too closely, Edinburgh, rising proudly from the lochs which then almost girdled it, must have seemed a stately and gracious city. One grim, grey tower dominated the castle rock, and in the middle of the town a much more beautiful St. Giles' than the St. Giles' of to-day thrust its lantern spire into the sky. And St. Giles' stood in a street that was not a narrow lane, like most medieval streets, but a great square, round which rose the new stone-built houses of noble and merchant, some of them with arcades underneath, where one found the best shops that Edinburgh could boast. The closes, too, were still closes in the old sense of the word—garden closes—for the long, narrow gardens that stretched behind the

High Street to the Cowgate and the Nor' Loch were still unbuilt on; apple and cherry trees still displayed their blossom within a few yards of the Mercat Cross.

But in this beautiful city, set among gardens on its lofty ridge, there were neither water-pipes nor drain-pipes; the refuse from the houses was flung into the streets, where pigs routed among the foul-smelling garbage, and the drinking water was drawn from wells, many of them in the public streets. It is little wonder that every few years Edinburgh, like the other towns in medieval Scotland, was devastated by a pestilence against which the medical science of the day could find no defence. In their despair people tried strange remedies: the Bishop of Dunkeld—if we are to believe his biographer—cured those who had been stricken down by the pestilence with holy water, in which one of St. Columba's bones had been dipped. The only man who did not recover, says the same veracious biographer, was a shameless wretch who wished that the holy water had been a pot of good ale.

But it was in those dark ages of medical science, in the year 1505, to be exact, that the College of Surgeons of Edinburgh received its charter from King James. For though the influence of the Renaissance was not felt in Scotland at this time, though the bishops and clerics who visited Rome came away quite untouched by the enthusiasm which they found there for the newly discovered art and literature of Greece, some attention was paid to learning. A second University, Glasgow, had been founded in 1451, and in 1495 Bishop Elphinstone founded a third at Aberdeen. These universities were attended for the most part by men destined for the priesthood, but the King and his advisers knew that a sheriff who was ignorant of law could do as much mischief as a priest who did not know the Latin of his service-book, and in 1496 an act was passed to compel country gentlemen to send their eldest sons, first to a grammar school "till they have perfyte Latin," and then to a university, to get instruction in law.

In those days, of course, one could not be a learned man without Latin, for it was the language of educated people all over Europe, the language in which all scientific books, and most histories, were written. The book of marvels which Hector Boece composed about this time and called a History of the Scots was written in Latin, like the more accurate work

THE MERCAT CROSS, CULROSS

Old Tolbooth, Dunbar

of John Major. These two historians wrote for the continental scholar, their books were printed, not in Edinburgh, but in Paris; but the poets Henryson and Blind Harry, and the forgotten bards whom Dunbar, the greatest of them all, celebrates in his *Lament for the Makars*, wrote in Scots for their own country-folk. For in this bleak northern land, in this too short interval between war and war, poetry had a strange brief blossoming, a spring which no summer followed.

But though people were now thinking of comfort as well as security, and of seemliness and beauty as well as of comfort, their desire for beautiful objects outran their skill; it was not a Scottish "wricht," for example, who fashioned the elaborately carved cupboard or linen chest which we saw in the dwelling of the wealthy merchant; that was imported from Flanders, like the tapestries on the wall, or the silver-ware that glittered on the "counter." In fact, if a really good manufactured article of any kind was wanted—from a feather-bed to a tombstone, from a cushion to a candlestick—it had to be imported from abroad. It was the same with books: though in 1507 two merchants, Walter Chepman and Andrew Millar, set up a printing press in Edinburgh, they ceased operations after they had published a few volumes, and most books came from abroad.

In return, Scotland exported no manufactured goods except woollen cloth of poor quality; the staple exports were salt fish, wool, and hides. In other words, Scotland paid in raw materials for the manufactured goods, and for the sugar and wine, spices and sweetmeats which it imported. But this trade was small in bulk and carried on under some curious restrictions. Only merchants in royal burghs were allowed to engage in foreign trade; they were forbidden to take their ships out of harbour in the stormy winter months, and when they did set sail they were all expected to make for the port of Middelburg in the Low Countries. Here the Scottish "Staple" was established; in other words, the town of Middelburg conferred certain privileges on Scottish merchants on the understanding that it would be granted a monopoly of the trade with Scotland in return.[1] Here the merchants found a hostel, and warehouses where they could store their goods. Usually they did not deal directly with the Dutch merchants, but put their affairs into the hands of the

[1] Removed to the neighbouring town of Veere in 1507.

Scottish Conservator—consul, we should call him. To him they sold their wool and their salted salmon, and he in return bought for them the medley of odds and ends which they required.

Though the Scottish merchant was a very small man beside the merchant princes of Bruges or Antwerp, he considered himself an exceedingly important person in his own town. He was tenacious of his own privileges and suspicious of what seemed

Printers' Device of Andrew Millar, 1508

to him to be the insolence of the craftsmen. For the craftsmen had taken a leaf out of the merchants' book: in every town the members of the separate crafts or trades organised themselves into separate gilds after the model of the merchant gild. When an apprentice shoemaker became a journeyman, he paid a fee to the boxmaster or treasurer, and was enrolled in the cordiners' gild or craft, the head of which was an official known as the dean or deacon. These craft gilds might be called medieval trade unions, but they differed from the modern trade unions in two important respects: they included both masters and men, and they were purely local associations; a member of the baxter craft in St. Andrews, for example, could not open a baker's shop in Cupar or Dundee.

In spite of the rise of the crafts, the merchants, for a time at least, tightened their hold over the towns. In the reign of James III the right of electing the burgh council was taken from the general body of the burgesses and conferred on the burgh council itself; after 1469 there was nothing to keep the retiring council from re-electing itself, and it usually did so. Further, in 1504 it was enacted that only a merchant trading within the burgh could represent it in Parliament. So the craftsman was excluded both from the burgh council and from Parliament, and so the merchants who represented the burghs in Parliament succeeded in securing the enactment of vindictive laws against the crafts and their deacons. But the crafts had come to stay.

Except for these squabbles between merchants and craftsmen, a deep peace seemed to have settled down on Scotland. Even the borders had been quiet ever since that November night in 1510, when the King, at the head of a great force of horsemen, rode out of Edinburgh, rounded up the border cattle thieves, and dealt out the local brand of justice to them at Jedburgh.[1] So law-abiding had the country become that the King would think nothing of riding from Stirling to the shrine of St. Duthac in Tain without an escort of any kind.

James played his part well, but at times he must have looked on Scotland as too narrow a stage for a king of his energy and political talent. The treaty with England was not the last of his diplomatic triumphs; he had succeeded in securing the friendship of England without losing the friendship of France, and in consequence he found himself courted by more than one continental prince. In 1506, for example, he sent a fleet to the help of the beleagured Queen of Denmark; in 1507 he urged the citizens of Lübeck not to aid the rebellious Swedes in their quarrel with the Danish King Hans; and when in the same year his kinsman the Duke of Gueldres appealed to him for help against the Emperor Maximilian and his son the Archduke, who were invading his territory, James, without actually fighting, succeeded in extricating the Duke from his perilous position. Even Louis XII of France did not disdain to ask the King of Scots for four

[1] "Jeddart Justice" meant hanging a man first and trying him afterwards.

thousand soldiers to help him in his invasion of Italy. For a time it seemed as if James would become the arbiter who would decide the fate of monarchs far mightier than himself.

James knew that he could not play that part unless he had the backing of a powerful fleet. Skilful and daring captains he had: he knew that on one occasion five English ships and on another three had been attacked by Sir Andrew Wood with only two ships, and had been forced to surrender. But he had few ships, and timber was scarce in Scotland. As early as 1506 he informed King Louis that he intended to build a fleet for the defence of his shores, and obtained permission for his agents to fell timber in the forests of Normandy; at the same time Scottish merchants went as far afield as Spain to buy anchors and cordage for the projected fleet.

One of the new ships was put under the command of Andrew Barton, who straightway sailed over to the Dutch coast and waged a vigorous war against the Dutch pirates who had been preying upon the Scottish merchant ships. But Barton leant a little too much towards piracy himself; again and again he captured Portuguese merchant ships, though Scotland and Portugal were at peace. When King Emmanuel of Portugal complained to King James, he was informed that Barton was quite within his rights, as, thirty years before, his father's ship had been captured in an encounter with a Portuguese vessel, and, in spite of repeated requests, no compensation had ever been paid for the slaughter of the elder Barton, or for the loss of his ship.

But the Portuguese complaints had not gone unheard at the English court. In the summer of 1511 the Lord Admiral and his brother, Lord Thomas Howard, attacked Barton's two ships in the Downs, as they were returning from the Dutch coast. If courage could have availed against superior weight of metal, Barton would have been victorious; when he lay on deck mortally wounded, with his leg shattered by a cannon ball, he insisted on beating a lively tune on a drum to encourage his men. But the Scots were completely outmatched; their ships were taken into the Thames and the crews lodged in the Tower.

James remonstrated as warmly with the King of England as Emmanuel had remonstrated with him; he could get nothing more than the answer that princes did not dispute about pirates,

CAST OF GOLD PATTERN COIN OF JAMES IV
This shows what is probably the Great Michael. (Original coin in British Museum.)

A contemporary (seventeenth century) impression of a sailing vessel. Reproduced from a Glasgow University student's notebook about 1680.

OLD BRIDGE OF FORTH, STIRLING
The ancient bridge, where the battle was fought, crossed the river higher up-stream.

TWIZEL BRIDGE
Where the English army crossed the Till before Flodden

and had to extract what consolation he could from a contemplation of his newest ship, the great *Michael*, with its towering castles and innumerable port-holes bristling with guns, the mightiest ship in Europe he believed it to be, to build which all the woods in Fife had been laid low. For already the "perpetual peace" was wearing thin; the dispute about Barton was only one of several questions, trivial enough in themselves, but serious enough to serve as a pretext for war. Had Henry VII been alive these questions might have been shelved, but Henry VII had died in 1509, and the ambitious and confident Henry VIII did not seem to care greatly whether James made war on him or not.

In 1512 came the test that strained the "perpetual peace" to the breaking point: the French King found himself confronted by a "Holy League"—a coalition organised by the Pope, in which England was a partner—and appealed to the King of Scots for help. James had to choose between the old alliance with France, never definitely abrogated, and the "perpetual" friendship with England. Elphinstone counselled peace, but the adventurous King rejected his policy of caution.

But Louis wanted more than expressions of friendship. In the early summer of 1513, when Henry was on the point of etting sail for France, an envoy from Louis was admitted to an audience with James and his Council at Edinburgh. To the King he presented, along with the letters from Louis, a turquoise ing and a letter from Queen Anne, in which she hailed him as her knight, and asked him to advance into England and strike a blow on her behalf.

Long afterwards stories were told of the strange and ominous happenings in the time of waiting which followed—how when the King knelt in his stall in the Church of St. Michael at Linlithgow an old man clad in a robe of blue appeared before him, uttered a solemn warning, and suddenly vanished, and how "there was a cry heard at the market cross of Edinburgh at the hour of midnight," a cry from ghostly heralds come from the realm of the dead to summon earls and lords, barons and burgesses, to appear before their Master within forty days.

On the 22nd of August James crossed the Tweed at the head of the most splendid army that a King of Scotland had ever commanded, and before September was well begun he had captured four castles. But the Earl of Surrey was hurrying north, gathering a formidable army as he went. "The crooked old carle" had not learned his strategy from romances of chivalry, but he thought that he knew how to deal with those who had: when he reached Alnwick, where he was joined by his son, Lord Thomas Howard, now Lord Admiral, he sent on a herald to James, offering to do battle with him at any time before noon on Friday, September 9. James accepted the challenge, but when Surrey advanced to meet the Scots he found them posted in an almost impregnable position on Flodden Hill. Instead of marching straight on the Scottish position from the south, he crossed the River Till, recrossed it a few miles farther north at Twizel Bridge, on the morning of September 9, and advanced on the Scots from the north.

When on that stormy September afternoon, the English vanguard, led by Lord Thomas Howard, neared Branxton Hill, about a mile and a half north-west of Flodden Hill, they saw the Scottish camp disappear in clouds of smoke. The Scots had set fire to the heaps of rubbish that had accumulated in their camp, and under cover of this smoke-screen had occupied Branxton Hill. Suddenly the air cleared, and the Admiral saw barely a quarter of a mile away, four glittering squares of spearmen. Taken by surprise, he halted his men till the main body under Surrey had come up on his left. The English were now facing southwards, the Scots northwards.

The battle began with an artillery duel, but the Scottish guns did little damage, and when the English gunners replied they not only silenced the Scottish batteries, but sorely galled the division under the immediate command of King James.

About half-past four in the afternoon the Scots moved silently down hill and closed with the advancing English, who like them were arranged in four divisions. Both sides fought on foot, and that they might move more easily over the slippery turf, the Scots had taken off their shoes.

At first it seemed that the Scots might be victorious: Lord Home and the borderers on the left routed the English division opposed to them. A sudden charge of the English reserves however, checked his advance, while on his right the Admiral's men smashed a way through the divisions commanded by the Earls of Crawford and Montrose. Farther to the east, the King's division crashed into the division commanded by Surrey. James's nobles and knights fought stubbornly, but they perished almost to a man, for here, as in the other parts of the field, the Scottish spears were outmatched by the English bills. The King himself lay among the slain; he had been cut down when he was only a spear's length from the English commander.

The battle ended when Sir Edward Stanley, coming up on Surrey's left, fell on the Highlanders commanded by the Earls of Lennox and Argyll and drove them headlong from the hill of death, but only darkness put an end to the pursuit, a pursuit in which no quarter was given.

One archbishop, two bishops, and thirteen earls had died beside their King. And with them perished a great multitude of "the mere uncounted folk." No chronicle preserves their names, but a heart-breaking old tune, "The Flowers o' the Forest," still played as a dirge in Scottish regiments, echoes the wail of anguish that arose from every town and hamlet as the news of the disaster spread over the land.

CHAPTER 14

JAMES V

NOT all at once did the Scots become fully aware of what had been lost at Flodden. The English army disbanded and did not venture north of the Tweed. The white-haired burgess of Edinburgh waited in vain for the bell that would warn him to grasp his rusty spear in his unaccustomed hand, and sally out to guard his town against the slayers of his son. For a time he tried to believe the comforting rumour that the King had not really been killed, that he had gone at last on that long-contemplated pilgrimage to the Holy Land, from which he would soon return. But for King James there could be no return; the country must fare as best it could with a boy-king seventeen months old.

Had Elphinstone been younger, had those great nobles who survived the wreck of Flodden, men like the Earl of Arran, the head of the great semi-royal house of Hamilton, and the Earl of Angus, grandson of old Bell-the-Cat, cared more for their country than for themselves, the Highland clans might have thought twice before they harassed the stricken Lowlands, and the border reiver might have herded his own, and not his neighbour's cattle. But Elphinstone was too old. After Flodden, says his friend and biographer Hector Boece, "he was never again seen to laugh, to enjoy jests or to make even the most modest pleasantry." He died in Edinburgh in October 1514, too soon, one trusts, to know that at the beginning of the month Louis XII of France, the king for whom his master had sacrificed his life and imperilled his kingdom, had married the younger sister of Henry VIII.

Angus married the Queen Dowager in 1514, and in the moves and countermoves of Angus and his rival Arran, Scotsmen soon ceased to look for any trace of a disinterested motive. They expected more from the great noble who appeared in the kingdom in the summer of 1515 and who was almost immediately appointed Governor or Regent of Scotland. This was John, Duke of Albany, a son of that adventurous and over-ambitious prince who had been forced to flee from the kingdom in the reign of James III. Albany had inherited his father's courage and his royal presence, though he never at any time tried to imitate his father by ousting the rightful king from the throne. But his policy was in the main designed to serve France. He had been born in France, had spent all his days in France and could speak no language but French. And the man who sought to govern a turbulent kingdom could not govern himself; if he was contradicted, he flung his hat in the fire, and dared any of the company to rescue it. It was soon obvious that he really cared little for Scotland; the cost of maintaining his French servants and his falconers, his private company of actors and his Italian trumpeters, emptied the already impoverished treasury; by the Treaty of Rouen in 1517 the Franco-Scottish League for mutual assistance in war was renewed, with the prospect that the Scottish King might be given a daughter of the King of France as a bride.

In 1517, Albany went off to France, where he was detained until 1521 because Anglo-French relations were friendly and France had no interest in stimulating the Scots against England. He left one of his French comrades, Antony de la Bastie, to be

JAMES V AND MARY OF GUISE

Plate 39 Linlithgow Palace
St. Michael's Church is to be seen behind the Palace.

Warden of the East March, the country of the Homes, whose head, Lord Home, had been executed by Albany. De la Bastie knew that the Homes would make trouble if they could, and when in the autumn of 1517 he heard that their confederates had seized the castle of Langton, he galloped out at the head of a few horsemen. But the castle would not yield, and he was forced to withdraw. As he rode off at some little distance from his men, the thunder of hoofs behind him told him that something was amiss. He looked round, to see a party of the Homes, led by David Home of Wedderburn, riding hard after him. For a time it seemed that he would outstrip his pursuers and reach the castle of Dunbar, but his horse fell and the Homes overtook him and slew him. The death of Lord Home had been avenged; the Laird of Wedderburn rode back in triumph, with the head of the murdered man tied to the saddlebow by its flowing hair.

Nor were strife and bloodshed confined to the borders; less than three years later a pitched battle was fought in the very High Street of Edinburgh, arising out of the feud between Arran and Angus, who had gained control both of the King's person and of the town and castle of Edinburgh. So when in the spring of 1520 a large party of the Hamiltons and their confederates, headed by Arran and his ally James Beaton, Archbishop of Glasgow, came to Edinburgh and lodged in the Canongate and those parts of the city outside the Flodden Wall, Angus and his friends judged it prudent to close the Netherbow Port and the other gates and remain on the alert all night. In the morning, while Angus drew up his forces in the High Street, his uncle Gavin Douglas, now Bishop of Dunkeld, went to the Dominican friary, where Beaton was, and urged him to put matters right before trouble began, for he knew how to do it.

"My lord, by my conscience, I know not the matter," cried Beaton, laying his hand on his bosom. There was a tell-tale clash as he did so, for under his clerical robes he wore an unclerical suit of armour.

"I perceive, my lord, your conscience be not good, for I hear them[1] clatter," remarked the bishop, calmly.

The Douglases stood firm and gave better than they got, and after a grim struggle the Hamiltons broke and sought refuge in

[1] The plates of armour, not the Archbishop's conscience, as Sir Walter Scott supposed.

the wynds and closes that opened off the High Street. Arran himself escaped only by flinging himself on a collier's horse and fording the Nor' Loch. Neither clerical rochet nor unclerical plate armour would have saved Beaton from the enemies who dragged him out from the altar in the church of the Blackfriars, had not Bishop Gavin magnanimously interceded for him. Altogether seventy-two combatants perished in this brawl, which the burgesses of Edinburgh long remembered under the name of "Cleanse the Causeway."

The return of Albany in 1521 constrained Angus to cross the border, but when Albany left Scotland for the last time in 1524, after involving it in an unsuccessful war with England, Angus promptly returned and was soon ruling the country in the name of a captive king.

So far every one had left the King out of his calculations. Soon after Albany's departure, James had been told that he was now king indeed. He was delighted, because the announcement brought release from what an old writer calls "correctioun at the schools," which in the sixteenth century was a formidable and painful business, even for a prince. But the ambitious youth of sixteen refused to be contented with the gilded captivity which had satisfied the boy of twelve. In the summer of 1528 he escaped by night from the Castle of Edinburgh and rode to Stirling, where he was joined by those lords who desired the downfall of Angus. A few weeks later, at the head of an army of 2,000 men, he advanced against the great Douglas stronghold of Tantallon, where Angus had taken refuge. After a siege, terms were agreed, whereby Angus and his kinsmen were allowed to retire to England.

The wild gallant stripling promised to develop into an excellent king, for if he had inherited something of his father's prodigality and love of adventure for adventure's sake, he also inherited his fierce passion for law and order. If his weakness for roaming about the country in disguise under the name of the Gudeman of Ballangeich got him into curious scrapes, it also taught him much about the people whom he ruled, and, when he went on a hunting expedition into Yarrow or Teviotdale with some hundreds of armed horsemen at his back, the deer was not always the only quarry that he sought, as John Armstrong, one of the most formidable of the border freebooters, discovered.

When in the summer of 1530 Armstrong heard that the King and his huntsmen were riding over the moors into Teviotdale, he rashly assumed that he had to deal only with a simple boy, and with more than two score followers behind him set out from his tower of Gilnockie to pay his respects to the King. James was not deceived by his sudden show of loyalty; he ordered Armstrong and his companions to be seized and hanged on the nearest convenient trees. Armstrong begged for mercy, but he looked in vain for any sign of relenting in the smooth young face of the prince. Then, the old ballad writer tells us, when he saw that his death was inevitable, he broke into a last hopeless taunt:

> To seek het water beneath cauld ice,
>   Surely it is a great folie;
> I have asked grace at a graceless face,
>   But there is nane for my men and me.

James's zeal for justice did not stop with the hunting down of robbers. There had been two courts which dealt not only with complaints brought straight to them but with appeals from the burgh and sheriff courts; the one was the Committee of Causes, a committee of the Parliament, which met only when Parliament was in session, and the other was the Session, a committee of the Council. Both the Lords Auditors, who sat on the first, and the Lords of Council, who sat on the second, were expected to perform their duties without payment; the result was that they sometimes accepted from the suitors that payment which they could not obtain from the King. Further, as knowledge of law was not too common in Scotland, the few legal experts were overworked, and had to be both Lords Auditors when Parliament was in session and Lords of Council when it was not. In both courts the same scenes were witnessed, crowds of bawling suitors at the door, each holding out a paper and demanding that his case should be heard first.

James knew the hardships of the ordinary suitor, he also knew that his own greatest hardship was a lack of money, so in 1531 he persuaded the Pope to allow him to impose a tax on the bishops and abbots of £10,000 a year, to be used to found and maintain a College of Justice—a body of expert judges who would be paid for their services and who would always be available for duty on the bench in a supreme civil court. There were to be fifteen of them, it was ordained by Parliament in 1532, eight clergymen, one of whom was to be President of the Court, and seven laymen, and the court was to sit regularly in Edinburgh all the year round. The bishops reluctantly consented; the original £10,000 yearly was soon whittled down to a large lump sum (which was used for entirely different purposes) and a small annual payment for the judges' salaries.

James's action had consequences of which he had little dreamed. The prelates, to raise the necessary money, set their lands in feu-farm and in so doing often dispossessed the original tenants in favour of new-comers who offered to pay a larger sum, thus loosening still further the bond, already dangerously slack, between the clergy and the poor country-folk. At the same time the bond between the King and the bishops was drawn dangerously tight, for he knew that he could wring money from them by defending them in the face of the attacks now being made on the Church.

By this time fifteen years had passed since Luther had nailed his theses to the door of the church in Wittenberg, northern Europe seemed already lost to Catholicism, and Henry VIII had even now definitely broken with the Pope. In Scotland, even among those who detested the new doctrines of Luther and looked on King Henry as a traitor to the faith which he had undertaken to defend, there were many who recognised that all was not well with the Church. There was no more bitter opponent of the new opinions than John Major, the Lothian youth who had become the most famous theologian in the colleges of Paris, but Major did not hesitate to say that the Church was far too wealthy and that it would have been better if David I had not lavished lands and money upon his newly built monasteries. Men entered the priesthood for what they could get out of it, and preferment in the Church went not to the man who was most worthy of it, but to the man who could call a powerful noble his kinsman or who could spend money more lavishly than his rivals at the court of Rome. Even the King was far from scrupulous in the use of the influence which he possessed with the Pope; if he could not have a bishop who was both saint and statesman, he chose a statesman rather than a saint. Sometimes, too, he wanted to provide for a needy kinsman without expense to himself; this explains why in 1492 James,

Duke of Ross, the brother of James IV, was made Archbishop of St. Andrews, and why he was succeeded in 1504 not by Elphinstone, but by Alexander Stewart, a boy of thirteen, whose main recommendation was that he was the King's illegitimate son.

The royal example did not lack imitators; the great nobleman provided for his younger sons by securing rich benefices for them, and by arranging that while they studied philosophy and theology at Paris or St. Andrews, their clerical duties should be performed by a poorly paid substitute. That was not all: there was nothing to prevent a priest being vicar of two or more parishes, even though one might be in Tweeddale and another in Caithness.

So it was almost inevitable that often the bishop or abbot should forget what he was supposed to be, and should sink to the level of a secular baron. John Major mildly suggested that twelve or fourteen servants would be a suitable number for a bishop. And when the bishops neglected to visit the parish churches in their dioceses, when they did not care who knew that their manner of life was no better than that of the ordinary self-indulgent, pleasure-loving landowner, it is little wonder that laziness and ignorance were the least of the faults of which the mass of the inferior clergy were accused.

Of one thing Major was assured: the fault lay not in the doctrines of the Catholic Church but in the fact that its discipline had been flouted by the very men who professed to be its servants, and not least by the Pope himself. The remedy for the evils which he deplored was simple: complete obedience to the precepts of the Church. So thought the old theologian, when in 1524 he returned from the turmoil of Paris to the courtyards of Bishop Kennedy's College at St. Andrews. So did not think the fiery young scholar, Patrick Hamilton, who in the same year came to the same quiet haven, but found no quiet there.

One could not purify the Church without changing the doctrines of the Church. The imaginations of medieval theologians must be swept aside; each man must shape his conduct and his beliefs, not according to the code of instructions laid down by the Church, but according to his own independent interpretation of the Bible.

So Hamilton thought, and what he thought he did not hesitate to declare openly. He was exiled, but in his banishment he talked with Luther himself face to face, and he returned to St. Andrews in 1528, more ready than ever to declare that his was the only faith in which to live and die. But he had walked into a trap; his enemies were watching him; at the end of February 1528 he was arrested by the command of James Beaton, now Archbishop of St. Andrews, adjudged to be a heretic, and burned in front of St. Salvator's College. The burning of Hamilton did not have the effect that Beaton intended; in defiance of an Act of Parliament of 1525 Protestant books were smuggled into the country, and the discussion of the new doctrines was by no means confined to the professional theologians at the universities.

But whatever his subjects might think, the King, dependent as he was on the support of the clergy, showed no disposition either to follow the example of some of the North German princes and become an out-and-out Protestant, or to take the middle course pointed out to him by his uncle Henry VIII, who in 1531 definitely repudiated his allegiance to the Pope, without making any attempt to alter the doctrines or ceremonies of the Church within his kingdom, and in 1535 began to plan an attack on the English monasteries.

Like many people of lesser rank both north and south of the border Henry not only doubted if the monasteries were fulfilling the purposes for which they had been founded, but wondered if they had any purpose to fulfil at all. For the monks did not consider themselves obliged either to preach or to teach; preaching they left to the parish clergy and to the friars, teaching they left to the grammar schools, which were to be found in almost every Scottish burgh, and to the three universities. Schools, it is true, were to be found in some of the monasteries, but their main function was to train the young novices who would afterwards become monks, or the boys who sang in the choir of the abbey church. What was more, the efficiency of the parish clergy was impaired by the fact that the revenues of the parish churches were often diverted to the monasteries. For example, to the Abbey of Arbroath came the revenues of thirty-three parish churches, to the Abbey of Kelso the revenues of thirty-seven; nearly nine-tenths of the parish churches of Scotland were annexed to abbeys, priories, cathedrals or other institutions.

Henry VIII knew what he meant to do with his own monks: he

meant to prove that not only one or two monasteries in his kingdom, but one and all, were sinks of iniquity, to turn the monks adrift, and annex their property. Some of it he would keep; the remainder he would sell or give to lay landowners who, knowing that they owed their new-gotten wealth to the King and to his change of faith, would be eager to support him through thick and thin. What is more, Henry had determined that James must follow his example. One would think that what James did or did not do to the Scottish monasteries was no business of his; but Henry was looking far ahead; he saw that if he went ahead with his policy of hostility to the Pope he might have need of an ally; he saw too that if he could persuade James to commit himself to an attack on the Catholic Church, James would find himself at loggerheads with the King of France, and would become the permanent ally—and in time the vassal—of England.

In vain was the net spread in the sight of the bird. James, instead of crossing the border to discuss theology with Henry and plan a combined attack on the monasteries, set sail for France, where, on the first day of the year 1537, he was married to the Princess Madeleine. But the fragile beauty of the tender-hearted girl withered away in the cold Scottish summer; only two months after she had bent down to kiss the soil of her husband's kingdom, she lay in her coffin in Holyrood. James married again, in 1538, and again his bride was a Frenchwoman, Mary of Guise.

Even these two marriages, even the declaration of the Scottish Parliament in 1541 that no one was to question papal authority under pain of death, failed to convince Henry that James had not the slightest intention of taking his advice; he tried to entice James to York, but after staying there for a few weeks he had to return south without his nephew. He was convinced now; in the summer of 1542 the fleet sailed for Scotland and at the same time the border townships and farm steadings began to go up in flame. But a strong force of English commanded by Sir Robert Bowes was intercepted and captured by the Earl of Huntly at Haddonrig.

The King, delighted with his success, urged Huntly and the other nobles to follow up the retreating invaders. But the nobles thought that they had done enough; they had no mind to obey a "priests' king," and though they knew that Henry had despoiled the English monasteries, they did not see why their king should quarrel with him over a policy which had brought wealth to many a needy baron and knight. Though a Scottish army crossed the border in November the King did not go with it, and the nobles were furious when they learned that the chief command had been delegated, not to one of themselves, but to the King's favourite, Oliver Sinclair. While they were disputing, while some of their men had begun to move off homewards, they were hotly attacked by a small body of English cavalry. They fled in panic, only to find themselves trapped among the pools of Solway Moss. Many of the nobles surrendered without striking a blow.

Almost mad with grief, with a mortal disease upon him, the King rode from Lochmaben to Holyrood and from Holyrood to his pleasant hunting-seat of Falkland. For the moment it seemed as if his melancholy might be lifted; news came to him from Linlithgow that a child had been born to his Queen. He asked anxiously if it was a boy. "A fair daughter," said the messenger. The King, remembering how the Scottish crown had come into the Stewart family through the marriage of Marjory Bruce with Walter the Steward, murmured, "Adieu, farewell, it cam' wi' a lass, it will pass wi' a lass," then, in the words of the old chronicler, "he turned his back unto his lords, and his face unto the wall."

CHAPTER 15

THE REFORMATION AND THE END OF THE FRANCO-SCOTTISH ALLIANCE

IN the two hundred and fifty-six years separating the death of Alexander III from the death of James V, the wheel had come full circle. As in 1286, a king had died, leaving only a little girl to succeed him; as in 1286, a hard and efficient king, a great-uncle, moreover, of the Queen of Scots, sat on the English throne. The same ambition which had burned in Edward I flamed up in Henry VIII: he would unite Scotland to his own kingdom, and he would do it in the same way, by securing the consent of the Scottish leaders to the marriage of their queen with Prince Edward, the heir to the English throne.

Henry's task seemed an easy one. His policy of hostility to the Roman Catholic Church had many admirers in Scotland; even the Governor of Scotland himself, the changeable Earl of Arran, had become something of a Protestant, more through hatred of his rival the great Cardinal Beaton than through zeal for reform in the Church. And in some of the too-willing prisoners from Solway Moss, the Earls of Cassillis and Glencairn and their fellows, Henry found Scotsmen who were ready to act as English agents in return for their liberty. Early in 1543 he sent them to Edinburgh in the company of the Earl of Angus, who had been in England since 1528, pledged to do their utmost to secure the consent of the Scottish Government to the treaty of marriage.

They succeeded; in July 1543, the Treaty of Greenwich was signed, by which the Scottish Government gave its consent to the marriage of the young Queen to Prince Edward, and to her removal to England as soon as she reached the age of ten. In their ecclesiastical policy, too, the Governments of the two countries seemed to be drawing closer together; the same Parliament that appointed ambassadors to discuss the treaties with the representatives of the English Government also announced that any man who chose might now read the Bible in an English translation without fear of punishment.

But before the end of the year the Scots realised that Henry VIII, like Edward I in his day, was aiming at nothing short of the complete incorporation of Scotland into his own kingdom. The Scottish Parliament promptly repudiated the treaty, and Arran, in his desperate need for the counsel of a wiser man than himself, found it necessary to make friends with his former rival, Cardinal Beaton.

Henry was furious. Still, as Edinburgh was far from London, the Scots thought that they had no cause for fear, and when in the early summer of 1544 a great fleet appeared in the Firth of Forth the Governor and the Cardinal persuaded themselves that it was only a fleet of fishing-boats returning from Iceland, and the burgesses of Leith who had paused to gaze at the strange spectacle on their way from church, sat down to their Sunday dinners with an easy mind. Most of them, however, left the meal untasted, when they heard the clash of weapons in the streets outside and commands shouted in the unfamiliar southern tongue. The English had come. But their commander, the Earl of Hertford, aimed at a bigger prize than Leith. On the morrow, when he had been reinforced by two thousand horsemen, he forced his way through the Canongate into Edinburgh and let his troops loose in it to burn and plunder as they pleased.

This was not the way to win the hearts of the Scots. Even the Scottish Protestants, who had shrunk from the Cardinal's policy of firm friendship with France, began to wonder if it might not be the lesser of two evils; even the Douglases lost their enthusiasm for the English alliance when, in 1545, they found their lands laid waste and the tombs of their ancestors in Melrose Abbey desecrated by English raiders. When on Ancrum Moor, in the half-light of a February afternoon, a strong force of English borderers, blinded by the smoke of their own guns, fled in panic from the terrible Scottish spears, the Scots knew that they had been successful because Angus, that master of shifts and stratagems, had for once consented to give his country the benefit of his skill. But Henry persisted in his rough wooing: in the autumn of 1545 Hertford appeared on the border once again; once again plundered monasteries and flaming towns advertised to the Scots the benefits of the English alliance and the merits of the faith that Henry had embraced.

Henry was not the only clever man who blundered. To his cleverest antagonist, David Beaton, Cardinal, Archbishop of St. Andrews and Bishop of Mirepoix in France, Protestantism and treason seemed to be one and the same thing. Questions of doctrine did not interest Beaton—why should he want to change the Church that had made him what he was? He did not see that the elevation of a man of notoriously evil life like himself to the ranks of the princes of the Church supplied the critics of that Church with a most damaging argument.

Of the few Scottish preachers who had dared openly to denounce the Cardinal and the Catholic Church none wielded more influence than George Wishart. Those who were not moved by his preaching were moved by his courage; when the pestilence broke out in Dundee, he had hurried back to the stricken town, and from the top of the East Port of the city had preached to the sick and dying outside the gate, and to those still untouched by the pest within. Of him Beaton resolved to make an example. He was arrested at Ormiston House, near Haddington, taken to St. Andrews and lodged in the castle there. Wishart seems to have had some premonition of the fate that was in store for him. He had narrowly escaped assassination in Dundee, and from that time, whenever he preached in public, a grim-visaged, black-bearded schoolmaster, John Knox by name, had stood on guard beside him, grasping a great two-handed sword. An hour or two before he was arrested Wishart ordered his friend to lay aside his sword and leave him, and when Knox protested, he quietly replied, "Nay, return to your bairns, and God bless you! One is sufficient for a sacrifice."

Wishart was found guilty of heresy, and early in 1546 was burned in front of St. Andrews Castle. The two greatest prelates in Scotland, the Cardinal and the Archbishop of Glasgow, sat at a window in the castle to watch his dying agonies. Men who detested Wishart's doctrines were constrained to admire his calm and cheerful courage. Even the executioner knelt and asked his pardon before he bound him to the stake. "Lo, here is a token that I forgive thee," said Wishart, kissing him on the cheek; "my heart, do thine office." But no sign of compunction came from the Cardinal.

This was not forgotten: three months later a party of Wishart's friends assembled near the castle early in the morning, rushed over the drawbridge before the affrighted porter could pull it up, knocked the porter on the head and made their way to the Cardinal's room. "I am a priest; I am a priest," cried the terrified Cardinal, "ye will not slay me." "The blood of Wishart cries a vengeance upon thee," said one of his murderers coldly as he raised his sword to strike, "and we from God are sent to revenge it." "I am a priest," moaned the dying man again as he fell to the ground, "fie, fie, all is gone."

During the next twelve months St. Andrews Castle became a city of refuge to all those who were disaffected to the government. Here, for example, at Easter in 1547, came John Knox. As yet he had never preached in public; now, urged by his friends, he not only attacked the doctrines of the Church from the pulpit, but administered the Communion in the manner advocated by the continental reformers.

In the meantime events of the greatest importance had happened elsewhere. Henry VIII died in January 1547, two months before his great rival, Francis I. The death of Henry made no difference to the relations between England and Scotland: though the nominal governor of England was the boy-king Edward VI, Hertford, now become Duke of Somerset and Protector, was the real ruler of the country. But if England had not grown any less hostile, with the accession of Henry II France became almost embarrassingly friendly.

It was not altogether sympathy for a small nation, faithful ally of France though it had been, that moved the French King to interest himself in Scottish affairs. It was something much less laudable: Henry of France had begun to think that he might succeed where Henry of England had failed; he would do his best to keep Scotland from becoming a province of England that he might ultimately make it a province of France. One advantage he had: the mother of the child-queen was a Frenchwoman, the sister, moreover, of the Duke of Guise and the Cardinal of Lorraine, the greatest men in France next to himself; he could count on her, therefore, to favour the marriage of her daughter to his son, the Dauphin Francis.

The defenders of the Castle became aware of this new activity on the part of France when, in the summer of 1547, a French fleet sailed into St. Andrews Bay and opened fire upon them. At first they were not dismayed, for the first broadsides only dislodged a few slates; even when they saw the brazen guns being pulled up the slope from the harbour and planted on the roofs of the Cathedral and of St. Salvator's College they still boasted that they would "keep their Castle against England, Scotland, and France all three." "Your walls shall be but egg-shells," was Knox's grim comment. Six hours after the bombardment had begun in real earnest a breach yawned in the wall through which a horse and cart could have been driven, and the garrison had no choice but to surrender. Their lives were spared, but they were taken to France, some of them to toil at the oar in the galleys.

So Knox disappears for a time from Scottish history. On his release from the galleys in 1549 he settled in England, where he gained so much fame as a preacher that he was appointed one of the chaplains to the young Edward VI, and it was proposed that

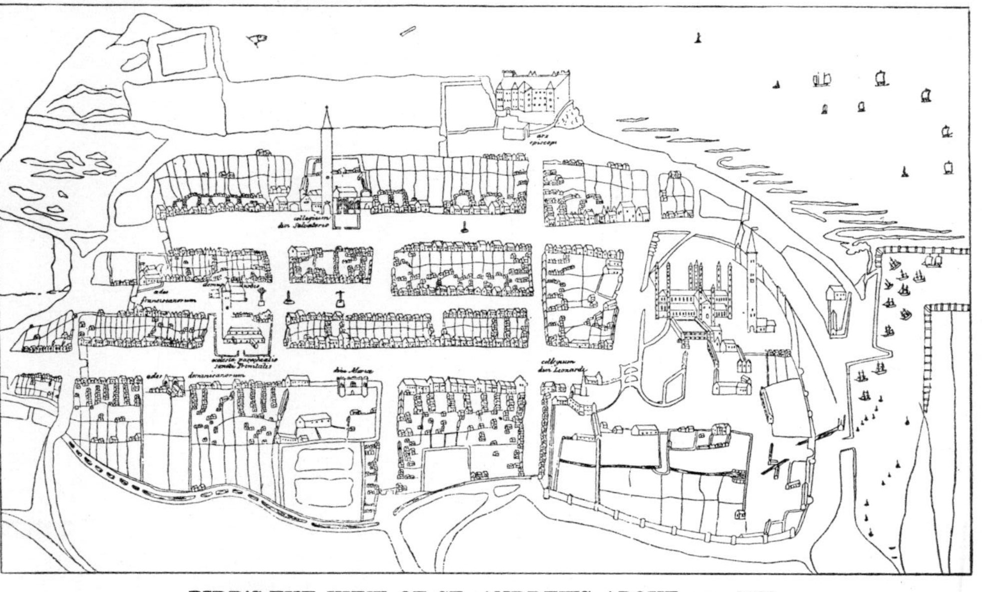

BIRD'S-EYE VIEW OF ST. ANDREWS ABOUT A.D. 1530

The Cathedral stands in the great walled enclosure to the east of the town. Notice the Castle (*arx episcopi*), St. Salvator's College (*collegium divi Salvatoris*), the Town Hall (*domus urbis*) with the market cross and the tron standing beside it, and the three ports guarding the western entrances to the town he should become a bishop. With the accession of the Catholic Mary Tudor in 1553 Knox had to flee from England. At Geneva he heard the great French reformer, John Calvin, explain his religious beliefs and he saw a city disciplined as he would fain have Scotland disciplined. From Geneva he went to Frankfurt, to be minister of the congregation of exiled English Protestants there; but wherever he went contention seemed to follow, and after a few months he returned to Geneva to wait for news from Scotland.

Meantime much had happened in Scotland. In 1547, a few weeks after the sails of the French fleet had sunk below the horizon, an English army, led by Somerset, crossed the border and, keeping in touch with a fleet, advanced up the east coast towards Edinburgh. On Saturday, 10th September—Black Saturday—they came upon the Scottish army at Pinkie, about six miles east of the capital. For a time it seemed as if the Scots might prevail; the spearmen in the Scottish vanguard crossed the River Esk and drove a part of the English army back in disorder. Then some of the lighter English ships, creeping close inshore, opened fire on the left flank of the Scottish army, and when the English field batteries joined in, the vanguard, after waiting in vain for reinforcements, retired on the main body; their comrades, blinded by the rain that was driving over the battlefield, mistook them for the enemy and attacked them fiercely. The English, encouraged by the evident panic and confusion in the Scottish ranks, laid aside their fears and advanced. At once the panic became general; in the biting words of an old Scots historian, his countrymen "fled but[1] order, like beasts." Many in their panic leapt into the River Esk and were drowned, many were so paralysed with fear that they allowed themselves to be cut down without attempting to defend themselves.

Somerset found, like many an English commander before him, that to defeat a Scottish army in battle was a very different thing from subjugating Scotland. After Pinkie an English expedition captured Broughty Castle at the mouth of the Tay and bombarded Dundee, and in the spring of 1548 the English occupied Haddington and used it as a base of operations for pillaging the surrounding country. The result was to convince the Scots that they must send their Queen to France and give

[1] without

their consent to her marriage with the Dauphin, should that marriage be the price of the French King's support. By the Treaty of Haddington (1548) it was agreed that Mary should go to France; companies of French, German, and Italian mercenaries crossed from France to Scotland; in the autumn of 1549 Haddington was recaptured; in the early spring of 1550 Broughty Castle surrendered to the Governor and his French auxiliaries.

Scotland had no more to fear from Somerset; the failure of his Scottish schemes had brought the great Protector low; he had fallen from power, and death on the scaffold was fated soon to be his portion. What is more, by the Treaty of Boulogne, which had put an end to the war which had broken out in 1549 between England and France, the English Government undertook to withdraw its garrisons from Scotland, to refrain from attacking Scotland in the future, and to raise no objection to the proposed marriage of the Scottish Queen and the Dauphin.

France had saved Scotland from England; who was now to save Scotland from France? Henry II could now boast that Scotland was as much subject to him as his own kingdom. Steadily the weight of the gilded chains increased, till in 1554 Arran, who some time before had received the French dukedom of Châtelherault, resigned the office of Governor to the Queen Mother.

Beaton had been succeeded as Archbishop by John Hamilton, Arran's half-brother, and Hamilton, though his private life was no better than Beaton's, did initiate a policy designed to reform the Church without revolutionary changes. The Council of the Scottish Church passed well-intentioned acts to tighten up discipline and ensure the better education of the clergy, while provision was made for the instruction of the people by the issue of a Catechism in the vernacular. Hamilton was not averse to certain concessions in the direction of reformed doctrine, and was quite ready to reduce the influence of the Pope and thereby increase his own power and that of his brother while the latter was Governor. But after Mary of Guise succeeded Arran the interests of the Archbishop and the government were no longer harmonious.

Mary of Guise had no lack of courage or of womanly charm; she could soften the hearts of her most stubborn opponents with tactful speeches, framed in the prettiest broken English;

but more than courage and charm was required in her new position. The Scottish nobles, seeing the French King change from an ally into an overlord, grew restive; in 1557 they protested strongly against being dragged into a war with England simply because Philip of Spain, the husband of the English Queen, had dragged an unwilling England into war with France, and though a Scottish army crossed the Tweed in October, it refused to risk another Flodden and had to be disbanded. But before the end of the year the Scottish Parliament had given its consent to the marriage of the young Queen Mary with the Dauphin of France and had appointed eight ambassadors to be present at the ceremony in Paris.

The chains were being drawn tight, tighter than the ambassadors knew. As they stood under the grey towers of Notre-Dame and gazed at the flower-like figure and candid face of their Queen, they could not know that this girl of fifteen had already played them false. She had signed one paper bequeathing her kingdom unconditionally to the King of France should she die childless, a second putting her kingdom in pledge to him for the cost of its defence and of her education, and also a third declaring that no document which she might sign thereafter could cancel the other two. Though the ambassadors knew nothing of this, and though they had already agreed that the Dauphin should take the courtesy title of King of Scotland, they refused to grant further requests without consulting the Scottish Parliament. Something sinister happened after their refusal: four of them died suddenly on their way home before they had left France.

Men whispered that they had been poisoned, but the rumour did not keep the Parliament from granting the Dauphin the crown. To outward appearance the two countries had never been more friendly: the French King had conferred an unheard-of privilege on his allies, for Scots who came to France were to be treated as naturalised Frenchmen and were not to be debarred from any benefice or office, or from inheriting any property in France, and the Scottish Parliament reciprocated by conferring a similar privilege on Frenchmen living in Scotland. In spite of her daughter's marriage, in spite of this generous naturalisation law, the Regent's position became more difficult every day. What was she to make of the Scottish Protestants, who were steadily gaining in numbers and becoming louder in their

HOLYROOD ABBEY

On the right are the foundations of the choir and transepts of the Abbey Church destroyed by the English in 1544. The great east window represents the repairs undertaken after the Reformation to preserve the nave, which remained roofed until 1768. The corner of the Palace seen here dates from Charles II's reign.

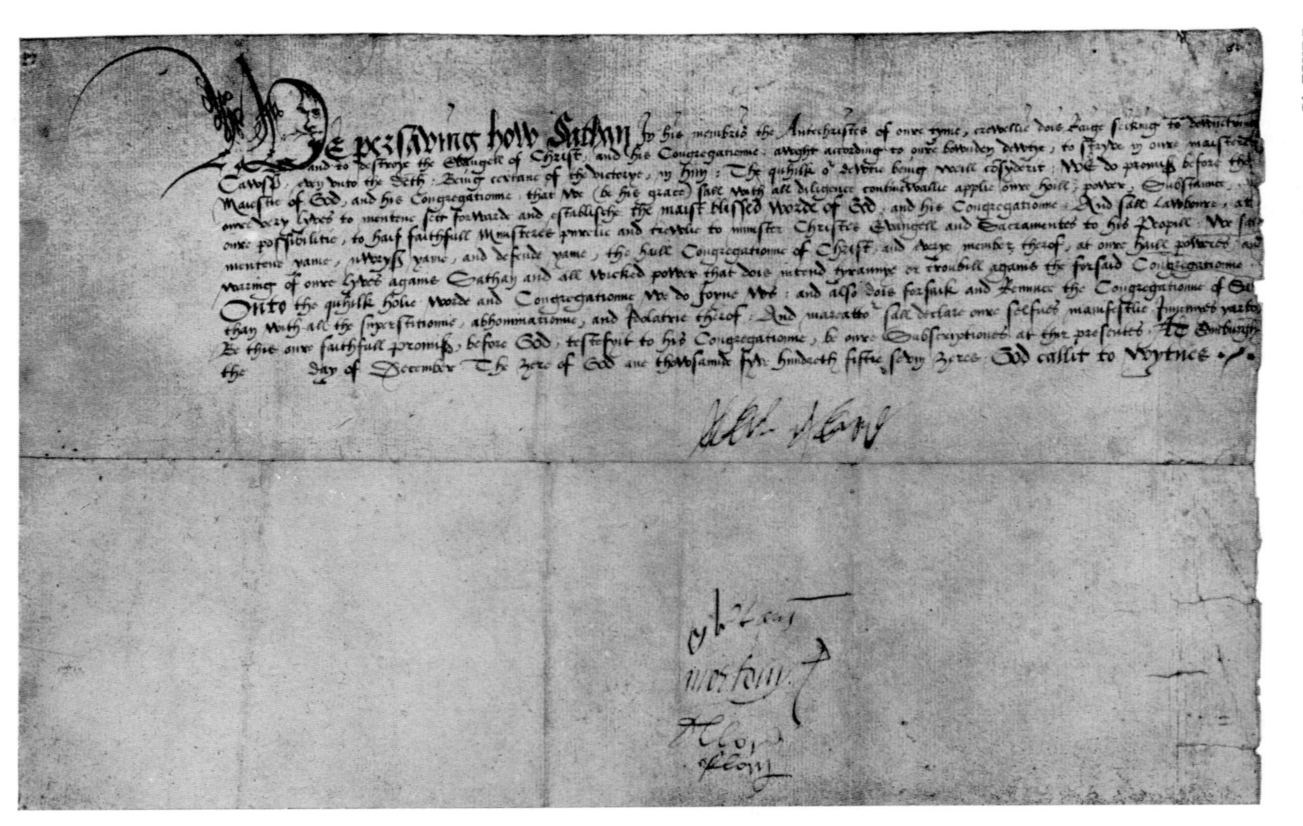

We persaving how Sathan in his membris the Antechristes of oure tyme, crewellie dois rage seiking to downthring
and to destroye the Evangell of Christ, and his Congregatioune: aught according to oure bounden dewtye, to stryve in oure maisteris
Cawss, evin unto the deth: Being certane of the victorye, in him: The quhilk oure dewtie being weill considerit, We do promis before the
Maiestie of God, and his Congregatioune, that we (be his grace) sall with all diligence continewallie applie oure haill power, substance, and
oure verray lyves to menteine sett forward and establische the maist blissed worde of God, and his Congregatioune: And sall labour, at
oure possibilitie, to haif faithfull Ministeres purelie and trewlie to minister Christes Evangell and Sacramentes to his People: We sall
menteine thame, nwryss thame, and defende thame, the haill Congregatioune of Christ, and everye member therof, at oure haill poweris and
waring of oure lyves agains Sathan and all wicked power that dois intend tyrannye or troubill agains the forsaid Congregatioune:
Unto the quhilk holie worde and Congregatioune we do joyne ws: and also dois forsaik and renunce the Congregatioune of Sathan,
thay with all the superstitioune, abhominatioune, and Idolatrie therof: And mareattour sall declare oure selfes manifestlie ennemeis thairto,
Be this oure faithfull promis, before God, testifeit to his Congregatioune, be oure subscriptiones at thir presentes: At Edinburgh
the day of December The zeir of God ane thowsande fyve hundreth fiftie sevin zeires. God callit to Wytnes.

BAND OF THE LORDS OF THE CONGREGATION, 1557

complaints? At first they had not absented themselves from the ordinary services of the Church, but in 1555 John Knox had paid a visit to Scotland and had succeeded in persuading many of them to stop attending Mass. The Regent was no persecutor, nor did she want to do anything that would make the French alliance unpopular; on the other hand she was an orthodox Catholic, and she knew besides that in the past the Catholic prelates had supported the alliance with France through thick and thin. So, though she was not unwilling to let the Protestants worship in their own way, provided they did it in secret, she would admit of no alteration in the organisation, ceremonies, or doctrine of the Roman Catholic Church in Scotland.

But the Protestants would not be content with mere toleration; at the end of 1557 certain of the Protestant Lords had signed a bond or agreement by which they declared that they forsook the Roman Catholic Church and pledged themselves to apply their whole power, substance, and very lives to establish and maintain a reformed Church in Scotland.

And though the Queen Regent was averse from persecution herself, she could not control the prelates; in the spring of 1558 Walter Myln, an old man of eighty-two, was burned at the stake as a heretic.

A thrill of horror ran through Scotland. The Protestants had been assured by the Regent, only a short time before, that she would not molest them; now they found it hard to believe either her original promise or her declaration that she had not consented to Myln's death. In vain the Lords of the Congregation tried to get their way by negotiation; neither the Parliament which met at the end of 1558 nor the Provincial Council of the Scottish clergy which met in March 1559 would concede their demand that the services of the Church should be in the vulgar tongue and that the reformed Communion service with the Communion in both kinds[1] should replace the Mass. Not only so, but just about this time the Regent became suddenly less conciliatory; she knew that as peace had been signed between France and Spain, she could now count on the support of French troops should any serious trouble arise in Scotland. So when

[1] Communion in which the wine as well as the bread is administered to the lay worshipper.

she heard that the people of Perth had become Protestant she ordered the Provost to make them Catholic again, only to be told that "he could make their bodies to come to Her Grace . . . but to cause them to do against their conscience he could not promise." She learned too that on Easter Day, despite her express commands, the people of Perth and Dundee stayed away from Mass altogether. It was too much; she peremptorily ordered the four preachers whom she considered responsible for this defection to appear before her at Stirling on the 10th of May.

Besides, at the beginning of the year there had appeared on the doors of Scottish friaries the "Beggars' Summons," giving the friars notice to quite their property in favour of the poor and infirm. This notice was due to become operative on the 12th of May, two days after the preachers were due to appear at Stirling.

The country gentlemen of Angus and Mearns assembled at Dundee, resolved that if the preachers went to Stirling they would go with them. From Dundee the Reformers went to Perth, where they were joined by John Knox, who had just returned to Scotland to put his fiery eloquence and rude but effective wit at the service of his brethren. On the 11th of May in the parish church at Perth, Knox preached a rousing sermon, in which he declared that the Mass was an idolatrous rite. When the sermon was over, a priest stepped forward to the high altar, intending to celebrate Mass as usual. "This is intolerable!" shouted a boy, only to be promptly cuffed by the priest. The youngster thereupon retired to a safe distance and threw a stone at the priest; it missed him, but smashed an image on the altar. Other bystanders joined in the stone-throwing and soon they had succeeded in demolishing every image in the church. Word spread that mischief was afoot, but the preachers and the country gentlemen prudently remained indoors at dinner and the "rascall multitude," as Knox called them, soon treated the beautiful buildings of the Charterhouse, even though its chapel contained the tomb of a king, and of the Franciscan and the Dominican friaries, as they had treated the parish church. Thus the "Beggars' Summons" took effect.

The Regent replied by getting an army together and advancing against Perth; but she could not be altogether sure of her followers. Two of them, the ambitious Lord James Stewart, a half-brother of Queen Mary, and the young Earl of Argyll, were really heart and soul with the Reformers, and before she could summon the city to surrender, the Protestant lairds and burgesses of the west, led by the Earl of Glencairn, had appeared on the scene. Neither side was over-anxious to come to blows; the Lords of the Congregation withdrew from Perth on the understanding that the Regent should not garrison it with her French mercenaries, and advanced on St. Andrews. There the same sorry story was repeated; the crowd, lashed into a frenzy by the reckless eloquence of Knox, sallied forth to the Cathedral, the fairest and greatest church in all Scotland, and smashed and battered to their hearts' content. The Regent was powerless, Argyll and Lord James had deserted her; though her army advanced against the Protestant forces, it found them strongly posted at Cupar and retired without risking a battle. From Cupar she withdrew to the capital, but even there there was no safety; the victorious army of the Congregation, after it had turned aside to capture Perth, after it had sacked the churches in Stirling and Linlithgow, was now heading for Edinburgh. The Regent retreated to Dunbar; hardly was her rearguard clear of the capital when the disorderly forces of the Protestants poured in at the gates. Even now the Regent did not lose heart. Her small, well-disciplined professional army held together in defeat; the motley hosts of the Congregation melted away in the hour of victory. Her sudden advance on Edinburgh three weeks later found the Lords of the Congregation with only a handful of followers; they were forced to promise that they would no longer molest priests or despoil churches, and to retire to Stirling.

The Regent's forces straightway occupied the town of Leith. Every day her position grew stronger; in the closing months of 1559 reinforcements from France poured into the fort at Leith, and though the Lords of the Congregation, accompanied by no less a person than Châtelherault, again occupied Edinburgh and prepared to lay siege to Leith, their forces were mauled so badly in a chance encounter that they again retired. Emboldened by this success, the Regent sent a detachment of her army to pursue them in Fife. So at the end of 1559 the cause of the Scottish reformers seemed hopeless. But help was at hand. In November 1558 the Protestant Elizabeth had ascended the English throne; in the following year the death of Henry II had made Francis and Mary King and Queen of France. But to faithful Roman Catholics, who did not regard Elizabeth as a lawful daughter of Henry VIII, her kinswoman Mary was not simply Queen of Scotland and France, she was Queen of England as well. And the Scottish Queen did not hesitate to make this claim; when she heard of the death of Mary Tudor she promptly assumed the coat of arms of England in addition to those of Scotland and France.

The French occupation of Scotland, then, might be but a step to a French invasion of England. On their side the Lords of the Congregation were forced to recognise that their volunteer armies were no match for the disciplined French mercenaries, that they must look outside Scotland for help, and that only from their old enemy England was help to be expected. They despatched the cleverest of their number, the wily Maitland of Lethington, to the English court with their appeal for help. His was no easy task; the help might be given at too great a price; if he called in the Englishman to expel the Frenchman, the Englishman might stay. But he was successful; by the Treaty of Berwick, signed in February 1560, the English Government agreed to send an army to Scotland to co-operate with the Lords of the Congregation and to continue the struggle until the French were driven completely out of Scotland.

Even before the Treaty was signed a fleet of English ships appeared in the Forth—to look for pirates, their commander said—and early in April a strong English army joined the forces of the Lords of the Congregation before the walls of Leith. The plight of the French garrison was desperate. In France, too, Catholic and Protestant were now involved in open war, and the King did not dare send forces sufficient to break through the English blockade. The Queen Regent lay in Edinburgh Castle stricken with a mortal sickness. But the French mercenaries fought stoutly, beat off attack after attack, and made more than one murderous sally into the lines of the besiegers. The Regent's death in the early summer made no difference to them; they fought on even when the English cannon had destroyed their stores and magazines and reduced them to scanty rations of horseflesh. The French king's advisers saw that the struggle was hopeless, and ambassadors were dispatched to the English court, whence, accompanied by two English ambassadors, they proceeded to the camp of the allies.

The treaty of Edinburgh, signed early in July, put an end to the French attempts to dominate Scotland. Only six score French soldiers were to be allowed to remain in Scotland; the French officials, too, had to go; in future no foreigner was to hold any office under the Scottish crown. But the English troops also were to withdraw, leaving the Scots free to settle their own affairs. Finally, the Scottish Queen must remove the arms of England from her royal insignia and so declare to the world that she considered Elizabeth to be the rightful Queen of England.

So with the signing of the Treaty of Edinburgh the Auld Alliance came to an end: the events of the previous ten years had convinced the patriotic Scot that France was no longer the champion of Scottish independence, but its foe. That the alliance should have ended when it did was partly the fault of Mary of Guise and her over-ambitious kinsmen; that it would have developed into a permanent partnership if they had been content to go slowly cannot, however, be maintained. Apart from the common fear of England, there was no real bond of union between the two peoples; the difference of language, even without the five hundred miles of estranging sea between the pier of Leith and Calais harbour, was sufficient to keep them apart. Some trade there was between the two countries, it is true, but it was Veere in Holland, and not Bordeaux or Havre de Grace, that attracted the bulk of the Scottish merchant ships. To one small though influential class the end of the old friendship made a change; though the Scottish soldier of fortune still took his sword and his valour to France, the Scottish scholar was in future to be more often content with such learning as he could get in St. Andrews or Glasgow or Aberdeen. The cultured Scotsman had no longer, as it were, one foot in Paris and one in Edinburgh; his horizon was contracting; in time he would become almost, though not quite, as insular as his English neighbour.

Though the Treaty of Edinburgh made no mention of religious matters it put the Scottish Protestants in an unassailable position. In August 1560 the Scottish Parliament met in Edinburgh to repudiate the supremacy of the Pope, to forbid the celebration of the Latin Mass, and to adopt a reformed Confession of Faith.

CHAPTER 16

MARY QUEEN OF SCOTS

To us the signing of the Treaty of Edinburgh and the abrogation by Parliament of the Roman supremacy, mark the end of a chapter in the history of Scotland. But to the thoughtful Scotsman of that day, everything must still have seemed dark and uncertain. The Treaty of Edinburgh had indeed been signed, but Queen Mary would not ratify it; in other words she still maintained that she and not Elizabeth was the rightful Queen of England. The Parliament of 1560 had indeed repudiated the authority of the Pope and prohibited the celebration of Mass, but how could acts of Parliament which had not been approved by the sovereign be lawful acts? Besides, it was doubtful if Parliament had the bulk of the nation behind it; though burgesses and country lairds in Angus, Fife, Lothian and other parts of the Lowlands were now solidly Protestant, different views still prevailed in much of the north and west. As abbots, bishops and other clergy still had their rank and most of their revenues, it did not seem as if the old church system had been overthrown. The events of 1560 cannot have seemed decisive.

The divisions among the leaders of the Protestant party made the outlook still more uncertain. Everything was clean-cut and definite in John Knox's dreams: dreams of a country kept free from the power of the Pope by fear of the prison and the gallows, dreams of a Church not unlike the Anglican Church, with bishops —only he would call them superintendents—and with a prayer book—the English Book of Common Prayer would serve till copies of a simpler one became available. If Knox had his way there would be no more ignorant clergy; he would cover the whole land with a network of schools. Every parish would have one, and so a clever boy, however poor he might be, would be able to proceed from the Parish School to the Burgh School, where he would learn Latin and Greek, and perhaps Hebrew, and thence to the University, to be equipped to serve either Church or State. A noble dream; easy of realisation if the revenues of the old Church could be handed over intact to the new. But the nobles and country lairds had different views. It is true that their zeal for the overthrow of the old order seemed to be equal to that of Knox himself; but the needy baron, with an eye to the revenues of the neighbouring abbey, had no mind to see them used to provide a minister for the parish church, or a schoolmaster for the school that was yet to be built.

And what of Lord James Stewart, half-brother of the Queen, what dream floated before his eyes? Wealth perhaps—the revenues from the broad lands of St. Andrews Priory flowed into his coffers—but power still more. If the accident of his birth had kept him from being crowned King of Scotland he could still be the uncrowned king, and perhaps—who knew?—something more. And his new ally Châtelherault? What had made him change from a half-hearted Catholic to a half-hearted Protestant? He too cherished ambitions, for he could not forget that he was the great-grandson of James II and that he stood next in the line of succession to the crown. He himself might never wear it, but could Elizabeth be persuaded to marry his son, the Earl of Arran, Mary's claims could be brushed aside and a Hamilton would become ruler of both kingdoms. There were others besides Châtelherault and his kin who favoured this scheme; the inscrutable, changeable Lethington toiled hard to bring it about, both because he wanted to see a Scot seated on the throne of England and Scotland, and because he believed that only through a voluntary union with England could his country ever gain lasting security and prosperity.

This project came to nothing; before the year was out Elizabeth let it be known that she would not consent to marry Arran, and in the autumn of 1561 Mary herself arrived in Scotland. Bereft of her husband, conscious that she had become an unwanted stranger at her own court, she had resolved to leave France. Seldom had Edinburgh looked more gloomy than on the day when she landed in Scotland: "The verray face of heavin," said Knox, "did manifestlie speak what confort was brought unto this cuntrey with hir, to wit, sorow, dolour, darknes and all impietie." Her heart must have sunk within her as she splashed through the rain with her bedraggled cavalcade, and saw the towers of Holyrood loom ominous through the mist. Her loyal subjects, some five or six hundred of them, came to serenade her that night, but the monotonous cadences of the psalms which they sang and the melancholy wail of fiddles none too well tuned, plunged her French attendants into even deeper gloom.

But in those days the shadows did not rest on her long. She was barely nineteen, with a girl's zest for enjoyment, with a gay confidence in her power to charm both friend and foe. The tap of dancing feet, the stately strains of pavan and coranto were heard once more in Holyrood, and sober citizens shook their heads when they heard how the Queen and her four ladies-in-waiting—the four Maries—had appeared at one of these dances disguised as swaggering young gallants, and how the Earl of Arran, mad enough already, had come near to losing what remained of his wits for love of his sovereign.

But as ruler of a country where the Protestants were in the ascendant, Queen Mary had a difficult part to play. On the very first Sunday after her return some of the more extreme Protestants, having heard that Mass was to be celebrated in the chapel at Holyrood, made their way into the palace, and would have broken into the chapel and slain the priest had not Lord James Stewart stationed himself in the doorway. The storm blew over; the Queen issued a proclamation declaring that she had no intention of changing the religion that she found established in Scotland, although she demanded liberty to worship in the ancient way for herself and for her household. Knox might declare in the pulpit that one Mass was more fearful to him than ten thousand armed enemies; the ordinary man saw nothing to fear from a ruler who made no attempt to shelter her Roman Catholic subjects from the rigour of the law, and who in 1562 accompanied Lord James Stewart in an expedition against the Earl of Huntly, that expedition which ended in the death on the field of Corrichie of the great earl who might have been an agent to restore the power of Rome.

But Mary's thoughts ranged far beyond the walls of Holyrood, far beyond the boundaries of Scotland. She had been Queen of France once, could she not still be Queen of England? She was Elizabeth's kinswoman, the daughter of Margaret Tudor's only son, and she knew that in the eyes of Roman Catholics, who refused to regard Elizabeth as the lawful daughter of King Henry VIII, she was the rightful Queen of England. If only she could marry some Continental prince who would put his fleets and armies

MARY QUEEN OF SCOTS

LORD DARNLEY AND HIS BROTHER, CHARLES,
AFTERWARDS EARL OF LENNOX

at her disposal, then—but only then—could she wrest her heritage from Elizabeth. But the long-cherished project of a marriage with Don Carlos, the eldest son of Philip II of Spain, had to be abandoned, if only because that prince turned out to be hopelessly insane. She might try another way: by tact and fair words, by accepting a husband whom her rival had chosen for her, she would persuade Elizabeth to acknowledge her as her successor.

But Elizabeth was adamant; she saw that if she acknowledged Mary's title to succeed to the throne, she would remove the only objection that the English Roman Catholics could have to her rival, and pave the way for her own deposition. It took long for Mary to recognise that there was no getting past this refusal, but after four years' fruitless efforts she realised that tact and patience would avail nothing, that Elizabeth had made up her mind to thwart her at every turn.

Unluckily for Mary, in the early months of 1565 Henry Stewart, Lord Darnley, appeared in Scotland. The Queen saw him at a dance, straightway fell in love with the tall slender youth who carried himself like a king, and made up her mind that she would marry him. The match had little to commend it; it is true that Darnley was, like Mary, a grandchild of Margaret Tudor, and that the English Roman Catholics regarded him with more favour than they did Mary, because, in spite of his Scottish descent, he had been born and educated in England; but Elizabeth could not view with equanimity the marriage of her two most dangerous rivals, and the Protestant nobles in Scotland feared that the marriage would be the first step to the destruction both of their power and of Protestantism in Scotland. Encouraged by Elizabeth, the Earl of Moray—to give Lord James Stewart his new title—and the other Protestant lords prepared to take up arms. Mary held to the course that she had chosen; in July 1565 Darnley and she were married in the Chapel of Holyrood according to the Roman Catholic rite, then, after declaring that she had no intention of attacking the Protestant religion, she gathered an army together, hunted the rebels all over southern Scotland, and finally forced them to retire across the border. Moray went to seek counsel of Elizabeth, but this Queen, who objected to his rebellion, not because it was a rebellion, but because it was unsuccessful, ordered him to "pack out of her presence."

This "Chaseabout Raid," as people called it, was Mary's last success. Too soon she learned that she had thrown away her affection on a foolish and petulant youth, one who, not content with being hailed as King Henry, grumbled perpetually because Mary would not give him the kingly authority which he was incapable of using. It was not to him that the Queen turned when she wanted advice, but to David Rizzio, "a merry fellow and a good musician," who had come to Holyrood in the train of an Italian ambassador and had remained behind to be the Queen's French secretary. Soon the supple musician became an all-powerful favourite, and though the haughty nobles might frown on him and thrust him aside, he bore himself with all the more arrogance, "disdaining all danger and despising counsel."

Darnley's jealousy of the foreign favourite gave the exiled rebels and their confederates the chance of striking a blow at the Queen. Early in 1566 he was persuaded to join in a plot against the favourite, and he formed one of that band of armed men who in the dusk of a March evening beset the Palace of Holyrood, barred all the doors, made their way by a private stair to the Queen's little supper-room and seized the unfortunate musician. It was in vain that the Queen stormed and wept, it was in vain that the terrified wretch clung to his mistress; his enemies dragged him out of the room and butchered him, leaving the King's dagger in his body for a sign.

The Queen found herself a prisoner in her own palace, with a man who had insulted her beyond all hope of forgiveness. But, knowing that wild outbursts of anger would be useless, she set herself to study revenge. It was an easy matter for Mary, consummate actress as she was, to throw her spell once more over the shiftless Darnley, and detach him from his fellow-murderers; it was an easy thing for her to greet Moray, suddenly come from England, as if she thought it was solicitude for her and not ambition for himself that had made him return. When, two nights later, Moray and his confederates waited on her in her room in Holyrood to ask that she should pardon the murderers, she agreed to do it on the morrow, drank to the health of each of them and asked that the keys of the palace should again be entrusted to her. When the morrow came, she and Darnley were thirty miles away at Dunbar, and the news that she was gathering an army soon sent the murderers of Rizzio scurrying across the border. At the same time she won over—to outward seeming at any rate—Moray and the other lords who had taken refuge in England after the Chaseabout Raid. She had ridden out the storm, and a season of calm weather seemed to be in front of her. The birth of a son, too, in the summer of 1566, should have strengthened her position. But her reconciliation with Darnley was a hollow sham: she was no longer merely indifferent to him, she despised and hated him.

Her hatred of her treacherous and contemptible husband grew more intense when she compared him with one among her nobles, the brave, impetuous, arrogant Earl of Bothwell, whom men might hate, but could not afford to despise. If only Bothwell could be her husband! It was a mad and wicked dream; not only would Mary's co-religionists regard her as a traitor to their cause if she married a Protestant, but Roman Catholic and Protestant alike would be horrified at the union of two persons both of whom were already married. The ecclesiastical courts might be cajoled into declaring Bothwell's previous marriage null and void, but a divorce from Darnley would not satisfy Mary, for she feared that it would damage her infant son's claim to the throne. But if not divorce—what?

Bothwell too wanted Darnley away, so did Moray and Lethington, and so did the actual murderers of Rizzio, whom he had first supported and then attempted to betray. Before the end of the year the Queen and these other enemies of Darnley met in council in Craigmillar Castle. Darnley must be got out of the way, they decided; the Queen consented to leave the precise manner of his removal to the nobles, provided they did it in such a way as to lay no spot on her honour or conscience.

Would we could say that her honour was unspotted! Early in the year 1567 the Queen journeyed to Glasgow, where her husband lay smitten with a horrible disease, coaxed him into a good humour and persuaded him to return to Edinburgh with her. Lest he should infect the young prince with his disease she lodged him, not in Holyrood, but at the Kirk o' Field, an abandoned collegiate church just outside the walls of the city, on the site now occupied by the older buildings of Edinburgh University. Here, too, the Queen spent most of her time till the night of the 9th of February, when after chatting with Darnley, and telling him, as if nothing lay behind her words, that almost a year had passed since Rizzio had been murdered, she suddenly announced that she had promised to dance at the wedding festivities of one of her servants, and returned hastily to the palace. An hour or two later the crash of an explosion shook the sleeping city; the Kirk o' Field had been blown up "so that there remained not one stone on another undestroyed." The dead body of the King was found in a garden close at hand. There was no mark of burning on him; the murderers had strangled him first and the house had then been blown up.

Even if there had been none to say that soon after the Queen's return they had seen Bothwell, arrayed as if for battle, steal out of the Palace, there would have been little doubt about the identity of the prime mover in the affair. But though rumours flew about Edinburgh, though placards accusing him of the murder were placed on the walls by night, though the Earl of Lennox, the father of the murdered man, cried out for vengeance, no one dared to touch him, knowing that he stood higher in the Queen's favour than ever. The Queen was persuaded to appoint a day for his trial, but nothing came of it, for, knowing that Bothwell had packed the town with armed men, Lennox prudently stayed away. Moray, too, judged it best to leave Scotland for a season.

Worse was to follow: as Mary was returning from Stirling, where she had been visiting her young son, she was waylaid by Bothwell at the head of a party of horsemen and borne off to Dunbar Castle. People suspected that Mary was a willing captive, and the manner in which Bothwell's divorce was hurried through the courts, the spectacular entry of the Queen into Edinburgh, with Bothwell holding her bridle to make the crowd think that she was his prisoner, and the dukedom which the Queen conferred upon him, served to confirm their suspicions. In vain the minister who proclaimed the banns declared that the marriage should not take place; on the 15th of May, in the Chapel at Holyrood, before a handful of the nobles, the Queen of Scots and the new Duke of Orkney were married "with neither pleasure nor pastime."

Mary was left without a friend in Scotland; even those who had striven to believe that she had no part in Darnley's death were horrified at her hasty marriage with the man universally believed to be her husband's murderer. That her subjects should

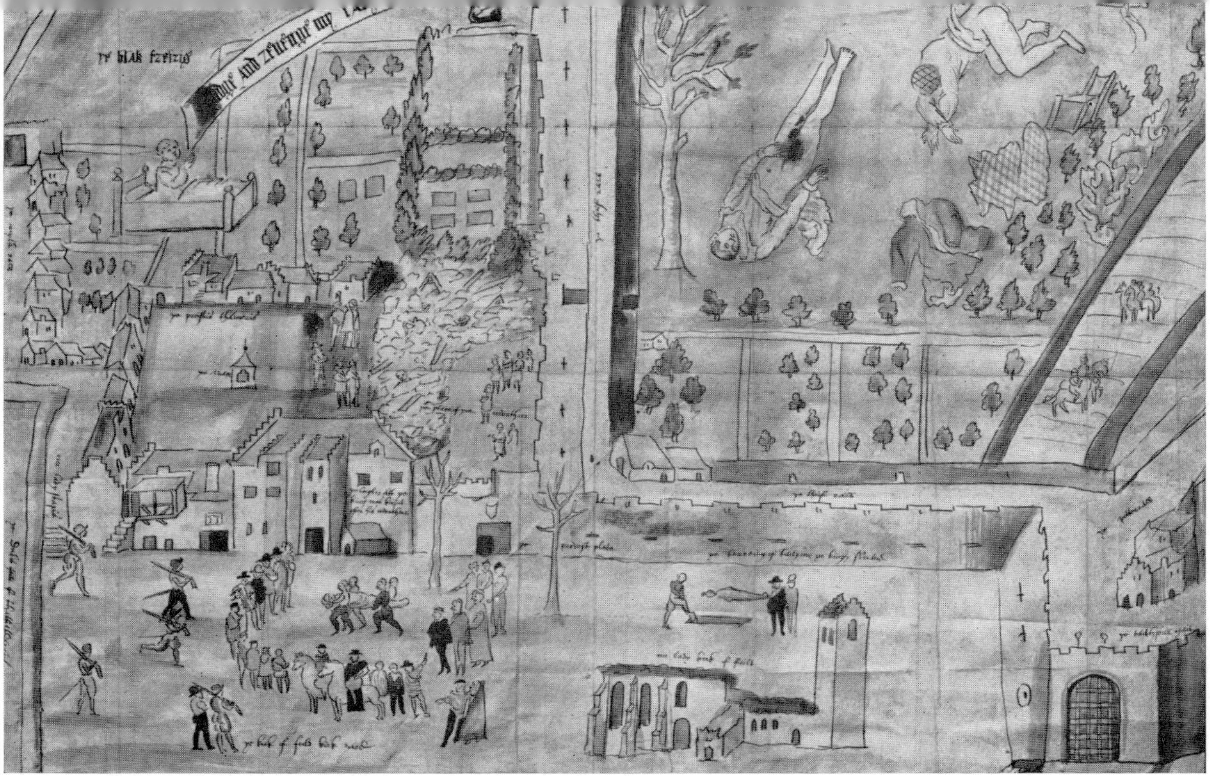

PLATE 44

This represents an accumulation of detail rather than an accurate plan of the whole scene. It is possible to see the devastation caused by the explosion. The bodies of Darnley and his Page in the garden, the Flodden Wall and the ruins of 'Our Lady Kirk of Field'. In the top left corner the infant Prince prays 'Judge and revenge my cause, O Lord'.

CONTEMPORARY DRAWING OF THE KIRK O' FIELD TRAGEDY

[illegible]
allyee
ce iourdhuy apres disner ma este denonsse
ma sentence pour estre executee demain comm
une crimynelle a huict heures du matin
ie nay eu loisir de vous fayre ung ample disco
de tout ce qui sest passe mays sil vous plaist
de croyre mon medesin & ces aultres miens
desolez serviteurs vous oyres la verite & com
graces a dieu ie mesprise la mort & fidellem

A SECTION FROM THE LAST LETTER OF MARY QUEEN OF SCOTS

Capten Craufurd, I haue hard sic report of your gud seruice done to me from ye
beginning of the weiris agains my onfreindis, as I sall sum day remember ye same,
god willing, to your greit contentment. In ye main quhyle, be of gud confort, and re-
serue you to that tyme wt patience, being assurit of my fauour. faire weil. 1575 [illegible] September
your gud freind, James R.

3 Ve aproue thir foure lynis aboue writtinn with oure awin hand bei[ng]
present. At Fa[lk]land the fift day of September 1584.

James R.

TWO EXAMPLES OF JAMES VI'S HAND, THE FIRST WRITTEN DURING HIS TENTH YEAR.

rise in rebellion was inevitable; in Moray's absence the Earl of Morton acted as leader, and Bothwell and Mary were forced to flee to Dunbar. They raised an army and marched again towards the capital, but when they reached Carberry Hill, not far from where the battle of Pinkie had been fought, they found their way barred by a stronger force under the rebel lords. The rebels protested that they had no quarrel with the Queen, but that they must have the traitor who had murdered her husband. Bothwell hotly denied that he was a murderer and offered to fight to the death with any one who charged him with the crime. Kirkcaldy of Grange and Murray of Tullibardine at once took up the challenge, whereupon Bothwell protested that one of his degree could not fight with a simple country laird. To Lord Lindsay's challenge he could not give the same reply; but the Queen, fearing for her lover's safety, gave him her purse and ordered him to flee to Dunbar, and then, as soon as she knew that he would be safe from pursuit, she surrendered to the Laird of Grange. From Dunbar Bothwell took ship, and, though closely pursued, escaped to Norway, where he fell into the hands of the kinsmen of a lady to whom he had earlier promised marriage. He ended his days in a Danish prison.

A different and a harder fate awaited the Queen. She entered Edinburgh that night, not as she had done a few weeks before, with a proud lover at her bridle; there was no look of triumph on her dusty and tear-stained face; instead of a royal banner a flag with a picture of her murdered husband was borne before her, and instead of the salvoes of welcome from the guns of the Castle, she had to listen to the curses and insults of angry women. From Edinburgh she was hurried a few days later to Lochleven Castle, where she was forced to abdicate in favour of her infant son James, and to consent to Moray's becoming Regent.

For almost a year Mary remained a prisoner in Lochleven Castle. But the Hamilton faction, though not for any love that they bore to Mary, resolved to secure her release: if they rescued her they might force her to marry Lord Claud Hamilton, a son of Châtelherault, but they were in any event opposed to the recognition of James as king, because from him the succession might pass not to them but to Darnley's family, the rival house of Lennox.

It seemed impossible that Mary could escape from her island

prison; all the gates of the castle were locked before dusk every evening, and even though she might have got into a boat unobserved during the day, she would have been seen long before she reached the shore of the loch. But escape she did; one evening, after supper, her guards discovered that though the doors were still locked, the Queen had disappeared. They broke open the gates and hurried down to the waterside. Away out on the loch they could hear the plash of oars; they pushed off their boats in pursuit, only to discover that the thole-pins had been removed, and that try as they might, they could not overtake the Queen. A party of horsemen was waiting for her at the water's edge and with this escort she rode off to Hamilton.

Mary had barely another fortnight of freedom, if to be in the hands of the Hamiltons could be called freedom. The Regent flung all the troops he could muster—only four thousand—into Glasgow; when the Queen and her allies attempted to march from Hamilton to Dumbarton, keeping a little to the south of Glasgow, they found their way barred by the Regent's troops at Langside. The Regent's horsemen were easily scattered, but his foremost company of spearmen stood fast for the space of half an hour, their spears interlocked with those of the Queen's vanguard. Even when their spears were shattered they fought on, attacking their opponents with stones or with anything on which they could lay their hands. The half-hearted soldiers behind them, encouraged by their example, came up on their right, charged the enemy and broke their ranks. Mary, seeing her followers flee in hopeless confusion, gathered a body of horsemen about her and galloped from the field. Dumbarton was barred to her now, and with Dumbarton the road to France; there was nothing for it but to go to England and throw herself on the mercy of Elizabeth. A few days later, at the Abbey of Dundrennan, on the shores of the Solway, she bade farewell to her followers and embarked on the vessel that was to bear her to England. She never returned. Elizabeth could not afford to be generous to a clever and ambitious princess who considered herself, and was considered by many of Elizabeth's Catholic subjects, to be the rightful Queen of England, and Mary, who had come expecting to be treated as an honoured guest, found that she was to all intents and purposes a prisoner. As the years passed, as plot after plot formed round her, her confinement grew straiter, till in 1587, having been found guilty of complicity in a plot to slay Elizabeth, she was executed in the hall of Fotheringhay Castle.

CHAPTER 17

JAMES VI AS KING OF SCOTS

THOUGH Queen Mary never set foot in her kingdom after 1568, for long her unquiet spirit seemed to trouble Scotland. None knew better than Moray, who continued to rule the country on behalf of the infant King James, how treacherous was the calm that followed her departure. In the west the Hamiltons, in the north Huntly, threatened rebellion. Some of his former allies, too, envious of the wealth and power to which they had helped him, began to curse the folly which had made them drive Mary out only to put Moray in; others, who had objected to Bothwell more than to Mary, asked why the Queen, who had now completely recovered from her mad infatuation, should not again wear the Scottish crown. With most of the malcontents, jealousy of the Regent and the party in possession, with some, loyalty to their former sovereign, led to the formation of a coalition which had for its object the securing of Mary's return to Scotland and her restoration to the throne.

Moray knew that behind all this plotting and planning of the Queen's Lords, as the malcontents were called, was the cunning brain of the chameleon Lethington. In the autumn of 1569 he caused Lethington to be arrested on a trumped-up charge and lodged in a citizen's house in Edinburgh. But Lethington's confederate, Kirkcaldy of Grange, the governor of the castle, promptly arrested him a second time and refused to give him up. War soon broke out—a war on which more depended than either King's Lords or Queen's Lords dreamed. The triumph of the Queen's Lords could have been a disaster for Scottish Protestantism. It is true that many of the Queen's Lords were Protestants, and that they aimed simply at the restoration of the Queen. Still, with Mary on the throne a Protestant Church would be in an exceedingly precarious position.

No story of chivalrous deeds brightens the sordid record of this "war of religion." It began with assassination: in January 1570 Hamilton of Bothwellhaugh, knowing that the Regent was to pass through the town of Linlithgow, concealed himself in a house on the main street, in front of which sheets were stretched as if an innocent washing had been hung up to dry. As the Regent rode slowly past, delayed by the pressure of the crowd, Hamilton shot him in the stomach, then flung himself on a horse and escaped. Moray was able to walk to his lodging, but died a few hours later. Both the house and the horse were the property of another Hamilton—the Archbishop of St. Andrews. The friends of the murdered Regent did not forget this. When, more than a year later, they captured the Archbishop in Dumbarton Castle, he was tried, found guilt of complicity in the murders of Darnley and Moray as well as of conspiring against King James, and hanged at the market cross of Stirling.

The Earl of Lennox, the grandfather of the young King, whom Queen Elizabeth had persuaded the King's Lords to accept as Regent, fared no better than his predecessor. In 1571 the King's Lords had been compelled to abandon the town of Edinburgh, swept as it was by the guns of the Castle, and to make Stirling their headquarters. So it came about that in the month of August two Parliaments, one in Edinburgh and one in Stirling, denounced each other as treasonable assemblies, and pronounced sentence of death and forfeiture on offenders who refused to be arrested. But the Parliament at Stirling was graced with the presence of the five-year-old king, attired in gorgeous robes, with a brand-new crown on his head—the old one being at Edinburgh. As he entered the unfamiliar building he asked what place this was and was told that it was a Parliament. His eyes roved round the hall while his grandfather made a speech, then rested on a gap in the roof; "I think there is ane hole in this Parliament," remarked the youngster solemnly.

Five days later something happened which made the superstitious remember the boy-king's idle remark. Between three and four in the morning shouts of "A Hamilton! A Hamilton!" followed by the crackle of musketry and the crash of splintering timber roused the sleeping burgesses. Lord Claud Hamilton and the Earl of Huntly had broken into the town with four hundred horsemen at their backs. In the darkness and confusion few cared or knew how to resist; within a few minutes Huntly had captured not only the Regent but every one of the King's Lords. Having done all that he meant to do, he prepared to ride back with his prisoners to Edinburgh, but his men were not satisfied; leaving the prisoners all but unguarded they roamed through the town in search of plunder, and began to break open shops and stables. Meantime the burgesses, having collected their scattered wits, sallied out, fell on the handful of men who had remained with Huntly, and rescued the prisoners. The alarm spread; soon cannon from the Castle were thundering through the darkness, soon the raiders were streaming in disorder along the road to Edinburgh, but not before one of Huntly's men had mortally wounded Lennox.

The death of Lennox did nothing to shorten the war; the Earl of Mar was elected in his place, and the weary struggle went on. It was like stalemate in chess: the Queen's Lords were not strong enough to smash the King's Lords, but, as long as the Queen's Lords held Edinburgh Castle, the King's Lords could not pretend to govern the country. And the Castle seemed impregnable; it was bombarded, but the besiegers feared to follow up the cannonade with an assault; it was blockaded, but provisions and reinforcements slipped through as before; appeals were sent to Elizabeth for guns and engineers, but only fair messages came from the parsimonious Queen.

In the autumn of 1572, when a truce gave a few months' rest to the combatants, Mar died—heart-broken it was said, because he could see no end to the struggle. His death opened the way for the more vigorous Earl of Morton. But the cause of the Queen's Lords was already lost: hitherto the douce burgess had looked on King's Lords and Queen's Lords alike as dangerous nuisances whose broils forced him to leave his booth and promenade the streets of his little burgh equipped with helmet and spear. The news of the Massacre of St. Bartholomew let him see what might happen in his own country if the Queen's Lords were victorious. In a moment indifference disappeared: the great mass of Scotsmen in the Lowlands ranged themselves behind the King's Lords. At the same time the announcement of the English Government that Mary would never be allowed to return to Scotland left the Queen's Lords with nothing to fight for.

But though most of the Queen's Lords made their peace with the Regent early in the following year, though Queen Elizabeth had at last granted the request of the Scottish Government and had sent engineers and artillery northward to Edinburgh, though Lethington was weakened by a deadly disease, the Castle still held out. Not till the end of May 1573, after English guns had bombarded it continuously for a week, killing more than a third of the scanty garrison, bringing down King David's Tower and another great tower, and pounding the battlements into sand, did Kirkcaldy consent to surrender. Respect for a gallant foe counted not at all with Morton; he ordered Kirkcaldy to be hanged, and would have served Lethington in the same fashion had not Lethington cheated him by dying.

There were none who loved the cold and forceful Regent, but he gave Scotland the peace which it required; he kept it clear of quarrels with England and entangling alliances with France, and maintained the new national church. Though his enemies forced him to resign the Regency in 1578, his eclipse was only temporary ; a few weeks later he was back in the Privy Council once more. But in the following year a fascinating stranger, Esmé Stewart, Seigneur d'Aubigny, a nephew of the late Earl of Lennox and, after the King, heir to that earldom, arrived from France. He quickly gained the heart of the young King, who made him Lord High Chamberlain and Earl of Lennox and admitted him to the Council. But Lennox, it was whispered, wanted more than titles and offices; he had come to bring Scotland back to the French alliance and to the Roman Catholic faith, not by deposing James, but by making the young King and his mother joint sovereigns. Morton, though he saw the ground crumbling beneath him, could do nothing. In 1581 he was accused by Captain James Stewart, one of the associates of Lennox, of complicity in the murder of Darnley, and arrested and beheaded. Lennox, no longer an Earl but a Duke, was now the master of Scotland. But the Duke's vigorous repudiation of the Roman Catholic faith failed to convince; in 1582 the Earls of Gowrie, Mar, and Glencairn, convinced that his influence over the King meant no good either to Church or State, lured the King to Ruthven Castle, made him a prisoner, and for ten months governed the country in his name. Lennox judged it prudent to flee to France, where he died a few months later. In 1583, however, James escaped from Ruthven, and the attempts of the Earl of Gowrie to bring the King under subjection once more resulted only in Gowrie's death on the scaffold and the flight of his supporters to England. The young King found in Captain James Stewart, now Earl of Arran, a counsellor whose policy was similar to that of Lennox. But, save for the King, Arran had few friends, and when the lords who had taken refuge in England returned with an army behind them, Arran followed the example of Lennox and fled.

Whatever may have been the King's private thoughts a year or two earlier, there seemed no likelihood now that he would renounce his policy of friendship with England and the maintenance of Protestantism. It is true that his subjects thought him unduly generous to the three Roman Catholic Earls, Huntly, Errol, and Angus, whose plots and rebellions disturbed the north of Scotland between 1589 and 1595; but he had excellent reasons for remaining a Protestant. Elizabeth of England was unmarried, she had now neither brother nor sister; the imprisoned Mary Queen of Scots was her next of kin. But the English would not have Mary at any price; they could not forget the other Queen Mary and the red glare of the fires of Smithfield. James, on the other hand, had only to stay Protestant, insinuate himself into the good graces of Queen Elizabeth, persuade her Parliament to set aside the will of Henry VIII, which barred the descendants of Margaret Tudor from the succession, and the rarest and juiciest of plums would drop into his mouth.

He had only to pay the price, and when Elizabeth died the crown of England would be his. A permanent alliance with England was the first instalment; in 1585 a treaty was signed whereby each country promised to come to the help of its neighbour if its neighbour should be invaded. At the second instalment James hesitated for a little—only a little—it was his mother's life. He knew what to do. When the sentence of death was pronounced against Mary he protested vigorously, and threatened to invade England, but there was nothing in his threats and though his subjects clamoured for war with England, they clamoured in vain.

But the will of Henry VIII was not set aside; never, till the end of her life, did Elizabeth declare that she wanted James to be her successor. On the other hand, she never declared that she did not want him to succeed her: she simply left the subject alone, unable to face the thought that at some time there would be an England, but no Elizabeth Tudor. But the King took comfort from the pension and the gracious letters that Elizabeth sent him, and lived in hope.

The years that followed the flight of Arran were comparatively peaceful. For one thing, until 1595, the young King allowed himself to be guided by Sir John Maitland of Thirlestane. Thirlestane, unlike his more brilliant brother the unfortunate Lethington, did not "steer too nigh the sands to boast his wit"; he directed his energies to the humdrum work of repairing the broken machinery of government. James might grumble at the advice which his Chancellor gave him, especially in ecclesiastical matters, but he always took it in the end. In 1587 an attempt was made to restore the prestige and authority of the Parliament—which had tended to become simply a meeting of whatever faction happened to be uppermost at the time—by fining heavily every member who had been summoned and who failed to attend. A more important Act was passed at the same time. Almost every one had forgotten that at one time anyone who held land of the Crown, however narrow his lands might be, was entitled also to attend Parliament; almost every one had forgotten the Act passed in 1428 which ordained that the free-holders of each county were to send two representatives to Parliament: when, indeed, in 1560 the country gentlemen insisted on being present at the Parliament which established Protestantism in Scotland, their action was looked on as something new and altogether exceptional. It was now decreed that the forgotten Act of 1428 was to be put into execution; before a Parliament assembled the freeholders in each county were to meet together and choose "twa wise men . . . of gude rent, and weel esteemed" to be their representatives in Parliament. The Commissioners of the Shires were to have the same number of representatives on the Committee of Articles, as the other three sections of the Parliament, prelates, nobles, and burgesses.

It had always been a comparatively easy business to get Parliament to pass sensible laws: it was still as difficult as it had ever been to secure obedience to these laws when they were passed. The long period of civil strife had interrupted the administration of justice, the circuit courts had fallen into abeyance, and serious crimes were tried only at Edinburgh. To remedy this the justice ayres were re-established in 1587; the country was divided into four districts, to each of which two competent judges were assigned. But this proposal seems to have had very little effect. Indeed, it was not always easy to get competent and honest judges even in the Court of Session; in 1579, Parliament, moved by the complaints that the King had often chosen "young men, without gravity, knowledge and experience" and that some of them had taken bribes, found it necessary to ordain that any Lord of Session found guilty of taking bribes should lose office and all his movable goods, and further, that any judge whom the King appointed in future must pass an examination conducted by the other Lords of Session before he could be admitted to the bench. The Parliament which met in 1592 supplemented this Act by declaring that no one who was under 25 or who had not a private income of at least 1,000 merks was to be appointed a Lord of Session.

The contempt into which the King's courts had fallen was not due simply to incompetent or corrupt judges; the wisest and most upright of judges found it difficult to make himself a terror to evil-doers. If one gentleman had a dispute with another he usually settled it out of court, "*à la mode d'Édimbourg*," as people said on the Continent, a fashion which involved the use of swords and pistols. If he killed his opponent he was summoned at the market cross of the nearest county town to deliver himself up and stand his trial. If, like a sensible man, he refused to come and be tried, nothing happened to him. There were no police to fetch him, and the score or two of soldiers who made up the royal bodyguard had their hands full protecting their own master. He would be outlawed, of course, but outlawry meant nothing to a laird whose country-house was built like a fortress and who could muster a body of stout retainers to defend it. What made it worse was that most of the disputes were senseless feuds inherited from a previous generation. In 1587, James, who was always apt enough to believe that men could be made to listen to reason, tried one ingenious plan for composing these endless quarrels. He invited the more troublesome of his nobles to a banquet in Holyrood, at which he drank their healths thrice, and urged them to live at peace in future; next day he marched them two by two—

each pair a brace of mortal enemies—up the Canongate to the Market Cross, where they found a large table prepared for them. There the performance of the previous day was repeated; to the blare of trumpets, the booming of cannon and the wild cheering of the astonished burgesses, the King drank the health of his nobles and made them drink to one another, then, as an appropriate conclusion to the ceremony, came a burst of fireworks in which the gallows crashed to the ground.

Neither this ceremony, nor attempts to establish justices of the peace after the English model, could break the Scottish country gentleman of his habit of taking the law into his own hands. And too often the King and his judges, while they punished friendless malefactors with furious severity, avoided a trial of strength with a powerful offender; in 1592, for example, the Earl of Huntly, hearing that his enemy the Earl of Moray was at his house at Donibristle with a handful of servants, galloped there at the head of forty horsemen, and slew the Earl as he tried to escape in the darkness. James decided that eight days' imprisonment was sufficient punishment for the murderer.

But the peace-loving king who now sat on the throne was just as determined as the most heroic of his ancestors had been to establish the reign of law and order in Scotland, and he came nearer to success than any of them had done. In some ways his task was easier: there was no longer a hostile government south of the border, ready to stir up rebellion and to offer fugitives from justice a convenient refuge, there was no ambitious Douglas or Albany capable of leading a coalition of nobles against the King. When in 1593 a wild Earl of Bothwell, after three unsuccessful attempts, broke into the King's bedroom and demanded his release from the sentence of treason, when in 1600 the Earl of Gowrie lured James to his house in Perth and attempted to make him prisoner, each was fighting for his own hand, with no backing from the other nobles. The nobles had every reason to be contented; in the scramble for the Church lands they had got almost everything, the Crown and the Reformed Church comparatively little; what possible cause of quarrel then could they have with the King? If he attempted to make them disgorge their spoil it would be a different story, they might talk of rebellion then, but since he let them digest it in peace there was no need for them to interfere with his experiments in kingcraft.

Not only did the central regions of Scotland become more peaceful, but James's attempts to maintain order in the Highlands and Islands and in the Borders were more successful than those of any previous king. James saw that the old problem of the Borders, which had always defied efforts by either Scotland or England separately, could now be solved through the action of joint Anglo-Scottish commissions, and the stricter patrolling of the frontier which was a sequel to the Union of the Crowns in 1603 made the Border cattle-raider's trade a more precarious one. In the Highlands, James ruthlessly suppressed the most lawless clan, that of MacGregor, and extracted promises from other chiefs that they would keep their clans in order. In Orkney and Shetland the Norse laws were abolished and the administration brought into line with that of the rest of Scotland. On every part of Scotland, and on every aspect of Scottish life, this reign left its imprint. Even the date of the beginning of the year was adjusted by James VI: hitherto the year had begun on 25 March, but it was ordained that from 1600 onwards the year should begin on 1 January—a change not made in England until 1752.

James's success was not altogether due to the weakening of the opposition to the Crown, it was due in large part to the ability of the monarch. For James was no mere conceited and bewildered pedant, drawing strange theories from half-understood books; he had a whimsical, but a clear and vigorous mind, sharpened by much painful experience. With little money, with no army behind him, James had learned to live by his wits, to read the character of those about him, to get by persuasion, intrigue, and bluff what he knew he could not get by an appeal to the sword. Timorous he might be, but his fears could not turn him from his goal, though he might approach it by devious courses; he might appear to relinquish a scheme; usually he had only postponed it to a more convenient season. And his goal was the establishment of absolute monarchy. It must be remembered that when he worked for it he was moved not by selfish ambition but by the conviction that it was the only thing that would save the country. A sensible king would call in honest and efficient servants to help him in his task of government, but he must be the sole judge of their honesty and efficiency; he would consult Parliament, but he must be free to reject its advice, or the advice of any other assembly, if he did not approve of it. Further, cases which concerned the King, problems which demanded an immediate solution, would be submitted, not to Parliament, but to the more manageable Privy Council, the members of which were appointed by the King.

In 1603 came the news for which James had waited so long. A little before midnight on Saturday, 26th March, a horseman galloped into the courtyard of Holyrood and aroused the sleeping household. Though he was bespattered with mud and reeling with fatigue—he had ridden from London to Edinburgh in less than three days—though the King had retired for the night, he insisted that he must see him at once. When he was admitted, he fell on his knees before James and saluted him as King of England, Scotland, France,[1] and Ireland. The King asked for a proof that Elizabeth was dead, whereupon Sir Robert Carey, for that was the horseman's name, showed him a ring that his sister had drawn from the finger of the dead Queen. James recognised it; it was a ring that he himself had given to Elizabeth. Even then he hesitated to believe his good fortune; not till he received a dispatch from the English Privy Council two days later informing him that he had been proclaimed King of England did he allow the news of his accession to the English throne to be made public in Edinburgh.

CHAPTER 18

PRESBYTERY AND EPISCOPACY

At last the dream of Edward I had come true, though in a fashion that would have seemed marvellous to him; the two kingdoms had been united, not by an English monarch succeeding to the throne of Scotland, but by a Scottish monarch succeeding to the throne of England. In such a union there could be little to wound, and much to swell the pride of the patriotic Scotsman. Scotland gave up her King to England, but

[1] The claim to the crown of France, first made by Edward III, was not abandoned till the time of George III.

she kept her Parliament, her Privy Council, her laws and law courts, and her own ecclesiastical organisation. What is more, James's English subjects, far from showing any desire to absorb the smaller in the larger country, strenuously resisted James's attempts to bring about a closer union. In 1606 the English Parliament rejected James's proposals for the establishment of free trade between the two countries and for counting all Scotsmen as naturalised Englishmen. In 1607, however, the English judges decided that the "post-nati," those born in Scotland after the accession of James to the English throne, should enjoy all the rights and privileges of English subjects, and the Scots passed an act giving reciprocal rights to Englishmen.

But though the English Parliament made no attempt to pass laws applying to Scotland, though no disappointed suitor ever dreamed of appealing from the judgement of the Court of Session to that of the House of Lords, the fact remains that Scotland was now governed not from Edinburgh but from Whitehall. The most important work of the Scottish Parliament, the drafting of new laws, was done not by the whole Parliament, but by a committee known as the Lords of the Articles; whoever controlled the Lords of the Articles controlled the Parliament. James introduced the practice of sending a list of those whom he wished to see on the Committee with a request that they should be appointed, a request which Parliament did not dare to refuse. A year or two later he refined on this plan; he arranged that on the first day of Parliament the bishops should choose eight nobles to sit on the Committee; they in their turn chose eight bishops, the sixteen then chose eight burgesses and eight commissioners of the shires. The Committee was completed by eight of the great officers of state. In appearance, the Parliament appointed the Committee without outside interference; in reality, since the bishops, like the officers of state, owed their places to the King, the Committee was appointed by James himself.

James found his Privy Council an even more useful instrument than a subservient Parliament. It was always in session; its ordinances had the weight of Acts of Parliament; it was a law-court as well, which never hesitated to deal with offenders who were too powerful or cases which were too difficult for the other courts to tackle. As the members of the Council were all royal nominees—capable judges and administrators perhaps, but men who did not dare to contradict the King—James was able to make the proud boast to his English Parliament, "Here I sit and govern by my pen; I write and it is done, and by a clerk of the Council I govern Scotland now—which others could not do by the sword."

In fact, James was more feared and respected by his Scottish subjects when he dwelt in Whitehall than when he dwelt in Holyrood. But they did not look on him as a tyrant, they looked on him as one of themselves, a prince who knew what was good for them and would let them have it if he could. The only quarrel which law-abiding Scots had with their sovereign arose from the objections of some of them to his ecclesiastical policy. But it was a serious dispute.

To see what the quarrel was about we must compare what happened at the Reformation in Scotland with what happened in England. In England, the passing of the Acts of Supremacy and Uniformity in 1559 had meant that the supremacy of the Pope and the doctrine of transubstantiation were repudiated, and that an English Book of Common Prayer replaced the Latin Service Books, but the ancient organisation of the Church was retained. The Church of England was still an episcopal Church; the new archbishops and bishops had many of the possessions and privileges of their predecessors; like them too, they were members of the House of Lords. Many of the prayers in the Prayer Book, too, were simply English versions of the Latin prayers in the old service-books, and while some of the festivals were allowed to lapse into oblivion, many were retained. But it was no longer the clergy who controlled the government of the Church: though a new bishop was nominally elected by the chapter—the clergy of his cathedral—the members of the chapter knew that they must appoint only that man whom the sovereign had given them permission to elect; moreover, the Parliament, including laymen of all ranks, representative of the whole community of the people of England, made laws for the Church.

But the Scottish reformers felt no tenderness towards anything associated with a Church which to them was altogether evil. The Roman Mass, they argued, was an idolatrous rite, therefore the worshipper must not kneel at Communion lest he should seem to be adoring the consecrated bread and wine; pictures and images were idols, therefore, whatever their beauty, they must be ruthlessly destroyed; the great festivals of the Church had no scriptural authority, therefore the burgess must on no account shut his shop on Christmas Day, and the minister must on no account administer Communion on Easter Day. As yet, however, the Scottish Protestants did not show that hostility to printed service-books and set forms of worship that they were afterwards to display. At first the English Book of Common Prayer was used, though it was gradually ousted by the Book of Common Order, which prescribed a less elaborate form of worship.

The Scottish reformers, unlike the English, had carried through their reformation not with the help of the Crown but in defiance of the Crown, and they could not, therefore, dispossess the existing bishops and other clergy. They appointed superintendents to do very much the same work which the bishops had done—and to do it much more efficiently—and the central government of the Church was committed not to Crown or Parliament but to a General Assembly, which was a kind of Protestant Parliament, containing barons and burgesses as well as superintendents and ministers. In each parish there was a kirk session of elders elected each year from among the congregation, to assist the minister in his work.

Altogether the differences between the Church of Scotland and the Church of England were not strongly marked in Knox's lifetime, and in 1572, the year of his death, arrangements were actually made, with his full approval, for appointing ministers to the bishoprics in almost exactly the same way as bishops were appointed in England, and those new bishops were to carry on the work of appointing and supervising ministers which had hitherto been done by the superintendents. But in 1574 a new leader appeared among the Scottish ministers, and he held very different views from John Knox. He was Andrew Melville, who had spent ten years in France and Geneva, and he returned to Scotland to an influential position as Principal, first of the University of Glasgow, and then of that of St. Andrews. Melville was opposed to bishops and superintendents alike, and as a result of his agitation the Second Book of Discipline, drawn up in 1578, proposed a Church organisation from which they were excluded. All ministers were to be of the same rank; there must be moderators, of course, for the various assemblies, but they were appointed by the assemblies and at the end of their limited period of office they became ordinary ministers once more. Some of the most important functions of the bishop were to be taken over by a new body of ministers and elders, the Presbytery, which administered a group of about a dozen parishes. It was the presbytery, for example, that was to examine candidates for the ministry and ordain them when they proved their fitness. According to Melville, moreover, elders were to be appointed for life, and such life-elders, along with ministers, were to compose presbyteries, synods and general assemblies, so that the Church was going to have an exclusive and self-sufficient organisation, quite unrelated to the polity of the State, and one in which neither King nor Parliament had any part.

James found that he must disentangle again the old problem which had perplexed Alexander I and William the Lion, the problem of the relations of Church and State. What was he to make of this new General Assembly, which met when it pleased, without any reference to the King's wishes, and before it dispersed appointed a Committee or Commission of Assembly to deal with any problem that might arise before the next assembly was summoned, so that in a sense it was always in session? This would not have mattered if it had shown an accommodating temper, but it seemed to be careless whether it thwarted the King or not. For to Presbyterian divines like Andrew Melville, who knew neither timidity nor tact, the problem of Church and State admitted of a simple solution, the solution propounded in the Second Book of Discipline. Let Church and State confine themselves to their own special provinces; let the Church confine its attention solely to religious matters and the State to secular matters. It was a doctrine familiar to the medieval Popes. But where was one to draw the line between the "external things" which were the exclusive concern of the State, and "the matters of conscience and of religion" with which the State was forbidden to deal? It seemed to the King that the Presbyterian divines drew it wherever it happened to suit themselves, that they wanted to have a finger in every pie, to make their churches echo one Sunday with denunciations of his clemency to his Catholic subjects or his suspicious friendliness with Catholic states, and

Twenty-pound Gold Piece of James VI, 1576

PLATE 47

WEST HIGHLAND TOMBSTONES

The figure represents a Highland Chief of fifteenth or sixteenth century date.

the next with outspoken criticisms of his personal faults, such as his habit of "profane swearing."

In 1584, when the Raid of Ruthven had shown the King to what lengths the Presbyterian leaders were prepared to go, James succeeded in persuading the Parliament—already jealous of the growing power of the Assembly—to pass what were known as the "Black Acts." No man, whether minister or layman, would in future be exempt from the judgement of the ordinary courts, whatever the charge against him might be. Any one who criticised the King—even in the pulpit—would be punished for spreading slanderous lies, and no ecclesiastical court was to sit in judgement on any case, ecclesiastical or other, except with the express consent of the King. But James was unable to maintain his challenge to the claims of the Presbyterian divines; in 1592 he had to give his consent to an Act which would in time have fully established the Presbyterian system and which admitted the jurisdiction of the new ecclesiastical courts in spiritual matters.

After the death of Thirlestane in 1595 James felt himself free to follow a bolder course. Convinced that a Church governed by bishops who owed their places to him would not impede and contradict him as a Church governed by independent assemblies had done, he resolved to modify the Presbyterian system and revive Episcopacy. But James moved forward cautiously at first, attempting as far as it was possible to get the consent of the Assembly to measures which in the long run would bring about his objects. A riot in Edinburgh during the closing days of 1596, which broke out because James insisted on the trial of a minister who had called Queen Elizabeth an atheist, gave the King the chance for which he had waited. His threats that he would move the court to Perth rather than be bullied in his own capital, and his refusal to restore the city to favour till it had paid him a sum of 20,000 merks, convinced many a burgess and many a minister too that the Presbyterian divines had gone too far in their claims to direct the policy of the State. James took care that during the next few years the General Assembly should meet not at Edinburgh, but in remoter towns like Dundee or Aberdeen, where it would be less influenced by the zealous followers of Melville, whose strength lay in the south. Interviews with royalty and grants of liberal allowances for travelling expenses weakened the objections of many of the ministers to Episcopacy; the General Assembly of 1600 agreed that the Church should be represented in Parliament just as the pre-Reformation Church had been. At first the Assembly was unwilling to give the name of bishop to these representatives or to appoint them for more than one year, but James soon succeeded in overcoming its scruples and the thirteen Scottish bishoprics were once again filled.

The King was not yet content, for the new bishops were bishops only in name; the government of the Church was still largely in the hands of the General Assembly and its subordinate synods and presbyteries. But the General Assembly was no longer in a mood to defy the King. In 1605 some ministers who had disregarded a royal edict postponing a meeting of the Assembly were found guilty of treason and banished for life. A few months later the King got rid of his most formidable opponent, Andrew Melville. Melville had visited London on the King's invitation and had been tactless enough to write some satirical Latin verses on the furnishings of the Chapel Royal. For this he was imprisoned in the Tower, and at the end of four years banished to France, where he died in 1622. In 1609 Parliament restored to the bishops their right to act as judges in all disputes about wills and divorces, as well as in all purely ecclesiastical cases, and in 1610 a tamed and subservient Assembly consented to the Scottish bishops being granted once more an essential place in church government.

But James had succeeded so far, largely because his innovations concerned only a small minority of his Scottish subjects; the country gentleman did not worry himself as long as James asked no questions about the land which he had filched from the Church; the ordinary worshipper did not worry himself as long as he saw no break in the accustomed routine of the service. On Sunday he sat in a building which contained little to remind him that it had once been a Catholic church. Whitewash covered the paintings on the walls, the windows were filled with plain glass, the great crucifix had been thrown down from its place above the rood-screen, the niches stood empty of their saints, and in place of an altar against the east wall there was a communion table around which the minister and the people could assemble. The organ had disappeared at the same time as the altar; the only music which one heard during the service was the unaccompanied singing of a metrical version of the psalms.[1]

When James visited Scotland in 1617—his one and only visit after he ascended the English throne—it became evident that he aimed at modifying the Scottish forms of worship. An organ costing £400 was fitted up in the Chapel Royal at Holyrood, and when James attended divine service the organ music, the chanting of the boy choristers, and the appearance of the officiating ministers, not in the black Geneva gown, but in the white Anglican surplice, grieved the more scrupulous. Protests, however, were not effective, and in 1618, after his return to England, he persuaded a General Assembly meeting at Perth to pass five Articles making important innovations in the worship of the Church. Services, to be attended by all, were to be held on Christmas Day, Good Friday, Ascension Day, Easter Day and Whit Sunday, communicants were to kneel when they received the Sacrament, and children were in future to be confirmed by a bishop. James had gone too far: it was impossible to enforce the Articles of Perth; a mere handful of people attended church on Christmas Day; shopkeepers not only opened their booths but strutted about in front of them during the service; and there were few ministers who dared to bar from the communion table the devout worshipper who refused to kneel.

Worse followed with the accession of Charles I in 1625. James understood his people through and through; Charles, though he was born in Dunfermline, had left Scotland when he was three years old and was now to all intents and purposes a foreigner. With James ecclesiastical questions were matters of policy; he revived Episcopacy because it buttressed the royal power: with Charles they were matters of conscience; he maintained Episcopacy because he believed that a Church without bishops was no Church at all. James had made few efforts to get the Church lands from those who had appropriated them, though he knew that some ministers were miserably poor; Charles, a few months after his accession, announced that all Church lands belonging to lay proprietors must be surrendered to the Crown.

[1] The version of the metrical psalms now used in the Church of Scotland was not introduced into Scotland till 1650. One or two of the psalms used in King James's time, like the famous Old 124th, are given in the Psalter as alternative versions distinguished by the heading "another of the same."

This Act of Revocation was soon whittled down, but the mischief was done; Charles had alarmed the nobles, and they now began to think of making common cause with the ministers who had opposed the King's ecclesiastical innovations.

Charles did not want money and lands for himself, and he did, out of his Revocation, make arrangements for the stipends of the ministers—arrangements which survived the collapse of so many of his schemes and indeed endured until the twentieth century. He wanted money for other purposes too, all designed in one way or another to improve the dignity of public worship or to embellish his Scottish capital. He created a new bishopric, at Edinburgh, and insisted that the church of St. Giles should be renovated to make it a fitting cathedral; Edinburgh had to find the money for a new church, the Tron; and the King demanded also the erection of a new Parliament House, close by his new cathedral. His manifold requirements drove Edinburgh to bankruptcy and it was poor compensation that Charles made it a city and formally declared it his capital. While financial pressure on Edinburgh was particularly severe, the whole country was undergoing the unpleasant and novel experience of being subjected to regular and heavier taxation and St. Giles' was not the only great church which the King insisted should be repaired.

The grievances which arose in one way or another from the King's ecclesiastical policy were closely linked with constitutional issues. There was already uneasiness, to say the least, at the management of Parliament through the Lords of the Articles and at the manipulation of the election of that all-important committee to ensure that only measures approved by the King could be passed. The question now was, by what means could criticism be put convincingly before the King and how could the opinions of his subjects be brought to bear on the shaping of government policy and the making of laws. It became clear in 1633 that nothing could be hoped for from Parliament. In that year, when Charles was in Edinburgh for his coronation as King of Scots, a Parliament was held at which the Committee of Articles was elected, as it had been before, through the use of the bishops as the King's creatures; when the recommendations of the Committee were put before the full house, the King was present in person and noted how men voted; and the measures passed included a ratification of the King's Revocation and an act

JAMES VI

DUNDERAVE CASTLE, ARGYLL

Re-roofed and restored in the twentieth century

stating that the clergy should wear surplices. It next became equally clear that it was useless to try to approach Charles by way of petition, for Lord Balmerino was tried for treason because he had been associated with a supplication by which it was proposed to lay constitutional and financial grievances before the King. Frustrated in other ways, the opposition must have come to the conclusion that nothing short of a violent outbreak could check the King and that such an outbreak, involving an appeal to the populace, could most easily be brought about over ecclesiastical issues. And the King played directly into their hands.

In 1633, when Charles visited Edinburgh, his more precise subjects noticed that an altar with candles upon it was erected in the Chapel Royal of Holyrood for his coronation, and that when he went to St. Giles' surpliced clergymen read the Anglican service. After the King's departure their fears were realised; in 1636 the publication of the Book of Canons, or rules for the Church, which every minister was obliged to say he accepted, let them see exactly where the King stood. Those who questioned the King's right to shape the organisation of the Church or criticised the Episcopal system and the Book of Common Prayer were to be excommunicated. All parish churches were to be fitted up like Anglican churches, with the communion table placed like an altar; ministers might hear confession, but were not to utter extempore prayers. Further, ministers must undertake to use a Prayer Book which was being prepared, but which none of them had seen.

There was widespread indignation, partly at what Charles was doing, partly at the way in which he was doing it. James had tried to carry his people with him if it was at all possible; he secured the co-operation of carefully tamed Assemblies for his reforms, but Charles seemed to be absolutely careless of the feelings and convictions of the ordinary minister and the ordinary worshipper. Prayer Books, he argued, were necessary to their spiritual welfare, though they did not know it; therefore Prayer Books must be forced upon them. It was only natural that the Scot should resent the King's attempt to take charge of his conscience, but behind his resentment at Charles's high-handed action lurked something else—the fear that the King's real aim was the restoration of Roman Catholicism. This fear was strengthened in 1637 by the publication of the new Service-Book: it was based on the English Book of Common Prayer, though a number of changes had been made to bring it into line with Scottish usage and opinions, but to the excited minds of the people it bore a suspiciously close resemblance to a Roman Catholic service-book.

The King had gone too far; not even all the bishops wholly approved of the book; when the Dean of Edinburgh attempted to read it in St. Giles' Cathedral he was at once interrupted by shouts and yells from the female worshippers. The Bishop stepped into the pulpit and tried to quiet the tumult, only to be greeted with cries of "Wolf!" "Beastly belly-god!" and "Crafty fox!" But worse followed; the ladies began to hurl bibles and folding stools at his head, so that, to quote an old writer, "jouking became his safeguard." No better fortune awaited the Archbishop of St. Andrews when he intervened; he was forced to appeal to the provost and bailies to restore order. Even when the brawlers were driven from the church they battered at the doors and threw stones at the windows, and when the Bishop emerged he was at once mobbed by a furious crowd.

Charles could not realise that every section of his people, laird and noble as well as peasant and petty craftsman, was opposed to his ecclesiastical policy; the riot, far from convincing him that he must retreat, only confirmed him in his determination to force the Prayer Book on a country that would not have it at any price. The news that the King did not intend to abandon the Prayer Book provoked another riot in Edinburgh later in the year, and the Privy Council was at its wits' end when the Lord Advocate suggested that the malcontents, instead of plunging the whole of Edinburgh into an uproar, should appoint a committee to confer with the Council and then disperse. His suggestion was acted on at once; four nobles, four lairds, four ministers and four burgesses were at once elected, and the Privy Council realised when it was too late that by giving an organisation to the King's opponents they had been made doubly dangerous. The "Tables," as this committee was called, resolved that a definite protest should be made, and early in 1638 the famous National Covenant was framed. We have seen how in earlier times private persons, like the Earls of Douglas, Crawford, and Ross in the reign of James II, often entered into "bands" or engagements to support one another against any one whatsoever. The National Covenant was a band to bind, not one or two individuals, but the whole nation: those who signed it bound themselves to defend the King with their lives, but to have nothing to do with his ecclesiastical innovations until they were approved by a free Assembly and by Parliament.

The Covenant became a standard round which the nation rallied; copies were carried to every quarter of the kingdom, and everywhere, except in the north, were signed with enthusiasm.

At last Charles gave way; he announced that a General Assembly was to be held in Glasgow in November. Before ever the Assembly met the result of its deliberations was a foregone conclusion; the presbyteries were instructed not to elect any minister who approved of the Canons and Prayer Book; the ministers, moreover, were accompanied by nobles and lairds, under the guise of elders, as well as by representatives of the burghs. The bishops, who knew that their colleagues had no intention of dealing kindly with them, protested that such a gathering was no true Assembly, and it was certainly no free Assembly. Their arguments convinced the Lord High Commissioner, the Marquis of Hamilton, who dissolved the Assembly. But the Assembly refused to be dissolved; under the guidance of the Moderator, Alexander Henderson, it proceeded not only to denounce Charles's innovations but to demolish the whole structure which his father had erected. Episcopacy was abolished, the bishops were deposed and some of them excommunicated, and with them disappeared the Five Articles of Perth, the Book of Canons and the Service-Book.

CHAPTER 19

SCOTLAND AND THE CIVIL WAR

THE abolition of Episcopacy by the Glasgow Assembly in 1638 and the restoration of the Presbyterian system were an open challenge to the King. Charles must either give way or fight, and, as he sincerely believed that a Church without bishops was no true Church, he could not give way. But could he fight? For he had neither a standing army nor money to hire mercenary troops, unless he summoned his English Parliament and asked it to finance the campaign, and he knew that any Parliament which he summoned now would be much more critical of his actions than the very unfriendly Parliament which he had dismissed in 1629. He did succeed, however, in raising an army of 20,000 men in the early summer of 1639, and moved with it to the border, only to find that the road into Scotland was barred by a force, equal in numbers, but far superior in discipline, commanded by Alexander Leslie, a veteran who had served in wars on the Continent. Charles made one half-hearted attempt to advance into Scotland, and then, before any serious fighting took place, he brought the campaign to an end by signing the Pacification of Berwick. This Treaty seemed to promise the Scots all that they wanted, for though Charles refused to recognise the Glasgow Assembly, he agreed that all disputed questions should be referred either to another General Assembly or to Parliament. Thus the First Bishops' War came to an end. But the Second Bishops' War followed speedily. When the General Assembly which Charles had sanctioned met a few weeks later, it simply re-enacted all the acts of the Glasgow Assembly. The Parliament would have gone further, if the Lord High Commissioner[1] had not prorogued it before it could ratify the proposals made by the Committee of Articles. At length, in June 1640, after ten separate prorogations, Parliament met in defiance of both King and Commissioner, abolished

[1] Name given to the nobleman who acted as the King's representative in Parliament or in the General Assembly.

Episcopacy, and freed itself from royal control by setting its own house in order. Hitherto new laws had been drafted, not by Parliament as a whole, but by the Committee of the Articles, to which men who were known to be critical of the King's policy had very little chance of being appointed. Now it was enacted that only when Parliament judged it necessary was a Committee of the Articles to be appointed, and further, that each estate, nobles, barons,[1] and burgesses, was to choose its own representatives.

This time the Parliament as well as the Assembly had challenged the King, and in the late summer of 1640 Leslie again led an army towards the border. Charles was even less able to meet the challenge than he had been in 1639, though he had summoned the "Short" Parliament earlier in the year. He had quarrelled with it at once and dissolved it without obtaining any money from it.

The ill-trained and disorderly troops that Charles got together were worse than useless. Ten days after crossing the Tweed the Scots captured Newcastle; four days later they were in Durham. As they could now cut off the coal supply of London, the King had no choice but to open negotiations with them, and, as they declared that they would accept no treaty of which the English Parliament had not approved, he was forced to summon the famous "Long" Parliament. Commissioners from both countries met in London to settle the terms of the treaty, but, as the English Commissioners knew that the presence of a Scottish Army in the northern counties was a check on the King, a year passed before the treaty was at last completed. It gave the Scots all that they wanted; the King promised to approve of the Acts of the Scottish Parliament of 1640, including the obnoxious Acts abolishing Episcopacy and limiting the powers of the Lords of the Articles; and, in addition, to give Parliament the right to challenge the actions of his ministers. At the same time the English Commons voted an indemnity of £300,000 to the Scots.

But much had happened in England between the opening of the negotiations and the signing of the treaty. Against his will, the King had been forced by the Long Parliament to surrender

[1] The name usually given to the country gentlemen who were Commissioners for the Shires.

what he considered inalienable rights: he could no longer summon or dismiss Parliament just when he thought good; he could no longer raise money to supplement his ordinary revenues without first consulting Parliament, and worst of all, as the execution of Strafford proved, his goodwill could no longer protect from the vengeance of Parliament a minister who carried out his policy. If he wanted to win back what he had lost, or even to keep what he had got, he would have to fight. Why then not make sure of the support of the Scots in the coming struggle? With this purpose in view he visited Edinburgh in the autumn of 1641, but, though he made concession after concession, though he scattered titles broadcast, no one trusted him; his visit was a failure. Of those who had appeared against him, the only one whom he won over to his side was the young Earl of Montrose, who had led the Scottish vanguard across the Tweed in 1640. Montrose was still a Presbyterian, but he had begun to suspect that some of his fellow Covenanters, like the great Marquis of Argyll, were more concerned to advance their own interests and perhaps pull down the monarchy than to set up Presbyterianism.

So when the Civil War broke out in England the Scots at first held aloof. They were not interested in the political question, in the attempts to decide where the King's authority ended and where the authority of the Parliament began: they were almost wholly occupied with the ecclesiastical problem. The King, it is true, had consented to the establishment of Presbyterianism in Scotland, but reluctant consent to the establishment of Presbyterianism in only one part of his dominions was not sufficient to make the Scots come into the war on his side. They wanted a much higher price for their assistance—nothing short of the establishment of Presbyterianism and the suppression of Episcopacy in England, Scotland, and Ireland.

One would have thought that men who had fought so bitterly against interference with their modes of worship and system of Church organisation would have been slow to interfere with the religion of other people. But this was not so. When they demanded freedom for the Church they demanded freedom for one Church only. Just as Charles thought that a Church which was not governed by bishops was no Church at all, and that therefore it was his duty to force all his subjects, in Scotland as in

England, to become Episcopalians, so the Scots thought that a Church which was not governed according to the Presbyterian system was no Church at all, and that therefore it was their duty to make a Presbyterian, not only of every Scotsman, but, if they could manage it, of every Englishman too.

It seemed as if they might succeed. One royalist victory had followed another, and in the summer of 1643 the English Parliament, confronted with the prospect of utter defeat, appealed to Scotland for help. At the same time they summoned an Assembly of Divines to Westminster, to remodel the doctrines and ritual of the national Church, and to this Assembly representatives from Scotland were invited. By the Solemn League and Covenant, signed in the autumn of 1643, the Scots agreed to intervene on the side of the Parliament, and the Parliament undertook "the reformation of religion in the kingdoms of England and Ireland, in doctrine, worship, discipline and government, according to the word of God and the example of the best reformed churches." The Scots had no doubt where "the best reformed church" was to be found, and were not likely to think for a moment that their Presbyterian system was capable of improvement, but the English were not so sure. However, at the beginning of 1644 Alexander Leslie, now Earl of Leven, crossed the frozen Tweed at the head of 26,000 men.

At the battle of Marston Moor, in July 1644, the battle which lost the north of England to the King, the Scottish contingent played an important part. We are often told of the irresistible charge of Cromwell's Ironsides; we are not told that when Cromwell was wounded and his horsemen thrown into temporary confusion, David Leslie saved the situation by hurling the Scottish cavalry against Rupert's victorious squadrons, that, in the rout of the Parliamentary infantry, the Scottish regiments alone stood firm, or that, in the last triumphant charge which ended the battle, Cromwell's cuirassiers and Leslie's light horsemen rode side by side.

A few weeks later the tables were turned. Montrose, now a Marquis, made his way to the Highlands and got together an army composed mainly of Highlanders, with an Irish contingent, and a sprinkling of Lowland gentlemen and their retainers. With this motley host, destitute of artillery and almost destitute of cavalry, he proposed to win back Scotland for King Charles.

It seemed a crack-brained scheme—to make the clans forget their feuds and jealousies and leave the security of their glens to fight for a distant King, for whom they cared nothing, in a quarrel which they could not understand. Yet it succeeded. The clansmen somehow knew that Montrose was not like other leaders, and that, if they followed him, they would have a chance of booty on a scale of which they had never dreamed.

Scotland soon learned how formidable these undisciplined, impetuous fighters could be. At the beginning of September, Montrose advanced against Perth, but found his way barred at Tippermuir by a Covenanting army twice as large as his own. The Highlanders fired one volley, then, flinging aside their muskets and their plaids, swept down with a wild yell on the wavering ranks of the Lowland infantry. The Covenanters lost their nerve and fled in terror, only to be cut down mercilessly by the pursuing Highlanders. Less than a fortnight later Montrose appeared before Aberdeen. Again the forces that tried to stop him melted away before the fierce onslaught of the Highlanders, who followed them up, and plundered and slew at will in the streets of the town. Then he disappeared into the Campbell country, where his great rival, the Marquis of Argyll, was wont to exercise a more than kingly authority; there he plundered at his pleasure until, in February 1645, he concluded his campaign in the west by swooping down on Argyll's army at Inverlochy, after a forced march through snow-bound passes and completely defeating it.

March saw him at the other side of Scotland, taking the walled town of Dundee by storm, then hustling his tipsy soldiers out by the East Port as the Covenanting army, under General Baillie hurried in at the West Port. In May he utterly smashed an army commanded by Hurry, Baillie's second in command, at Auldearn, near the Moray Firth. In July he routed Baillie himself at Alford. Baillie escaped, and was put in command of another army, but at Kilsyth, in the following month, Montrose defeated Baillie a second time and occupied Glasgow.

It was a glorious record, a record that no other general living at that time, not even Cromwell himself, could have equalled. But Montrose had gained nothing but honour. He had failed to win over the Lowlands to his side, for the Lowland Scot could not forgive the man who had let his wild Highlanders and Irish

Hamilton Dower House
Prestonpans, 1628

Before and after its restoration by the National Trust for Scotland.

Plate 51

Kinross House

men loose on Aberdeen to slaughter defenceless burgesses. He had failed to reinforce the hard-pressed Royalist armies, and though he had given Alexander Leslie some anxious moments, he had failed to divert a single regiment from the Scottish army in England. What could he do with an army which threatened to dissolve after every victory, with troops who went home after every battle, and did not return till they had seen their booty safely stowed away? Even if he could have invaded England after Kilsyth he would have been too late, for the King's hopes of victory had been destroyed a month earlier, in the crowning disaster of Naseby.

Now that the power of the King was shattered, the Scottish army in England could be used to deal with Montrose. David Leslie crossed the Tweed at the head of four thousand veterans and, on a misty September morning, surprised the remnants of the Royalist army at Philiphaugh, near Selkirk. In vain Montrose galloped out from the town and charged at the head of his cavalry; the battle had been lost before it was well begun. Montrose's friends hurried him from the field. It was well, for the victors, remembering Aberdeen, showed no mercy to the prisoners. The bulk of them, including the women and children who had followed the army, were butchered on the battle-field. Those who were spared were spared only for trial and execution.

Meantime the Scots were sore perplexed. They had entered into an alliance with the English Parliament because they wanted to establish Presbyterianism in England, and they thought that Parliament had promised to establish it. Further, as if to show that the Parliament was sincere, the Westminster Assembly still continued its deliberations, and still showed itself anxious to defer to the wishes of the Scottish representatives. But it was evident that the English Parliament could not keep to the bargain which it had made in the Solemn League and Covenant; the destinies of the country were controlled no longer by Parliament but by the Army, and the Army did not favour the establishment of Presbyterianism in England. Many of the officers and men were, like Cromwell, Independents, who thought that each congregation should manage its own affairs and mind its own business. They would not dream of interfering with the Presbyterians, if the Presbyterians left them alone, but that the

Presbyterians should compel any Protestant to become a Presbyterian was intolerable to them.

The perplexity of the Scots grew deeper when, in 1646, the vanquished King threw himself on the mercy of the Scottish army. Since the English Parliament had disappointed them, they were ready to fight for the King, if he would undertake to establish Presbyterianism in England. Charles refused. The Scots handed him over to the English Parliament, and withdrew beyond the Tweed.

So the attempt to establish Presbyterianism in England, through the co-operation of the King or of the English Parliament, had utterly failed. But though the Westminster Assembly failed to transform the Church of England into a Presbyterian Church, it has left its mark upon the Church of Scotland: to this day Presbyterian services are supposed to follow the order prescribed by that Assembly. The Longer and Shorter Catechisms were framed by it, and, what is stranger still, the metrical psalms, which make the exiled Scot think of the "clinkum clank o' Sabbath bells" at home, were largely composed by a Cornishman, and recommended to the use of a somewhat unwilling Church by that same Westminster Assembly. The Confession of Faith of the Church of Scotland, and its Form of Church Government, are still those drawn up at Westminster.

Meantime, some of the Scots began to think that they had been in too great a hurry to give up their King; though they objected to his ecclesiastical policy, they did not wish to see his lawful authority diminished, and now it seemed that the Parliament and the Army between them were doing their best to deprive him of every shred of kingly power. Before the end of 1647 the representatives of the Scottish Parliament signed a treaty—the Engagement—by which they pledged themselves to send an army into England to support the King, in return for his promise to give Presbyterianism a three years' trial in England. The Engagement split the country into two; the more bigoted Presbyterians were furious because the Commissioners who negotiated the treaty had not insisted that Charles should undertake to establish Presbyterianism for good. For their leader they had that statesman who had been suspect to Montrose, the Marquis of Argyll. The prophets of woe were justified: at the end of the following summer the Duke of Hamilton led an army across the border, but Cromwell came upon the Scots when they were strung out from Preston to Wigan, and, in a three days' battle, drove them out of Preston through Wigan, and finally rounded them up at Winwick, about two miles from Warrington. The remnants of the army surrendered. Hamilton himself escaped death on the battle-field only to be executed a few months later. Preston was an unmitigated disaster; it extinguished the King's last hopes of safety, for the army leaders now hardened their hearts against him, and it led to civil strife in Scotland. The Anti-Engagers of the south-west, known as the "Whiggamores"[1] or "Whigs," marched on Edinburgh and overthrew the government: Argyll was now master of Scotland.

But it soon became apparent that Cromwell was master of Argyll. When he visited Edinburgh he was entertained as if he had been a Scottish general who had triumphed over a foreign army, not an English general who had vanquished a Scottish army, and before he left he insisted that no one who had fought for King Charles was to hold any office in Scotland. A subservient Parliament hastened to obey him by passing the Act of Classes in January 1649. But the execution of the King a few days later horrified even those Scots who had hitherto been the King's bitterest opponents, and swung the whole country round into opposition to Cromwell and the Commonwealth. There was all the difference in the world, they felt, between opposing the King's policy and laying violent hands upon the King. That Scotland should be without a King was unthinkable; now that Charles I had been slain, the only thing to do was to proclaim his son as King in his stead.

To proclaim Charles II as King was one thing: to invite the exiled monarch to Scotland and defend him against the inevitable attacks of the Commonwealth armies was a very different one. The Scots, however, were willing to do it, but for a price. Charles must sign both Covenants. Charles did not wish to sign if it could possibly be evaded, and he had commissioned Montrose to invade northern Scotland. Montrose knew from the start that his enterprise was hopeless; his force of unwarlike Orcadians and foreign mercenaries was routed at Carbisdale in Ross-shire, and he himself was captured, taken to Edinburgh, and executed.

[1] They got their name because West-Country carters were supposed to cry "Whiggam!" when they wanted to encourage their horses.

He met disaster as he had met triumph; on the day of his execution his calm and simple dignity silenced the brawling Edinburgh mob, and brought tears to the eyes of those who had wept for sons slain at Kilsyth or Tippermuir.

There was no help for it now: Charles undertook to observe both Covenants, and about midsummer 1650 he appeared in Scotland. A month later Cromwell crossed the border. The independence of Scotland was at stake now, but by the Act of Classes the privilege of fighting for his country was denied to any man who had followed Montrose or Hamilton, and so thousands of the bravest and most experienced soldiers were excluded from the army with which David Leslie confronted Cromwell. Even then the Scots outnumbered the English by two to one. Their Commander, too, had made up his mind to play a cautious game, and give no opening to Cromwell. He kept him marching and countermarching, through country from which all food-stuffs had disappeared, in a vain attempt to get between the Scottish army and Edinburgh; then, when Cromwell, finding his army weakened by sickness and starvation retreated to Dunbar, Leslie promptly occupied Doon Hill, about two miles to the south of the town. The northern slope of the hill is defended by a deep ravine, through which the Brocksburn flows to the sea. Cromwell was at his wits' end: though his confidence seemed unshaken, he admitted to one of his friends that he could not escape "without almost a miracle."

The miracle happened: Cromwell could hardly believe his eyes when, on the afternoon of the second of September, he saw the Scottish infantry descend the slopes of Doon Hill and take up their position on the plain. "The Lord hath delivered them into our hands," he cried. The Scots made no attempt to continue their advance. When the night came on with wind and rain they bivouacked on the southern side of the stream, confident that no one would be fool enough to fight in such dirty weather. But it was dangerous to make such an assumption when Cromwell was in the neighbourhood. In reality, his whole army was standing to on the other side of the ravine, for he was resolved to attack before dawn the next day. While it was still dark fighting began away on the left of the Scottish position. As a wan light broke over the North Sea, the cannon began to thunder against the Scottish centre, and the trumpets sounded the advance

Under cover of the artillery fire detached bodies of red-coated cavalry and infantry, with shouts of "The Lord of Hosts," forced their way across the stream. At first the Scottish centre stood fast, and the Scottish cavalry on the right charged and drove the advancing English back towards the ravine. But the counter-charge of Cromwell's second line hurled back the horsemen upon their own infantry in the centre. The centre held for a little and then gave way, and soon the whole Scottish army was rolling back in wild confusion. Of the army of 23,000 men, three thousand fell on the field of battle and another ten thousand were made prisoners.

But the upholders of the Covenant did not know when they were beaten. Cromwell followed up his victory by occupying Edinburgh. Argyll and his associates still refused to have anything to do with a man who was ready to allow every Protestant to cleave to his own special form of Protestantism. They turned instead to the prince who believed in his heart that Presbyterianism was no religion for a gentleman, but professed himself willing to impose it on his English subjects, and on 1st January Charles was crowned at Scone. They had learned some sense, however. Despite the protests of the stricter Presbyterians,[1] the Act of Classes was rescinded. No man was now debarred from fighting for Charles II because he had fought for Charles I. So the small force of famished and disgusted men, with which Leslie had guarded the approaches to Stirling throughout the winter, had grown to be a formidable army in the summer of 1651. And Leslie seemed to have learned his lesson; he refused to be lured from his position in front of Stirling. But Cromwell was too clever for him; he moved his army over into Fife, and marched on Perth, thus at the same time threatening to take Leslie in flank and leaving the road to England uncovered. The little stratagem worked beautifully; when Cromwell reached Perth, he heard that Charles and the whole Scottish army had left Stirling and were bound for the border.

Leaving Monk behind to deal with Stirling and Dundee, Cromwell hurried after the Scots, collecting reinforcements as he went, till his army had swelled to 31,000 men. The 3rd of September had come round again, and it was not among the

[1] Known as Protesters: those who were willing to co-operate with the former followers of Charles I were called Resolutioners.

gorse and bracken of some Scottish moorland, but where the spires of Worcester look down on the meadows watered by the Teme and the Severn, that the last scene of this grim tragedy was enacted. For five hours the Scots fought bravely against foes who outnumbered them by two to one. They were forced over Severn Bridge and into the town on the west side only to sally from it gallantly on the east side, but they were beaten back, their guns captured and turned upon them, and they themselves forced to surrender. The King escaped, but not many more.

Five days earlier one of Monk's officers had captured the Committee of the Estates,[1] the last remnant of the Scottish Parliament; two days earlier Monk's troops had stormed and sacked the town of Dundee, next to Edinburgh the wealthiest town in Scotland.

The spirit of the Scots was completely broken. In a little over three years they had raised three armies, only to see each of them ground to powder by Cromwell, and now they could do no more. The English garrisons in their chief towns, the great new fortresses at Leith, Perth, and Ayr, reminded them that they belonged to a conquered country. They were not treated harshly. They were treated rather as children—but as children who might blunder into mischief if they were not carefully watched. A Committee of eight English officials replaced the old Privy Council, seven English judges, "kinless loons," replaced the old Court of Session, but did not inherit that weakness for taking bribes which the "Auld Fifteen"[2] had manifested. The Scottish Parliament did not meet again after 1651, and in 1654 it was arranged that thirty representatives should go from Scotland to the English Parliament at Westminster.

In return for her loss of independence, Scotland gained trading privileges that had hitherto been reserved for Englishmen. Scottish captains were allowed to bring goods from foreign harbours into English ports and ports in the English colonies. She gained too, what she did not value, a respite from religious strife. But the Presbyterians had not yet learned their lesson. They would still have refused to others the freedom which they claimed for themselves.

[1] The committee of the Scottish Parliament which met when Parliament was not in session.

[2] The fifteen judges of the Court of Session.

CHAPTER 20

THE RESTORATION AND THE REVOLUTION

THE Scots greeted the Restoration of Charles II in 1660 with a delight untroubled by any forebodings of evil; defeat and humiliation were over; Scotland was an independent kingdom once more—a kingdom, moreover, ruled by a Covenanted King. But Charles had no intention of being bound by the Covenant, or of letting the Scottish Parliament enjoy the powers which his father had been forced to concede to it. In defiance of a statute of 1641, he chose his Privy Council and the great officers of state without ever consulting Parliament. And the Parliament, in its first raptures over the return of the King, came pretty near to signing its own death-warrant. It passed a Rescissory Act, annulling all Acts passed by its predecessors since 1633, thus automatically re-establishing the Committee of the Articles. It agreed that the King was supreme governor of his kingdom, over all persons and all causes; it again gave bishops a place in the House, and it restored the old method of choosing the Committee of the Articles which James VI had introduced, which made it practically impossible for a member of whom the King did not approve to be appointed to the Committee.

But most people were less concerned about the changes in Parliament than about the rumours of changes in the Church. Different people looked forward to different things: the nobles and country gentlemen, for example, in their relief at the passing of the long years of war and banishment, were set only on enjoying themselves; they bitterly regretted their short-lived alliance with the Presbyterian ministers against Charles I, and were ready to go to any length to help his son, Charles II, to put them in their place.

In the north-east of Scotland, too, the people honestly preferred Episcopacy to Presbyterianism. In other parts of the Lowlands burgesses and country folk expected to see Presbyterianism again established, but Dunbar and Worcester had taught them the folly of attempting to impose Presbyterianism on England, or to hold Charles II to a Covenant which he had accepted under compulsion. In the south-west, however, where the spirit of the Protesters was still strong, ministers and people alike were out and out "Covenanters," who would be satisfied with nothing less than the establishment of Presbyterianism in England as well as in Scotland, as required by the Solemn League and Covenant.

But in 1661 it was discovered that when Charles spoke of protecting the Church as established by law, he meant the Church as established by Charles I in 1633, and further, that James Sharp, who had been sent to London to represent the moderate Presbyterians, had himself been persuaded to become Archbishop of St. Andrews. Parliament not only consented to the reintroduction of bishops into the Church, but also declared that ministers who had been appointed since 1649 must resign their charges, and receive them again with the approval of the bishop of the diocese.

Most of the ministers gave in for the sake of peace. They had to admit that the bishops made no attempt to interfere with the doctrines or services of the Church. No prayer-book was used; surplices were not worn; communicants did not kneel. Besides, kirk sessions and presbyteries continued to act very much as before.

Nearly three hundred ministers, however, most of them from the south-west, left their churches rather than have any dealings with the bishops. Their places were filled, but the people refused to listen to the "curates," as the new ministers were called. They stayed away from church, to go to some secluded spot among the hills, where they could listen to their own banished minister. The Government retaliated by imposing heavy fines on all who ventured to attend these conventicles or even stayed away from church, and by sending dragoons into the west to collect the money at the sword's point. This severity, instead of frightening the enthusiasts for the Covenant in the west, only goaded them into resistance. In 1666 some hundreds of them marched to Edinburgh, but, finding that the citizens did not mean to support them, they turned about and began to retreat homewards. They were overtaken, however, at Rullion Green in the Pentlands, by Sir Thomas Dalziel and his dragoons, and completely defeated. More than thirty of the prisoners were hanged; the remainder were sent to work as slaves in the sugar plantations of Barbados.

HOGENBURG'S PLAN OF EDINBURGH

Gives an impression of the Castle as it was before the siege of 1573 and its subsequent reconstruction.

The Duke of Lauderdale, to whom Charles had entrusted the direction of Scottish affairs, now attempted a policy of conciliation. By his advice, Letters of Indulgence were issued in 1669 and 1672, giving permission to the banished ministers to return to their churches without submitting themselves to the bishops, on certain conditions. Many ministers availed themselves of the Indulgences, but a remnant refused to give way, and although in 1670 attendance at conventicles had been declared to be a treasonable offence, they did not lack congregations. The worshippers were more careful now; they came to the conventicle fully armed and posted sentries to keep watch while the preaching went on. Their attempts to avoid arrest only made the Government all the more anxious to arrest them. Lauderdale and Charles looked with suspicion on these musterings of armed men, and guessed that another rebellion was afoot. So the screw was tightened; in 1678, 3,000 Lowland militia men and a "Highland Host" of 6,000 clansmen were sent into the south-west. The Highlanders were not cruel, but their habit of helping themselves to whatever they fancied in the houses where they were billeted did not endear them to their unwilling hosts.

These measures for preventing a rebellion only made a rebellion inevitable. At the beginning of May in 1679 Archbishop Sharp was dragged from his coach as he was crossing Magus Muir, near St. Andrews, and brutally murdered. A month later Captain John Graham of Claverhouse rode out from Hamilton with three troops of horse to disperse a conventicle. When he reached Drumclog, however, a stretch of marshy ground near Loudoun Hill, he found that he had to deal with a formidable body of armed men. His life guards and dragoons could not withstand the furious onslaught of the blue-bonneted country folk; they galloped pell-mell for Glasgow, leaving more than thirty of their comrades dead on the field. A few days later Glasgow itself was in the hands of the rebels. Their triumph was short lived; they could not agree on what they were fighting for, and a fortnight after they had entered Glasgow they were completely defeated by the Duke of Monmouth at Bothwell Brig. Fourteen hundred prisoners were taken to Edinburgh to be herded into Greyfriars Churchyard. A few were executed, but most were released on condition that they promised never again to take up arms against the King; almost three hundred, however, refused to make this promise, and were shipped off to America, but all except about forty of them were drowned when their ship was wrecked on the coast of Orkney.

Some of the Covenanters, however, refused to be taught anything by defeat. In 1680 a few of them, headed by the preacher Richard Cameron, rode into Sanquhar, and at the market cross declared war against the King and all who supported him. The government could see nothing ludicrous in the sight of one minister and a few score of west-country rustics "taking on" the whole forces of the British monarchy. Cameron himself was killed in a skirmish at Aird's Moss; his followers were hunted down and shot. They were declared rebels, men who had drawn the sword against the King, and so could not complain if they perished by the sword of his officers. Grim, unlovable men these Cameronians must have been, immovable in their opinions, certain that they were right and that the rest of the world was hopelessly wrong. Yet, if we cannot admire their intolerance, we must admire the courage which made them continue in a hopeless venture long after they knew it to be hopeless, and, when tortured by the thumb-screw or the boot, refuse to utter the word that would have saved their lives.

The government was now, however, pursuing a policy which was offensive to others besides the irreconcilable Cameronians. In 1681 a "Test" was imposed upon all ministers and all who held public office: they were required to repudiate the Covenants, to declare their adherence to the Confession of Faith of 1560, to acknowledge the King as "supreme governor of the realm, over all persons and in all causes as well ecclesiastical as civil" and to renounce any opposition to the government of church and state. Several of the Episcopalian clergy found it impossible to accept such obligations. The President of the Court of Session resigned rather than swear in these terms, and the Earl of Argyll, son of the Marquis who had opposed Charles I, was condemned for treason because he was willing to take the oath only "as far as it was consistent with itself," but he escaped to Holland. In 1684, too, proceedings were taken against several Presbyterian ministers who had availed themselves of the Indulgence, but were held not to have observed the conditions laid down, and they were forbidden to preach again.

When Charles II was succeeded in 1685 by his Roman Catholic

brother, James VII, the Earl of Argyll returned from his exile in Holland to head a rebellion. Disputes broke out among his followers; he disbanded his army, was captured, taken to Edinburgh, and executed. His attempt brought fresh misery upon the Covenanters: when word of his coming arrived, two hundred prisoners were packed off to Dunnottar Castle and lodged in a miserable dungeon, open to the sea wind and the east coast "haar." Their guards made them pay, not only for their food, but even for their drinking-water. If they refused, their portion of water was spilt on the prison floor. Many died, and some who tried to escape were tortured by having pieces of lighted tow tied between their fingers. After Argyll's rebellion had collapsed, those who agreed to accept the Test were released; the remainder were transported to the American Colonies.

The King meant, after he had undermined the Episcopalian establishment by granting freedom of worship to all his subjects, to establish Roman Catholicism in its place. Though everybody knew the purpose which lay behind the Letters of Indulgence issued in 1687, most of the Presbyterians, wearied out with persecution, were in no mood to look a gift horse in the mouth. Only the followers of Cameron remained obdurate. They would accept no favours from a King who had not taken the Covenant.

The resistance to the episcopalian policy of Charles II, though strenuous, had been limited to a few districts and largely to the lower classes: but the opposition to the popish policy of James VII was nation-wide. James had similarly alienated his English subjects, and in 1688 a revolution resulted in his flight to France and the acceptance of William of Orange, his son-in-law, as King of England. A number of Scots had already been in touch with William in Holland, and other Scottish peers and gentlemen met him in London and invited him to take over the administration of Scotland and summon a convention of estates. When it met, and showed that it had a majority for William, the supporters of James, or Jacobites, withdrew, under Graham of Claverhouse, now Viscount Dundee. William was then proclaimed King of Scots.

But the cause of James was not yet lost. Dundee had ridden to the Highlands to raise the clans for King James. A force of regulars, commanded by General Mackay, was sent after him.

The royal troops threaded the dangerous Pass of Killiekrankie unmolested, but when they emerged on the open ground at the head of the Pass they found Dundee waiting for them. It was the story of Tippermuir over again. One crashing volley, and then, before the soldiers could fix their bayonets, they saw, breaking through the smoke, a horde of half-naked Highlanders, yelling and brandishing their claymores and leathern targes. It was too much for them. They wavered and broke under the impetuous charge. Mackay, with a remnant of his troops, escaped, but hundreds of his soldiers lay dead on the battle-field or in the black pools of the Garry.

The victory of Killiecrankie availed James nothing, for Dundee was among the slain, and without a leader the Highlanders were useless. It is true that they advanced to Dunkeld, but Dunkeld was garrisoned by warriors as fierce as they were and far more obstinate—the Cameronians, who had been formed into a regular regiment. The Highlanders outnumbered them by four to one, but they held on after their colonel was killed, after their ammunition was exhausted, till finally Lowland "dourness" prevailed against Highland fire and dash, the attacks ceased, and the clansmen melted away.

The fear of the rebellion in the Highlands had not altogether disappeared when in 1690 the Scottish Parliament attempted a final settlement of the ecclesiastical problem. The Presbyterian majority in the Convention had forced William to accept a statement that "prelacy" was a grievance and ought to be abolished, and in the Covenanting south-west the Episcopalian ministers had been "rabbled" or driven out by the mob. But it was by no means clear that these actions represented the prevailing state of mind throughout the country, and William himself would have been quite ready to maintain Episcopacy had the bishops agreed to support him. However, when the bishops and many of the clergy declined to accept him as King he gave way, and agreed to a statute which established the Church of Scotland very much as we know it to-day. Presbyterian ministers who had been expelled during the two previous reigns were brought back to their parishes, and commissioners, appointed to exclude ministers whose life and doctrines seemed to be unsatisfactory, deprived hundreds of Episcopalian clergy. King William was not satisfied; it seemed to him that the triumphant

Presbyterians were persecuting the Episcopalians, as the Episcopalians had persecuted them, and he did not see why an Episcopalian clergyman should not remain undisturbed in his parish as long as he took the oath of allegiance, and kept his ideas about Church government to himself. Besides, comparatively few Presbyterian ministers were available, and it seemed foolish to deprive the Episcopalians and leave parishes without ministers. But King William's plan for a really comprehensive Church broke down, for the Presbyterians were afraid that if the numerous Episcopalian clergymen were allowed to remain in the Church they would recapture it and make it an Episcopal Church once more.

CHAPTER 21

SCOTLAND IN THE SEVENTEENTH CENTURY

THROUGHOUT much of the seventeenth century, Scotland, to outward appearance, differed little from the Scotland of 1513. Travellers from England, usually quick to criticise, admired the great unenclosed fields of oats and barley in Fife and the Lothians, but in reality very little additional land had been brought under the plough, and the old-fashioned, wasteful methods of cultivation still persisted. The old, simple economy still persisted too. When the countryman wanted a new suit, he handed the wool which he had shorn from his own sheep to his wife or daughter, who carded it and spun it on her own spinning-wheel. Next he took it to the local webster, who wove it into hodden grey cloth on the handloom which stood in his cottage. Even now he did not go to the tailor, he waited for the tailor to come to him. For the country tailor had no shop; he wandered from house to house, staying a day here and a day there, cutting out and sewing together the homespun garments. In the same way the careful housewife filled her linen cupboard: she spun the thread from flax gathered in the fields about her home, then made the webster weave it into sheets and napery. Just as the farmer often contented himself with growing only as much corn as his family could consume, so the housewife spun only as much yarn as her household would require.

Nor was there much change in the houses of the country folk; few of them could boast any better dwelling than the low-roofed hut of turf, where the only flooring was trodden earth or clay, and where the smoke from the hearth in the centre of the floor escaped through the unglazed windows, as well as through the chimney of clay in the thatched roof overhead.

Altogether, even in the well-cultivated, long-settled Lothians, it was not a smiling landscape that presented itself to the traveller from the south. Save in the neighbourhood of the houses of the country gentlemen, no trees or hedgerows gave variety to the monotonous expanse of cornland and pasture, and, in the first half of the century at least, even the lairds' mansion-house, with its iron-barred windows and pepper-box turrets, looked as grey and grim as a medieval fortress. In the second half of the century, however, the attempt to combine security with comfort was at last abandoned, and fine country houses, designed for purely domestic purposes, appeared. A close inspection of a seventeenth-century mansion would, moreover, have revealed some signs of an increasing regard for beauty and comfort, though the panelled walls seemed more gloomy than the old variegated tapestries. One or two pictures—mostly family portraits—added a little colour here and there. A ceiling, covered with frescoes or, more usually, intricate ornamentation in plaster-work, replaced the open rafters. Carpets appeared on the floors of the principal rooms; chairs were more plentiful, and also more comfortable, for they were padded and upholstered in leather and tapestry; the beds were now vast structures with four elaborately carved wooden posts supporting a wooden canopy, from which heavy curtains depended. Marble chimney-pieces were brought from Italy, and the Duke of Lauderdale believed that his were better than any he had seen in England.

Other changes were taking place in the country house. The hall now stood empty or was abandoned to the servants: the master of the house had dinner with his family or his guests in the smaller but more convenient dining-room; then, after the dishes of meat were removed from the table, he retired to the new withdrawing-room,[1] where dessert was served. Earthenware dishes now appeared on the table, though it was long till

[1] The modern form "drawing-room" began to displace the older form about 1642.

the old-fashioned pewter and tin plates disappeared; and since the establishment of a glass-works at Wemyss in 1619 drinking-glasses were quite common, though even the most fastidious hostess did not think it necessary to set forks before her guests.

Similar changes in the direction of increased comfort were taking place in the houses of the wealthy burgesses. There was one "improvement," however, that we can hardly admire—the bedrooms were now fitted with box-beds. The English traveller too, though his own standards of cleanliness were not too high, was shocked at the indifference to dirt and foul smells which the average Scotsman seemed to display. He was not astonished that he should be expected to convey his meat to his mouth with his fingers, or that all the water used in the house should be conveyed from wells in the street, or that the house should be devoid of drains and baths—it was what he was accustomed to at home—but he thought that the water might be fetched from the wells oftener than once in two days, that garbage should not be allowed to accumulate until the whole house reeked of it, and that the pewter platters need not appear with traces upon them of the previous meal—or previous week's meals! One consequence of the prevailing disregard for cleanliness was the pestilence which every few years devastated the crowded and noisome towns. To the pious, the pest was a judgement from heaven, sent to warn them against the Popish tendencies of their rulers; they observed a solemn fast, but made no attempt to cleanse their polluted highways and houses.

With the smell of Edinburgh in his nostrils the traveller found it difficult to do justice to the appearance of the town. It was now enclosed by the lofty Flodden Wall, pierced here and there by fortified ports or gates. The wall kept the town from spreading outwards, but it could not keep it from spreading upwards. The newer buildings rose six or seven stories into the air, and towered high above their predecessors.

The "closes" too, had ceased to be garden closes, and had become the closes that we know to-day—narrow covered passages leading through the older houses facing the street to the newer houses that now covered the sites of the vanished gardens. But among the dark and evil-smelling wynds and closes there was one noble thoroughfare; just as the modern visitor admires Princes Street, the seventeenth-century travellers admired the spacious street, lined with lofty stone houses, that stretched from the Castle to the Netherbow Port—a great fortified gateway guarding the lower end of the High Street—and thence, under the name of the Canongate, to the outer courtyard of Holyrood. In the Canongate there were now some spacious mansions, the town-houses of the nobility, and Holyrood Palace itself was reconstructed in Charles II's reign, most of it in an entirely new and very pleasing style. Travellers lamented, however, that the burgesses should spoil their houses by building projecting wooden galleries in front, which they usually boarded up to form additional rooms, with the result that the handsome stone buildings seemed to be only ramshackle structures of wood. Only two new churches—Greyfriars and the Tron—had been built in Edinburgh since the Reformation, for there were plenty of old ones. But a stately Parliament Hall rose a few yards to the south of St. Giles', and the ruins of the Kirk o' Field had been cleared away to make room for the buildings of the University.

There was little of the repose and quiet that one expected of a University town in the crowded wynds and streets of Old Edinburgh. The scholar who did not wish to be distracted by the skirling of fish-wives, the brawling of caddies or street porters, even the occasional clash of weapons, would find the quiet which he desired in—Glasgow! Travellers seemed to find some peculiar charm in this quiet little town, with its few streets set among gardens and orchards, its Bishop's Palace and its University, above which rose the stately Cathedral in almost all its ancient beauty. It reminded one visitor of Oxford. It is true that the trade of Glasgow increased rapidly during the century, so that it outstripped Dundee and became the most important town in Scotland next to the capital; as long, however, as the river on which it stood was so choked up with sand that no vessel of more than six tons could reach the wharf, it seemed impossible that it could ever be a port of any consequence.

It seemed impossible, too, that Scotland would ever be able to support its inhabitants, who by 1700 numbered about a million. To the Englishman, the Scot of this period seemed to be cautious and unenterprising; at a time when the English trader had taken his friezes and kerseys to the very ends of the earth, the Scottish trader cautiously followed the old trade routes to Veere and

THE TRON CHURCH, EDINBURGH

Built at the instance of Charles I, it was later reduced in size when the South Bridge was constructed.

Bordeaux. And he had little to bring to market except salted salmon, coarse woollen cloth, and coal, for the Scottish craftsman was as unenterprising as the Scottish trader, and, like him, was bound hand and foot by the rules of his gild. When we remember that the stagnation in trade was matched by the stagnation in agriculture, we cannot wonder that Scotland was confronted with an apparently insoluble unemployment problem.

In those days there was no Canada to beckon to the workless Scot. It is true that in 1621 Sir William Alexander had planned the colony of Nova Scotia, but this "New Scotland" was not seven days' but seven or eight weeks' voyage distant, and besides, in 1632 it had passed into the hands of France. So the wandering Scot kept on this side of the Atlantic; if his tastes lay in the direction of trade, he made his way to Poland, which was then a great kingdom, and, with a stock of merchandise small enough to be carried on his back, trudged from village to village. But he kept his Scottish pride; however small his pack, he called himself not a pedlar, but a merchant. The more adventurous Scot found employment of a different kind waiting for him on the Continent. In 1618 war had broken out between the Emperor [1] and the Protestant Elector Palatine, the son-in-law of James VI. It developed into a great struggle between the Catholic and Protestant princes of Central Europe, which dragged on for thirty years. During this period, Scottish soldiers crossed the seas in thousands—more than 3,000 left Scotland in 1626 and 6,000 in 1631—some to fight in the armies of the Emperor, some, like Dugald Dalgetty, to zigzag from one side to another, going where pay and rations seemed most attractive, most of them to follow the banner of Gustavus Adolphus of Sweden, the Protestant Champion.

Still there remained crowds of unemployed at home, drifting about the country with strange tales on their lips: those dark-complexioned folk who called themselves "Egyptians," [2] and

[1] The (Holy Roman) Emperor, in theory the successor of the Roman Emperors of the West, and of Charlemagne, was in practice the elected head of a loose confederacy of states, occupying in the seventeenth century much the same territory as Germany, Austria, and Czechoslovakia today. It became customary for the Emperor to be chosen from the ducal House of Austria. But the Hapsburg Emperors ruled Austria and Hungary as hereditary monarchs, not merely in their imperial capacity.

[2] Gipsies.

announced that they could see into the future—for a consideration; vagabond students requiring money to enable them to continue their studies; sailors, lately shipwrecked—if their story was to be believed; jugglers, minstrels, and story-tellers—all that joyous crowd for which there was no room in a Scotland that had grown serious. In 1579 Parliament had declared that all such vagabonds were to be arrested, flogged, and burned on the ear with a hot iron, but the Act had little effect. In 1616 the Privy Council complained bitterly that countless beggars lay in the Canongate, bawling for alms, or rising and crowding round any passer-by who chanced to stop for a moment, so that decent people were "fashed and wearied by them," but it could think of no better remedy than ordering the magistrates to expel them from the burgh. The gipsies met with sterner treatment. In 1636, for example, when the Privy Council heard that some gipsies had been lodged in the prison at Haddington for a month, it ordered the men to be hanged, and the women to be drowned, "because the keeping of them longer there is troublesome and burdenable to the town."

Parliament showed itself much more considerate to those whom it called aged, poor, impotent, and decayed persons. It was only fair that it should take some thought for them, for one of the complaints against the unreformed church had been its neglect and oppression of the poor and the reformers had professed an especial tenderness for "the poor labourers of the ground" and for those unable to work (but no sympathy for "stout and strong beggars"). The Parliaments of 1574 and 1579, which thundered against persons "able in body, living idly and fleeing labour," gave orders that beggars who could not work were to return to their own parishes, which were now authorised to tax themselves for the relief of their own poor. But few parishes were heroic enough to impose an adequate tax on themselves; in most places the kirk-session was content to draw upon the weekly collection in the plate at the church door and upon the income from "mortifications" or charitable bequests; when these sources proved insufficient, licences were issued to the poor people, allowing them to beg from house to house. A further Act of Parliament in 1672, which remained the foundation of the Poor Law until 1845, made little difference to the position.

The reformers had proposed the building up of a great educa-
ional system. At the time, nothing came of the plan; the men
vho had got the Church lands had no intention of giving them
ıp; and so the Reformation left the Scottish schools and colleges
oorer, if anything, than they had been before. But the plan
vas there; others in succeeding generations reared the structure.
lmost every burgh had its burgh school, and probably the major-
y of parishes in the Lowlands had schools, in terms of Acts of
rivy Council and Parliament passed in 1616 and 1633. These
cts, and also one passed during the Presbyterian ascendancy in
646, proposed that the heritors should be assessed for the upkeep
f the parish school.

The founding of Edinburgh University in 1582 gave Scotland
our Universities to England's two. Nor was the University
arred against the poor man's son. At the beginning of Novem-
er, when he had finished helping his father with the harvest,
he poor student came up to college, there to "cultivate the Muse
n a little oatmeal," till the end of the session in April when he
ft his books and returned to the plough and the harrow. But
he Universities had comparatively little to offer. Without
noney, they could not attract scholars of European renown to
e their professors nor build up a library like the Bodleian, in
vhich the student, weary of a ten times repeated lecture, could
xplore the realms of knowledge for himself. Yet they benefited
y gifts: the library of Edinburgh University had begun with a
equest from Clement Little, and in 1627 Drummond of Haw-
hornden, the poet, presented five hundred volumes to it. The
nost important development of the century, however, was the
oundation in 1682 of the Advocates' Library in Edinburgh,
vhich grew until in the twentieth century it became the National
ibrary of Scotland. If libraries were growing, laboratories
ardly yet existed, for though lectures on science were given,
hey were based on the teachings of Aristotle, who had died more
han two thousand years before, and neither lecturer nor student
hought it desirable to check Aristotle's statements by actual
xperiment. On the other hand, there were many developments
n scientific studies outside the universities: Scotland produced
ogarithms, the invention of John Napier of Merchiston; the
irst Scottish atlases were prepared, based on the work of Timothy
ont; James Gregory was one of the leading astronomers in

Britain; the Physic Garden, as the Royal Botanic Garden was at first called, was established in 1670; the Royal College of Physicians of Edinburgh was founded in 1681; and it was Sir Robert Moray, a Scot, who was first President of the Royal Society of London.

The seventeenth-century schoolboy went to school at six in the morning, and, although he was allowed to go home for breakfast and dinner, he was not dismissed finally till prayers had been said at six at night. Saturday was like other days, though once or at most twice a week the boys were allowed to go to some convenient field and play games under the watchful eye of one of the doctors, as the assistant masters were called. On Sunday they had to go to school before the morning service, to be catechised by the head master, and then conducted by him to the parish church. Holidays were given grudgingly, and the Protestant suspicion of the old festivals of the Church tended to make them fewer and shorter. And even when he played with his fellows in the school yards, the schoolboy could not be quite at his ease; he was required to speak Latin all the time If he used his own Lowland tongue, his words would be noted by one of the "lupi," or secret censors, and carried to the head master, who would promptly apply the rod. For Latin was still a spoken language. All the lectures in the Universities, both in Britain and on the Continent, were delivered in Latin; scientist and philosophers still wrote in Latin, and so in those days the man who knew Latin had a tremendous advantage over the man who did not.

There was too much Latin altogether in their school curriculum. It was not the business of the Grammar School to deal in such vanities as Art and Science, French or English, and one shudders to think of what would have happened to any venturesome "doctor" who put English play-books into the hands of his pupils, and made them study *The Merchant of Venic* as carefully as they studied Terence's *Phormio*. The literature o the period, both in prose and verse, when it was not in Latin was not in Scots either, for the Reformation, followed by the Union of the Crowns, had led to the adoption of English as th literary language of Scotland. A great deal of verse was produced but against the mighty array of English writers headed by Shakespeare and Milton we can put only the figure of Drummond of Hawthornden, a true but not a highly original poet.

Although the reformed Church was critical of drama, and the nore puritanical utterly condemned it, it was hardly ever ntirely suppressed, and in the Restoration period it flourished, n Edinburgh at least, under the patronage of the Lord High Commissioner and his court. The rising standards of culture nd taste which are apparent everywhere we look in this century —house-building, church-building and church-restoration, educaion and intellectual activity—can be seen also in music. James VI had been interested in music, at least to the extent of patronising English musicians and restoring revenues to the Chapel Royal, and Charles I continued his policy. The much-maligned Prayer Book of 1637 laid a new emphasis on music, and a new ersion of the metrical psalms—attributed to King James but argely the work of Sir William Alexander, Earl of Stirling—was published, far superior by literary standards to earlier ersions, but doomed to be discarded along with the Prayer Book. In 1635 there appeared also a new Psalter with musical ettings, all the tunes being arranged in four-part harmony and ome of them having elaborate versions requiring highly-trained hoirs; musicians have never ceased to praise this Psalter.

No doubt the disturbances caused by the Civil War checked or a time the full blossoming of Scottish culture, and the victory f the Presbyterians, whose thought was so largely dominated by English Puritanism, gave the kirk-sessions and presbyteries an pportunity to curb many expressions of artistic impulses. It must not be forgotten, too, that the kirk-sessions felt that they ad to deal with more dangerous enemies than actors or singers. Were there not in every town and village warlocks and witches, men and women who had sold themselves to the Devil? Proably some old pagan creed that had lain half-remembered in ne minds of men for centuries had come to the surface again. Certainly there were people who professed to have some magical ower, spae-wives who assured their dupes that they could see nto the future, find stolen goods, cause winds to blow or cease, crops to flourish or wither at their pleasure. Usually they were uilty of nothing more than obtaining money under false retences. It made no difference: should the minister suspect ne of his parishioners of dealing in magic and spells, she was aled before the kirk-session, and, if possible, bullied into an dmission that she had gained her skill from the Devil himself.

The kirk-session then reported to the Privy Council, whicl commissioned special judges, usually local lairds or magistrates to go on with the case. If the accused had confessed nothing cruel and senseless tests were employed. She might be bound anc flung into a pond; if she floated, it was a sign that the pure elemen would not receive her guilty body, so she was taken out, strangled and burned. No one was safe, for an accusation of witchcraft wa discovered to be a convenient way of getting rid of an incon- venient enemy. And the shadow showed no sign of passing The triumph of the Presbyterians in 1638 increased instead o diminishing the tyranny of superstition; in 1643 thirty witche were burned in Fife alone.

One wonders if, from the terror-laden streets of the Lowlanc towns, people sometimes looked curiously to the blue Highlanc hills, to the land where the new religion sat on men as lightl as the old and where murder never masqueraded as zeal for th purity of the Church. Probably they did not: to them th Highlands were still an alien and hostile land that they woulc never dream of visiting. Scotland was to all intents and purpose two countries; there was more difference between a burges from Perth and a MacGregor from the braes of Balquhidde than there would be between a burgess of Perth and a burges of Paris. Let us imagine them standing together. There is th man from Perth in his broad blue Scots bonnet, his close-fittin doublet, with a narrow linen collar at the neck, his voluminou breeches, rather like the modern "plus fours," stockings of cloth and buckled shoes. Beside him stands the Highlander; his chie garment is a tartan plaid wrapped round his body and held i place by a belt at the waist, his legs are bare, on his feet are shoe of untanned deerskin. They cannot communicate, for th Highlander speaks nothing but Gaelic. Should the burges invite the Highlander to spend the night with him, if we ca imagine such a thing happening, his guest would scorn the box bed. He would place the mattress on the floor, and even the be uneasy because of the unusual comfort. For to the mos luxurious feather-bed in the world the Highlander preferred hi own couch made of bundles of heather, though, when he ha no choice, he could sleep out of doors in the winter snow, with hi plaid wrapped tightly round him. In other ways he was mor of a Spartan than the burgess; he could march for a whole da on a mouthful of oatcake or barley-bread. Work at the loom or the bench he despised, and he preferred fishing or hunting or rounding up the cattle of the Lowland laird to handling the spade or the sickle.

Furthermore, while the bond between baron and vassal had slackened in the Lowlands, the bond that united the Highlander to his chief was as strong as it had ever been. For the Highlander could not think of himself as a solitary individual fighting for his own hand; he belonged to a special community—the clan—all the members of which followed a chief. Although the rank and file of a clan neither bore the same surname as the chief—or as yet bore any surname at all—nor were related by blood to the chief, yet the clansman regarded the chief as more worthy of respect than his own father. To obey him without question was the first and plainest of his duties, to die for him the highest of privileges. The chief, for his part, knew that something was expected of him in return. He had to keep open house; to suffer scores of idle clansmen to live within the walls of his castle and to eat at his table. It was a sad expense, but wealth in fighting-men was preferable to wealth in money or cattle, when one had to do battle with a rival chieftain.

Even the Highlands, however, grew more orderly in the course of the seventeenth century and throughout Scotland generally one of the most important things that happened between 1600 and 1700 was that the country was transformed from one in which the law had been often ill-enforced and often disregarded to one in which the law was generally obeyed. After the troubled minority of James VI, Scotland had enjoyed a period of continuously stable government such as she had hardly ever enjoyed before, and after 1603, with the King in remote security in England, there could be no more "raids" or palace revolutions on behalf of this or that faction among the nobles. James was, besides, a peace-lover by temperament and a peace-maker by policy, ever ready either to reconcile or to repress such of his subjects as were disposed to revive old feuds. After the troubles of the 1640s, Scotland was again subjected to a period of severe disciplining at the hands of the Cromwellian army of occupation, and it was said that this brought about conditions more orderly than had ever been known before. Throughout the whole century the Privy Council was assiduous in its attention to breaches of the law, and in 1672 Scotland at last got a permanent central court for criminal justice—the High Court of Justiciary. Very remarkable results in the extension of law and order were obtained, in the reigns of James VI and his successors, without anything like a modern police force, in the main without a standing army and with only occasional resort to military force. Very likely a good deal of the credit is due to the bishops, the ministers and the kirk-sessions and their persistent work, in alliance with central and local authorities, to uphold certain standards of conduct. But it is hard to escape the conclusion that the essential change was a change in the outlook of the people of Scotland, who were in the main becoming more interested in peaceful pursuits and more satisfied with the slowly, but steadily improving economic conditions in which they lived.

CHAPTER 22

DARIEN AND THE UNION

THE Union of the Crowns had not removed the danger of disputes with England. To all appearance, that union left Scotland a completely independent country, with its own Parliament and Privy Council, its own laws and law-courts. To all appearance, allegiance to the same sovereign was the only tie that bound the two countries together. But had that independence been as complete as it seemed, it would have involved both countries in serious difficulties. Suppose England wanted to enter upon war with France or Holland, and suppose Scotland was determined to stay out—what then? As a matter of fact Scotland never could stay out of a war in which England was involved. The war between England and France which broke out in the reign of Charles I resulted in the loss to Scotland of her one colony—Nova Scotia—and though the Dutch had granted valuable trading privileges to Scottish merchants, though the bulk of the Scottish exports to the Continent passed through the Dutch port of Veere, Scotland was twice dragged into war with Holland in the reign of Charles II. For Scotland was not

PARLIAMENT HALL, EDINBURGH

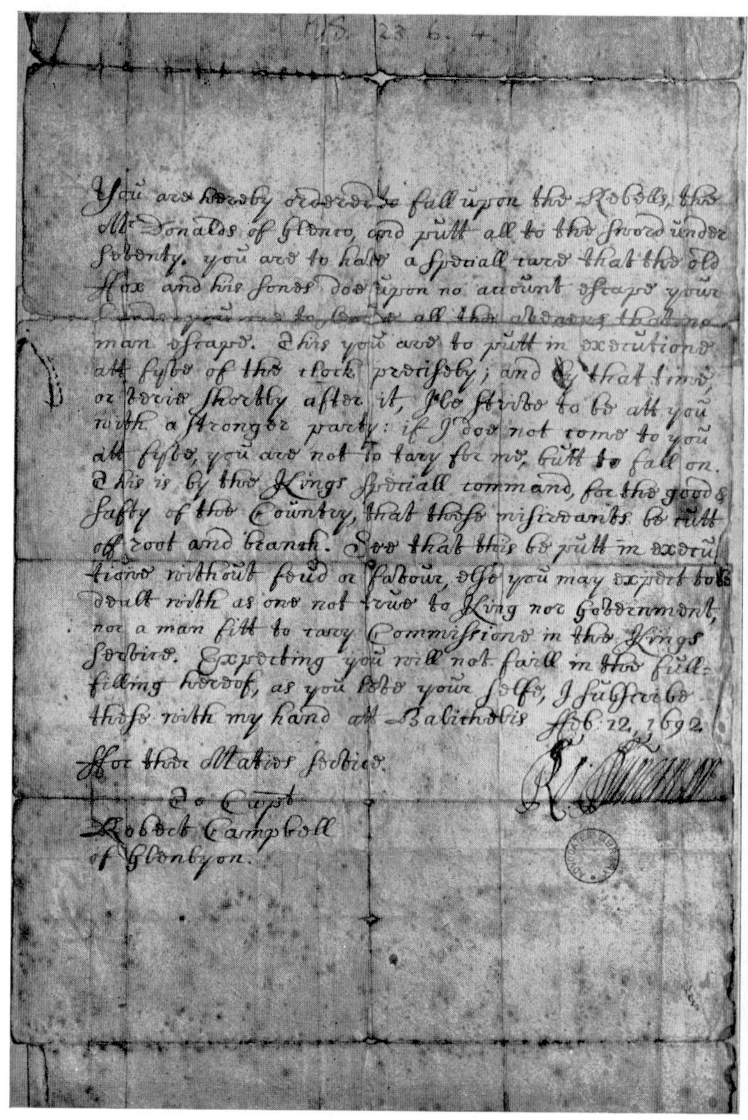

You are hereby ordered to fall upon the Rebells, the
Mc Donalds of Glenco, and putt all to the sword under
seventy. you are to have a speciall care that the old
Fox and his sones doe upon no account escape your
hands, you are to secure all the avenues that no
man escape. This you are to putt in execution
att fyve of the clock precisely; and by that time,
or verie shortly after it, I'le strive to be att you
with a stronger party: if I doe not come to you
att fyve, you are not to tarry for me, but to fall on.
This is by the Kings speciall command, for the good &
safty of the Country, that these miscreants be cutt
off root and branch. See that this be putt in execu-
tione without feud or favour, else you may expect to be
dealt with as one not true to King nor Government,
nor a man fitt to carry Commissione in the Kings
service. Expecting you will not faill in the full-
filling hereof, as you love your selfe, I subscribe
these with my hand att Balicholis Feb: 12, 1692.

For their Majties service.

R. Duncanson

To Capt.
Robert Campbell
of Glenlyon.

Order for the Massacre of Glencoe

Directed by Major Duncanson to Captain Robert Campbell of Glenlyon.

really independent: James VI and his successors chose and dismissed their ministers without consulting the Scottish Parliament, nor did Parliament object, for the control which the sovereign exercised over the election of the Lords of the Articles made it a most obliging and accommodating body.

At last, in the year 1690, King William consented to the abolition of the Committee of the Articles, though he refused to surrender the right of appointing what ministers he pleased. At the same time, the abolition of Episcopacy meant the elimination of bishops from Parliament, and the new Presbyterian Church showed no desire for parliamentary representation. At last the Scottish Parliament seemed free. But it soon found that it was not free to do what most Scots now thought it was most desirable to do, and that was to expand Scotland's overseas trade.

England was the obstacle. In 1651 the English Parliament had passed a Navigation Act, which forbade goods to be imported into England and its colonies unless they were carried in English ships or in ships belonging to the country in which the goods were produced. The complete union of the two countries two years later shielded the Scottish merchants from the evil effects of the Act, but at the Restoration, when the countries once more had their separate Parliaments, a Navigation Act was again passed and Scots were deprived of the privileges which the English merchants enjoyed. The captain of a Scottish ship could no longer bring French silks and wines into an English port; he could take Scottish goods only, and on these he had to pay higher customs dues than his English rival. He might, if he chose, take Scottish linens and woollens into a port in the North American Colonies, but he did not choose, for he knew that though he was allowed to bring Scottish goods in, he was not allowed to take Colonial goods out.

To make matters worse, the powerful English trading companies considered that they had the sole right of trading with certain regions; a Scottish merchant who attempted to trade with India must expect the implacable hostility of the East India Company, if he thereupon took his goods to any part of Africa he would be warned off by the African Company. Turn where he might, the Scottish merchant found his English rival blocking the way.

William of Orange has been reputed to have been a wise and conscientious ruler but, as we shall see, the black business of Glencoe and the blacker business of Darien seemed to prove that he did not care what happened to his Scottish subjects.

Since, in spite of the failure of the Killiecrankie campaign, many of the Highland chiefs still remained faithful to the exiled King, a proclamation was issued ordering every chief to take the oath of allegiance to King William before January 1st, 1692. All the chiefs but two, MacDonnell of Glengarry and MacIan of Glencoe, took the oath before the appointed date. Glengarry was head of a formidable clan and master of a powerful fortress; MacIan was the chieftain of a small sept or branch of the Clan MacDonald, and dwelt in a narrow glen four miles long, the outlets from which could easily be blocked. William, advised by Sir John Dalrymple, the Master of Stair,[1] sent a letter to the general commanding the royal forces in the Highlands, ordering him to give Glengarry a second chance but adding, "If MacIan of Glencoe and that tribe can be well separated from the rest, it will be a proper vindication of public justice to extirpate that sect of thieves."

Dalrymple was aware, and perhaps William was aware too, that MacIan had really meant to take the oath and had made his way to Fort William before the end of the year, only to be told by the officer there that he should have gone to the Sheriff at Inveraray, that he had struggled through snow-blocked passes and arrived at Inveraray three days late, but three days in front of the Sheriff, and that when the Sheriff did appear on the 6th of January he was so much moved by the old chieftain's tears that he allowed him to take the oath. It mattered nothing to Dalrymple, he had intended to make an example of MacIan all along, and now MacIan had delivered himself into his hands. William, his mind full of weightier matters, did not trouble to find out precisely what Dalrymple meant to do.

At the beginning of February 1692 the inhabitants of Glencoe were alarmed by the appearance among them of a company of soldiers. They soon recovered from their alarm, however, when they discovered that the commander of the royal troops was Captain Campbell of Glenlyon, whose niece was the wife of MacIan's second son. The soldiers were billeted in the cottages

[1] Master: the title given to the eldest son of some Scottish noblemen.

scattered up and down the glen, and soon made friends with the clansmen. Glenlyon spent much of his time drinking with old MacIan or playing cards with his sons, and when MacIan invited him to bring two of his officers with him to dinner on the 13th of February he did not refuse.

MacIan little knew that his guest had just received a letter containing the following words: "You are hereby ordered to fall upon the McDonalds of Glencoe and put all to the sword under seventy; you are to have a speciall care that the old fox and his sons doe on no account escape your hands." He little knew that four hundred soldiers were being moved up to block the southern end of the glen, and that another four hundred were making for the northern entrance.

Very early in the morning of the 13th the work of slaughter began. Parties of soldiers went from house to house, shooting the sleeping or half-awakened occupants, driving off the cattle and setting fire to the thatch. MacIan was shot down by one of the officers whom he had invited to dinner; a soldier tore the rings from his wife's fingers with his teeth. Among the slain were three or four women and a boy of six, who clung to Glenlyon's knees and offered to be his slave if only he would spare his life. As if to add to the terrors of the morning, snow began to fall heavily. But the snow acted as a screen to the dwellers in the more remote cottages, who, warned by the sound of firing, escaped by the unguarded outlets from the pass. For the plot had miscarried: the soldiers who should have guarded the northern end failed to arrive in time. Mischief enough had been done, for twenty-five or thirty people were slain by the soldiers, and others, who escaped for a time, perished in the snow.

At first the average Lowlander looked on the affair as nothing more than an ordinary clan fight and refused to listen to the Jacobite pamphleteers who insisted that William was at the bottom of the business. But William's reluctance to order an inquiry, his strange action in pardoning Dalrymple after being compelled by the Scottish Parliament to dismiss him from office, and his neglect to send the guilty soldiers home for trial, made the average Lowlander feel that there must be some truth in the accusations of the Jacobites.

And soon the Lowlander too had cause, or thought he had cause, to curse King William's lack of regard for his Scottish subjects. So far the Scottish merchants had complained bitterly of the privileges which English traders and trading companies enjoyed, but they had done nothing more. Now in 1695 there appeared in Edinburgh a man who claimed to have found a remedy for Scotland's worst ills. This was William Paterson, the roving financial genius who in the previous year had founded the Bank of England. Paterson's plan was a simple one: the English Parliament had granted monopolies to English trading companies; let the Scottish Parliament therefore grant a monopoly of trade with Africa and the Indies to a Scottish trading company. The Scottish company must then make haste to gain what Paterson called "the Door of the Seas, the key of the Universe"—the unoccupied Isthmus of Darien. For Paterson was confident that sooner or later Darien would become the centre of the world's commerce, that goods destined for India, instead of being sent round the Cape of Good Hope or the more perilous Cape Horn, would simply be shipped to some port on the eastern side of Darien, then carried across the narrow isthmus to a port on the western side, where ships that had come from India would be waiting. Thus the merchandise of Europe and the merchandise of Asia would be exchanged, not in Europe or Asia, but in Darien.

To plant a settlement like this, with its harbours and roads, forts and fleets, would be an expensive business, too expensive for a poverty-stricken country like Scotland; but Paterson knew that there were other English merchants besides those who were members of the African or East India Company who wanted to trade with Africa and India, and he knew that these unprivileged merchants would be glad to become members of a Scottish trading company.

In June 1695 the Scottish Parliament passed an Act establishing "the Company of Scotland Trading to Africa and the Indies," or the Darien Company, as it is usually called. Its capital was to be £600,000, but only half that sum was to be subscribed by the Scottish shareholders.

At first everything went well; English investors speedily subscribed the £300,000 which was their share of the capital. Meantime the directors of the English East India Company saw that if they did not act their monopoly would be broken and their Company ruined—already the price of its stock was falling with disastrous rapidity—so they set to work, and soon the English

Parliament declared that it meant to impeach the leading English members of the Scottish Company. The threat was enough; the English investors at once withdrew their money. William himself frowned on the scheme. He could not support the Scots Company without breaking the monopoly of the English companies, and the privileges which the English merchants enjoyed, legally conferred by the English Parliament, could not be disregarded without creating indignation in England. And William was all along conscious of something to which his Scottish subjects hardly gave a thought: he was endeavouring to settle the question of the succession to the Spanish throne by negotiations which he hoped would prevent a war in which Britain and Holland would be fighting for their very existence against the forces of Louis XIV of France. It was of the utmost importance that he should have Spain on his side, but if he were to support a scheme for planting a Scottish colony in territory claimed by the Spanish government, he would certainly drive Spain into the ranks of his enemies.

The opposition of the King and of the English Parliament raised the enthusiasm of the Scots to a veritable frenzy; £400,000 of the necessary £600,000 they would find themselves, the remainder they would get on the Continent. But though agents of the Company crossed to Hamburg they found that the representative of the English Government had been there before them; the foreign merchants would not subscribe a penny unless they could get a definite assurance from King William that he approved of the Scottish Company, and this assurance the King was careful not to give.

Though it was hopeless to go on with insufficient capital, national pride would not permit the scheme to be abandoned. A great effort was made, the whole of the £400,000 was subscribed, and in July 1698 the ships *Caledonia*, *St. Andrew*, and *Unicorn* with twelve hundred emigrants on board, freighted besides with the hopes of a whole nation, set sail from the port of Leith. Paterson himself accompanied the expedition.

In November Darien was reached. The emigrants were enchanted by the first prospect of New Caledonia, as they had decided to call their settlement. "The Soil is rich," said one of them, "the Air good and temperate, the Water is Sweet, and everything contributes to make it healthful and convenient. . . .

We are certainly much bound to Providence in this affair." The natives were not unfriendly, the gift of a hat laced with gold won them the good favour of the most important chief, a pompous little Indian called Andreas, who appeared before them in a gay scarlet coat, but with no shoes or stockings. On a little promontory they built a fort, to which they gave the name of Fort St. Andrew, and busied themselves in putting up huts and in making clearings in "the legion of monstrous plants," where they tried to grow yams and maize.

The glamour soon faded from the scene, they grew tired of the chattering monkeys, and the brilliant but songless birds which flashed through the gloom of the tropical forests. The captain of the *St. Andrew* might declare that the harbour beside the fort could easily contain a thousand of the greatest merchantmen in the world; what did that matter when only one or two ships appeared—ships whose business was not to trade but to spy? The Indians were willing to accept presents, but showed no anxiety to buy the wigs, stockings, and Bibles which the colonists tried to sell to them.

The prospect of financial ruin was bad enough, but the prospect of starving to death in a foreign land was worse. The colonists had been sent off with only six months' provisions, instead of the supplies for nine months which had been promised them. They tried to get provisions from Jamaica, but in vain; King William had issued a proclamation forbidding the English colonists in America to have any dealings with the Scottish settlers. And behind the spectre of famine loomed the spectre of pestilence; fever broke out and slew one out of every four among the wretched adventurers. There was nothing for it but to abandon the colony, and in July 1699 the survivors re-embarked. But they took the fever aboard with them, and little more than half of those who set sail from Darien put into port in the English colonies.

News travelled slowly in those days, and so it came about that a few weeks after the survivors of the first expedition had left, a second contingent of three hundred colonists arrived. They could do nothing but turn about—not, however, before one of their two ships was burned—and make for Jamaica.

At the end of September, just when a third expedition of 1,300 settlers was ready to sail, vague rumours of the disaster reached Scotland. The commander of the expedition, however, started off without waiting to find out what truth was in the rumours and involved the third expedition in a bigger disaster than had befallen the first.

Hitherto the unhealthy climate had been the worst enemy that the settlers had to contend with, but now they had to reckon with another foe. Though the Spaniards knew better than to attempt to settle in this extremely unhealthy part of the coast, they were firmly resolved that no other European colonists must be allowed to establish themselves there. So, soon after they landed and reoccupied the deserted Fort St. Andrew the colonists learned that a Spanish army and fleet were moving against them. In vain the gallant Campbell of Fonab attempted to delay the Spaniards by storming their encampment; Fort St. Andrew was soon blockaded both by land and sea. Already the fort was no better than a pest-house, but the Scots stubbornly defended it for more than a month; only when the number of men able to handle a musket was reduced to three hundred did they surrender.

The Spaniards had admired their bravery, and allowed them to march out as if in triumph, with drums beating and colours flying, but they had to leave Darien. The sorry history of the first expedition was repeated; fever slew them by the hundred on their voyage to the English colonies.

The Darien Scheme had ended in complete and disastrous failure. Two hundred thousand pounds, and what was worse, the lives of more than two thousand men, had been flung away.

It is easy for us to apportion the blame, to say that people who knew nothing about tropical medicine—who tried to fight yellow fever with whisky—had no right to complain if they fell mortally ill when they went to a tropical country. But to the Scotsman of the time the villain of the piece was King William.

The lesson of Darien was clear, and the more far-sighted statesmen in both England and Scotland began to realise what William realised: the only way to avoid the confusion caused by the Scottish Parliament granting to Scottish merchants privileges which the English Parliament had already granted to English merchants, the only way to keep the Scottish Parliament from ruining his carefully calculated foreign policy, was to unite the Scottish Parliament to the English Parliament. William made an attempt to get the English Parliament to consider a scheme for union, but the Commons would have nothing to do with it. Even when he lay on his death-bed in the early weeks of 1702, he sent a second appeal to the English Parliament, but again no heed was paid to his request. Queen Anne's appeals were more successful, but though in the first year of her reign representatives of the two countries met at Whitehall to draw up a treaty of union, nothing came of the negotiations; the Scots would accept the Union only if they were to be admitted to the trading privileges which the English enjoyed, privileges which the English representatives obstinately refused to part with.

It is little wonder that the Scottish Parliament which met in 1703 showed rather an ugly temper. Two years previously the English Parliament had declared in the Act of Settlement that if Anne died without children the crown would go to the Electress Sophia of Hanover, a grand-daughter of James VI, and her descendants; now the Scottish Parliament passed an Act of Security, which declared that unless Scotland received the same trading privileges as England, the Scots would choose a sovereign of their own after the death of Queen Anne. This Bill, which could have effected the complete separation of the two kingdoms, the Queen naturally refused to accept, whereupon the Scottish Parliament refused to vote supplies, and forced her to give her assent before the end of 1704. But intimidation was a game at which two could play. In February 1705 the English Parliament passed the Alien Act, which prohibited the importation of cattle, linen, and coals—almost the only commodities which the Scots could export—from Scotland into England, and declared that if at the end of the year the Scottish Parliament still refused to fall into line with the English Parliament about the question of the succession or, alternatively, to agree to treat for union, then all Scots would be treated as aliens.

Meantime English interference with Scottish trade continued. After the settlement on the Isthmus had been abandoned the Darien Company attempted once or twice to send merchant ships to Africa and India, but one of these, the *Annandale*, was captured and retained by the English, and another, the *Speedy Return*, disappeared. So when the English merchant ship *Worcester* was driven into the Firth of Forth in August 1704 it was promptly seized to compensate for the *Annandale*. That was not all. The rumour spread that the apparently innocent

PLATE 56 GEORGE HERIOT'S SCHOOL, EDINBURGH

George Heriot (1563-1624), jeweller to James VI, left his fortune to endow a 'hospital' or boarding school for boys. The building, completed about 1650, is an outstanding example of the architecture of the period.

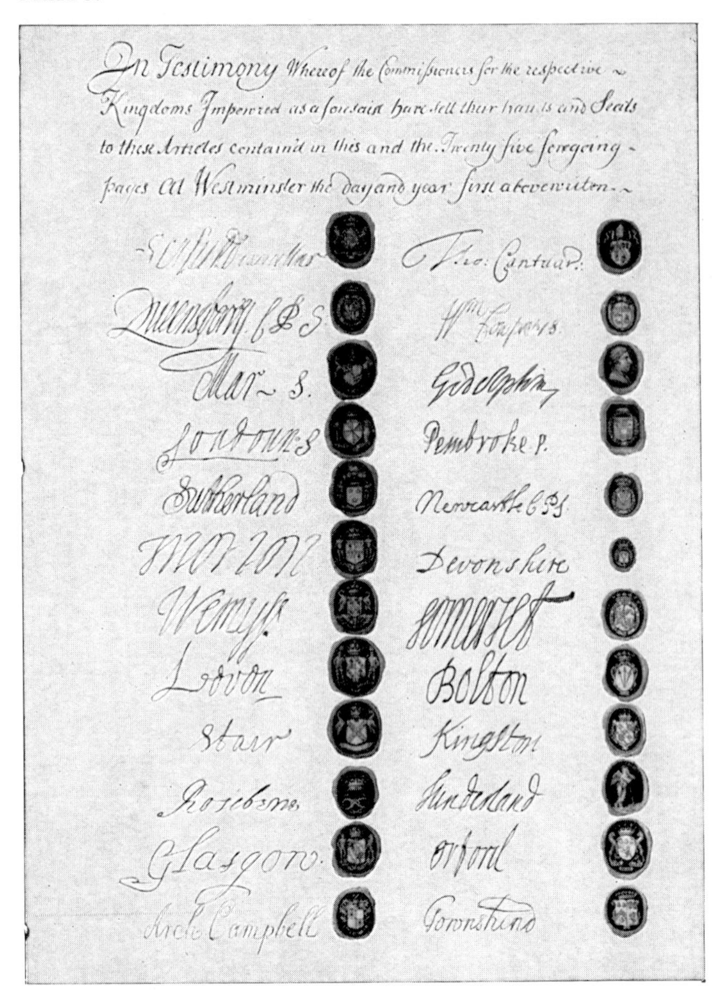
In Testimony Whereof the Commissioners for the respective Kingdoms Impowered as aforesaid have sett their hands and Seals to these Articles contain'd in this and the Twenty five foregoing pages At Westminster the day and year first abovewritten.

Seafield Cancellar — Tho: Cantuar:
Queensberry C P S — Wm Cowper C S
Mar S. — Godolphin
Loudoun S — Pembroke P.
Sutherland — Newcastle C P S
Morton — Devonshire
Wemyss — Somerset
Leven — Bolton
Stair — Kingston
Rosebery — Sunderland
Glasgow. — Orford
Archd Campbell — Townshend

THE TREATY OF UNION

The articles of Union, signed by the Scottish and English Commissioners on 22 July 1706.

merchant ship was a pirate, and that it had sunk the *Speedy Return*. As a matter of fact there was not a word of truth in the story; the *Speedy Return* had itself turned pirate. It made no difference; the captain and crew were arrested, and though there was not a shred of evidence to justify the verdict, they were found guilty. The knowledge that two of the crew of the *Speedy Return* had actually landed in England, the Queen's orders that a reprieve should be granted, weighed less with the judges than their fears of the Edinburgh mob; in April 1705 Captain Green and two of his men were hanged on the sands of Leith, between high and low water mark.

This was nothing less than murder, though murder disguised under the forms of justice, and for a time it seemed as if war could be its only sequel. But though the English people were furious, the English Government did not want war with Scotland at a time when it required all its resources for the struggle with France. The alternative to war was a closer union, so in summer the Duke of Argyll was despatched to Edinburgh as High Commissioner to persuade the reluctant Scottish Parliament to open negotiations for a treaty of union. After more than a month of fierce debate the Scottish Parliament consented; it was arranged that thirty-one Scottish Commissioners should be appointed by the Queen to meet an equal number of English Commissioners.

With the repeal of the Alien Act at the end of the year the relations between the two countries became less strained, and in April 1706 the representatives of the two countries met in the palace at Whitehall. Though each side wanted some sort of a union, each side was determined to keep as much and to give away as little as it could. The Scots, for example, contended that the union of the two countries need not involve the disappearance of the Scottish Parliament, that questions which affected both nations might be settled either in a joint session of both Parliaments, or by a body of members drawn from both Parliaments. They demanded, in other words, a federal union. But the English contended that this was too small a price for the Scots to pay for complete commercial equality with England, and demanded an incorporating union. It was agreed, therefore, that there should be one Parliament for the whole of Great Britain, and that to it Scotland should send sixteen Peers and forty-five members of the House of Commons. England had five hundred and twelve members in the House of Commons, and the Scottish proportion was fixed by striking a balance between the population of Scotland, which was about a fifth of that of England, and the revenue of Scotland, which was estimated to be only one-fortieth of that of England. On the death of Queen Anne, the Electress Sophia of Hanover and her descendants were to be sovereigns of this now United Kingdom. In return for the loss of their Parliament the Scots would be granted "full freedom and intercourse of trade and navigation," but with equality of privileges went equality of burdens; customs duties in Scotland would be raised to the English level. On the other hand, a sum of £398,085 10*s*.—the Equivalent as it was called—was to be paid over by the English Government, mainly as compensation to the shareholders in the Darien Company. Further; there was to be a common coinage—at this time the pound Scots was worth only twenty pence in English money—and a common system of weights and measures. But the smaller country was not to be entirely absorbed into the greater: it was still to have its own law courts and its own code of laws; the private law courts of the great nobles—abolished at the Restoration in England—were to be retained in Scotland, and the royal burghs were to keep their peculiar privileges.

At the beginning of October 1706 the Scottish Parliament met to consider whether it should accept or reject the Treaty. Rejection seemed more probable than acceptance, for the Country Party or Opposition outnumbered the Court Party or Government Party, and the clamorous mob which filled Parliament Square every day did their best to make rejection certain. Even the Duke of Queensberry, the High Commissioner, was not safe; the mob on one occasion tried to attack him and chased his coach down the Canongate to Holyrood. Not till three regiments of soldiers had been called in to keep order in the city were the members of Parliament able to go on with their deliberations without fear of disturbance. Things were worse in Glasgow, where a minister had wound up his sermon on the Treaty with the words, "Up and be valiant for the city of our God." As a result of his eloquence a riot broke out; the Provost, far from being able to control the disturbers of the peace, was forced to hide in a box-bed, and the town remained in the hands of the mob for more than a month.

But the Opposition was not really united. One section, the Jacobites, would not have the Treaty at any price; another, the "Squadrone Volante," had hovered between the Court Party and the Country Party, and had committed itself to neither. When at the beginning of November the first article of the Treaty was discussed, Lord Belhaven's stately rhetoric, his impressive description of "our ancient mother Caledonia . . . sitting in the midst of our senate . . . waiting for her own children to deal the fatal blow" moved the house less than the short speech of Lord Marchmont which followed it: "Behold, he dreamed, but lo! when he awoke, he found it was a dream." When the article was put to the vote, the "Squadrone Volante" went over to the Government side and voted for acceptance.

The Opposition, however, could not see that they were beaten; they insisted on a lengthy discussion of every one of the twenty-five articles in the Treaty. Meantime the passing of an Act of Security, giving a definite assurance that no alteration in the Church of Scotland would be attempted, removed the fears of the Presbyterians, and in January 1707 the High Commissioner touched the Act with his sceptre, in token of the royal approval.

From Edinburgh the Treaty, in which the Act of Security was now embodied, went to Westminster, but it met with no opposition in the English Parliament, and on 6th March, 1707, the royal assent was given.

A few days later, on the 25th of March, 1707, to be exact, the Scottish Parliament met for the last time. There were no displays of stately oratory, no moving farewells, only the transaction of a few trivial pieces of business. Why should the members feel shame for what they had done and shed tears over it? They were not traitors who had been bribed by English gold to sell the independence of their country, but practical men confronted with the task of extricating their country from an exceedingly perilous position. Perhaps they had conceded too much to the English Government, but they could console themselves with the thought that the terms were the best that could be obtained in the circumstances. And if there was no impassioned eloquence there was cold common sense in the words with which the High Commissioner brought the Session—and the Parliament—to a close.

"The public business of this session now being over, it is full time to put an end to it.

"I am persuaded that we and all posterity will reap the benefit of the Union of the two kingdoms, and I doubt not . . . that you will promote an universal desire in this kingdom to become one in hearts and affections, as we are inseparably joined in interest, with our neighbour nation."

CHAPTER 23

THE MAKING OF INDUSTRIAL SCOTLAND

The Scots had been enticed into the Union by the prospects of economic advantage. The ultimate results, as this chapter will show, fully justified their far-sightedness, but the Union did not bring immediate prosperity to Scotland and its first effect was to depress, not to stimulate, the trade of the country. A major change like the union of two countries had inevitably to be followed by a period of adjustment, in the economic field as in others, and about half a century passed before it was clear that Scotland as a whole would gain. At first, free trade with England meant the end of the system of controls which previously, and especially since the Restoration, had been imposed to foster Scottish manufactures. There had been restrictions on the import of manufactured goods which could compete with the home products and on the export of the raw materials which, policy dictated, should be kept in Scotland and used for manufacture at home. Patents and monopolies had been granted by the Scottish government, and companies had been formed to finance various manufactures, such as the weaving of woollen and linen cloth, the making of soap and glass and the refining of sugar. With the union and the abolition of the customs barrier between England and Scotland, all the import duties which protected Scottish manufactures were swept away and English manufactured goods, often of better quality and in any event produced on a large scale and in consequence cheaper, were able to flood the market in Scotland and drive Scottish manufacturers out of business. Much the same thing had happened before, during the Commonwealth period, when there had likewise been free trade between England and Scotland.

It is true that if Scotland had the same burdens as England it now had the same privileges, for trade was opened between Scotland and America and the restrictions removed which had previously made it almost impossible for Scottish merchants to trade legally with the colonies. Yet it seemed at first that even this might profit Scotland little, for, as we know so well in our own day, imports have to be paid for, and in general paid for by the export of other goods. Now, Scotland had few goods to export, for the colonies did not want hides and only the West Indian slave-owners wanted salt-fish—for their slaves; what the colonies did want were manufactured goods, for they themselves had few manufactures and were indeed restrained from the manufacture even of some of their own raw materials. Nor could the Scots become, like the Dutch, carriers of goods manufactured in other countries, because for this they required capital and a greater skill in ship-building than they seem to have possessed at that time.

Yet a colonial trade did begin, and within a few years there were spectacular results from the treaty of union—the treaty, as Scott makes a Glasgow bailie say in *Rob Roy*, "that opened us a road west awa' yonder." By the middle of the century millions of pounds of tobacco were coming into the Clyde each year, and Glasgow became the premier tobacco port of Great Britain. In addition, there was sugar and rum. Not more than a small proportion of the tobacco was for Scottish consumption, and most of it was for re-export to the Continent, since the colonies were forbidden to export tobacco directly except to Britain and other British territories.

The exports sent out in exchange for the goods from the colonies were at first the old staple Scottish products—salt-fish, coarse cloth and knitted goods. Linen became for a time the most important export, but as the years passed the need for more and more goods to export became apparent. Scottish manufactures sprang up to meet the demand—wrought iron work, leather goods, pottery and crystal, rope-making, hat-making and furniture, all of which developed in the west of Scotland in this period.

But it would scarcely be an exaggeration to call the eighteent century, or at least a part of it, the linen era in Scottish industry The dominance of cotton did not threaten linen until toward the end of the century, the age of the heavy industries was t come only in the nineteenth. The manufacture of linen was nc a new industry, and as it was one in which England did nc compete it had not suffered from the change at the union, bu there was room for development and for improvement in th quality of the linen produced. In 1727 Acts were passed whic provided for the supervision of the industry and which place funds (available in terms of the Treaty of Union) at the dispos of the Board of Trustees for Manufactures. This Board offere prizes and subsidies and arranged for instruction and for th assistance of skilled workers from Picardy (who gave their nam to Picardy Place in Edinburgh). The Scottish Society for th Propagation of Christian Knowledge and the Commissione who administered the estates forfeited after the Jacobite risings— both of them bodies which we shall encounter again in thei various schemes for the betterment of Scotland—were active i similar ways from the middle of the century.

Flax, the raw material, was grown in Scotland, but the nativ crops soon could not meet the demand, and much was latterl imported from the Continent. The many processes involved i the industry were, one or more of them, carried on in nearl every parish in the kingdom—the preparation of the raw flax b separating the fibre from the stalk, spinning, weaving, bleachin and dyeing. While there were many factories, the industry w still in the main a domestic one. Every spinster really was spinster in those days, for spinning was the main part-tim occupation of every Scottish country-woman. But, whi spinning long remained a part-time occupation, weaving, eve though still done in the home, came to be full-time and to l largely concentrated in particular areas like Glasgow, Paisle Dundee, Dunfermline, and Perth, and the finishing process were even more localised. The production of linen cloth ro about twelve-fold between 1728 and 1800.

The phase in which the main pillars of the Scottish econom had been tobacco and linen came to an end suddenly whe the American War of Independence (1776-83) brought abo the immediate collapse of the lucrative tobacco trade. Aft the independence of the colonies was recognised, tobacco was of course again imported, but only for Scottish consumption, as the Americans were now free to send their tobacco directly to any country. Since there could be no resumption of the tobacco trade on its previous scale, those who had engaged in the tobacco trade had to find other markets, and the capital which had accumulated in commerce had to find new outlets. The commerce which had previously provided the incentive to industry now produced the capital for industry.

The industry which came along to absorb the capital which had been accumulated in the tobacco trade, to make use of some of the skill acquired in the linen manufacture, and to dominate the Scottish economy for nearly a century, was the cotton industry. It so happened that in the 1770's English inventors had devised machines for spinning cotton thread—the spinning jenny of Hargreaves and the water frame of Arkwright—and in 1785 came the "mule" of Crompton. Thus the possibilities of extending the use of cotton emerged just at the time when the American war set free capital and business experience, and it was in 1783, the very year when the American war ended, that David Dale, a Glasgow merchant, showed Arkwright the Falls of Clyde and asked him how he thought they would do for a cotton mill. Glasgow capital, English inventive genius, Scottish natural resources and textile skill, and Clyde shipping to bring in the raw cotton, combined to give Scotland a great new industry. The spinning of cotton was in factories from the start, and within a few years there were many mills by Scottish riversides, especially in Renfrewshire and Lanarkshire. The production of cotton thread tended to exceed the powers of the weavers, who still at this time worked by hand, and the weavers were in consequence very prosperous.

There was a third textile industry which, like linen, was not new but was greatly developed in the later eighteenth century. This was wool. One side of woollen manufacture was revolutionised by the appearance of knitting machines; and the cloth-making industry began to take something like its later shape in the Border area. The term "tweed," however, did not originate in the name of the Border river, but in a happy misreading of the term "tweel."

While the textiles, and especially linen and cotton, were far and away the most important features in the Scottish industrial scene well into the nineteenth century, there had already been certain developments in the utilisation of Scottish minerals which pointed the way forward to a time when they would become dominant. The coal industry was still much hampered by two things. One was the difficulty of keeping the mines free of water, and the solution of this problem was in sight with James Watt's improvement of the steam engine, though only one of Watt's engines had been brought into use in a Scottish colliery by 1800. The other difficulty was that of transport, for so long as roads were bad and there was no mechanical means of transport, coal could hardly be conveyed in large quantities except by sea along the coasts. But the eighteenth century saw the introduction of wagonways on which coal was conveyed in wagons drawn by horses, and, as we shall see, the making of canals made it easy to carry coal into Glasgow and other centres; it remained, however, to apply steam to the means of locomotion both by land and water.

The Scottish iron industry likewise laboured under difficulties. Its serious beginnings are dated from the opening of the Carron works near Falkirk in 1760. As in the case of the first cotton mills, this venture represented a combination of English capital and technical skill with Scottish business acumen, designed to exploit Scottish natural resources—in this instance the native iron ore, coal, and wood, as well as water power, which was used to blow the blast for the furnaces and drive other machinery. But existing processes were not capable of making the best use of much of the Scottish ore, and in any event there could be no great growth of this industry until the steam engine was further developed and more efficient machinery invented. Consequently, development was very slow in the seventy years after the foundation of the Carron works, and only with the invention of the hot blast in 1828 did the Scottish iron industry really begin to flourish. Until then iron was a negligible item in comparison with linen and cotton.

The commercial developments and the industrial expansion which followed from them were alike of benefit primarily to the west of Scotland. The population of Glasgow, only 12,000 at the time of the union, reached 100,000 a hundred years later, and towns like Paisley and Greenock expanded in a similar way.

Glasgow had before the Union hardly been a port at all, for, although there was a quay at the Broomielaw, stretches of the Clyde below it were so shallow as to make it almost useless, and Port Glasgow had been founded in 1662 as, quite literally, the port of Glasgow. Ships of any size had to be unloaded there or at other points lower down the river until well through the eighteenth century. Glasgow was ultimately connected to the western seas by a deepened Clyde which was in effect an artificial waterway, and it came to be connected with the Firth of Forth by another artificial waterway—the Forth and Clyde Canal.

The towns of eastern Scotland, which had at first found the Union detrimental, in time came to share in the economic expansion. Some of the imports from America did come into eastern ports, and the linen industry was developed in Fife and Angus as well as in the west. In Edinburgh a great variety of industries started or expanded, and the Leith shipping figures show a tenfold increase in the hundred years after the Union.

Edinburgh illustrates some of the changes for the better which were coming over town life in this period. Down to the closing years of the eighteenth century the prosperous merchant or shop-keeper had been content to live above his shop, in a flat that contained at the most four rooms. One might admire the carved stone fireplace, the panelled walls, and the graceful lines of the new mahogany furniture; still one had to admit that a house lighted at night by flickering candles, a house without water-pipes or drains, left much to be desired. Water could be got only by sending one's servants for it to the public well in the street below or else by waiting till the water caddie appeared with his water-cart. Household refuse had to be thrown from the window after dark, and woe betide the benighted wayfarer who did not have the presence of mind to shout "Haud your hand" when he heard the warning shout of "Gardyloo" [*Gardez l'eau*] from a window above.

Such a house, with its tiny windows which were seldom opened, with the cavernous box-beds in every room, would have seemed dark and stuffy even if it had stood in the middle of a ten-acre field. But it was hemmed in on all sides by tall "lands" or blocks of flats, often reaching a height of ten or eleven storeys. For down to the closing years of the eighteenth century additional accommodation was found for the increasing population by building higher, and by packing the houses more tightly, within the old boundaries of the town. The "closes," the gardens which had once brought a country fragrance into the very heart of towns like Edinburgh and Glasgow, disappeared altogether under the great bulks of stone and mortar, or survived only as dark passages leading into narrow and sunless courtyards. It was in a flat in one of these tall "lands," approached by a malodorous common stair, that not only prosperous merchants, not only ministers, lawyers and doctors, but judges and lords and ladies "wi' a lang pedigree" were content to dwell. This shortage of accommodation had one curious consequence: the fashionable doctor prescribed for his patients, the busy lawyer interviewed his clients, not in his own house, but in the tavern at the close end.

In the closing years of the eighteenth century, however, a big change took place. It was most marked in Edinburgh, where merchant and minister, doctor and lawyer, judge and lady of high degree, forsook their cramped and lofty quarters in the Old Town and settled in the New Town of broad streets and stately houses that sprang up as the town at last began to spread beyond the ancient site on the ridge between the Castle and Holyrood. The North Bridge spanned one valley in 1763 and plans were drawn up for building on the north side of what had been the Nor' Loch and which became Princes Street Gardens; the South Bridge spanned the other valley in 1785, and even before that houses had been built to the south of the old town, especially in George Square (1766). The change was not confined to Edinburgh; in Glasgow, in Dundee, in Aberdeen, splendid terraces spread along broad streets and some prosperous manufacturers or merchants built themselves roomy villas, set in spacious gardens, on the outskirts of the town. The new houses had their disadvantages: water, for example, had to be drawn from a well in the garden; the architect, in his anxiety to make the house look dignified, tucked the kitchen and scullery away underground; at night the light of candles scarcely revealed the design of the textile or paper wall-coverings which were taking the place of panelling. Still, they were a great improvement on the old insanitary dwellings.

The old, simple economy, in which most of the people of Scotland were fed and clothed by the produce of their immediate neighbourhood and in which few men were employed full-time in specialised work, began to give way to a more complex structure. Hitherto comparatively little transport had been necessary, but if the industrialisation of Scotland, with the increase in the size of towns and the concentration of manufacturing processes in certain areas, was to proceed, vast improvements in transport had to come. Wheeled traffic of all kinds had until this time been far from common: goods were carried by packhorse, on sledges or in creels borne on the back; men and women, when they did move about the country, usually rode on horseback. The roads, inadequately maintained in terms of an act of Parliament which compelled a certain number of days' labour on the roads each year, were in such poor shape that a coach, constantly breaking its axles or foundering in ruts and mud, was a liability rather than an asset. Travellers passed so seldom that Scotland, it was said, had few highwaymen, since they would have found no employment. But from the middle of the eighteenth century there was a long series of acts setting up local turnpike trusts and empowering them to levy tolls on vehicles and apply the proceeds to the maintenance of roads. The toll-house and the white toll-gate became familiar features of the Scottish landscape—too familiar, for they impeded traffic and added to its cost. It was not an ideal arrangement, and some time elapsed before the principles of good road construction were discovered, but by the early nineteenth century a great improvement had taken place. Nor was the traveller on the new roads compelled to trust himself and his horse to treacherous fords or overloaded ferry-boats, for this was the age of the great bridge builders, Rennie and Telford. In every part of Scotland rose the stately and beautiful structures which they designed and which are still often carrying twentieth century traffic, of dimensions the designers never dreamed of. In the Highlands, the military roads made by Wade between the Jacobite rebellions and by other commanders after the Forty-Five were maintained after they ceased to be of military importance, but they were often too steep for the needs of peaceful traffic, and after 1800 were replaced by new roads constructed by a Commission for Highland Roads and Bridges.

At the same time as the roads were improved, the arrangements for providing changes of horses were perfected, so that not only could more loads be carried but transport could become much more rapid and frequent. The service between London and Edinburgh had taken from twelve to sixteen days in 1750, and was a monthly service; but thirty years later there was a daily service and the time had been cut to sixty hours. Not till 1763 did a stage-coach ply regularly between Edinburgh and Glasgow, and then, even with four or six horses, twelve hours were required for the journey and the service operated only three times a week.

For heavy goods, however, the value of roads was limited as long as there were only horses to pull the loads. The greater ease of pulling heavy loads on water drew men's attention to the possibilities of canals, which had a brief but brilliant career at the end of the eighteenth century and the beginning of the nineteenth. A link by water between the Firth of Forth and the Firth of Clyde had often been spoken about in the past, and it finally took shape in the Forth and Clyde Canal, from Grangemouth to Bowling, completed in 1790. The canal was an extraordinary success, and very profitable to its promoters, with three thousand vessels a year passing through it at its busiest. Two other canals in central Scotland were associated with it: the Monkland canal, designed to connect the rich coalfields of the Coatbridge area to Glasgow, had a branch connecting it with the Forth and Clyde Canal and was opened in 1790; and the Union Canal, running from the Forth and Clyde Canal near Falkirk to a basin near the centre of Edinburgh, was completed in 1822. Thus, apart from through traffic from sea to sea, the Forth and Clyde Canal was part of a system which enabled coal and iron to be moved by water throughout a large part of central Scotland and into the big centres of population, and there was also considerable passenger traffic when water still offered far greater comfort and almost as much speed as the roads. So successful were canals for a time that the movement for their construction spread to many parts of the country. There was a plan for a canal from Glasgow to Ardrossan (designed to eliminate the tortuous stretches of the Clyde), but it never went further than Johnstone; there was a successful canal from Aberdeen to Inverurie; and there were plans for canals to join many other towns, like Brechin and Forfar and Elgin, to the sea, but they never materialised. There were also two canals of a different type—planned not to aid inland transport but to shorten sea-passages: the Crinan Canal, from Ardrishaig to Crinan, to cut out the voyage round the Mull of Kintyre, and the Caledonian Canal, joining up the three lochs in the Great Glen between Fort William and Inverness.

While so many of the developments of this period pointed the way to a change in the emphasis of the Scottish economy from agriculture to industry, there was also a revolution in agriculture itself. One of the greatest weaknesses hitherto had been the lack of winter feeding for cattle, and this was remedied by the cultivation on a large scale of root crops like turnips and by the introduction of artificial grasses which produced abundant hay crops. When fodder thus became plentiful, the wholesale slaughter of animals at Martinmas ceased to be necessary. Not content with increasing the number of his sheep and cattle, the new-fashioned farmer wanted an improvement in the quality too, and did not rest until he had succeeded in rearing animals that were far larger and healthier than their predecessors. New breeds of sheep, too, were introduced, especially in the Borders, to supply raw material for the woollen industry, and sheep-raising spread to the Highlands, where it largely displaced cattle. Mutton was in demand for food in the growing towns of Scotland, and both sheep and cattle were exported to England as well.

Other changes took place in the rural districts. Large farms became the rule; not only would four or six little farms be thrown together to form one big one, but land once regarded as good for nothing would be included in the new-fashioned farmer's holding. Shallow lochs and marshy hollows and flat green carses by the riverside were drained and brought under the plough, loose stones were collected from land hitherto untilled—and from much of the tilled land as well—and piled up to form "dry stane dykes." For in Scotland, as in England, enclosures came in with the new methods of farming; the days of the unfenced corn-rigs, of the pasture shared by the cattle of half a dozen owners, were at an end; farms, big and little, were rearranged as compact parcels of land, which had to be fenced off from neighbouring farms by a march dyke or boundary wall. So the go-ahead farmer was freed from the interference of stupid or lazy neighbours; he was freed, too, from the fear of being hustled out of his farm before he had time to carry out the improvements that he had planned, for he now held his farm on a lease, not of two or three, but of nineteen or twenty-one years; he was freed, finally, from the labour services to the landlord which had in earlier times often formed part of his rent and which had sometimes interfered with his attention to his own crops.

So instead of growing oats and barley year after year on the infield, and letting the outfield lie fallow for three or four years on end, exhausting the one and not getting nearly enough from the other, the new-fashioned farmer increased the yield from his acres by manuring the land more heavily and by varying the crops in different fields from year to year; after oats he might sow, not more oats, but turnips, after turnips, wheat, after wheat, clover, then in the fifth year he would return to oats again. As soon as he could he got rid of the old-fashioned wooden plough, and adopted the new swing plough, invented by John Small of Dalkeith in 1750, which required only one man and one pair of horses. The flail followed the old wooden plough into oblivion: in 1787 Andrew Meikle, a millwright of Dunbar, invented a threshing-machine, and soon threshing-machines, driven by horses or by water-power, were installed in every up-to-date farm. There were also horse-drawn hoes to tend the root-crops, and heavy harrows of iron to break up the ground effectively after it had been ploughed. The sleds and the "tumblers" with their solid wooden wheels, which had satisfied the farmers of an earlier day, no longer satisfied the up-to-date farmer; he insisted on the "wricht" supplying him with carts like those which are in use to-day. The crops produced under the new agricultural system, being both heavier and of better quality, helped to feed the growing urban population. The acreage under wheat very greatly increased, and of course the extensive cultivation of the potato provided an article which did more than anything else to feed the poorer classes in town and country alike.

The new-fashioned farmer made money, especially in the years of the long war against the French Revolution and Napoleon (1793-1815), when the price of corn rose to dizzy heights. His prosperity was shown in the changed appearance of the farm buildings. Not for him now the "auld clay biggin'" with its thatched roof; the tenant of two or three hundred acres must live in a substantial stone house of two or three storeys, as big as the manse and three or four times as big as the schoolhouse. And the farmhouse itself was only one of a group of massive stone buildings, forming a steading that sometimes dominated the rolling cornfields almost like a medieval fortress. Thatched roofs went out of fashion with walls of turf and unmortared stone: in Fife and the Lothians the red-tiled roofs of farm steading and cottage added a new note of colour to the landscape, while in the south-west, and north of the Tay, slate roofs gave a somewhat chilly and forbidding look to the new stone buildings, except where the walls themselves were of red sandstone.

Landlords were taking the keenest interest in their properties, and one of the ways in which they sought at once to adorn their estates, shelter their crops and provide for the wealth of future generations was by afforestation. There was a perfect passion for planting. Men like Grant of Monymusk in Aberdeenshire and the Duke of Atholl in Perthshire sowed and planted trees, especially larch, literally by the million. Atholl is said to have used a small cannon to fire canisters of seed to inaccessible parts of the hillsides, so determined was he that all should be wooded. It was not an absence of all trees, but only an absence of old trees, that moved Dr. Johnson to scornful speech when he visited Scotland in 1773. On almost every estate, rows of beeches or chestnuts lined the avenues and clustered about the mansion-house. And the mansion-house itself, now that landholding in Scotland had become highly profitable, was often palatial in its luxury and extent, and its design sometimes represented the noblest architecture known in recent centuries.

In a matter of a hundred years after the Union, therefore, and directly or indirectly as a result of it, the Scottish economy had ceased to be primarily a rural economy and the population and wealth of the country were no longer distributed mainly according to the fertility of the soil. There was now a large concentration in the Clyde Valley, based partly on the textile (linen and cotton) industry, partly on commerce; there was the beginning of an industrial area between the Forth and the Clyde, based on coal and iron; new life had come to towns in Fife, Perthshire, and Angus from the linen industry; some of the east coast towns, while their commerce was quite overshadowed by that of the west, had recovered from their post-union depression and were thriving on new industries; the industrial belt, which runs from south-west to north-east, from Ayrshire to Angus, was taking shape. The main cause of the transformaton had not been the mechanical inventions of the period or the exploitation of Scottish minerals, but had been commerce, which had stimulated the rise of a variety of industries. But at the end of that century after the Union many of the developments conspicuous in later times—particularly machinery, the engineering industry and steam transport—had little more than started.

CHAPTER 24

THE GOVERNMENT OF SCOTLAND AFTER THE UNION

THE treaty of union laid it down that on and after the 1st of May 1707 the kingdom of Scotland and the kingdom of England should alike come to an end and that there should be in their place a single kingdom of Great Britain. But, while it was explicit that the united kingdom should have a single Parliament, it was far from explicit on the future arrangements for the administration. To people at the time, that question did not seem a very vital one, because the activities of the central government were then very limited. The State was not concerned with education, the relief of poverty and unemployment, communications, public health, agriculture and other matters which nowadays require vast departments and regiments of civil servants. In so far as such matters were dealt with at all, they were the concern of local authorities only, and the central administration confined itself mainly to the negative function of maintaining the law and order within which individuals could freely conduct their affairs.

The general tenor of the treaty suggests that those who framed it were thinking in terms of a unitary administration for the whole of Great Britain. At the same time, however, the treaty contained certain provisions which made a unified, or at any rate a uniform, administration not quite practicable. The Scottish law courts, with their judges and officials, were to remain separate from those of England; the Scottish seals, from the great seal downwards, were to remain in use; the registers and records of Scotland were "to continue to be keeped as they are within that part of the united kingdom now called Scotland"; and even the retention by the Church of Scotland of its separate identity had some administrative significance in an age when establishment was a reality and not a mere form and when kirk-sessions and presbyteries had many secular functions. There would have to be at least a member of the government able to advise on the affairs peculiar to Scotland, and such an adviser might easily become an administrator. Even the maintenance of law and order necessitated the existence of someone to act as a liaison officer between the government on one side and the law officers and the military in Scotland on the other. The Scottish Privy Council was not abolished by the treaty of union, though the possibility of its discontinuance was foreseen, and it was in fact abolished in 1708, leaving a kind of vacuum, for some of its wide powers in day to day business could not be readily undertaken by the Privy Council of Great Britain.

In this situation, the administrative implications of union had to be worked out by trial and error, and the period of some forty years after 1707 was a time of experiments and expedients, with no settled policy. Sometimes there was a separate Secretary of State for Scotland, but when there was he often found little to do, and sometimes Scottish affairs were handled by one of the two British Secretaries of State who at that time shared the responsibility for both home and foreign affairs. But in the years when there was not a separate secretary for Scotland, real responsibility for Scottish affairs tended to lie not with a Secretary of State but with some Scottish official—the Lord Advocate or the Lord President of the Court of Session—or with a Scot who was pre-eminent for his influence rather than for any office he held, notably two successive Dukes of Argyll. And after 1746, when the secretaryship for Scotland lapsed, the same state of affairs continued. Nominal responsibility for Scotland lay at first with one of the two secretaries, and later with the Home Secretary (after his office was created in 1782), but the Lord Advocate was often in effect the minister for Scotland and most Scottish business passed through his office.

Of the forty-five members who represented Scotland in the Westminster Parliament, thirty went from the counties and fifteen from the burghs. The county franchise remained as it had been settled in the seventeenth century and was still governed by the concept that Parliament was an assembly of the king's tenants, with the result that the only voters were those who held charters from the Crown relating to lands of specified values. Owing to the persistence of the feudal procedure whereby a Crown tenant granted charters of lands to his own "vassals" and remained the "superior" of lands so granted, the Crown tenant might not himself be the occupier or even the proprietor of the lands qualifying for the vote, but he retained the vote in virtue of his "superiority." Thus it was possible to find qualifications for new voters not only by splitting actual estates, but also by splitting the mere superiority without altering the proprietorship of the lands. Several statutes attempted to prevent abuse by imposing oaths to be taken by electors, but they were sometimes evaded, and it was remarked in 1792 that "all these precautions have been constantly defeated by the ingenuity of the learned profession, who have always succeeded in finding salves for weak consciences. Gentlemen of the fairest character, nay clergymen, have been induced by subtle explanations, and the nicest verbal subterfuges, to take these oaths, contrary to the evident intendment of the legislature, contrary to the received meaning and usage of language and in defiance of the general sense of the country." An elector, it was tersely said, might have no property in a county except the right to vote. The various devices used to create additional votes were not intended to broaden representation, but were designed to enable one party or another to secure its hold on the county.

Even with the creation of additional votes, the number of electors in Scotland was still small. While Ayrshire had the largest electorate—235 voters in 1781—the sheriffdom of Bute had no more than twelve, only ten counties had over 100 and the total for the whole country, in 1788, was less than 3,000. And the number of persons who really counted was very much smaller because there were all kinds of ways by which influential men could dominate the voters: family relationship, personal friendship, the judicious distribution or promise of offices and pensions, commissions in the armed forces and livings in the church, as well as discussion and persuasion, all played their part. A list of all the county voters drawn up in 1788 contains notes illustrating the varied considerations which had to be kept in mind by those who sought to influence the course of Scottish county elections: "would like promotion in his profession as a writer"; "has a family to provide for. Sons in the army"; "his son wants a kirk"; "his predecessors went with the Grants. His niece is married to Baron Gordon"; "in ill health. His son of age; may think differently from his father"; "a widower. A very independent man, if he does not marry again."

The fifteen burgh members were representative of the sixty-six royal burghs, but they were not elected by the burgesses or even, except in the case of the member for Edinburgh, directly by the town councils. The burghs other than Edinburgh were arranged in groups of four or five, and the process of election was by two stages: the town council of each burgh appointed a delegate, and the four or five delegates from the burghs in the group met together and chose the member. The councils themselves were very largely co-opted and self-perpetuating. In Aberdeen, for example, the town council met every year about Michaelmas (29th September) and elected four of their own number, thirteen members of the merchant gild and two of the six deacons of trades or craft gilds, to form the new town council for the ensuing year. The old and new council then together elected the provost, the four bailies and the other burgh officials. Thus the number of councillors concerned in the first stage of a Parliamentary election—totalling some 1,300 for the whole of Scotland—were not themselves the elected representatives of the burgesses. Several burghs were wholly dominated by a local magnate, and in some the office of provost remained in the same family generation by generation. So the problem of reforming the representation of the burghs in Parliament was bound up with the problem of reforming the burghs themselves.

Defective as the system was, its faults became even more conspicuous as the economic changes brought about a redistribution of the population. Thus the Fife burghs, some of which were only hamlets, returned three out of the fifteen burgh members; Glasgow, with 200,000 people, shared a member with three other burghs; Paisley and Greenock, with 40,000 and 20,000 inhabitants respectively, were not royal burghs and had no burghal representation at all.

The entire system, with its small number of voters interested less in policy than in the material interests of themselves and their friends, lent itself to "management," and Scotland was "managed" in this sense, for a time by the Duke of Argyll and later in the century by Henry Dundas, first Viscount Melville (1742-1811) Dundas made his career through the law and the law offices of the government, but, as a colleague and friend of William Pitt the younger, he was between 1783 and 1805 successively President of the Board of Control for India, Treasurer of the Navy, Home Secretary and Secretary for War. With English and Indian as well as Scottish patronage at his disposal, Dundas had exceptional opportunities to attach voters to his own faction, but on making appointments he did not overlook ability. In days when entrance to the public service was not guarded by competitive examinations, Dundas became a dispenser on a large scale of comfortable Government jobs and of posts in the East India Company's service. Many a poor Scots youth owed his start in life to this genial despot, who, even after he became Viscount Melville, remained faithful to the homely Scottish speech. At the height of his power, Dundas controlled elections in no less than thirty-six of the forty-five Scottish constituencies.

With a single British Parliament in which the Scottish members were a very small minority, and with no consistently effective independent administration for Scotland, the policy pursued in Scotland was shaped partly by what was conceived to be the interest of Britain as a whole, but partly also by personal and party considerations. Scottish needs and Scottish sentiment received scant attention, and a good deal of popular resentment was aroused. The series of grievances began very soon after the Union. In 1709, for example, an Episcopalian clergyman, called Greenshields, was thrown into prison by order of the Court of Session, because he had used the English Book of Common Prayer. He appealed to the House of Lords. It was not the first appeal to the House of Lords since the Union, and, while the treaty had been clear that there should be no appeal from a Scottish court to an English court, there seems to have been no hesitation about accepting the principle of the appellate jurisdiction of the British Parliament. But when the appeal of Greenshields was sustained by the House of Lords many Scots were furious: that the decision overturned was intolerably harsh counted for nothing with them; all they saw was that the decision of the central Scottish court, in a matter relating to the exclusive position of the Presbyterian Church of Scotland, had been overturned by a decision in London.

More serious blows to the Church of Scotland followed in 1712. It was logical to follow the decision in favour of Greenshields by a Toleration Act which permitted Episcopalians who were not Jacobites to meet for worship and use "the liturgy of the Church of England," and this measure was contested by the Presbyterians as a clear breach of the security granted to the Church of Scotland in the Union agreement. It did not help matters that the Abjuration Oath, by which Episcopalian clergy were required to renounce their belief in the Pretender's claims, was to be exacted from Church of Scotland ministers as well, because while Presbyterians had no love for the Pretender they objected to the imposition of an oath on them by Parliament. Another controversy arose over the method of appointing ministers in the Church of Scotland. The Presbyterians had always maintained that no minister should be forced on a congregation without its consent and that on the contrary he should be elected either by the congregation or by a body which represented it. The power of the individual lay patron—usually the most important landowner in the parish, but often the Crown—to appoint the minister, had, however, continued since the Reformation without a break except between 1649 and 1661, but in 1690 that system was abolished; in every parish the right of selecting a minister was given to a body consisting of the elders and the Protestant heritors or landowners. Now, in 1712, the British Parliament, by restoring to the individual lay patron his right of patronage, laid itself open again to the charge of flouting the Treaty of Union.

In those same years after the Union the Scots were acutely conscious of the economic disadvantages they suffered through the removal of favourable protective duties, and in 1712 the Scottish fisheries were almost ruined by an increase in the salt tax, designed to bring it up to the English level. The prosperity of the fishing industry depended on the export of cured fish to the Continent, and the increase in the tax made salt so dear that the fish-curers could not afford to buy it.

It was another fiscal grievance which led to the first riots after the Union—the Malt Tax riots of 1725. Walpole, the head of the British administration, had first of all proposed a tax on ale in Scotland, but withdrew this in face of opposition and substituted a tax of 3d. per bushel on malt; this was only half of the duty levied in England, but rioting followed, especially in Glasgow, where the house of the Member of Parliament, Campbell of Shawfield, was wrecked by a mob. The military were called out, but they were attacked by the populace and had to fire in self-defence. The provost and bailies were arrested for their complicity, but neither they nor the rioters could be convicted, and the captain whose troops had fired was actually tried and condemned and saved only by a royal pardon.

Somewhat similar circumstances attended the Porteous riots in Edinburgh in 1736, when the captain who had fired on the crowd was not in the end saved from the vengeance of the mob. This episode, so well narrated in Scott's *Heart of Midlothian*, arose out of the popular attitude to smuggling, which was itself a symptom of the lack of sympathy with the government and its regulations. The Scots resented the efficient collection of excise which had been introduced after the Union, with the result that the "free trader," as the smuggler was euphemistically called, was a hero, and "to jink the gauger" or evade the exciseman was an honourable exploit. When two smugglers were sentenced to death in Edinburgh, one helped the other to escape (with the connivance of the people) and at the execution of the solitary victim the onlookers became restive, whereupon Captain Porteous, of the City Guard, commanded his men to fire causing some casualties. Porteous was tried and condemned but reprieved by Queen Caroline, acting as Regent for George II whereupon the mob broke into the Tolbooth one night, seized him and hanged him. The government, thoroughly outraged proposed to suspend the city's charter, disband the City Guard and demolish the Netherbow Port, and the Queen declared that, sooner than submit to such an insult to her government she would make Scotland a hunting-ground (to which the Duk of Argyll retorted, "In that case, Madam, I shall take leave o your Majesty and go down to my own country to get m hounds ready for the chase").

It was inevitable that, in the political field as in the economic there should be a period of rather painful adjustment, durin which the Scots had at least to learn what it meant to be governe as part of a larger whole. No doubt many felt, as Scott makes one of his characters say, "When we had a king, and a chancellor, and parliament men o' oor ain, we could aye peeble them wi' stanes when they werena guid bairns—but naebody's nails can reach the length o' Lunnon."

There were more profound aspects of this process of political adjustment. There was, for one thing, the acceptance of the fact of Union as an enduring feature in Scottish life. The grumblings which had gone on for a generation after 1707 gradually receded, and for about a century (1750-1850) the existence of the Union was hardly challenged. It was a more difficult process, and a longer one, for the Scots to develop a political life within the framework of British politics. What had to be created was a Scottish political outlook or consciousness which shared in British politics, so that Scots could learn to regard British politics as their own. The process was long and difficult because the system of Parliamentary representation was such that Parliamentary elections provided no outlet for political interest: those who had an effective voice in choosing the Scottish members of Parliament were very few, and among those few the issue was usually personal rather than political. Nor did the Scottish representatives at Westminster show much political vitality, for they were usually the unhesitating supporters of the government of the day which had managed their election, and they exercised no independent judgement. At one point, it was said, a Scottish M.P. complained that the Lord Advocate was not tall enough: "the Scottish members," he explained, "always vote with the Lord Advocate, and we therefore require to see him in a division. Now, I can see Mr. Pitt, and I can see Mr. Addington, but I cannot see the Lord Advocate."

A Scotland which had, broadly speaking, no electoral rights, no active Parliamentary representation, and no political concern beyond an occasional outburst of resentment when some Scottish interest was affected, showed little enthusiasm for the doings of the Westminster Parliament and the issues which engaged British statesmen, until nearly the last quarter of the eighteenth century. The crisis of the 1770's was the quarrel with the American colonies which led to the American War of Independence (1776-83). While the Scottish M.P.'s, or most of them, continued to support the Cabinet, among thinking Scots there was a great deal of criticism of the official policy. The growing interest in current affairs at this point is reflected in a sharp increase in the number of periodicals, which doubled in a decade, and in the space given in the reports of news to American affairs—at one point, as an editor apologetically remarked, to the exclusion of items relating to the General Assembly of the Church of Scotland. There was much sympathy with the cause of the colonists, and the advantages of granting them independence were being weighed in Scotland even before the beginning of the war which ultimately compelled the British government to take that course.

From discussion of the political rights of the Americans it was a short step to discussion of the political rights of Scotsmen, which meant primarily the extension of the franchise, a subject which was being canvassed as early as 1775, and also what was called "economical reform" or the reform of the administration, which found support in an address by the Synod of Glasgow in 1782. It may be of some significance that whereas the frustration of the Scots in the realm of civil politics had probably stimulated them to concentrate on ecclesiastical politics, with the result that there was a series of secessions and schisms, the church courts were being used as channels for the expression of public opinion on matters of government policy. However, by this time associations for political purposes and agitation were making their appearance in England, and from England they were spreading to Scotland. There was much discussion of matters like the proper duration of Parliaments (which at that time lasted for seven years) and of the elimination of abuses in county elections; but more important at that point was consideration of the reform of the burgh constitutions, which of course indirectly affected the Parliamentary franchise. The economic changes were producing not only the movements of population already referred to but also the rise to wealth of industrialists and the attainment of a regular wage by numbers of workers in the factories. A new social structure was arising which was wholly unrelated to the existing political system.

Further impetus to the reform movements came in 1789, with the outbreak of the French Revolution, which was at first widely welcomed as being likely to be as beneficial to France as the Whig revolution of a hundred years earlier had been to Britain. Interest in the stirring events in France as well as in the activities of organisations advocating political reforms in Britain again led to a sharp increase in the number of newspapers in Scotland. As the French revolutionaries proceeded to more and more extreme measures they lost the support of moderate reformers in Britain, but their actions stimulated extremists like Thomas Paine, whose *Rights of Man* advocated the abolition of the monarchy and the use of force if necessary to bring about a radical reform of Parliament. The Society of Friends of the People, founded in England, spread to Scotland, where Paine's work was widely circulated and even translated into Gaelic, and there were riots on the King's birthday, an attempt to assassinate Dundas and much wild talk about "the last verse of the last chapter of the last book of Kings." Extremism would in any event have alienated moderate support, but its association with the inauguration of the Reign of Terror in France made matters worse for it, and in 1793, when Britain went to war with France, the cause of revolution, and even of reform, came to be looked on as unpatriotic. Those who persisted in pressing for reform prejudiced their cause by corresponding with the French revolutionaries and by adopting plans which appeared to threaten not merely reform, but revolution, and government policy, prompted partly by the needs of national security and partly by mere panic, proceeded to severe repression. "Conventions of Friends of the People" met in Edinburgh and went so far as to propose giving support to a French army should one invade Britain, as well as providing for the summoning, in certain circumstances, of a British "National Convention," along the lines of the assembly which in France had abolished the monarchy and executed the King. The government took strong action: Thomas Fyshe Palmer, a Unitarian clergyman, was sent to Botany Bay for seven years, and Thomas Muir, an advocate, was sentenced to transportation for fourteen years. The judge who condemned them was Braxfield, who made no pretence of judicial impartiality. While many of the radicals were intimidated, there was still a zealous remnant, advocating the use of force and planning armed rebellion, with the result that in 1794 two men were tried for treason and one of them executed. In 1795 there was a stricter Treason Act and a Seditious Meetings and Assemblies Act.

These measures were severe, but they are parallel to the action taken against British Fascists in the second World War, and were undoubtedly supported by the mass of public opinion. The situation was such that all sympathisers with reform of any kind were apt to be suspect. Had not those who began the French Revolution, it was argued, been respectable middle-class people,

Thomas Muir

just like those plausible Whig lawyers, and had not their apparently reasonable and moderate demands led to wholesale confiscation and massacre? The wife of one wholly respectable burgh reformer was credited with guillotining hens in her backyard, in preparation for dealing with bigger game when the time came. Even the imitation of French fashions in dress, like trousers in place of breeches, and the disuse of hair powder, aroused prejudice. Old loyalists could be heard to thank God that they had always stuck to the constitution and to breeches and one conservative laird would hardly admit to his house anyone wearing trousers or gaiters.

Only a very resolute minority adhered to the cause of reform without any taint of fanaticism or radicalism, but there were some young advocates and other lawyers, like Henry Erskine and Francis Jeffrey, who remained pledged to the cause of reform and were responsible for the foundation of a progressive magazine, the *Edinburgh Review*, in 1802. The war, first against the French Revolution, later against Napoleon, went on until 1815, but in its later years and during the aftermath the support for reform again grew. Moderate men ceased to be afraid of every kind of change, and many professional men went over to the side of reform. At another level of the social scale there was a good deal of distress, leading to strikes and riots with both economic and political objectives. In 1820 the whole of Glasgow was on strike, and fighting took place at Bonnymuir between a handful of Radical weavers and a detachment of cavalry, but this "Radical War," as it was called, rather confirmed the Government in its opposition to sweeping changes.

The period of reform legislation began in the 1820s. Interest centred once more for a time on the burgh constitutions. Committees of enquiry between 1819 and 1821 reported that there were many abuses in burgh administration, and the outcome was, not yet the granting of the demand for the abolition of self-election by burgh councils, but the provision of a rather ineffective measure of financial control by the court of exchequer, before which burgesses could summon corrupt magistrates. Secondly, there was reform in the administration. In 1829 and 1830 many Scottish offices, some of them lucrative sinecures, were abolished, so reducing the amount of patronage at the government's disposal, and the system whereby Scotland had been largely in the hands of a "manager" came to an end. Third was the more difficult and controversial subject of the Parliamentary franchise. Proposals for reform in both the county and burgh elections were brought forward between 1823 and 1826, but were rejected. In 1830, however, a government came to power at Westminster which was pledged to the cause of Parliamentary reform and during the next two years, while the reform bills for England and Scotland made their stormy passage through the Commons and the Lords, there was wild excitement in Scotland, with marches, demonstrations, riots, and petitions, as well as remarkable victories for the reformers at elections even under the existing system.

The Reform Act of 1832 increased the number of Scottish members in the Commons from forty-five to fifty-three. The number of county representatives was left unaltered, but changes were made in the burgh representation: Edinburgh and Glasgow were each given two members, and Dundee, Aberdeen, Paisley, Perth and Greenock, one apiece; the smaller burghs were still arranged in groups, but eight new burghs were added to their number. In the counties the Act enfranchised only the actual proprietors of land or houses worth more than £10 a year, and tenants paying a rent of more than £50 who held their farms on a lease of more than seven years. In the burghs all householders paying an annual rent of £10 a year or more were entitled to vote, and the system of indirect election by delegates of the burghs in a group was abandoned. The dismal prophecies of the Tories, the exultation of the Radicals over the passing of the Bill, alike seem strange to us nowadays, for the 1832 Reform Act enfranchised only the middle classes; the £10 qualification shut out the great bulk of the working classes, for few even of the highly skilled workmen could then afford to pay £10 a year for house rent—at a time when, in Dundee, the wages of masons were from 7s. 6d. to 15s. a week, of carpenters from 10s. to 13s., and of weavers from 7s. to 10s. But the reform was startling enough, and produced a remarkable change in the political complexion of the Scottish members: under the Dundas regime, all but half a dozen of the forty-five Scottish members were pledged to support the Tory government; in the first reformed Parliament, which met in 1833, all but nine of the fifty-three Scottish members were Whigs, or Liberals as they were now coming to be called.

Parliamentary reform brought burgh reform in its train: before the end of 1833 the Scottish Burgh Reform Bill placed the power of electing town councils in the hands of those householders who were now entitled to vote in Parliamentary elections. Later in the century several populous places were erected into burghs—the new "Police Burghs" as they were called.

A further Reform Act, in 1868, increased the number of Scottish members from fifty-three to sixty, and gave the vote to virtually all householders in the burghs, as well as to lodgers paying a rent of £10 a year, though in the counties the franchise was restricted to the owners of property worth more than £5 a year and tenants paying a rent of more than £14. The Act of 1885, however, besides raising the number of members to seventy-two, gave the vote to householders and lodgers in the rural districts: and the Act of 1918, besides admitting women over thirty to the vote, and all men over twenty-one, gave Scotland two additional members of Parliament. In 1928 the age limit for women was reduced to twenty-one.

CHAPTER 25

THE JACOBITE RISINGS AND THE HIGHLANDS

THERE were some people who drew comfort from the discontent in Scotland after the Union; to the Jacobites it seemed a sure sign that Scotland was ready to fight for the exiled Stewarts. When James VII died in 1700, Louis XIV of France had promised to support the cause of his son—James VIII and III, as the Jacobites called him, the "Pretender," as he was known to his enemies. Why, then, should not the Pretender, with a French army at his back, land in Scotland, rally his faithful Scottish subjects to his standard, and, at the head of a great Franco-Scottish force, make his way across the border, and recall England to its allegiance? A French fleet did indeed escort the Pretender to the coast of Fife in 1708, but when British warships were sighted at the mouth of the Firth of Forth, it slipped back to France without landing its royal cargo. The next Jacobite attempt was not made until 1715, by which time Scotland had not only been united to England for eight years but had been ruled for a year by the German Prince who, in 1714, was proclaimed as King George the First. The Pretender was not altogether without support in the Lowlands: in Angus, Aberdeenshire, and part of the south-west, most of the country gentlemen were enthusiastic Jacobites, who drank valiantly to the health of the exiled King. The profound dissatisfaction with the Union seemed an admirable foundation for Jacobitism, and, combined with the sentimental attachment to the old native dynasty, made Jacobitism a much stronger force in Scotland than in England, where a Stewart restoration seemed to offer little advantage save to the Roman Catholics. Yet Scotland was far from unanimous, for national resentment against England proved a weaker force than ecclesiastical opinions. While the Roman Catholics were naturally Jacobites, and so were many of the Episcopalians, to whom the House of Stewart had been almost consistently favourable, the Presbyterian Church was resolutely opposed to a Stewart restoration. The Lowland support for the Jacobite cause in 1715 was mainly in those areas where the Episcopalians were strong.

More was to be expected from the Highlands, which had changed little since the days of Montrose. The average Highland chief had grown more like an ordinary Lowland gentleman. He was better educated, and had travelled more than his predecessor of eighty years before, but his relations to his clan remained the same. It was not simply a feeling of loyalty and gratitude that bound the clansmen to their chiefs. The chief still retained the powers which his ancestors had enjoyed of deciding disputes and imposing penalties. So if the clansman refused to obey his chief, he would probably find that his cattle disappeared, or that his house was set on fire; yet he could not hope for redress, since the only judge to whom he could appeal might be the chief himself—the man who was responsible for his troubles.

But why was Jacobitism stronger in the Highlands than in the Lowlands? For one thing, the ecclesiastical situation was different, for the chequered history of the Church in the seventeenth century, which had not been to the advantage of the religious life of Lowland Scotland, had been latterly even more detrimental in the Highlands. At the Reformation, John Carswell, superintendent of Argyll and Bishop of the Isles, had been a forceful agent in the extension of the reformed faith in the south-western Highlands at least and had translated the Book of Common Order into Gaelic. After him there were other worthy bishops in Argyll and the Isles, so that by the 1630s the hold of the reformed church was widespread, and in the 1640s and 1650s the presbyterian Synod of Argyll was very active, but its work was interrupted by the disturbances caused by Montrose's campaigns and other military operations, as well as by an influx of Roman Catholic missionaries from Ireland. The Restoration caused no dislocation in the Highlands, for there were few dissidents from episcopacy in that area, but the consequences of the Revolution were a catastrophe. The new Presbyterian Church was for years hopelessly undermanned, and the resources of the now disestablished Episcopal Church were quite inadequate to maintain anything save a dwindling number of itinerant ministers. The result was a kind of vacuum, of which full advantage was taken by Roman Catholic missionaries. Hitherto Romanist effort had been intermittent, but from the 1690s it was consistent and sustained, with the appointment of bishops, the planting of settled priests and the establishment of a seminary to train youths for the priesthood. The Highlands were, throughout the eighteenth century, mainly Episcopalian and Roman Catholic, and in some areas there was no Presbyterian church until well after 1800. Education, as well as religion, was seriously hampered by the vast extent of the parishes and by poor communications: even if there were a church and a school, they could serve few people in a parish which might extend to three hundred square miles, intersected by high mountains, trackless deserts and stretches of water.

But the clans were far from unanimous in their Jacobitism, and part of the explanation lies in the position of Clan Campbell. In the sixteenth century the house of Argyll had been a principal instrument of the Crown against surrounding clans and its policy of aggrandisement had earned bitter hatred. Then, in the covenanting period, the house of Argyll became conspicuously the enemy of the house of Stewart, and this tended to throw its enemies on to the royalist side. By this time the Campbell power was dominant from the Mull of Kintyre to Loch Creran and from the Firth of Lorne to the east end of Loch Tay, and all its neighbours—Stewarts, MacDonalds, Camerons, MacPhersons and Robertsons—made a kind of anti-Campbell coalition which formed the core of the Jacobite strength in the Highlands in 1689, 1715, and 1745. Even the mere fact that the Campbells were Presbyterians went a long way to ensure that their neighbours would be Episcopalians.

In 1715 the Pretender, having persuaded himself that the time had come to start a rebellion in Scotland, wrote from France to the Earl of Mar, urging him to raise the clans at once. It was a curious time to choose, for the Treaty of Utrecht, ending the war between France and Britain, was only two years old, and James could no longer count on the help of the ruler of France, or, indeed, of any of the continental princes. And Mar was a curious leader, with nothing of the Highland dash and fire, a trimming politician who had taken a long time to discover which side he should stick to.

Mar for once acted speedily; he hurried north to Scotland and issued invitations for a great tinchal or hunting-party. But the real business of the meeting was the discussion of plans for a rebellion; the guests dispersed, only to assemble a few days later with their tenants and clansmen at Castletown in Braemar. Here the old Scottish standard was raised as a sign that the struggle had begun, but the fall of a golden ball from the top of the flag-staff damped the enthusiasm of the superstitious Highlanders. For a time, however, everything went well; most of the northern towns declared for King James, and Mar occupied Perth without the slightest difficulty. As the Jacobite army advanced, the recently appointed Presbyterian ministers fled before it and the congregations received Episcopalian clergy once more—and when, some months later, the Jacobites retreated, the Presbyterians came back in the wake of the government forces and one Episcopalian after another found himself on trial for "intruding" into parish churches. Meantime, between Mar and England there was a force of only two thousand government troops, under the Duke of Argyll, in the neighbourhood of Stirling. Yet having reached Perth about the middle of September, only twelve days after the campaign had begun, Mar refused to advance farther until he was joined by the clans from the West Highlands.

At the beginning of October the news that the border Jacobites were astir roused him from his inactivity. Lord Kenmure on the Scottish side, and Lord Derwentwater and Thomas Forster on the English side, had each gathered a small force of a few hundred horsemen, and, having got them, began to ask what they should do with them. Mar resolved to send some two thousand men southward under Mackintosh of Borlum to co-operate with them, while he himself stayed at Perth with the main part of the army. But the Duke of Argyll barred the road to the south at Stirling; the only alternative route to England was across the Firth of Forth, and this was no safer, for the Forth was patrolled by British warships. It was this second route, however, which Mackintosh decided to take.

Mackintosh had learned his business in an excellent school—the French army. He marched a small detachment of his force ostentatiously to Burntisland, where it was bombarded by the fleet. Meantime, the rest of his men had slipped across Fife undiscovered, occupied the little towns near the mouth of the firth, and helped themselves to such fishing-boats as they required. In these they crossed under cover of darkness to the Lothian coast. Mackintosh, instead of making straight for the border, turned westward and marched upon Edinburgh and Leith. Everything seemed in his favour, for Argyll was still in Stirling, more than thirty miles away, and had very few horsemen in his little army. Yet he was prompter than Mackintosh; he mounted two hundred of his infantrymen on cart-horses, and with these, and a body of three hundred cavalry, he clattered into Edinburgh. Mackintosh, fearing that he would be trapped behind stone walls, led his men out of Leith when darkness had fallen, flitted silent and unobserved along the shore of the firth, and then struck southward for the border, where the forces of Kenmure and Forster had already effected a junction. He found his allies at Kelso, disputing what they were to do next. Forster's plans for an advance into Lancashire were accepted in place of Mackintosh's more sensible scheme for co-operating with Mar, and at the beginning of November the motley force crossed the Tweed. Five hundred of the Highlanders, however, deserted, rather than follow Mackintosh into what they considered a foreign country. Meantime, Mar lingered irresolute in Perth. He had advanced on Dunblane when Argyll dashed to rescue Edinburgh, only to withdraw again to Perth when Argyll returned to Stirling. In the second week of November, after the western clans had come in, he discovered that he had no longer any excuse for delay, and advanced on Stirling. Argyll had advanced too, and on the morning of the 13th November the two armies blundered into each other at Sheriffmuir, a mile or two north of Dunblane, where the "heighs and howes" on the heathery moorland made it difficult for the commanders to see what was happening except in their immediate vicinity.

The Highlanders, after their custom, flung off their plaids, fired one volley, then, throwing away their muskets and grasping their claymores, they rushed on the enemy. Their right wing broke the ranks of the regulars opposed to them, but the Jacobite left wing had to meet Argyll himself. While the Highlanders were in mid-career, before they had reached the red lines of the waiting infantry, they were thrown into confusion by the sudden cavalry charge which Argyll launched against their flank. Seizing his opportunity, the Duke ordered the whole right wing to advance, and drove the Highlanders back to their camp on the Allan Water.

It was an absurd situation, if not an uncommon one in battles of those days. The right wing of each army had been victorious, the left wing had been defeated. Who, then, was the real victor? As the old ballad writer put it:

> There's some say that we wan,
> Some say that they wan,
> Some say that nane wan at a', man:
> But ae thing I'm sure,
> That at Sheriffmuir,
> A battle there was, that I saw, man.

There was really no doubt about it. Mar's retreat to Perth immediately afterwards converted a drawn battle into a victory for King George's men; Argyll still remained in front of Stirling, the road to the south was still closed to the Jacobites.

Meantime the Jacobites in the north of England had occupied Preston, where, on the day before the battle of Sheriffmuir, they were attacked by the Government troops. They beat off the small force which tried to drive them from the town, but reinforcements arrived, and two days later they surrendered unconditionally. The seemingly indecisive battle of Sheriffmuir had really decided the campaign. Mar's Highlanders, tired of inactivity, and disappointed in their hope of plunder, slipped off to their native glens by dozens and scores every day, while Argyll's army, reinforced by some regiments from Holland, and by the troops that had been employed against the Jacobites in northern England, now outnumbered that of his opponent by almost three to one.

And now, at the end of the year, when all hope of a Jacobite victory had disappeared, the Pretender himself arrived in Scotland.

Alas! this too clear-sighted prince was not the leader who could rekindle a dying enthusiasm, and convert defeat into victory. "For me it is no new thing to be unfortunate," he declared to his officers, "since my whole life from my cradle has been a constant series of misfortunes." The Highlanders were puzzled by his cold, reserved manner. Their bewilderment turned to rage when, at the end of January 1716, they learned that, though Argyll was at last advancing to attack them, their leaders had decided to abandon Perth and to retire to the north.

It was useless to point out to them that Argyll's army was superior in numbers and equipment, and that there was no sense in waiting to be defeated. "What can we do?" asked one of the officers. "Do?" was the indignant answer. "Let us do what we were called to arms for, which certainly was not to run away." When the officer urged that the King's safety had to be considered he was silenced by the reply: "Trust his safety to us, and if he is willing to die like a prince, he shall see that there are ten thousand men in Scotland willing to die with him."

James was not willing to die like a prince: he consented to Perth being abandoned, and to the northward march being begun; what was more, when he reached Montrose, he gave his followers the slip, and, along with Mar, embarked on a ship which was bound for France. The Highlanders marched on to Aberdeen, where a message from the Pretender was read, simply thanking them and advising them to shift for themselves. With rage in their hearts, they straggled on to Ruthven in Badenoch, where they dispersed. The "Fifteen" Rebellion was over.

Obviously the danger of a similar rebellion was not over as long as each clan was a private army, taking orders from its chief. The Government had already made an attempt to break down the bond between chiefs and clansmen by passing the Clan Act, which declared that the lands of any chief who rebelled would be forfeit to the Crown, while, if his tenants remained loyal in spite of his orders to rebel, they would be excused the payment of rent for two years; on the other hand, if tenants engaged in treason and their landlords were loyal, the tenants' lands reverted to the landlord. Immediately after the Rebellion, a Disarming Act was passed, imposing fines for the possession of arms and inviting the surrender of weapons; but the effect was to disarm only the loyal clans: the clans who still preferred

King James to King George did indeed hand over a curious assortment of obsolete weapons, but anything that was really serviceable they usually managed to keep. The estates of Jacobite landlords were of course forfeited, and instead of being conferred on rival families in the old fashion they were vested in Commissioners, but this well-intentioned attempt to administer forfeited estates in the public interest was not a success at this stage.

In 1719 the hopes of the Jacobite party rose again: Cardinal Alberoni, the all-powerful Spanish minister, had come forward as champion of the Pretender. It was arranged that while the Earl Marischal, with two frigates and some three hundred Spanish soldiers, attempted a landing on the west of Scotland, a large expedition, consisting of five warships and twenty-two transports, with five thousand soldiers on board, should sail for England. But a storm scattered the larger expedition, and though the Earl Marischal and three hundred Spaniards landed in Loch Alsh and marched into Glenshiel, they soon found their advance barred by the Government troops, and their retreat cut off by the fleet. The Spaniards surrendered; the Earl Marischal and the Scottish Jacobites who had joined him scattered, and lived to fight another day.

This "Nineteen" Rebellion, then, had been easily snuffed out, and, when General Wade, as Commander in Chief for Scotland, undertook to pacify the Highlanders in 1724, it seemed as if another attempt at a rebellion would be impossible. A more stringent Disarming Act was passed in 1725, and General Wade congratulated himself that the Highlander no longer went to kirk and market armed with claymore and pistols, but was content with a stick. The Highlander had learned caution, that was all; he had his claymore and pistols, dirk and targe still, though he did not swagger abroad with them—unless, indeed, he enlisted in one of the six Highland Companies raised by Wade to co-operate with his regulars. These companies, their number now increased to ten, were in 1739 formed into the Black Watch regiment and initiated the policy of using the Highlanders' fighting qualities for the benefit of Britain.

But Wade was not content with the Disarming Act. He saw that while the Lowlands could easily be invaded from the Highlands, the absence of roads and bridges made a counter-invasion

Cairns and Graves of the Clans, Culloden

General Wade's Bridge across the Tay at Aberfeldy

Plate 61 Carrington Church, Midlothian, 1710

of the Highlands very difficult—absolutely impossible in fact for an army equipped with artillery. He therefore set his soldiers to construct a network of roads—roads such as had not been made since the Romans left Scotland—where once there had been only rough tracks or no tracks at all. In eleven years two hundred and fifty miles of road and forty-two bridges were constructed. Wade's own principal routes were those linking Fort William with Inverness, Inverness with Dunkeld, and Crieff with Fort Augustus, but his name is often attached to other roads which were in fact constructed later in the century. The Highlands were being conquered by pick and spade.

In 1739, however, the outbreak of war between Britain and Spain aroused the old hopes and the old fears, and when, a year or two later, the relations between Britain and France became strained, nothing seemed more certain than that the restoration of the Stewarts by a French army of invasion would be attempted. An invasion was indeed planned, but nothing came of it. The warships and transports which had been collected were scattered by a tempest when they left their harbours at Brest and Dunkirk, and in 1744 the French Government, convinced that the Scottish and English Jacobites were too weak to co-operate effectively with an invading force, abandoned the scheme altogether.

Without help from France—and very substantial help—it would be madness to attempt anything; of that all the most experienced Jacobite leaders, from the Pretender downwards, were firmly convinced. The trouble, it seemed, had blown over. And then, in the autumn of 1745, news reached the capital that Prince Charles Edward, the Pretender's elder son, had landed in the West Highlands, and that the clans were flocking to his standard.

Charles Edward, moved partly by the persuasions of Irish exiles like Sir Thomas Sheridan and Scottish plotters like Murray of Broughton, who had everything to gain and nothing to lose, but mainly by his "young adventurousness," had resolved "to put it to the touch, to win or lose it all." To him it seemed that at such a time only boldness could command success. The French Government, he knew, would do nothing, because the Jacobites in Britain would not move. The Jacobites in Britain would not stir until the French had done something. The only way, then, to get this all-important help from France was to go to Scotland, win over the clans, not by appealing to the common sense, but to the honour and loyalty of the chieftains, sweep through the Lowlands into England, and thus show the hesitating French statesmen that the Scottish Jacobites were no mere backboneless intriguers, but formidable warriors, and that it would profit France to give them generous support. The occasion was favourable to the extent that the British army on the Continent had been heavily defeated by the French at Fontenoy.

At his own expense he fitted out a ship of the line, the *Elizabeth* and a frigate, the *Du Tellier* or *Du Teillay*, and in July 1745 he set sail from France. The *Elizabeth* was intercepted by a British warship, and so badly battered that she had to put back to harbour. The *Du Tellier*, however, evaded her pursuers, and at the beginning of August Charles landed on the island of Eriskay, in the Outer Hebrides. There MacDonald of Boisdale advised him to go home. "I am come home," said the Prince and ordered his ship to set sail for the mainland. He landed in Moidart with seven followers. But some of the chiefs flatly refused to have anything to do with the expedition, others hung back and would not commit themselves.

While the whole affair hung in the balance, Lochiel, head of Clan Cameron, one of the most faithful supporters of the exiled Stewarts, made up his mind to see the Prince and convince him that it was his duty to abandon the enterprise and go back to France. His brother, knowing his romantic and chivalrous disposition, advised him not to venture into the Prince's presence but to carry on the debate by letter. Lochiel refused to take his advice, was granted an interview with the Prince, and explained to him why the expedition was certain to fail.

"Be the issue what it will," said the Prince, "I am determined to display my standard, and take the field with such as may join it. Lochiel, whom my father esteemed the best friend of our family, may stay at home, and learn his Prince's fate from the newspapers."

"Not so," cried Lochiel. "If you are resolved on that rash undertaking, I will go with you, and so shall every one over whom I have influence." Lochiel's decision represents all that was best in Jacobitism, and there were other high-minded men who were prepared to risk all as a matter of conscience, although they had no hope of success. But others who joined the rising did so because they had nothing to lose. Life had always been hard in the Highlands, with their dearth of fertile ground and their excessive rainfall, and it was made harder by the reluctance of the inhabitants to adopt improved agricultural methods, their lack of initiative, and the indolence on which all observers remarked. Perhaps even before the eighteenth century the population exceeded the level which could be maintained by an unintelligent and conservative economy, and it had in practice been maintained partly on the proceeds of raids on the more settled Lowland countryside. If the Highlands were going to be peaceful and orderly, habits of industry had to be instilled, partly so that the people could make the most of their resources and partly so that they should find an occupation other than brigandage; but even so, a drastic reduction in the population was probably necessary. As things were, the period since the Fifteen had seen an increase in order, a certain amount of demilitarisation of the clans and also the beginnings of certain changes in the social structure. There were those who were failing to adapt themselves to changing conditions, and to them the prospect of a large-scale raid into the Lowlands had its attractions in 1745.

Outside the Highlands, the Forty-Five gained far less broadly-based support than the Fifteen. The Episcopalian meeting-houses, where King James was always prayed for, had kept the Jacobite cause alive, but the Presbyterian Church was now entrenched throughout Lowland Scotland as it had not been in 1715. Some Lowland towns, like Aberdeen, Dundee, and Perth, and many Lowland noble and landed gentlemen, had welcomed Mar, after whose rising no less than nineteen Scottish peerages had been forfeited. By contrast, the support which Charles Edward received in the Lowlands was negligible. And even in the Highlands the area of Jacobite sympathies had contracted: the clans of the north-east, the north and the western isles were mostly neutral or on the side of the government. Had money and a properly constituted authority been available in the north when Prince Charlie landed, the Forty-Five would have been nipped in the bud. As it was, Forbes of Culloden, the Lord President, strove almost single-handed, with no resources save "pen and ink, a tongue and some reputation", but, even so, twenty independent companies were formed in the north under the command of Lord Loudoun, and, besides intercepting reinforcements which might have reached the Jacobite army, they held Inverness in its rear throughout very nearly the whole of the campaign.

The main strength of Prince Charlie's army came from a relatively small area—Appin, Glencoe, Lochaber, Loch Shiel, and Moidart—a region which was still solidly Episcopalian or Roman Catholic; among the prisoners taken in the rising were fifteen Roman Catholic and ten Episcopalian clergymen. It is significant of the contrast between the Fifteen and the Forty-Five that, whereas Mar had raised his standard in Aberdeenshire, Prince Charlie's was raised in remote Glenfinnan, before a small army of MacDonalds and Camerons. Soon he found himself in command of a force of over two thousand five hundred men. It was true that they were not as well equipped as the regular soldiers; though the men in the front ranks bore not only a musket, but a sword and dirk and a targe—a leather shield studded with nails—the men in the rear rank would probably have only a single weapon, and often no weapon at all, except a scythe blade stuck straight in a pole.

But the regular troops in Scotland were few in number, not more than three thousand altogether. Many of them were raw recruits, and their commander—Sir John Cope—an unenterprising, over-methodical officer, was no match for Lord George Murray, the clear-headed, scientific soldier, whom Charles had made his chief of staff.

Cope, hearing that the Jacobite army was moving eastward, making for Perth and the Lowlands, marched his troops into the Highlands, meaning to bar the advance of the Jacobites at the Pass of Corryarrick. He changed his mind, however, and went on to Inverness.

Thus the road to the capital was open: the Highlanders captured Perth, crossed the Forth by the Fords of Frew, a mile or two above Stirling, and got to Coltbridge, within two miles of Edinburgh, before any opposition was offered to them. Here two regiments of dragoons were drawn up to do battle with them, but as soon as the valiant horsemen heard the bullets from the Highland muskets whistle past their ears, they turned about, fled along the country road which is now George Street, and did not draw rein till they had reached Leith. Even there their halt was a brief one; the cry that the Highlanders were at hand sent them galloping in headlong haste to Prestonpans and beyond.

In Edinburgh itself, panic reigned. The old walls and gates would not stop an army, and the garrison consisted only of a few decrepit veterans of the City Guard, and a regiment of volunteers which melted away when it was ordered to march out and meet the rebels. A message from the "Young Pretender," demanding the instant surrender of the city, found the Town Council in two minds. The councillors knew that their present defenders could not be trusted, but they also knew that Cope's transports had been sighted off Dunbar. In the end, late at night, they sent three of the bailies in a coach to the Pretender's headquarters, to ask for time to consider the demand.

Meantime, after darkness had fallen, the Camerons made a detour to the south of the city, and, creeping in silently, took up their position in the wynds leading up to the Canongate, just outside the well-guarded Netherbow Port. Back to the city and through the West Port rumbled the coach with the three bailies, disconsolate because their request had been refused. The gates clashed behind them, they dismounted and made their way back to the Council, while the coachman whipped up his horses and drove down the street towards their stable in the Canongate. The sentinels at the Netherbow Port recognised him and opened the gate, but, as the coach lurched out, the Camerons rushed in, and made themselves masters of the sleeping city. Next day the unwilling heralds proclaimed James the Eighth at the Market Cross, and Charles Edward entered the palace of his ancestors.

To some at least of those who knelt to kiss his hand, this tall handsome youth with the light of triumph in his eyes, must have seemed like a prince out of a fairy tale. The spell was lifted from the dark forsaken palace; again lights gleamed from the windows; again one heard the strains of music and the tap of dancing feet. On the other hand, many Lowlanders looked on with a kind of detached amusement rather than with either hopes or fears, at "a popish Italian prince, with the oddest crew that Britain could produce, with plaids, bagpipes and bare buttocks . . . tag, rag, and bobtail."

The revels in Holyrood were interrupted by the news that Cope had landed, and was approaching Edinburgh from the east.

Charles led out his men and came upon Cope's army near Prestonpans, drawn up at the western end of a stretch of level ground. Cope had chosen his position well: his front was protected by a series of high walls, on his right was the firth, and on his left an apparently impassable marsh. He had, moreover, six pieces of artillery with him, and two regiments of cavalry, the heroes of Coltbridge. But, led by a Lowland volunteer who knew a path through the marsh, the rebels filed across it in the darkness, and took up their position on the level ground in the rear of Cope's army. When it was too late, Cope discovered what had happened, and in the grey light of dawn he made his army turn about, so that it now faced the east. The artillery he moved to his right flank: as before, the infantry were drawn up in line in the centre, with a regiment of cavalry on each flank.

When the morning mists suddenly lifted and revealed the glittering scarlet ranks of the regular infantry, the hearts of the Highlanders sank for a moment, but after muttering a prayer, they pulled their bonnets down over their brows, and then, at the word of command, they rushed wildly at the royal troops, firing their muskets as they ran. They formed a splendid target for Cope's artillery, but the gunners had lost their nerve when they saw the hordes of plaided warriors bearing down upon them, yelling and waving their claymores; they fled without firing a shot. The two cavalry regiments followed their example, and left the flanks of the infantry unsupported. The infantry fired one volley, but before they could fire a second, the Highlanders were among them, slashing them with their claymores, and warding off the bayonet thrusts with their leathern targes. Soon the thin line was broken in half a dozen places by the weight of the Highlanders' onslaught. Retreat was impossible; behind the royal troops stretched the line of high walls, so they had no choice but to surrender or die fighting. Most of them chose to surrender. Cope himself galloped to Berwick with news of the disaster—"The first general in Europe," said a wit, "who had brought the first tidings of his own defeat!" He is remembered to this day in the impudent strains of the Jacobite ballad, "Hey, Johnnie Cope, are ye wauken yet?"

But Charles made no use of his spectacular victory. He lingered in Holyrood while regular troops poured into English harbours from the Continent. Not till the beginning of November did he cross the border to advance on London by the western route.

Disappointment followed; though the Prince captured Carlisle and advanced as far as Derby without meeting with any opposition, it was plain that the English did not want him. He obtained in England only three hundred recruits. Every day, too, the number of the Government troops was increasing. Wade, with one army, watched Charles's rear from Newcastle; the Duke of Cumberland, son of George II, was marching through the Midlands to meet him with a second; a third was encamped at Finchley for the defence of London—altogether thirty thousand regular troops were ranged against the five thousand Highlanders. And though the French Government had at last definitely promised to support him, its promise mattered little as long as the British fleet had command of the seas; a body of a few hundred Irish soldiers enlisted in the French army was the only force that it succeeded in sending to Scotland. In spite of the heavy odds against the Jacobites, their approach caused panic in London, where King George was preparing for flight.

Charles's officers pointed out to him that it was folly to advance farther, and with London only a hundred and thirty miles away, the Highlanders reluctantly turned about and trudged back by the way that they had come. They succeeded in outmarching Cumberland's army; at Clifton, however, Cumberland's advance-guard of cavalry blundered into the Jacobite rear-guard, which was commanded by Lord George Murray himself. The Highlanders, instead of retreating or remaining on the defensive, charged the dismounted troopers in their usual fashion, and drove them back with heavy loss. After this the royalist vanguard kept at a respectful distance from the Jacobite rear-guard.

At mid-winter the Highlanders, arm-in-arm, struggled across the flooded Esk, and stood once more upon Scottish soil. All was not lost, for other clans had declared for the Prince in his absence, and so he now found that he had at his disposal a force almost twice as large as that which had invaded England. On the other hand, such enthusiasm as there was in the Lowlands was rather on the other side. To Lowlanders, the Prince, the Hero, the Deliverer, was not Charles Edward, but William, Duke of Cumberland, who was soon to be hailed by the General Assembly of the Church of Scotland as "the brave defender of your royal father's throne, the happy restorer of our peace, and the guardian of all our sacred and civil interests." Cumberland's army was not an "English" army, but a government army, including Scottish regiments, and all in all there were actually more Scots in arms on the government side than on the Jacobite side.

At the beginning of 1746 Prince Charles moved against Stirling, but his siege operations against the Castle were interrupted by the news that General Hawley was marching from Edinburgh at the head of nine thousand regular troops. The two armies met near Falkirk; the Highlanders fired one volley which turned the advance of Hawley's cavalry into a panic-stricken flight, then, flinging away their muskets, they drew their swords and hurled themselves upon the long red line of infantry. The elements seemed to fight on their side; they were whirled along by a great storm of wind and hail which blinded and confused their antagonists. It was Sheriffmuir over again: on the right, one or two regular regiments stood firm, fired steadily, and repulsed every attack of the clansmen; on the left, the infantry gave way before the tremendous onslaught of the Highlanders, and fled in confusion. But in the tempest and gathering darkness the Highlanders could not follow up their advantage, and Hawley withdrew unmolested to Linlithgow, where some of his men set fire to the noble palace.

A few days later Charles abandoned the siege of Stirling and retired to the regions beyond the Tay, where in the late winter and early spring his followers captured a number of posts garrisoned by Government troops. But these minor successes could not stop the flow of deserters from the Jacobite army, or delay the day of reckoning. In April, Charles learned that Cumberland had led an army of nine thousand men up the east coast to Aberdeen and was advancing on Inverness, where the Jacobite headquarters were. At once the stragglers were summoned, but only five thousand Highlanders assembled on Drummossie Moor, near Culloden House, about five miles to the east of Inverness.

The government army soon forced the passage of the Spey and encamped outside the town of Nairn, about twelve miles from

Culloden. Lord George Murray, seeing that victory was impossible by ordinary means, proposed that a night attack should be made on Cumberland's camp. The plan miscarried; though the night march was begun, the men, weary and half-starved, dragged themselves along at such a pace, that, if they had reached the enemy's camp at all, it would have been in broad daylight. there was nothing for it but to order the dispirited troops to turn about and march back to Culloden. They struggled back to their camp, which they reached just as dawn was breaking, flung themselves on the ground, and at once fell asleep.

They were roused two hours later by the drums beating to arms; Cumberland's army was at hand. Half asleep, they moved forward to their battle positions. Their right flank was protected by a wall which ran southward to the River Nairn, a few hundred yards to the south, their left flank by the walls enclosing the grounds of Culloden House. Cumberland was confident of success. Not only were his troops twice as numerous as the Jacobites, they had been carefully trained, and knew now what to do when they had to meet the headlong charge of the Highlanders. He put only seven of his fifteen infantry battalions in the front line, and between each battalion and the next he placed two pieces of artillery. Should the Highlanders break through the front line, they would find themselves confronted by a second line consisting of six more battalions drawn up three deep, flanked by guns to right and left.

And now Cumberland's artillery thundered out, and the grape-shot whistled through the air. The rebel guns replied, but did little damage, while the Highlanders began to grow restive as they saw their comrades go down beside them. Meantime, the Argyll Highlanders, who were fighting for the Duke, crept up to the wall on the left flank of the regular infantry and began to pull down the stones to make a passage for the cavalry.

After the cannonade had lasted for an hour, the Prince told Lord George Murray to give the word to charge. The clans on the right swept down into a storm of snow that at once changed into a storm of grape-shot and musket bullets. It seemed as if nothing could stop them; they broke through the first line of the stubborn infantry and advanced upon the second. Their valour availed them nothing, for a battalion from the Duke's reserve advanced on the left of the second line and formed up at right angles to it. The Highlanders as they surged forward were caught between two fires: they crumpled up as volley after volley was poured into them, not only by the troops facing them but by the regiment on their flank.

The left wing advanced too, but something seemed to be amiss. It was composed of MacDonalds, and the MacDonalds, it is said, were indignant because they had been removed from the post of honour on the right wing, a position which they claimed had been theirs since the Battle of Bannockburn. Thrice they rushed forward, but thrice, as they looked at the long rows of levelled muskets, they hesitated and retired. The third time they noticed that the right of the army had been broken and was streaming back in disorder. There was nothing for them to do now but join in the general flight.

Meantime, Cumberland's horsemen had made their way through the gaps in the wall and fallen upon the flank and rear of the retreating army, which, indeed, could hardly be called an army any longer. The survivors had passed the limits of what men could endure. Though some of the clans kept together and retired in good order, it was for the most part a panic-stricken mob that fled westward, begging in vain for quarter from the pursuing dragoons.

The Prince watched the rout of his army with tears in his eyes. It would have been better for him if his had been the fate of James IV at Flodden, but when one of his Irish officers laid hold of his horse's bridle, he allowed himself to be led from the field. Soon after, he separated himself from his officers, and made his way to South Uist, in the hope that from that remote island he might be able to escape to France. But his chances seemed ridiculously small, for the island was overrun by hundreds of soldiers, every one of whom knew that a reward of £30,000 would be his if he captured the Prince, while the surrounding seas were patrolled by innumerable small war vessels.

From his perilous plight he was rescued by the quick wit and courage of a lady, Flora MacDonald, who disguised him in woman's clothes, obtained a passport for an imaginary maid-servant called "Betty Burke," and so succeeded in smuggling him over to the Isle of Skye. There "Betty" attracted a dangerous amount of attention. "I have never seen such a tall, impudent jaud in all my life," said a genuine maidservant to Flora MacDonald; "see what lang strides she takes."

But Skye, like Uist, was too hot to hold the Prince. He was forced to cross to the mainland, where he hid for a time in a cave occupied by seven robbers, till he was able to make his way to "Cluny's Cage," a hut hidden in a tangle of brushwood on the side of Ben Alder, where he dwelt some time with Macpherson of Cluny, the owner of the cage, and Cameron of Lochiel. Not till September 1746, five months after Culloden was fought, did he succeed in embarking on a French frigate and escaping to France.

It would have been well for him had he fallen "when the clans faced the bayonets and died on the guns." Though he lived on for another forty-two years, "the name died before the man," the gallant and chivalrous adventurer was forgotten in the querulous, drink-sodden voluptuary. Long before his death in 1788, the most devoted of his followers knew that he would never—could never—be their leader again. His younger brother, Henry, had renounced all secular ambitions and had become a priest. He died in 1807, a Cardinal and a pensioner of King George III.

Long before the death of the last Stewart prince, peace had descended upon the Highlands. The victorious Cumberland resolved to terrorise the Highlanders; not only did he instruct his troops to give no quarter to the fugitives fleeing from the battlefield, he ordered detachments of his soldiers to march into the country occupied by the rebel clans, burn their houses, destroy their corn, and drive away their cattle. He was backed up by the Government. Of the three thousand five hundred prisoners taken during the campaign, one hundred and twenty were executed, over eleven hundred were transported or banished, and almost seven hundred died as a result of their confinement in filthy and overcrowded prisons.

The Government went further. It was convinced that the clan system was the source of all trouble. In 1746 Parliament passed a Disarming Act—one which, this time, really did disarm—and an Act prohibiting the wearing of the kilt, plaid or any tartan garment. An Act of 1747, abolishing heritable jurisdictions throughout Scotland, had a much more limited effect in the Highlands than is often believed. It abolished the regality courts and so restricted the competence of baron courts that these soon passed out of existence, but very few Highland chiefs had regalities and many of them were in no way affected by this act. It was, however, important that chiefs now ceased to be judges and that, at the same time, the old inefficient hereditary sheriff was replaced by a competent lawyer appointed by the Crown. The disappearance of tenure by military service, in terms of another act, loosened still further the hold which the landowner had over his principal tenants.

But military operations and government legislation were not in themselves sufficient to transform Highland life and society and fit them into the new Scotland of the eighteenth century. It was not enough to impose such order that men no longer needed to carry arms for security, it was not enough even to induce such a change of habit and outlook that peaceful pursuits would occupy the time and thought of the Highlanders. Economic changes were necessary if the too numerous inhabitants of the Highlands were to be kept alive. A certain amount had been done between the risings to improve Highland agriculture, for some enterprising landlords introduced the potato. Some new industries had been introduced too: iron smelting, in a few places, utilised the native timber, lead mines were opened and, most important, the linen manufacture was extended—and it was remarked in 1745 that the weavers did not "quit their looms to dance after the Highland pipes." But much more was needed if the poverty of the Highlands was to be eliminated.

As we have seen, it was the pinch of hunger rather than sheer love of mischief which made the Highlander drive off the cattle and sheep of his Lowland neighbour. The best of the houses—with the exception of the dwellings of the chiefs—were miserable hovels, like the one which Dr. Johnson and Mr. Boswell visited on the shores of Loch Ness in 1773. The thick low walls were built of unmortared stone, with a core of turf or earth, and loose thatch covered the roof, held in place by ropes of heather or straw, weighted by stones, which rested on the top of the wall. As the thatch left the core of turf uncovered, the rain soaked in between the inner and outer surfaces of the walls, and kept the house damp even in the rare spells of dry weather. Often there was neither window nor chimney; at best, the window was a hole in the wall, closed by a piece of turf in stormy weather, and the chimney a hole in the roof. Within, a fire of peat smouldered night and day on the flat hearth-stone placed in the middle of the earthen floor, and, as the occupants of the house always refrained from placing it directly under the hole in the roof, the hut was always full of the odour of peat smoke. But the inhabitants did not mind. On the contrary, they wanted the interior of their houses to be properly smoked, for every few years they pulled down the sooty thatch and spread it on their fields as manure.

Unfortunately there were less pleasant odours in the hut than that of "peat reek"; one end of the house served as a shelter for the sheep and cattle, which in those days were kept under cover all winter. They entered by the same doorway as the human occupants, from whom they were separated, in the more carefully arranged houses, by a flimsy wicker-work partition. A similar partition somctimes separated the living room from a bedroom at the other end of the hut, where the bedsteads were wooden boards, and the spring mattresses closely packed bunches of heather.

All this time the people were living on the verge of starvation, working not too energetically—for in winter and summer alike, the rain-laden winds of the Atlantic prevented that—and with no special skill. But even if they had used the new iron swing plough instead of the spade or the old wooden plough, even if they had learned all the new lore of drainage and manure and the rotation of crops, they could have expected only a trifling increase from the crops grown on their sterile and rain-sodden soil. There were only a few places in the Western Highlands or the Hebrides where a farmer could succeed in growing corn for profit. To people in this position, a single bad harvest meant not only scarcity but actual starvation. Before the Forty-Five, however, they knew that they had the chief behind them. He counted his wealth, not in money, but in men; his rents were paid for the most part in kind, so that he got far more food than he or his family could consume. It was only natural, then, that he should keep open house, and in times of scarcity see that his clansmen had sufficient food. But the changes after the Jacobite risings put an end to all this. The estates forfeited after the Forty-Five were administered by Commissioners for nearly forty years, and by the time the former owners or their heirs were restored they had learned new ways of life. The chief became a landowner, to whom the existence of a multitude of half-starved dependants was a perplexity and not a pleasure. There was nothing now to bind him to the grim old feudal keep in which he had spent his boyhood, and so he often became an absentee, living in Edinburgh or London, and drawing his rents from tenants whom he never saw. Sometimes he sold his estates altogether, to a Lowland or English proprietor.

The Commissioners for the Forfeited Estates did some excellent work, not only in encouraging agricultural improvements but in other ways. The assistance given to the linen industry, involving the establishment of stations where the various processes were carried on, and the giving of instruction in schools, had the result that the amount of linen cloth produced in Perthshire more than trebled between 1748 and 1788, and in Inverness-shire, where production had been of small account in 1748, the increase was sevenfold. The Commissioners also spent thousands of pounds on roads and bridges, and concurrently the making of military roads continued, along routes for which Wade is given the credit.

It was seldom, before the Forty-Five, that the poorer tenant paid his rent directly to the chief, or that the chief received the whole of his rent from the poor tenant. Large estates were usually leased to tacksmen, petty magnates, who were often kinsmen of the chief. Each tacksman paid an annual rent to the chief, but the rent which he paid to the chief was much less than the rents which he in his turn received from the sub-tenants among whom his portion of the estate was divided. These sub-tenants, though their fathers, and their fathers' fathers, might have cultivated the same amount of ground, had no security of tenure. Their land was let to them from year to year, and if the chief or the tacksman chose to raise their rent or put another tenant in their place, they would have no remedy. The tacksman had performed a useful function in the days when the chiefs wanted a numerous body of fighting men, for he had been the organiser of armed retainers, but it was hard to justify the system in a peaceful society. The Commissioners for the Forfeited Estates regularly granted leases to tenants and gave them a new security.

The changing attitude of the chiefs towards their tenants and their estates is shown by three great changes which took place in the second half of the eighteenth century and the earlier part of the nineteenth century. The Highland landowners found that the system of running their estates with the help of tacksmen was extremely extravagant, so, by refusing to renew a tacksman's lease when it expired, they gradually eliminated the tacksmen altogether. This proceeding, of eliminating the tacksman, as a superfluous middleman, had begun on the Argyll estates in the 1730s. The landlord's rents, now received directly from his tenants, amounted to far more than he had received from the tacksman, and the commercial value of estates thus rose sharply. The landlords had discovered, too, that another way to make money out of their estates was to encourage sheep-farming, but sheep-farming required large stretches of land. Some of the sheep-runs were on ground hitherto little used except by deer, but others were formed at the expense of cultivation, for the landowner sometimes obtained them by transforming a group of small farms into one large farm, which he offered at a rent sometimes six times as much as that which the tenants had formerly paid. Sometimes there was no tenant on the estate who could pay the new rent, and so the dreamy, improvident Highlanders were often elbowed aside by some hard-headed Lowlander, who had enough money in his purse to enable him to stock the farm properly, and to pay the rent without difficulty. Often one of the original tenants, more provident and enterprising than his fellows, would take over the new farm, and at the end of a very few years live in comfort such as his fathers had never known, in a "white house," with wooden floors, glazed windows, and plastered walls. With the great demand for wool for the textile factories and for mutton to feed the people in the towns—among whom the consumption of meat rose sharply—the introduction of sheep-farming enormously increased the value of Highland estates.

Some of the dispossessed tenants, but only a few, found occupation as shepherds on the new farms, others moved from the inland glens to the sea-coast, where they were placed on crofts or small farms by their landlord. Others drifted south to Edinburgh and Glasgow, where they bent their spirits to such menial tasks as carrying sedan-chairs. Thousands of the more enterprising crossed to America, or enlisted in the new Highland regiments which were raised during the Seven Years' War.

The third change to be chronicled, besides the disappearance of the tacksmen and the appearance of the big sheep-farms, was the introduction of the crofting system. Hitherto, the arable land had been let out, not to individuals but to groups of men. Now the residue that was not transformed into sheep-walks was divided into crofts or compact holdings, each of which was assigned to a single tenant. When this arrangement was first made, it was calculated by the landowners that each croft should support a household, for, though they had only a few acres of arable land, they were still allowed to graze sheep and cattle on the hill pastures around their crofts, and as they were usually not far from some sea loch, they could combine fishing with agriculture. This change had the advantage of emancipating the individual from the hampering effect of communal conservatism, but crofts were apt to be divided and subdivided to accommodate new families as the population grew, until they became quite uneconomic.

CHAPTER 26

THE CHURCH SINCE THE UNION

THE settlement of the Church at the Revolution in 1690 had been a kind of middle-of-the-road settlement which made a certain appeal to the many Scots who were not zealots either for the Covenants and exaggerated theories of ecclesiastical independence on one side or for the episcopal order on the other; and it had an assured future in an age when the emphasis in many men's minds was moving away from the niceties of ecclesiastical politics to more mundane affairs. Yet there was no possibility that it could comprehend all Scots, and the period of the Revolution and the Union does in fact mark the end of the ecclesiastical unity which had on the whole been maintained, at least externally, in all earlier generations. While adherence to episcopacy dwindled sharply as the old Episcopalian incumbents were deprived or died and were replaced by Presbyterian ministers, there remained a core of Episcopalians who refused to be

STEWART TOMB AT ROME

PLATE 63

THE GENERAL ASSEMBLY

absorbed into the new establishment. On the other wing, the Cameronians and all who adhered rigidly to the Covenants repudiated a settlement by which Parliament continued to legislate for the church in Scotland and by which "prelacy" was established in England, and they went so far as to withhold acknowledgement of the civil sovereignty of uncovenanted monarchs. Moreover, even within the Church of Scotland itself there were divergent opinions on so many topics that it is questionable whether it could have long continued without schism and secession.

There were those who, while not rigid Covenanters, felt that the Covenants had been too lightly laid aside and that the community should not have been emancipated from the civil penalties formerly attached to excommunication. There were those who, while they had accepted the parliamentary decision for presbytery in 1690, were not prepared to accept the continued interference of Parliament, and especially a British Parliament at Westminster, in Church affairs. They objected not only to the restoration of patronage and the granting of toleration to Episcopalians, but also to the Abjuration Oath imposed on Church of Scotland ministers by the Toleration Act. And there were differences of opinion in theology as well: while one school of thought—the "Evangelicals"—adhered firmly to the strict doctrines of Calvin, especially on the subject of Predestination, others maintained the more liberal "Arminian" traditions which had been associated with many of the Episcopalians, and others again moved towards a religion from which the supernatural had been largely eliminated and which became little more than a pagan philosophy. To hold faith and works in an equilibrium has always been a central problem for Christianity, but as controversy developed in Scotland in this period many abandoned the notion of an equilibrium altogether and emphasised either faith or works to the exclusion of the other; some argued that the faithful were not bound by any moral law, others that only the moral law mattered and that Christianity was a mere code of ethics. In this situation, the operation of patronage was likely to cause peculiar difficulties, for it was not unlikely that patrons would hold more liberal views than congregations and would appoint ministers whose sermons might be despised by those who heard them.

The so-called First Secession, in 1733, reflected all the current trends and controversies. Ebenezer Erskine, minister at Stirling, the leader, had long been one of the most popular "Evangelical" preachers, he had opposed doctrinal modification, he had denounced the Abjuration Oath and he defended the rights of congregations against patrons. Refusing to accept the ruling of the General Assembly against him when he condemned those who held different views from his own, he seceded with some other ministers and formed a separate church, based not only on conservative theology but on a revival of the Covenants and the ultra-Presbyterian tradition of 1650. The First Secession split in 1745-7 because some of its members scrupled to take an oath in which burgesses had to acknowledge "the true religion presently professed within this realm," and which, the precise contended, implied an acknowledgement of the Established Church. Each section—Burgher and Anti-Burgher—split again at the end of the century into "Old Light" and "New Light" sections, this time over the question of the power to be ascribed to the magistrate in matters of religion and the duty of the state to enforce ecclesiastical discipline—though this was, it may be observed, a purely academic question in a non-established church. There were thus for a time four churches stemming from the First Secession.

About the middle of the eighteenth century disputes over patronage became more serious, and ministers who sympathised with the claims of popular rights began to decline to take part in the induction of men who had been presented by patrons. Thomas Gillespie, minister of Carnock, was deposed in 1752 for so declining, and was joined within a few years by two other ministers who had been chosen by parishioners in disagreement with patrons and had been established by their supporters in "meeting houses." Those three formed in 1761 the Relief Church —"a presbytery for the relief of Christians oppressed in their Christian privileges"—and, its origins being what they were, it moved towards what was called the "voluntary" principle, that the church should not seek official endowments or State support but that each congregation should make itself responsible for the maintenance of church and minister and should be largely responsible for running its own affairs.

The Established Church, thus rid of some of the disturbing

elements, settled down to acceptance of the *status quo* in its relations with the State, and accommodated itself to the changing thought of the times. The century saw a growing attachment to "reason," which sometimes involved rationalism in the sense of a denial of the supernatural, but always meant at least a stress on moderation and common sense, a distrust of emotion and "enthusiasm." As the literature, music, and architecture of the eighteenth century show, the tone of the period was correct, formal and restrained, and these qualities became characteristic of the Church as well. Patronage was accepted, and the protest against it, made annually by each General Assembly since 1736, was dropped in 1784. The emphasis of the "Moderates" who now ruled in the Assembly was on cultural, intellectual and social attainments, and they shocked the more precise by unashamedly playing cards and attending the theatre. Some of them no doubt were really preaching the essentials of Christianity, stripped of the theological verbiage and the obsession with ecclesiastical politics which had so often obscured it, but others neglected spiritual matters. One minister, it was said, had only two sermons, although he varied the texts; in one presbytery, when a minister did write a new sermon, it was passed round all his fellow-presbyters.

But there were other elements, besides the antiquated politics and theology of the Seceders and the devitalised religion of so many Moderates. The century was the century which in England saw the rise of Methodism, and John Wesley, its founder, himself paid many visits to Scotland. Methodism as a separate sect did not gain many followers among the Scots, but it encouraged, within the Church of Scotland itself, a new type of evangelicalism, spontaneous and emotional and quite at variance with the Moderate distrust of "enthusiasm." At the end of the century, partly in association with the preaching tours of the brothers Robert and James Haldane, there was a wave of religious awakening which touched all ranks of society. By this time there were stirrings in politics as well, and the appeal of the lofty aspirations associated with the French Revolution in its early stages encouraged a new humanitarianism which could link up more easily with the warmth of the Evangelicals than with the coolness of the Moderates.

Conflict between the two opposing outlooks emerged on such

an issue as foreign missions, into which Evangelicals were prepared to throw themselves wholeheartedly, while the Moderate majority in the Assembly (though not repudiating the obligation to propagate Christianity) declined to countenance inter-denominational foreign mission societies. Conflict appeared also over the question of the welfare of the churchless masses in the growing industrial towns. The Evangelicals were enthusiastic for the new Sunday Schools, while the Moderates were suspicious—and perhaps not entirely without reason, for the schools were not for children alone and were apt to provide opportunities for political propaganda and agitation. The Evangelicals, again, raised money for the provision of additional churches or "chapels of ease," to supplement the parish system, while the Moderates looked askance at a movement which threatened to withdraw congregations from their legal parish ministers, and they foresaw legal difficulties in the relations of such churches to the laws governing the parish system.

The issues between the two parties covered the whole range of the question of how the Church could best perform its spiritual and humanitarian functions. The Evangelicals were not primarily ecclesiastical politicians, as many seceders had been, but they were driven to ecclesiastical politics because the existing system frustrated them in their aims. Patronage again became a much canvassed grievance, partly because it seemed contrary to the liberal thought which advocated popular rights in the state and partly because it was believed to perpetuate the domination of the Moderates. Almost equally important was the question of incorporating the new chapels of ease and their ministers into the legal polity of the Church. The Evangelicals contended that the Church could create a *quoad sacra* parish, a parish which was an entity for ecclesiastical purposes only; but it was not so easy to disentangle what was ecclesiastical from what was civil, since the Church was then responsible for education and poor relief, and if the ministers of *quoad sacra* parishes were admitted to presbyteries and General Assemblies then the validity of the acts of these courts might be open to question. In 1833 the Assembly passed a "Veto Act," which declared the disapproval of a congregation to be conclusive against the acceptance of a presentee, and a "Chapel Act," which admitted the ministers of chapels of ease to full membership of the church courts.

As the Assembly had now challenged statute law, case after case arose in which the law courts inevitably pronounced the Assembly's actions to be illegal. The consequence of the recurrent conflict was the decision of the more determined Evangelicals to withdraw from the State connection, and in the "Disruption" of 1843 about thirty-nine per cent of the ministers of the establishment gave up their stipends and their manses to "cast themselves on such provision as God in His providence may afford." About a third of the people followed them, and the Free Church of Scotland was formed. The Free Church had many wealthy and influential supporters, and the generosity and enthusiasm of its people made it possible to erect churches and schools and maintain ministers and teachers throughout the length and breadth of the land, on such a scale that there was a duplication of the entire ecclesiastical and educational systems.

The Disruption was the greatest of the secessions from the Church of Scotland, but it was also the last. Indeed, already before the Disruption, there had been the first indication that there would be a new trend, this time towards reunion. The two sections of New Light Seceders had come together in 1820 to form the United Secession Church, and in 1842 most of the Old Light Seceders had joined to form the United Original Secession Church. Four years after the Disruption the Relief Church combined with the United Secession to form the United Presbyterian Church. The Free Church then attracted into its fold in 1863 the majority of the United Original Secession and in 1876 the majority of the Reformed Presbyterians (the descendants of the Cameronians). Thus, by the end of the century there were, besides the Church of Scotland, only two other large Presbyterian bodies—the Free Church and the United Presbyterian Church. There were also three small denominations—the minorities of United Original Seceders and Reformed Presbyterians who had declined to enter into unions, and the Free Presbyterians, who had left the Free Church in 1893 on theological grounds.

The next stage in reunion was reached in 1900, when the United Presbyterian Church joined with the Free Church to form the United Free Church. This union attracted more notice, and that not merely because it was on a larger scale than earlier unions. The United Presbyterians stood for the "voluntary" principle, and renounced the whole concept of State support, but the Free Church, although it had in fact been organised and maintained as a voluntary Church, had adhered to the principle of establishment. It was therefore contended that when the Free Church joined the United Presbyterians it was renouncing a cardinal point in its policy, and for this reason a section of the Free Church refused to go into the Union. Not only so, but this continuing Free Church, claiming that it was true to principles which the majority had renounced, successfully asserted its right, in a lawsuit which went to the House of Lords, to the entire property of the Free Church. The intervention of a Royal Commission was then necessary to arrive at an equitable division of the property between the majority and the minority.

The United Free Church, as thus formed in 1900, was a more serious rival to the establishment than any previous non-established Church, for it could muster 1,700 ministers against 1,400 in the Church of Scotland. It was clear that, should union be carried a stage further, the United Free Church would be able to dictate its terms. Some of the obstacles which had stood in the way of union between the Free Church and the establishment had been removed shortly after the Disruption, and in 1874 one old-standing grievance was eliminated by the abolition of patronage. When negotiations for union began—they went on intermittently from 1909 to 1929—it emerged that what was to be required was little less than surrender by the Church of Scotland of its whole historic position as an endowed and established Church, and almost complete victory for all that the Free Church had contended for in 1843. In 1921 Parliament approved certain Declaratory Articles in which the Church of Scotland asserted its "right and power, subject to no civil authority, to legislate and to adjudicate finally, in all matters of doctrine, worship, government, and discipline," which was tantamount to Parliament's final abdication of its ecclesiastical authority in Scotland. (Rather oddly, however, no steps were taken to abolish the oath by which each sovereign, on his or her accession, still asserts his or her determination to maintain the Church of Scotland as it was established in 1690.) In 1925 the system, established by Charles I, whereby the stipends of parish ministers were provided from the teinds of the parish or dues paid in place of such teinds, was swept away, and with it went the duty of the heritors of the parish to maintain the church and manse; although large funds, derived from a fixed charge on land, continued to be drawn each year by the Church of Scotland, it had made a great financial sacrifice, paid as part of the price of union. Taken along with certain minor changes, these measures satisfied the scruples of the majority of the members of the United Free Church and extinguished many prolonged controversies. A small minority of United Free Church ministers and people declined, however, to enter into the union of 1929.

In 1956 the remnant of the United Original Secession Church wound up its affairs and was absorbed into the Church of Scotland, so that as a result of all the schisms and secessions among the Presbyterians there remained only the tiny remnant of Reformed Presbyterians (Cameronians), the Free Church and the Free Presbyterian Church (neither of much account outside certain Highland areas) and the United Free Church.

Successive schisms and reunions are the most conspicuous feature in Presbyterian history since the Union, but the Presbyterian churches have undergone many internal changes, especially within the last hundred years or so. The distaste for liturgical worship which stemmed from the reaction against the policy of Charles I and the subsequent alliance between the Scottish Presbyterians and the English Puritans led to a bleak austerity in Church services which has taken a long time to die. Throughout the eighteenth century and into the nineteenth public worship did not include even the reading of the Bible—which the people were supposed to read at home for themselves—and still less the recitation of "set forms" like the Apostles' Creed and the Lord's Prayer. The minister preached a long sermon, he delivered rambling prayers which were in themselves partly sermons, and the congregation took no part in the service save when, led by a precentor, they sang metrical psalms to a monotonously small selection of tunes. The proceedings were enlivened by the denunciation from the pulpit of the "penitents" whose breaches of morality had been found out by the kirk-session. Celebrations of Holy Communion remained infrequent, and the most conspicuous feature of sacramental worship in the eighteenth century was the gathering of large numbers of people from a wide area for a joint service—the "holy fairs" described in the verse of

Robert Burns, those "jostling, promiscuous assemblies" where reverence and devotion were often at a minimum.

The last hundred and fifty years have brought about a great transformation. The ordered reading of the Scriptures has been restored to its place in public worship, sermons have become shorter and a more liturgical character has been given to the services in some churches, with congregational recitation of the Lord's Prayer and the Creed. Service-books reappeared, introduced by individuals and societies in the nineteenth century, and a *Book of Common Order* was officially approved by the General Assembly in 1940. The general aim has been to go back beyond the period of English Puritan influence and to recover the principles of the first reformers. In music, the metrical psalms were supplemented first by the Paraphrases and then by successive Hymnaries which comprehend a wide range of Christian praise and devotion and abundant variety of musical settings. The restoration of better musical standards, involving the supersession of the precentor by a choir and an organ, had for a time the effect of making churches look rather like concert halls, dominated as they were by the organ casing and the platform for the choir, but in the twentieth century the tendency has been to re-plan churches in such a way that the focus of worship is unmistakably the Holy Table. The harsh kirk-session discipline was for the most part quietly laid aside in the course of the nineteenth century. Doctrinally, the Westminster Confession of Faith retains an official position, but subscription to its *formulae* in all their rigour is no longer required.

In the eighteenth and nineteenth centuries there had sprung up a number of churches, representative mainly of a more evangelical type of religion than was provided by the Presbyterian Churches —Methodists, Congregationalists and Baptists as well as smaller denominations. None of these can be said to stem from the main Scottish tradition. The Episcopal Church, however, has a continuous history linking it directly with those members of the Church of Scotland who declined to accept the Parliamentary establishment of Presbyterianism in 1690. Those of them who agreed to acknowledge Queen Anne and the Hanoverian kings enjoyed toleration from 1712, but a great many of them were Jacobites, who acknowledged "James VIII" and then "Charles III" as their kings until the death of Bonnie Prince Charlie in

1788. For those "non-jurors" there was sometimes severe persecution, especially in the aftermath of each Jacobite rising, and they were not able to qualify for toleration until 1792. The two sections of the Episcopal Church—the former jurors and non-jurors—drew together thereafter and ultimately organised their churches throughout the country under seven bishops, who retain among them the titles of the fourteen historic sees.

The Roman Catholic Church, as a regularly organised institution within Scotland, hardly existed until the 1690s. While there had been widespread lack of sympathy with the Reformation, and sometimes stubborn opposition to it, in some parts of the country, practically nothing had been done to rally that opposition, and the Counter-Reformation of the sixteenth century had made little impact on Scotland in a religious sense, whatever its political effects. By the early seventeenth century, Roman Catholic effort in Scotland was virtually extinct, and as the century went on the missions conducted by Irish priests were so intermittent and short-lived that about 1680 the Roman Catholic population was estimated, by a friendly observer, as being no more than 12,000—a few of them in Dumfriesshire, a few in the highlands of Aberdeenshire and Banffshire and the bulk of them to the north and west of the Great Glen. As a result of the more consistent and sustained effort which began in the 1690s considerable gains were soon claimed. Even so, the Roman Catholic population does not seem to have exceeded 30,000 throughout the eighteenth century and the beginning of the nineteenth. The situation was then transformed by the great immigration from Ireland, and in a hundred years the number of Roman Catholics increased twentyfold. Over the whole country the nominal Roman Catholic strength is about fifteen per cent of the population, but in the Glasgow area it is nearly a third.

A survey made in the late 1950s shows that some sixty per cent of the adult population of Scotland are members of one church or another. There are well over twenty denominations, but of the total church membership 63.5 per cent belongs to the Church of Scotland and twenty-five per cent to the Roman Catholic Church, while no other body can claim more than about two per cent. Nominal membership, however, is a very different thing from active support: on an average Sunday only one in four of the people of Scotland attends a church service, and only one in eight attends a service of the Church of Scotland. Strenuous efforts were made, in the 1950s, to attract greater support for the churches, but their results, so far as statistics show, were trivial.

CHAPTER 27

SCOTLAND'S INDUSTRIAL ECONOMY IN THE NINETEENTH CENTURY

THE rule of "King Cotton" over the heart of industrial Scotland continued until the middle of the nineteenth century and even a little later. About seventy-five per cent of the output came from mills in Lanarkshire and Renfrewshire, and there was an especially heavy concentration in Glasgow and its immediate neighbourhood. After 1800 power was increasingly applied to weaving as well as spinning, and the factory system became characteristic of both sides of the industry. The hand-loom weavers in general suffered severely from the change, though some of them continued to make a good living by producing fine, specialised work, such as the Paisley shawls, where the power-looms could not compete. The point of maximum expansion of the industry as a whole seems to have been reached by the 1850s, and there was already a tendency to a slight decline when the prosperity of this major part of the Scottish economy was shattered, as the tobacco trade had been shattered in the previous century, by events on the other side of the Atlantic. This time it was the American Civil War (1861-65), which cut off the supplies of raw cotton and brought the Scottish factories almost to a standstill. After the war, recovery was only partial, for there was increasing competition from other countries and from Lancashire, which showed itself more adaptable to the changing demands of the consumers. Only certain specialised work continued in Scotland, such as "lace" curtains and the cotton thread required for the recently invented sewing machines.

Other textiles, unaffected by the disaster which had overtaken cotton, continued to flourish into the twentieth century. In the linen industry also, though more slowly than in cotton, the factory system at length prevailed throughout, partly because the competition of cotton made the hand-production of linen no longer economic and partly because the agricultural changes made farming a full-time occupation and made it difficult to continue part-time spinning or weaving in the countryside. The linen industry, once so widespread over the country, was driven from the west by cotton and came to be concentrated almost entirely in Angus and Fife. Even in that area there was increasing specialisation, and the introduction of a new textile material, jute, drove linen from some of its former centres. Dunfermline remained a great linen centre, but Kirkcaldy came to specialise in linoleum and in Dundee all other textiles were ousted by jute. Jute imports were negligible in 1838 but by 1883 had reached a quarter of a million tons, and Dundee was the outstanding example of a town where a single industry dominated the scene.

With the decay of cotton, however, the emphasis of the Scottish economy, especially in the west, was no longer on textiles, but on the heavy industries—coal, iron, steel, engineering and shipbuilding—which rose to a dominating position in the second half of the nineteenth century.

The demand for coal was increased by many developments—the extension of the employment of steam engines in textile factories, in ships and in locomotives, the expansion of the iron industry, and the use first of all (from the 1820s) of coal gas, later of electricity, for lighting and heating; and at the same time railways and coastal steamships made it easier than ever before to make coal available in every part of Scotland. There was, too, a very large export trade from the east coast ports to London and the Continent. Far and away the majority of the collieries were in Lanarkshire and Ayrshire, and the total output rose from seven and a half million tons in 1854 to thirty-nine million tons in 1908.

Scottish iron was given an assured future by the invention of the hot blast by James Neilson in 1828. Heating the air used in the blast furnaces made it possible to use coal and iron which had hitherto been thought unsuitable for smelting, and in particular to exploit the blackband ironstone of Lanarkshire, which contained rich iron ore and a considerable proportion of coal but which had hitherto been cast aside as "wild coal." In ten years the number of furnaces more than doubled, and production increased more than fifty per cent, with a heavy concentration in Lanarkshire and Ayrshire. By 1860 a million tons of pig iron were being produced annually, and production remained at a little above that figure until 1914, despite the fact that the Scottish iron fields were becoming exhausted and the bulk of the iron ore had now to be imported. Cast iron was in use for a wide range of products, from domestic utensils to railway-bridges, and the invention of Nasmyth's steam hammer in 1839 made it possible to produce malleable iron which would stand the strains and stresses of the new machine age. Later in the century, however, interest began to centre on steel, the efficient manufacture of which began with the invention of improved processes about 1860. Once its production was established it rapidly replaced malleable iron for many purposes; for example, in a single decade (1879-89), steel almost completely ousted iron in shipbuilding.

Engineering was virtually a new industry. There were men who had been engaged on the construction and maintenance of machinery in cotton mills, there were intelligent and adaptable smiths, and there were foundries with considerable specialised skill in the forging of plates, bars, and rods. But, apart from the vast scale of production now necessary, there had to be a new precision which required improved lathes, power-driven tools for cutting, planing, boring and slotting, and accurate measuring apparatus. The experience acquired in the manufacture of stationary steam engines was rapidly applied first to engines for steamships, from almost the beginning of the century and then to locomotives for the railroads, from about 1830.

The earliest marine engines were fitted in wooden hulls, but iron ships appeared about 1830 and by 1845 more iron than wooden ships were being built. The Clyde had the raw materials and the skilled labour of workers in the iron industry, and was ready to turn to iron in place of wood, with the result that Clydeside took a foremost place in the world's shipbuilding. Between 1859 and 1889 the tonnage of shipping built on the Clyde showed a tenfold increase, and came to represent a third or more of the total British tonnage. By this time most of the

THE UNION CANAL

View of Edinburgh Castle and St. Giles from Port Hopetoun. This is a reproduction of an oil painting (artist unknown) of the canal basin opened in 1822.

new ships were steamers, but some of the finest and fastest of the clippers—the final glory of the sailing ship—were built in Scotland, either on the Clyde or in Aberdeen.

Scotland had a variety of other industries. There was, for example, the old-established but always expanding paper-making, printing and publishing; there was the distilling of whisky, which was put on a commercial basis in the early nineteenth century; and there was the manufacture of such wholly new articles as sewing machines, in the great Singer Factory at Clydebank (1884). Yet the core of the Scottish economy lay in a narrow range of textiles and heavy industry.

Both the roads and the canals had just reached their maximum efficiency, within the limits imposed by dependence on horses for traction, when the railways appeared and transformed interior communications. Railroads or wagonways, over which wagons drawn by horses slowly rumbled, had appeared in the eighteenth century, mostly as a means of conveying coal from the pits to the nearest point where waterborne transport was possible—from Tranent to Cockenzie, for example. And even when the steam locomotive first appeared in the 1820s the railways were mainly associated with coalfields and were an adjunct to canals or shipping. About 1830, however, lines independent of the canals, and designed for passengers as well as minerals, made their appearance, for example Glasgow to Garnkirk (1831), Dundee to Newtyle, Edinburgh to Dalkeith. Development was piecemeal, for Scotland was divided geographically into regions separated from one another by natural obstacles. One landmark was the Glasgow-Ayr line (1840), which connected Glasgow with the watering-places on the coast of the south-west, another was the Edinburgh-Glasgow line (1842), a trunk line which joined the two biggest centres of population in the country—and which at one stroke went a long way towards putting the canals in that area out of business. The mid-forties were a period of railway mania, when it was remarked that "Britain is at present an island of lunatics, all railway-mad." There was much loss of amenity, both in rural and urban areas, for neither antiquity nor beauty was considered when railway lines were planned.

The principal extensions were to the south and on the east coast. Both the eastern and western routes to the Border, connecting with English lines, were open by 1850, and the routes from Edinburgh and Glasgow to Aberdeen were completed a little later. Northwards, the line from Perth to Inverness was completed by 1863, and its extensions to Strome Ferry and Thurso by 1870 and 1874 respectively. Expansion in the west came in the main somewhat later—Oban in 1880, Fort William in 1899, Mallaig in 1912—and the west was to the end relatively ill-served, for practicable routes were few. Yet ultimately nearly all Scotland was within at most twenty miles of a railway and far and away the greater part of the country was within ten miles of one. In the mid-twentieth century, when the tale is of the progressive withdrawal of train services and the closing of lines, we are apt to forget the enormous enterprise, capital, engineering skill and manual labour which went to the making of the railways. By the beginning of the twentieth century the railway companies had already bridged estuaries and lochs some of which are not even yet crossed by road bridges. From the very outset, the railways attained speeds which put them in a position far in advance of their competitors, and indeed some of the schedules were as good by the 1880s as they have ever been.

The developments in sea transport were in some ways of even greater importance, in an age when the Scottish economy was becoming ever more linked with world-wide commerce. Glasgow, with further deepening and widening of the Clyde and the creation of a dock system, became the third port in Britain (after London and Liverpool) and also the headquarters of great shipping lines trading all over the world—the Clan Line, the City Line, and the Anchor Line. On the east coast, too, there was considerable development, with docks and wharves at Leith, Dundee, and Aberdeen and the creation of a new port at Grangemouth, which (though not until well through the twentieth century) was to displace Leith as the second port in Scotland. The increasing size of ships necessitated concentration in a few large ports, and all round the shores of Scotland the ancient small harbours declined into nothing more than fishing ports or decayed altogether.

As early as 1802 the people of Kirkintilloch had been astonished to see a strange monster, breathing smoke and steam, churning its way through the water of the Forth and Clyde Canal at the rate of almost six miles an hour, and pulling two barges after it.

They were looking at the first steamboat, the *Charlotte Dundas*, which William Symington had designed after years of experiment. But the *Charlotte Dundas* was allowed to make only a few voyages, for it was feared that the wash would undermine the banks of the canal, and the importance of the new invention was not fully realised until 1812, when the *Comet*, built by another Scotsman, Henry Bell, began to ply, first of all between Glasgow, Greenock, and Helensburgh and later between Crinan and Oban. While sailing vessels long retained the advantage of economy for long voyages, and were not displaced in the eastern trade until the opening of the Suez Canal in 1869, the steamship almost at once prevailed in estuary and coastal traffic and from the outset developed speeds which put it ahead of its rivals. The earlier marine engines were extravagant in their coal consumption, but in the course of the century there was a series of improvements which effected economies and gave higher speeds and more efficiency—the screw propeller (which displaced the paddle except for certain specialised work), the compound and then the triple expansion engines, and finally, at the turn of the century, the steam turbine. With all those developments Clydeside engineers were closely associated.

Steam navigation, besides establishing closer links between Scotland and other lands overseas, also revolutionised internal communications within Scotland, for a major part in the transport of both goods and passengers was played by coastal shipping. Apart from traffic to and from the western and northern islands, there were places on the mainland which were not accessible by road or rail and there were routes where the sea offered a more rapid and convenient means of travel than either coach or train. Steamers plied on inland lochs like Loch Tay and Loch Awe, on a route from Glasgow to Inverness via the Crinan and Caledonian Canals, and also on the east coast, linking London with Leith, Dundee and Aberdeen. Even when the steamship was slower than the train it offered cheaper rates for both cargoes and passengers. After the First World War, when coal became much more expensive, coastal traffic declined, and since the Second World War the competition of road transport has gone a long way towards driving coastal shipping out of business.

Everywhere in a review of Scottish industry in the nineteenth century there is the same tale of progress, of prosperity, of great fortunes accumulated by shrewd and thrifty Scotsmen who had begun with no capital but their brains. There were, however, occasional setbacks: from about 1870 to 1900 a world shortage of bullion led to falling prices and industrial recession; and the Scottish banking system, which had greatly aided the expansion of industry, was temporarily shaken by the collapse of the City of Glasgow Bank in 1878. Again, when we leave industrial Scotland, and turn to survey what was happening in the country districts, the picture is not so pleasing.

The changes in agriculture spread through the country only very gradually, and some of those which are thought characteristic of the eighteenth century were still going on in some areas in the nineteenth. In many districts small farms of the old type, worked by the tenant and the members of his family, were numerous long after 1820, and indeed are far from being extinct in some areas to-day. But in the more productive areas of the Lowlands, at least, the small farmer was fighting a losing battle, and the new-fashioned farmer went on from one novelty to another. Even by 1830 the tall brick chimney rising from the farm-steading showed that some of the farmers had installed steam engines to drive their threshing mills; others were experimenting with the primitive reaping machine which an Angus minister had invented. In time a whole range of mechanised implements appeared—not only reapers, but binders, hay-gatherers, hay-spreaders and potato diggers. The horse, however, was not in general displaced for traction until the advent of the motor tractor in the twentieth century.

Farming of every kind was at first stimulated by the growth of the towns and the demands of their populations. The repeal of the Corn Laws, in 1846, desirable though the step was in the interests of cheap food, was bound in the long run to be detrimental to British agriculture, for the country could be fed more cheaply on wheat imported from the virgin lands of North America. To make matters worse, in the 1870s there was a series of bad harvests and only farmers with capital behind them could weather the storm which assailed them from two quarters at once. As prices fell, the acreage under wheat fell catastrophically, there was a sharp decrease also in barley and a decrease even in oats, and there was a serious agricultural depression. In 1857 almost a quarter of a million acres were under wheat; in

OPENING OF THE GLASGOW-GARNKIRK RAILWAY, 1831

THE HIGHLAND RAILWAY

An early Highland Railway passenger train on the tracks between Dingwall and Strathpeffer. The Highland line had Inverness as its headquarters and opened up inland areas which formerly relied

1877 this had shrunk to about 81,000 acres, and in 1928 to 58,000 acres. In 1877, 269,845 acres were under barley, in 1928 only 117,369; in 1877, 1,024,882 acres were under oats, in 1928 only 878,436. Of course, stock-raising, with continued improvements in the quality of Scottish cattle, to some extent took the place of arable farming, but was not complete compensation, and there was an over-all decline in the importance of agriculture.

Whilst agriculture declined, there was an unprecedented development of the fishing industry. From the seventeenth century to the early nineteenth, one effort after another had been made to encourage the exploitation by the Scots of the rich fishing grounds around their shores, but they had met with only indifferent success. Only in the late nineteenth century did Scots at last begin to profit substantially from the herring fishing of the east and north, which had for so long been in the hands of foreigners, especially the Dutch. Larger, decked boats went further afield in search of herring, and the advent of the steam drifter made it possible for the same boats to follow the herring on their seasonal movements round the coasts not only of Scotland but of England as well. The number of barrels of herring cured in Scotland rose from 100,000 in 1812 to 1,500,000 in 1880, and in 1905, when at least 300 steam drifters were at work, over 1,000,000 barrels were cured in Shetland alone. With the employment of coopers, gutters, packers, and so forth at the various ports, and of ships to carry the cured herring to the Continent, the industry was of very great importance. Shore-workers, like the girls who gutted the herring, accompanied the boats as they moved from Stornoway and Lerwick down to Fraserburgh and then on to Yarmouth and Lowestoft.

The inshore fishing for white fish, conducted from innumerable small ports, had always been considerable, and it continued—the fish still being caught by lines, for the seine net was not introduced until 1920. Deep-sea white fishing was transformed with the beginning of trawling in the 1880s, and when steam trawlers appeared they were able to go to more distant waters in the north. Aberdeen became the third trawling port in Great Britain, and Leith and Granton also were important Scottish centres.

If there was a contrast between the prosperity of industrial Scotland and the difficulties of the rural areas of Lowland Scotland, there was an even greater contrast with the Highlands, which had their special difficulties. In spite of emigration overseas and of movement of population within Scotland, the number of people in the Highlands continued to rise until well into the nineteenth century. The small crofts could, after the introduction of the potato, yield enough food to keep body and soul together in a good year, but at the best they provided a bare subsistence.

DOMESTIC UTENSILS FOUND IN CROFT HOUSES BEFORE THE INDUSTRIAL REVOLUTION

1. Whisky jar 2. Bread spade 3. Salt jar: 'kit' slipware
4. Girdle 5. Toaster used for toasting oatcakes in front of fire after leaving girdle
6. Horn spoons 7. Pewter pot 8. Spirit flask
9. Skirlie pot 10. Mustard pot 11. Pepper mill

Occupations subsidiary to crofting were essential. The development of fishing in certain areas provided a suitable supplement to crofting, and the employment of local labour in the making of the Crinan and Caledonian Canals and in the construction of roads gave work and wages to Highlanders who could not otherwise have made ends meet. The most important industry, however, was the manufacture of kelp—the making of soda from the burning of seaweed. At the beginning of the nineteenth century this gave employment to 50,000 Highlanders and Islanders, but the kelp industry had grown up behind the shelter of an import duty on barilla—soda prepared in Spain from the barilla plant—and a similar duty on salt, heavy enough to keep it from being used in the manufacture of soda. The reduction of the duty on salt in 1817, followed by the halving of the duty on barilla in 1822, killed the kelp industry. While it had flourished it had, in conjunction with the subdivision of crofts, led to spectacular increases in population in some of the island parishes, and their position was now extremely precarious.

Then in the 1840s there were disastrous years for the potato crops, resulting in widespread distress and actual famine. The Government was slow to act, but some landlords spent vast sums on relief and there was much organisation of assistance by charitable societies designed to raise subscriptions in the Lowlands. Emigration, too, was arranged and aided by landlords and by societies. In 1847, the Board of Destitution organised the employment of Highlanders in railway and highway construction, and the same year brought the Medical Relief Grant, to subsidise medical practitioners in the Highlands and Islands. It began to be realised that there was something wrong with a country where the difference between potatoes and no potatoes was also the difference between life and death: there were far too many people in the Highlands—that was the chief cause of the trouble, and none but the most obstinate could doubt it.

Already, early in the century, there had in Sutherland been widespread clearances of tenants from land which was to be utilised for sheep. Many of the tenants were settled in crofts on the coast, where they were intended to prosecute the fishing. In the second half of the century there was another wave of clearances or evictions, in other parts of the Highlands, now sometimes in the interests of deer forests, and some of the islands, as well as mainland areas, had their population drastically reduced in consequence: Rum, for example, was virtually depopulated. Yet some of the islands still had far more people than they could support, and in the 1880s several factors combined to produce a new crisis—there was again a failure of the potato crop, the grain crops were poor, the price of cattle fell and the fishing was unsuccessful. There were land raids, when crofters seized by force land which they claimed they could cultivate, and elsewhere attempts to collect rents led to rioting.

In 1886 the Crofters' Holdings Act gave crofters security of tenure, with in effect the privileges but not the responsibilities of ownership, fixed rents, provided for the payment of compensation for improvements effected by tenants and set up the Crofters' Commission, with power to enlarge holdings and reduce rents. This met the popular demand at the time, but it has since become only too plain that to grant security of tenure to the extent of abandoning all control over the use to which the holdings were put was a grave mistake. Tenants were under no obligation to cultivate their holdings or even to reside on them, and, at least in some areas, far more land has passed out of cultivation and been allowed to degenerate into rough grazing under the operation of the Crofters' Act than happened in the course of earlier clearances and evictions. Nor did the new legislation do much, if anything, to arrest emigration, for the drift southwards and westwards went on. It is undeniable that when the exile left the languid, moist-laden air and sterile soil of his native glen he generally gained, if not wealth, at least comfort. To be owner of two hundred acres of good cornland in Manitoba, or to be an engineer in Sydney, was far better materially than to remain tenant of two or three or half a score of acres in Skye or Sutherland. But it is hard to remember this when one looks at the roofless cottages, overgrown with nettle and foxglove, that are to be seen in every Highland glen, or stranger still, when one comes on a whole village, once the home of two-score families, now as dead as Pompeii or Herculaneum.

The population of Scotland as a whole continued to increase steadily throughout the nineteenth century—1,608,420 in 1801; 4,760,904 in 1911—for the decreases in counties like Argyll and Sutherland were far more than offset by the enormous increases in the industrial areas: Lanarkshire increased tenfold and by 1911 had nearly as many people as the whole of Scotland had had in 1801. Part of the increase was due to a large immigration from Ireland. With the potato famine in the 1840s, Irishmen by the thousand crowded into central Scotland, and since they were fleeing from starvation they were content to accept any wage that would put food into their stomachs, and to herd together in any house, however small and squalid it might be. This influx of Irishmen gave the Scottish employer an unlimited supply of cheap labour, but it tended to lower the wages of the less highly skilled among the Scottish workmen. Again, this peaceful invasion of Scotland by people of a different race, with different traditions, different ways of looking at things, created some difficult problems. There were regions of industrial Scotland which practically ceased to be Scottish; their inhabitants regarded themselves as Irish and looked on Ireland as their home. And, while Irish were coming in, many Scots, often of the most intelligent and enterprising types, were emigrating from their homeland, some of them to England but a great many of them to the United States and the British Dominions.

CHAPTER 28

SOCIAL CONDITIONS AND ADMINISTRATION IN THE INDUSTRIAL AGE

A WALK through the stately terraces and squares and past the white villas set among new planted trees, in a Scottish city in the middle of the nineteenth century, would have shown nothing but signs of increasing prosperity and increasing comfort. But if we had turned to the unfashionable quarters of the town, abandoned by the owners of these new houses, we should have found that they had a very different story to tell. They were far more dirty, crowded and uncomfortable than they had been a generation before. The population of the ordinary Scottish industrial town was growing at a tremendous rate—Glasgow for example had 77,385 inhabitants in 1801, and 202,420 in 1831; Dundee, fewer than 27,000 in 1801 and over 45,000 in 1831. The increase was caused largely by an influx of strangers—not only country folk from neighbouring parishes, but immigrants from the Highlands and from Ireland, lured thither by hope of work. The newcomers had to live somewhere, and accommodation was found for them partly in the old "lands" which had recently been abandoned by their more prosperous tenants. The old dwelling-houses were divided and subdivided;

few Scottish working men could boast of a house containing more than two rooms; many had to be content with one. And though the town broke through its ancient boundaries in more directions than one, though the villas on the west were balanced by row after row of grim tenements on the east, "these additional suburbs," as a Dundee minister remarked, "were built without any general plan and without the least regard to health, elegance or cleanliness." Here, as in the older quarters of the town, one-roomed and two-roomed houses were the rule.

Part of the trouble had been that the expansion of the cities had started at a time when there was not only far too little regard for amenity but when municipal affairs were often grossly mismanaged. Under the old system, the councillors could do very much what they liked with the burgh and its revenues, knowing that their voteless fellow townsmen could not drive them from office. Again and again a provost or bailie would help himself to a big slice of the common land of the burgh, paying a ridiculously low price, and his comrades on the council, instead of protesting, lay low until they could follow his example. And to sins of commission they added sins of omission: the rapidly expanding towns were allowed to grow anyhow, without plan or arrangement; it was none of their business if houses and factories were mixed up in hopeless confusion, if new tenements were planted in already over-crowded areas and if green spaces in the heart of the town disappeared under masses of stone and lime. Every big Scottish town, even Edinburgh, even Aberdeen, glittering in all the splendour of granite, has its story to tell to-day of opportunities wasted through the shortsightedness, the lack of imagination of those who ruled in those critical years.

The cities had far outgrown the medieval methods of disposing of refuse, but progress lagged far behind the needs of the time. It was inevitable that in the crowded tenements, some of them looking on to sunless and malodorous lanes or courts, all of them without drains and without a proper water-supply, there should be breeding grounds of disease. Apart from the refuse heaps in the streets, unhealthy conditions arose from fishmarkets and slaughter-houses, as well as from the vermin of all kinds which infested many of the houses. One ancient scourge—smallpox—had been very largely eliminated by the introduction of vaccination at the end of the eighteenth century, but other diseases succeeded it, especially "fevers" like typhus, which always lurked in unhygienic conditions, and also cholera, epidemics of which caused thousands of deaths in 1832, 1848–49, and 1853–54.

It may be asked why self-respecting Scotsmen should have been content to live in such conditions. Some were quite satisfied; they did not understand—most medical men even did not understand—how closely connected dirt and over-crowding were with disease, and if you had found fault with them they would at once have quoted the proverb "the clartier the cosier." Higher wages would do such people no good, it was argued, for they would simply drink the increase. But though there was a great deal of unnecessary drinking in early nineteenth century Scotland—it was said in 1835 that Glasgow could boast one public-house for every fourteen families—the hardships which the majority of Scotsmen had to endure were not self-inflicted. Low wages and long hours were the rule everywhere, and, strange as it may seem, the conditions were worst in some of the most prosperous industries. The older generation of linen weavers, for example, found it more and more difficult to make ends meet. The boom in the linen industry had attracted newcomers, many of them starving Irishmen who were willing to accept a lower wage than the Scot could live on; women, too, who had once worked only in the spinning-mills, made their way into the weaving-sheds in larger and larger numbers. So, with a superabundance of workers to choose from, the manufacturer could reduce wages and disregard the protests of the old-fashioned weaver. A weaver was lucky if he got ten shillings a week; he might have to be content with seven, while many of the women had to accept five. Nor was that all. Hours of work were intolerably long: in Dundee, for example, the spinners and weavers began work at half past five in the morning, winter and summer, and finished at seven in the evening. They were not pent up in the factory all the time, it is true; they were allowed one interval of half an hour for breakfast and another half-hour for dinner. Nowadays we should count it an intolerably hard day's work for a grown man; then it was not thought too hard for boys and girls, for hundreds of these mill and factory workers had not reached the age of fourteen.

The plight of some miners was even worse than that of the factory workers. Till 1799 many Scottish miners were bound for life to the mine in which they worked, as their fathers and grandfathers had been before them. The act of 1799, which abolished this system, did nothing to remove some even worse evils connected with the Scottish mines. The very worst were too hideous for description; one may say, however, that women and girls were employed to do the work which later was done by pit ponies, and that the hours of work for all, men, women, and children, were cruelly long.

The legislation which by successive stages reduced working hours in industry and eliminated child-labour was British legislation, and is part of British history. But such legislation was only one small part of the answer to the problems raised by the industrial revolution.

The care of the poor, traditionally a function of the Church as the agency of Christian charity, did not become the responsibility of the civil authorities until nearly the middle of the nineteenth century. Although earlier acts of Parliament had made provision for the levying of an assessment for the relief of the poor, few parishes had found it expedient to operate such an assessment. The main burden had therefore remained with the Church, and was organised by the kirk-session of each parish. Funds came from "mortifications" or bequests, fines imposed by the session on offenders against morality, various fees collected by the session and, still the most important item, the collections taken at services (which, of course, in days when the minister's stipend was paid, and the church built and maintained, by the heritors, were not required for the general expenses of the congregation). The collections, however, were meagre, too often consisting mainly of the smallest coins and, what was worse, of base money, with the consequence that the allowances paid to paupers were insignificant. The system was not hopelessly inadequate in a mainly rural Scotland, where cash was a relatively small item in almost everyone's budget and where the community spirit of the neighbourhood could be relied on to produce assistance to the poor in the form of enough food to keep body and soul together. But its breakdown was almost inevitable as people concentrated in the growing industrial towns. In Glasgow an attempt was indeed made, under the valiant ministry of Thomas Chalmers, to maintain the whole welfare work of a large slum parish from the alms collected by the kirk-session, but

PLATE 67

THE 'NAIRNSHIRE'

Built as a full-rigged iron ship, of 1027 tons gross, by Dobie and Co., Glasgow. She was engaged for many years in the wool trade to Australia and her rig was later reduced to that of a barque, as seen here.

PLATE 68 THE R.M.S. QUEEN MARY

Laid down in the yard of John Brown and Co., Clydebank, in 1930, this famous Cunarder was not launched until 26 September 1934, as work on her was suspended during the depression. Her gross tonnage is 81,237 and on her sea-trials (seen here) her sixteen steam turbines, geared to four propeller shafts, gave her a speed exceeding 30 knots.

this last effort of the old regime worked only because of the personality and energy of Chalmers himself. In general, the urban parishes could now hardly avoid adopting assessment for a poor rate, and this in turn attracted paupers to the towns, so that the rate became a considerable burden. It was, however, the Disruption that dealt the final blow to the antiquated system of poor relief: now that the majority of the inhabitants of Scotland had no longer any connection with the Established Church, it seemed hardly fair that its kirk sessions should retain the exclusive burden of administering relief to the poor; besides, earlier secessions had already reduced church-collections, and it now became clear that they could no longer be regarded as a serious source for a poor fund.

The new Poor Law of 1845 made such provisions that it became almost essential for a parish to impose an assessment. There was to be an inspector of poor in each parish, and a parochial board, subject to a central Board of Supervision. Paupers were to be rigorously removed to their parish of "settlement" (that is, where they had been born or had lived for a certain period), and this relieved the towns. Poor relief continued to be administered on a parish basis until well into the twentieth century, but in the course of time a distinction was made between the different kinds of poverty, and provision for the relief of some kinds was taken over by the government. For example, one principal cause of pauperism was simply old age, and this burden was removed from the parishes with the introduction of the Old Age Pension in 1908. Unemployment, again,—the problem of "the able-bodied poor"—had never in earlier times been recognised as qualifying for relief, and was still not so recognised in 1845, but in the twentieth century Unemployment Insurance on a national basis dealt with this problem too. Finally, "Public Assistance," the successor of Poor Relief, became "National Assistance," also the concern of the central government. The Parochial Boards, as established in 1845, had consisted of all owners of land over a certain value, the magistrates in burghs, and the kirk-sessions, as well as elected representatives. They were large and unwieldy, and in 1895 were replaced by small Parish Councils, elected by the people. About the same time the central Board of Supervision was replaced by the Local Government Board.

Next to the relief of poverty was the problem of public health. One essential, if there were to be sanitary conditions in the towns, was a plentiful piped water supply. To supplement local wells by water piped from the nearby hills was not a novelty, for in Edinburgh water had been brought into the town from the springs at Comiston in the late seventeenth century, but the introduction of water directly to houses came much later, and only in the late nineteenth century did it become the invariable practice to lay water into each individual house or flat as it was built. Glasgow, dependent earlier largely on polluted streams, was furnished with an ample supply of pure water from Loch Katrine in 1859, and this had an immediate effect in reducing the deaths from epidemics. In Edinburgh a supply from the Pentland Hills was developed about 1820, and another from the Moorfoots in 1879.

Another necessity was medical attention. Again it was not a novelty for local authorities to pay physicians, but such efforts had in the past been intermittent, and, besides, there was need for medical action to *prevent* disease, which was almost a completely new idea of the nineteenth century. "Medical police," as it was called, included the appointment in the middle of the century of local medical officers of health in parishes and burghs and there was a succession of Public Health Acts giving powers for the removal of nuisances and the notification of infectious diseases. Hospitals, which had previously been inadequately provided by private charity, also became in part the responsibility of local authorities in the nineteenth century, when separate hospitals for infectious diseases made their first appearance.

As to housing conditions, one of the difficulties arose from the very merits of Scottish buildings, which were constructed to endure, and too often lasted until they deteriorated into slums. It is true that a tall "land" occasionally fell down, the best known instance being in Edinburgh, when the cry of a boy buried in the debris—"Heave awa', lads, I'm no deid yet"—has been immortalised. But usually they had to be pulled down, and it was here that the authorities first intervened. Already by the middle of the nineteenth century housing conditions in Glasgow were so bad that the municipality had to consider acquiring the worst tenements and destroying them, and in 1866 and 1867 both Glasgow and Edinburgh had slum clearance schemes. Regulations were also made, from 1862 onwards, for a minimum size of rooms and for the proportion between the height of houses and the breadth of the streets. The building of new houses, however, continued to be almost entirely a private responsibility, and it must be remarked that down to 1914 private enterprise did provide the houses, in numbers more adequate than they have ever been since, and also, latterly, of very high quality. In the nineteenth century the population more than doubled, and all these additional people were housed, with houses to spare. The improvement in quality is illustrated by the fact that the number of one-roomed houses was halved between 1861 and 1911, while in the rural areas the windowless "black house," of which there were 8,000 in 1861, had virtually disappeared by 1911. In fact, new Scottish housing for all classes reached a peak in the early years of this century; but of course there was still a vast heritage of unsatisfactory property left over from earlier generations. It was only after the First World War that the provision of houses became to any extent a function of the government or of local authorities, and those bodies have not yet succeeded in making houses as plentiful as they were in the days of private enterprise before 1914.

Poor relief, public health, town planning, and housing all tell the same tale of the extension of the work of the government and the local authority. The same applied in the education of youth, which, like the care of the poor, was a function traditionally pertaining to the Church. An Education Act of 1696 had been in the main a repetition of acts passed earlier in the seventeenth century. In every parish the heritors were to provide a schoolhouse, and the master's salary (of 100-200 merks Scots) was to be borne half by the heritors and half by the tenants. This act was little more effective than earlier acts had been, for heritors were, not unnaturally, reluctant to impose taxes on themselves. In 1758 there were said to be one hundred and seventy five parishes without schools—that is, nearly one parish in five. And in the larger parishes a single school, even when one existed, was quite inadequate. In 1803 there was another Education Act, still within the framework of the old system. The schoolmaster's salary was now to be not less than 300 merks Scots and he was to have a "commodious house," which, however, was not to contain more than two rooms. Many of the occupants of these "palaces for dominies," as the heritors who had to find the money indignantly called them, were sound and enthusiastic scholars, willing to teach Latin and Greek to the son of the ploughman or of the village tradesman who aspired to enter the University. The main trouble was that there were not enough "dominies."

There were, however, other agencies which in one way or another supplemented the parochial schools. We must not forget the old grammar and other schools in the towns, which hammered away at the classics in the traditional manner and which had their imitators in a number of other schools which arose sometimes as a result of charitable bequests and sometimes as self-supporting bodies. Some of the charitable foundations, originally boarding schools or "hospitals," became day-schools in the nineteenth century, and some of them had a broader curriculum than the old grammar schools.

In rural areas, especially the Highlands and Islands, much was done by the Scottish Society for the Propagation of Christian Knowledge, which was founded in 1709 and which in 1711 established its first school—in St. Kilda of all places, where "nothing had been taught for many a dark and dreary generation but the art of catching fish and solan geese." By the beginning of the nineteenth century the Society had nearly 200 schools, with 13,000 pupils. The Society had to be careful not to take action which would relieve heritors of their legal obligations, and therefore could not establish a school in a parish where there was not already a parish school, but their schools were a very valuable supplement to the parish system in the extensive Highland parishes. At first these schools used English only, but latterly they were permitted to use Gaelic as well. The advantage of using Gaelic in the Highlands, however, led early in the nineteenth century to the foundation of various societies specifically for the foundation of Gaelic schools, and among them they established no less than 190 schools.

The "adventure" schools of which we hear so much were private ventures, and might include highly reputable establishments in towns but also a great many schools where some old man or woman would impart, in return for a small fee, the little knowledge which he or she had acquired. In 1833 there were in the northern and western districts 300 adventure schools, with 11,000 pupils.

BERWICK-ON-TWEED

From left to right the bridges are:—The railway bridge, the modern road bridge, and the old bridge of the early seventeenth century construction.

Sunday Schools must not be left out of account, because originally they were intended to give secular rather than religious education and were held on Sundays simply because that was the only day on which factory workers could attend.

Towards the middle of the nineteenth century there were two important developments which to some extent altered the general picture of Scottish education. Arising out of provision for the erection of schools in the new *quoad sacra* parishes, a Parliamentary grant was made towards the cost of Scottish education—the first intervention of the central government in this field; and the granting of money from the State involved the appointment of Inspectors by the State. Secondly, with the Disruption, the Free Church made it part of its function to provide schools to duplicate those which were in the hands of the establishment, and within ten years over seven hundred Free Church Schools had been established. The Episcopal Church and the Roman Catholic Church already had their own schools, and all the churches set up their own training colleges for teachers. This denominational element was the necessary consequence of the exclusion from the parish schools, until 1861, of any teachers who were not members of the Church of Scotland.

While, therefore, the number of schools throughout the country was very considerable, and had been growing in the nineteenth century, the changes brought about by the industrial revolution meant that great numbers of children were not receiving any schooling. Not only was there a vast migration of people from the country to the towns, with relatively little provision for increased schools and teachers to cope with them, but the demand for juvenile labour meant that many children were working long hours and had no time for schooling. In the country as a whole it was estimated in 1865 that two thirds of the children were at school, but in Glasgow only half were at school.

The Education Act of 1872 marks the beginning of the modern system and the end of the responsibility for education which had so long been shouldered mainly by the Churches, partly by voluntary agencies. A School Board, to be specially elected by ratepayers, was set up in every parish, and to these boards were transferred the parish schools; they could also purchase private schools and could accept the gift of denominational schools. Schools had to be adequate to receive all the children of the parish, and parents were compelled to send their children to school. Finance came from Parliamentary grants, fees and a local rate; the fees of paupers were to be paid by the Poor Fund. The payment of fees was abolished in 1894. From 1908, when school boards were permitted to provide meals, transport, maintenance and books, and compelled to provide medical inspection, the scope of education has continued to increase. The school leaving age, which at first was on the attainment of a certain standard, became fixed at fourteen, without exemption, in 1901. A central "Scotch" Education Department, as it was officially called until 1918, had been organised to supervise and co-ordinate the work of the School Boards, to provide Inspectors and to control examination standards.

The best parish schools had always proceeded to university entrance level. Otherwise, secondary education had been provided by the old grammar schools and their imitators. Such schools were allowed in 1872 to participate in Parliamentary grants for the erection, but not the maintenance, of school buildings. In 1878 school boards were given wider powers to provide secondary education, but the parish was as a rule too small a unit for this purpose, and the boards were also reluctant to incur the expense. They were driven towards it, however, by the need for providing teachers, who were trained through the pupil-teacher system, later the junior student system. The inspection of secondary schools was instituted in 1886, the Leaving Certificate in 1888.

In 1905 the Scottish Education Department took over the training colleges of the Church of Scotland and the United Free Church. In 1918 the denominational schools were transferred to the new education authorities, which gave grants, regulated the curriculum and appointed the teachers (who had, however, to be approved by the appropriate Church authority) and religious instruction was given as before.

The eighteenth century had seen many changes in the universities. One was the substitution of a system of professors, each responsible for a subject or subjects, for the old system of regenting, whereby one regent conducted the same class through all subjects for the whole of its academic life. In consequence it became easier to widen the curriculum, and this was done to some extent, especially in Medicine, but the really wide variety of university studies did not come until much later. Latin was abandoned as the language of lectures and there was a movement away from residence. In the nineteenth century the curriculum was further widened, and specialisation on the part of both teachers and students increased; there were many new chairs, there were new degrees in Law and Science, there were honours degrees in Arts, there was encouragement of research and the institution of research degrees. Numbers increased throughout both the eighteenth and nineteenth centuries. Edinburgh had erected new buildings—the present "Old College"—in the late eighteenth century, and Glasgow abandoned its old quarters for the new buildings at Gilmorehill in 1870. Women were admitted in the last years of the nineteenth century. Acts of 1858 and 1889 gave the universities new constitutions, setting up University Courts with control in financial matters and the right to hear appeals from the Senatus, and also General Councils to represent the graduates and Students' Representative Councils to represent the undergraduates.

The universities, unlike the schools, have so far preserved their administrative independence, but in the twentieth century, and especially after the Second World War, rising costs made financial independence no longer possible. The sums derived from endowments and fees had increasingly to be supplemented by government grants, which now make up four-fifths or more of the income of the universities. While there is as yet no question of the universities being taken over by the State, there is a tendency towards uniformity throughout Great Britain and towards the elimination of distinctive characteristics.

The school and university education available in Scotland in the eighteenth and nineteenth centuries may seem limited and narrow, and the lives of scholars and teachers poverty-stricken, when we look back from an age when education is something like a first charge on the budgets of local authorities and when money is expended lavishly on sumptuous buildings and equipment and on the subsidising of study. Yet Scottish education, in the days of greater austerity, was superior in quality to that of England and most other countries, because the Scots were then inspired, if not by a love of learning, at any rate by a respect for learning. At every level, from elementary schooling to the universities, Scottish standards were high, and Scottish achievements were outstanding. Again and again, in the eighteenth century and the early nineteenth, it was a Scot who led Britain in one field or another—David Hume in philosophy, William Robertson in history, Adam Smith in economics, Walter Scott in fiction, to mention only a few. In the very days when Scotland was only finding its feet economically, and hardly counted at all politically, its cultural importance was higher than at any other period.

The vast increase in administrative activity which arose in the nineteenth century from the social problems of industrial Scotland led to a transformation of the machinery of local government. Not only were new organs set up throughout the country to deal with poor relief and education, but in the burghs, where local councils, now democratically elected, already existed, these councils became responsible not only for the maintenance of order but also for the construction and maintenance of streets, lighting and cleansing, transport and water-supplies, and latterly the building and letting of houses. The county had hitherto been a less important administrative unit than either the burgh or the parish, and such county administration as there was had been largely in the hands of the commissioners of supply, who were the proprietors of land over a certain value and had originally been appointed in the seventeenth century merely to make assessment for the land tax. In 1889 the county was given its first real organ of local government, when elected county councils were set up.

The trend in the nineteenth century was to multiply local authorities, some of them responsible for only a single function, and ultimately there were the following: town councils, county councils, district committees, commissioners of supply, standing joint committees, parish councils, school boards, district boards of control (for lunacy) and distress committees (for assistance to the unemployed). It proved unsatisfactory to have a multitude of separate elected bodies, for it was difficult to maintain interest in the elections; and, besides, for certain purposes, such as the provision of secondary schools, the parish was too small a unit. The first move away from the smaller units came, in fact, in the Education Act of 1918, which gave only the largest towns their own Education Authorities and merged the smaller units in the counties; but the new Education Authorities were still separately elected bodies.

The Local Government Act of 1929 amounted to a revolution. All the *ad hoc* bodies were suppressed, so that of the existing units there remained only the county councils and the town councils, but new district councils (which had very limited powers) were established. The town councils of the smaller burghs, too, were stripped of many of their functions: burghs were divided into three categories—the four cities of Edinburgh, Glasgow, Dundee, and Aberdeen, where the town councils had full powers over all services, including education; twenty large burghs, which retained control of most public services except education; and one hundred and seventy eight small burghs, which lost most of their powers to the county councils and retained control of only such purely local matters as lighting and cleansing. In more recent years fire services, gas and electricity, have been taken over from the local authorities by national boards.

In central administration, too, the tendency in the nineteenth and the early twentieth centuries had been to appoint separate authorities for special purposes—the Board of Supervision (for Poor Law), the Board of Commissioners in Lunacy, the Prison Commissioners, the Fishery Board, the Board of Agriculture and the Education Department. The Board of Supervision became the Local Government Board in 1895 and the Board of Health in 1919. A separate Secretary for Scotland at last reappeared in 1885, and in the course of time centralised administration under his supervision took over the work of most of the old Boards, which were in 1928 nearly all replaced by "Departments" responsible to the Secretary. The Secretary's increased powers were marked by his elevation to the dignity of a Secretary of State in 1926 and he has subsequently been supplied with Under-Secretaries, each with a certain special responsibility for a particular branch of the government's work.

CHAPTER 29

MODERN SCOTLAND

EVER since 1603, and to a much greater extent since 1707, there had been a steady increase in the comings and goings between Scotland and England. Free trade between the two countries had meant that there were many business links, and we have seen how, in the eighteenth century, there was co-operation between Englishmen and Scotsmen in industrial projects. Government, too—wholly in its legislative aspect and largely in its administrative aspect—was centred in London, to which many Scots were in consequence drawn. England also became an educational centre for Scots. Despite the qualities of Scottish education, Oxford and Cambridge became the goal of ambitious Scots for university education, the English public schools for pre-university education. The Scot who had been entirely educated in England made his appearance, and his contribution to his own country was its further anglicisation, besides the introduction to Scotland of a class distinction in education which had previously been unknown. Again, the Union had opened to the Scots careers south of the Border, at every level from Cabinet ministries, through medical appointments, down to gardening. In the diplomatic service, for example, Scots were established in most of the important British embassies on the Continent in the second half of the eighteenth century; they owed their success to their sound education, their readiness for hard work, and their ability as linguists. By the later eighteenth century the success of the Scots in England was so strongly marked as to incur a good deal of resentment. It was the time of Dr. Johnson's remarks: when Boswell admitted, "I do indeed come from Scotland, but I cannot help it," Johnson retorted, "That, Sir, is what I find a very great many of your countrymen cannot help," and he added later, "The noblest prospect which a Scotchman ever sees is the high road that leads him to England." But the success of the Scots in England continued, throughout the nineteenth century and on into the twentieth: out of ten successive prime ministers of Great Britain six were Scots, and out of five successive archbishops of Canterbury three were Scots—to mention only the two highest dignities in Church and State.

So far as literature was concerned, Scots had been abandoned as a literary language early in the seventeenth century, after the Union of the Crowns, and the great series of Scottish contributions to English literature began quite early in the eighteenth century, with James Thomson, author of *The Seasons*, David Malloch (who changed his name to Mallet for the convenience of the English) and Beattie, author of *The Minstrel*. Among prose-writers one of the earliest to attain fame was Tobias Smollett. And besides learning to write English, the Scots were by the middle of the eighteenth century deliberately cultivating English speech. Boswell had not been long in London when it pained him to associate with Scots fresh from Scotland, and, although himself an Ayrshire man, he was presently remarking, "Mrs. Miller's abominable Glasgow tongue excruciates me."

Many influences, some of them unobtrusive, were all the time at work, helping to weld together the two peoples. There was, for one thing, the acceptance in Scotland not only of English literature but also of English history. For two hundred years now the two countries have been sharing an ever-growing body of English literature (much of it, indeed, written by Scots, and some of it by Irishmen), and this common heritage has given an English slant to education as conducted even in purely Scottish schools. But it has been even more telling that far more instruction has been given in English history than in Scottish history: the notion has been instilled into Scottish children that the two countries share the same past, the same historic heritage, which is by no means true; not only so, but the predominant view of Scottish history has tended to be that of English historians, who regard anything which is not English as quaint, backward or even (ignoring the tumultuous and bloodstained annals of their own country) barbarous.

Then the industrial revolution and the great social changes which accompanied it intensified class divisions in Scotland and emphasised the horizontal division into classes at the expense of the vertical division into nations. The Scottish "worker" has been easily persuaded that his interests are at one with those of the English "worker"; the unity of some industries throughout Great Britain, and in general the Trade Union movement and the Socialist Movement have militated against a sense of distinctness between the two countries.

A new unity of feeling has been fostered also by the relations between Britain and the rest of the world. In the exploration, colonisation, and development of the lands which used to form the British Empire, Scots played a part far out of proportion to their comparative numbers, and Scotland's share in this field has increased her sense of unity with England. At least of equal significance was the penetration into Scotland of a sense of sharing in British foreign policy and British wars. The many wars of the eighteenth century did not make much impression on the Scots, but a change came with the long wars against the French Revolution and Napoleon between 1793 and 1815. For a time war was really brought home to the people of this island, for there was serious danger of invasion and of defeat. The Scots by this time hated and feared the French as much as did the English, and the effects of that critical period in drawing the two peoples together were far-reaching. Anyone familiar with Scottish towns knows how often there is commemoration, in street names and monuments, of the Napoleonic wars—Wellington and Nelson, Trafalgar and Waterloo—whereas one will look in vain for memorials to the names of Wolfe and Clive, Plassey and Quebec (though an episode in a war with Spain is recalled by the place-name Portobello). The recurrent colonial and imperial wars of the nineteenth century gave many opportunities for Scottish regiments to show their fighting qualities, and the people of Scotland followed the campaigns with interest and pride.

The earlier monarchs of the House of Hanover made no attempt to appeal in person to the loyalty of their subjects in Scotland, but in 1822 George IV came to Edinburgh on a visit which did much to shape the future pattern of the relations of the royal family with the Scots, for he was presented as the heir of the House of Stewart and arrayed in the trappings of a Highlander. Queen Victoria acquired an Aberdeenshire home at Balmoral and established the tradition of a lengthy stay in Scotland each autumn by the sovereign and other members of the royal family. George V and his successors have paid fairly

Plate 70 A Clyde 'Puffer'
Familiar Hebridean transport: one of the ubiquitous Clyde 'Puffers' delivering coal on the beach at Iona.

Plate 71 Disused crofting land: Mingulay, Outer Hebrides

The human population of Mingulay left the island in 1910. After the immense labour of creating these acres of cultivable ground, clearing the stones to demarcate the crofts, and tilling it all by

A shepherd's cottage of modern type looks an incongruity here; but throughout the West we find that the sheep and their owners of today are gathering benefit from the toil of cultivators of regular summer visits to the Palace of Holyroodhouse as well. The links between Scotland and the reigning family were drawn closer when the Duke of York, afterwards George VI, married Lady Elizabeth Bowes-Lyon, of the ancient Scottish house of Earls of Strathmore, and their younger daughter, Princess Margaret, was born at her mother's family home, Glamis Castle.

One obviously important factor in bringing England and Scotland together was the vastly greater speed and ease of communications in the nineteenth century. Edinburgh was cut off from London in the days when a lumbering stage-coach was the only means of communication between the two. But in 1821 steamships began to ply between Leith and London. "The convenience of going to London by the steam-packet," wrote Sir Walter Scott in 1824, "which carries you on whether you wake or sleep, is so much preferable to a long land journey, that I took it . . . . The extreme rapidity of communication . . . is like to be attended with a mass of most important consequences—some, or rather most, of them good, but some also which are not to be viewed without apprehension. . . . Formerly in Edinburgh and other towns . . . the cry which was raised in the great mart of halloo and humbug (London) was not instantly echoed back, as it may be in the present day and present circumstances, when our opinion, like a small drop of water brought into immediate contiguity with a bigger, is most likely to be absorbed in, and united with, that of the larger mass." Soon after the steamship came the railway, and in more recent times the telegraph, the telephone and wireless, which have all helped to diminish the individuality of Scotland.

In the twentieth century, therefore, Scottish history has been, even more than in the nineteenth century, British history, and the development of Scottish life and institutions has been shaped mainly by trends affecting Britain as a whole, and often, indeed, by trends affecting the whole world. Communications have continued to be accelerated: as a result of the invention and improvement of the aeroplane, America may now be reached from Scotland as quickly as Glasgow could be reached from Edinburgh in a mid-eighteenth-century coach, and the significance of space and distance is in a fair way to being eliminated altogether. To take another example, in a different field, the wide extension of the activities of the government in the planning of the national economy, in the control of public services like transport, and in the provision of "National Insurance" to relieve the individual citizen of responsibility for his own welfare, from birth and before it until death and after it, has come out of what seems to be a general demand of the present age.

Not least important was the fact that Scotland, as part of Great Britain and as part of a world-wide Empire, was involved in two World Wars. She escaped very lightly in respect of material damage by direct enemy action, for, apart from some very heavy raids on Clydeside in the Second World War, destruction through air attack was negligible in comparison with what was suffered by England and by many continental countries. But the loss of life on the battlefield, in the Merchant Navy as well as in the Royal Navy, and in air operations, was heavy, and its effect imponderable. Certainly no consideration of the difficulties of Scotland since the First World War can leave out of account those one hundred thousand Scotsmen who were no longer alive after 1918 to help in shaping their country's future.

The history of the period between the wars is dominated by one feature—industrial depression. Like so much else in the twentieth century, this was not a phenomenon peculiar to Scotland, and at its peak, in 1931, it was actually part of a world-wide crisis. But Scotland, or at any rate certain parts of Scotland, suffered with exceptional severity. All the heavy industries and some of the textiles slumped, with devastating consequences in unemployment. At no time between 1919 and 1929 was the percentage of unemployed less than ten, and in 1931 the figure was nearly thirty per cent; in Dundee in 1931 the figure was thirty-seven per cent and among Clyde shipbuilders it was as high as sixty-five per cent. What this all meant in human suffering, not only material but moral, is unlikely ever to be understood except by those who experienced it. One incidental result of the depression was a further wave of emigration, which carried off still more of the young and enterprising Scots who might have made great contributions to the life of their country.

The underlying cause was a change in the emphasis of the world's economy. In the nineteenth century Britain's rapid industrialisation had given her an advantage over lands only partially or not at all industrialised, and had made practically the whole world a market for her products. Those days are gone, never to return. Scotland suffered severely during the depression between the wars precisely because her economy was over-concentrated in a limited field of heavy industry and textiles in a period when there was increasing competition from overseas and when there were also unexpected fluctuations in markets and in fashions. The world's steel-making capacity, for example, doubled between the end of the First World War and the end of the Second, and most of the increase was in countries which had previously been importers of steel. With a world-wide development of heavy engineering, Scotland can never again be a provider of the world's needs in ships and locomotives as she was in the nineteenth century. Linen, again, suffered after the First War largely because of a change of taste, which went far to eliminate the table-cloth. More recently another staple Scots product, coal, has begun to feel the effects of the competition of oil, which has superseded coal in ships and locomotives and for many other purposes. Another competitor of coal, in the production of electricity, is water-power, but in this field Scotland herself is a producer, on an ever-increasing scale.

Apart from world-wide changes, Scotland suffered also from the tendency of industry, within Britain itself, to move to the south. Some at least of the economic troubles were not peculiar to Scotland, for similar complaints came from the north of England. It would seem that the northward drift of industry, which set in during the eighteenth century, has recently been reversed; the tide has of late been flowing to the south, with its result in the continued development of the English Midlands and the London area, and it is hard to see what could have been done to check this process.

Whatever may happen within Britain, it is clear that competition from overseas, as other countries become industrialised, will go on, and markets will continue to be lost, so that in many branches of industry Scottish products will be mainly for Scottish needs and there can be export only of those products in the making of which Scotland has special advantages. Compensation is to be sought in the development of a variety of lighter industries—the making of electrical apparatus of every kind, typewriters and clocks, fountain-pens, furniture, and clothing. There have already been healthy developments along these lines. There are also some older light industries in which Scotland has certain advantages and which remain valuable for both British and foreign consumption—some branches of the woollen industry, brewing and distilling, for example.

The period since 1918 may emerge in perspective as one of those periods of rather painful adjustment through which the Scottish economy had passed more than once in earlier generations. We reviewed the difficulties in the period immediately after the Union and saw how they were overcome by the development of overseas commerce and of the linen industry. We saw in the late eighteenth century the collapse of the tobacco trade on which the prosperity of Glasgow had been founded, and the turning from tobacco—and also from linen—to cotton. That lasted less than a hundred years, when it in turn collapsed. Concentration was then, and not until then, on the heavy industries. Has Scotland been adjusting herself again, this time to the decline of the heavy industries? Whatever else it may do, history does teach us to take long views.

Behind and beyond modern industry of every kind there still lies the other part of Scotland's dual economic heritage—the industries based on the products of her soil, her rivers and her seas. These industries include the production of grain and other crops for human and animal consumption, the raising of cattle and sheep, the processing in various ways of hides and wool, and also the fisheries. We regard, quite rightly, the second and later heritage, based largely on the exploitation of Scotland's mineral resources, as the core of the Scottish economic structure; but we must not forget that the older heritage is the more constant of the two.

Recent years have seen great strides in the mechanisation of nearly all operations connected with agriculture, and this development at once compensates for the shortage of labour in the rural areas and, by making every operation more speedy, to some extent overcomes the difficulties caused by adverse weather. There are, it must be admitted, certain factors working to the detriment of Scottish agriculture, and they are the more regrettable in that there is, and is likely to continue to be, a world shortage of food: extravagant inroads have been made on agricultural land by the wanton extension of the towns, which have in the main been planned of late in ways foreign to the traditional Scottish type of building, which favoured compact terraces and flats; people continue to migrate from the country to the towns, and the educational system, which removes most country children from their homes at the age of twelve to give them an urban education, threatens rural communities with extinction; and there is a tendency for countryfolk to make no attempt to rely on their own resources but to look to the towns for the supply even of commodities like bread and milk. In the Highlands and Islands land continues to go out of cultivation, but here and there a good deal of energy is going into the breaking in of moorland and the re-seeding of land which has been only rough pasture; moreover, the Highlands are being used as never before for the growing of trees, which now cover hundreds of square miles of formerly bare mountain-sides.

The fisheries present a picture of fluctuation. The great days of the herring industry proved to be short-lived, and that branch of fishing is now a mere shadow of what it was a generation ago. Nor have Scottish deep-sea trawlers competed with entire success against their English rivals. As a result, many once-flourishing ports are in decay, and the export of fish is almost a thing of the past, while more and more foreign fishing vessels—Polish, Russian, Norwegian, German, Belgian, and others—are constantly at work in Scottish waters. On the other hand, the small Scottish seine-netters and liners (many of them adaptable also for herring-fishing during the season) bring their crews a very good living and provide fish of superior quality.

There has never, since the Second World War, been a reversion to anything like the unemployment figures of the inter-war depression. Yet employment figures themselves are not necessarily an indication of a healthy economy: the trouble is that an increasing proportion of the employment is now in occupations like entertainment, transport, administration, distribution, and other services. Besides, owing to the lower birth-rate of recent times and the greater expectation of life, the proportion of aged people in the community has grown, while at the other end the raising of the school-leaving age has also reduced the number of workers. To this extent the burden on the productive workers has steadily become greater.

Yet the fact remains that there has been a high level of employment in recent years, and wages have soared. These developments, taken along with the provision by the State of pensions and allowances, have eliminated want and have brought about a startlingly improved standard of living for those who used to be called the working classes. At the same time, the pressure of taxation, ever since the First World War, has gone a long way to impoverishing, comparatively, the upper and middle classes of society. Up and down the country, estates have had to be sold, and it is very rare to find a great mansion still in use simply as a private residence: some have been demolished, others turned over to some institutional purpose, and a few pay their way by being turned into showplaces. At last stirred to an awareness of the great cultural loss to the nation resulting from the levelling effects of taxation, the government has recently made grants for the maintenance and restoration of historic buildings in private hands, and the National Trust for Scotland (a voluntary organisation) has also done much to relieve owners of the burden of trying to maintain the fine houses characteristic of a very different Scotland.

Scottish politics, like the Scottish economy, were in the nineteenth century essentially British rather than peculiarly Scottish. Yet there were one or two significant differences. For Britain as a whole there was a recurrent swing of the pendulum between the two great parties, but this was the result of the oscillations in England. In Scotland, only once between 1832 and 1918 did a general election fail to produce a majority of Liberal members of Parliament. After 1918, however, the Liberal party decayed. Already, as a result of a split over the question of Home Rule for Ireland, in 1886, the Liberal Unionists had broken away, and had in time become merged in the Conservative Party. Now the radicals among the Liberals went over to the growing Socialist Party. The Scottish Liberal M.P.'s dwindled in number until by the middle of this century there was only one. In the new situation, the two principal parties—Conservatives and Socialists—were more evenly balanced; the pendulum swung in Scotland after 1918, but recent general elections have shown that the number of voters who change their allegiance is now small and that there is something like a new stability, this time in the shape of an approach to equilibrium between the two parties. Moreover, while between the wars representatives of smaller groups—the Independent Labour Party and the Communist Party—were able to win and hold seats, more recently the chances of any candidate other than a representative of one of the main parties have been remote indeed.

From the middle of the eighteenth century until the middle of the nineteenth the Union had been virtually unchallenged, but during the last hundred years and more there has been recurrent agitation against the Union—not a steadily mounting opposition, but rather a series of waves, each of which has, after a few years, spent its force. In 1853 there appeared a National Association for the Vindication of Scottish Rights, which had some influential support and which organised well-attended meetings in both Edinburgh and Glasgow at which resolutions were passed asking for a Secretary for Scotland and for increased Scottish representation in the House of Commons. There was criticism also, as there has often been since, of the use of the style "Queen of England" and of the proportions in which the expenditure of public money was distributed between the two countries.

A second phase of agitation began about 1880, when the term "Home Rule" was "distinctly and loudly mentioned." One result was the appointment of a Secretary for Scotland (1885), another the foundation of the Scottish Home Rule Association (1886). The Liberal Party was now officially committed to Home Rule for Ireland, and it was logical to consider a similar arrangement for Scotland. Besides, a separate Scottish legislature made a very special and practical appeal to the Scottish Liberals, since the voting record of Scotland suggested that in such a legislature they would have a permanent majority. The party as a whole, however, was not profoundly moved, and although resolutions in favour of Scottish Home Rule were brought forward in the House of Commons in 1893 and 1894 they attracted little interest, let alone support.

The Liberal Party was out of power from 1895 to 1906, but when it returned to office a fresh wave of Scottish sentiment did produce results. A request, often made before, for a special standing committee to deal with Scottish bills in the House of Commons, was granted in 1907, and this Scottish Grand Committee has functioned ever since, latterly with increased powers. Home Rule Bills were drawn up and introduced in 1908 and 1911, without reaching a decisive stage, and yet again, with better prospects, in 1913 and 1914. Thereafter the First World War meant that such an issue would have to be shelved, but in 1922 a Home Rule Bill was again produced and the Liberal Party remained formally committed to the cause of Home Rule. After 1922, however, the Liberal Party ceased to be an effective force in British politics, and the prospects of the achievement of a separate legislature through the support of a great political party faded. The Socialist Party did seem for a time in the 1920s likely to inherit the Liberals' interest in devolution, and some individual Scottish Socialists did support Government of Scotland Bills in 1926 and 1929. But no Socialist government in power has ever shown any disposition to further such a cause.

The obvious futility of relying on one of the great parties led to the foundation of separate Scottish Nationalist Parties, which have repeatedly, during the last thirty years, put forward candidates at elections. But the fortunes of such candidates at general elections have been an unbroken tale of defeats and often of lost deposits. Only once, at a by-election in 1945, has a Nationalist candidate been returned, and he was promptly unseated at the next general election. There is no doubt whatever not only that a strong sentiment in favour of Home Rule persists and also that some separate Scottish legislative body offers certain advantages which are apparent to men of very diverse views and interests. Yet, however much can be said in favour of Home Rule, when the Scottish voters go to the polls they vote on British political issues and for one of the British political parties—a measure of the absorption of Scotland in Great Britain.

The general picture of the last two hundred and fifty years, since the Union, is one of a process of the assimilation of Scotland to England. But there have been trends running the other way, for many recent developments have fostered Scottish national sentiment and the sense of Scotland's distinctness. While political agitation has not led to a measure of legislative devolution, it has led to administrative devolution, with the setting up of separate Scottish departments for a great many governmental functions like Education, Health, Agriculture and so forth. Although the Scottish vernacular, as a spoken tongue, has gradually given way to English, it was revived as a literary language in the eighteenth century by Allan Ramsay, Fergusson and Burns, and has been kept alive ever since. Even although not one

Plate 72 St. Andrew's House, Edinburgh
Headquarters of the Scottish Government Departments.

PLATE 73

THE 'HONOURS OF SCOTLAND', EDINBURGH CASTLE

person in a hundred may ever read the vernacular works of Scottish poets, the fact that they exist has helped to maintain a sense of national identity. Early in the nineteenth century there was the romantic movement in historical writing, associated mainly with the name of Sir Walter Scott, and this spread widely, if perhaps inaccurately, among the people of Scotland and of other lands, some acquaintance with Scotland's past as something of marked individuality. In the same period there began the serious study of Scottish history from original record sources, which has gone on ever since. In recent years a little has been done in schools, and more in universities, to study Scottish history as a serious subject and so to counteract the influence of the much more general attention still given to English history. On a very different plane—probably in descent from the romantic movement of the early nineteenth century—there has been a lively cultivation, most of it deplorably unhistorical, of clans and tartans, kilts and bagpipes, and a very successful attempt to persuade the people of Scotland that they are a Celtic people. It is something of a curiosity that the Highlands, which ceased two hundred years ago to play an important part, relatively, in Scottish political and economic life, are now in a fair way to conquering the whole country in the social and cultural sphere. The outcome of all those varied developments is that after two and a half centuries of political union, and after perhaps ten centuries of southern influence, Scotland still preserves a national identity which may be difficult to define but is none the less real.

LIST OF CHIEF EVENTS

	A.D.
Agricola invades North Britain	80
Battle of Mons Graupius.	84
Invasion of Severus	208
St. Ninian at Whithorn	*circa* 400
End of the Roman government in Britain	*circa* 430
St. Columba lands in Iona	563
Battle of Nechtansmere (Dunnichen)	685
Northmen plunder Iona	802
Kenneth MacAlpin becomes king of Picts and Scots	843
Battle of Carham won by Malcolm II	1018
Duncan, grandson of Malcolm II, succeeds to Strathclyde	1018
Duncan I defeated and slain by Macbeth	1040
Marriage of Malcolm Canmore and Margaret	1070
Magnus Barelegs acquires the Western Islands	1098
Battle of the Standard	1138
The Treaty of Falaise, by which William the Lion surrenders the Independence of Scotland to Henry II	1174
Richard I acknowledges the Independence of Scotland	1189
Alexander II conquers Argyll	1222
Treaty of York defines the Border	1237
Battle of Largs	1263
Western Islands acquired by Scotland	1266
Accidental death of Alexander III at Kinghorn	1286
Death of the Maid of Norway	1290
Edward I awards the Scottish Crown to John Balliol	1292
John Balliol dethroned by Edward I	1296
Battle of Stirling Bridge	1297
Battle of Falkirk	1298
Execution of Wallace	1305
Coronation of Robert Bruce	1306
Battle of Bannockburn	1314
Burgh representatives at Parliament	1326
Treaty of Northampton	1328
Death of Robert Bruce	1329
Accession of David II	1329
Edward Balliol invades Scotland	1332
Battle of Halidon Hill	1333
Battle of Neville's Cross	1346
Accession of Robert II, the first of the Stewart Kings	1371
Battle of Otterburn (Chevy Chase)	1388
The Clan Fight at Perth	1396
Death of the Duke of Rothesay	1402
Burning of the Lollard, James Resby	1407
Battle of Harlaw	1411
Foundation of the University of St. Andrews	1412
Burning of Paul Crawar	1433

LIST OF CHIEF EVENTS

Event	A.D.
Assassination of James I at Perth	1437
Foundation of the University of Glasgow	1451
Fall of the Black Douglases	1455
Accidental death of James II at the Siege of Roxburgh Castle	1460
Orkney and Shetland Islands acquired by Scotland	1468-9
St. Andrews made an Archbishopric	1472
Execution of James III's favourites at Lauder Bridge	1482
Battle of Sauchieburn and Assassination of James III	1488
End of the Lordship of the Isles	1493
Foundation of the University of Aberdeen	1495
Education Act	1496
Marriage of James IV and Margaret Tudor	1503
Battle of Flodden and Death of James IV	1513
Burning of Patrick Hamilton	1528
Endowment of the College of Justice	1532
The Rout of Solway Moss and Death of James V	1542
Burning of George Wishart	1546
Murder of Cardinal Beaton	1546
Battle of Pinkie	1547
Bond of the Lords of the Congregation	1557
Return of John Knox from the Continent	1559
"The Reformation Parliament" : First Book of Discipline	1560
Return of Mary from France	1561
Marriage of Mary and Darnley	1565
Murder of Riccio	1566
Murder of Darnley	1567
Marriage of Mary and Bothwell	1567
Battle of Langside	1568
Mary's Flight to England	1568
Murder of the Regent Moray	1570
Regent Lennox slain	1571
Death of John Knox	1572
Death of the Regent Mar; Morton Regent	1572
Fall of Edinburgh Castle	1573
Second Book of Discipline	1578
Raid of Ruthven	1582
University of Edinburgh founded	1582
Execution of Mary	1587
Act authorising Presbyterian Government	1592
Gowrie Conspiracy	1600
Union of the Crowns of England and Scotland	1603
Episcopacy re-established	1610
Education Acts	1616, 1633
The Five Articles of Perth	1618
Death of James VI	1625
Act of Revocation	1625
Charles's Visit to Scotland	1633
Scottish Prayer Book	1637
Riot in the Church of St Giles	1637
The National Covenant	1638
Episcopacy abolished by the General Assembly at Glasgow	1638
First Bishops' War	1639

	A.D.
Second Bishops' War	1640
Solemn League and Covenant	1643
Battle of Philiphaugh	1645
The Engagement	1647
Battle of Preston	1648
Execution of Charles I	1649
Charles II proclaimed King	1649
Execution of Montrose	1650
Battle of Dunbar	1650
Battle of Worcester	1651
Scotland under the Commonwealth	1651
Scotland under the Protectorate	1653
Restoration of Charles II	1660
Restoration of Episcopacy	1661
The Pentland Rising	1666
First Letter of Indulgence	1669
Establishment of High Court of Justiciary	1672
Murder of Archbishop Sharp	1679
Battle of Drumclog	1679
Battle of Bothwell Bridge	1679
Sanquhar Declaration	1680
Test Act	1681
Death of Charles II	1685
Earl of Argyll's Invasion	1685
Three Letters of Indulgence	1687
James VII deposed	1689
Battle of Killiecrankie	1689
Highlanders defeated at Dunkeld	1689
Presbyterianism re-established	1690
Abolition of Committee of Articles	1690
Massacre of Glencoe	1692
Education Act	1696
The First Darien Expedition	1698
Death of William III	1702
Scottish Act of Security	1704
Union of the Parliaments of England and Scotland	1707
Attempted French Invasion of Scotland	1708
Patronage restored	1712
Death of Anne	1714
Jacobite Rising	1715
Battle of Sheriffmuir	1715
Malt-Tax Riots	1725
Death of George I	1727
Porteous Mob	1736
Jacobite Rising	1745
Battle of Culloden	1746
Abolition of Heritable Jurisdictions	1747
Death of George II	1760
Accession of George III	1760
Carron Iron Works founded	1760
James Small invents the swing plough	1763
James Watt patents his steam engine	1769

LIST OF CHIEF EVENTS

	A.D.
Deepening of the Clyde begun	1770
Andrew Meikle invents his threshing machine	1784
Opening of Forth and Clyde Canal	1790
Thomas Muir sentenced to Botany Bay	1793
David Mushet discovers blackband ironstone	1801
Bell's Steamboat—"The Comet"	1812
"The Radical War"	1820
James Neilson patents his hot blast furnace	1828
First Reform Act	1832
Burgh Reform Act	1833
The Disruption	1843
New Poor Law	1845
Second Reform Act	1868
Education Act	1872
Patronage abolished	1874
Secretary for Scotland restored	1885
Third Reform Act	1885
County Councils established	1889
Union of the Free Church and the United Presbyterian Church—the United Free Church	1900
Representation of the People Act	1918
Union of the United Free Church and the Church of Scotland	1929

LIST OF SOVEREIGNS

	A.D.
Malcolm II	1005–1034
Duncan I, grandson	1034–1040
Macbeth	1040–1057
Malcolm III (Canmore), son of Duncan I	1057–1093
Donald Bane, brother	1093–1094
Duncan II, son of Canmore	1094
Donald Bane (second reign)	1094–1097
Edgar, son of Canmore	1097–1107
Alexander I, brother	1107–1124
David I, brother	1124–1153
Malcolm IV, grandson	1153–1165
William the Lion, brother	1165–1214
Alexander II, son	1214–1249
Alexander III, son	1249–1286
Margaret (The Maid of Norway), grand-daughter	1286–1290
First Interregnum	1290–1292
John Balliol, descendant of David I	1292–1296
Second Interregnum	1296–1306
Robert I, descendant of David I	1306–1329
David II, son	1329–1371
Robert II, nephew	1371–1390
Robert III, son	1390–1406
James I, son	1406–1437
James II, son	1437–1460
James III, son	1460–1488
James IV, son	1488–1513
James V, son	1513–1542
Mary, daughter	1542–1567
James VI, son (James I of England)	1567–1625
Charles I, son	1625–1649
Charles II, son	1649–1651
Commonwealth and Protectorate	1651–1660
Charles II	1660–1685
James VII (II of England), brother	1685–1689
William II (III of England) and Mary II, nephew and daughter	1689–1694
William II (alone)	1694–1702
Anne, daughter of James VII	1702–1714
George I, great-grandson of James VI	1714–1727
George II, son	1727–1760
George III, grandson	1760–1820
George IV, son	1820–1830
William IV, brother	1830–1837
Victoria, niece	1837–1901
Edward VII, son	1901–1910
George V, son	1910–1936
Edward VIII, son	1936
George VI, brother	1936–1952
Elizabeth, daughter	1952–

GENEALOGIES

GENEALOGY OF THE FAMILY OF DUNCAN I

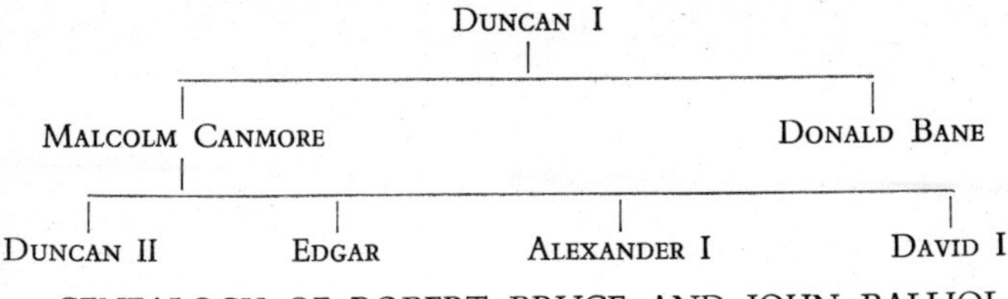

GENEALOGY OF ROBERT BRUCE AND JOHN BALLIOL

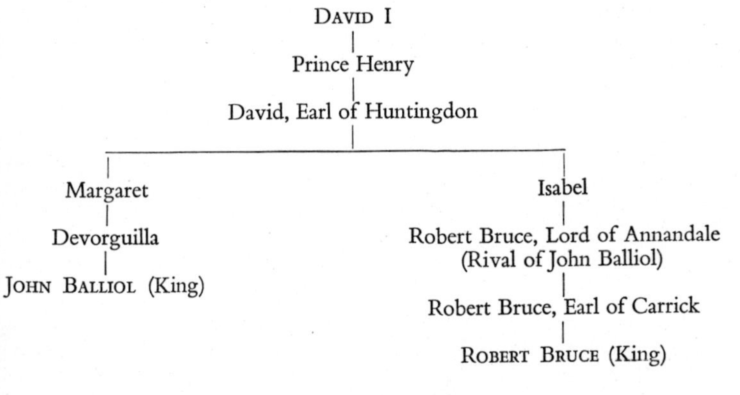

THE STEWART LINE

ROBERT I (The Bruce)

Marjory, married to Walter the High Steward

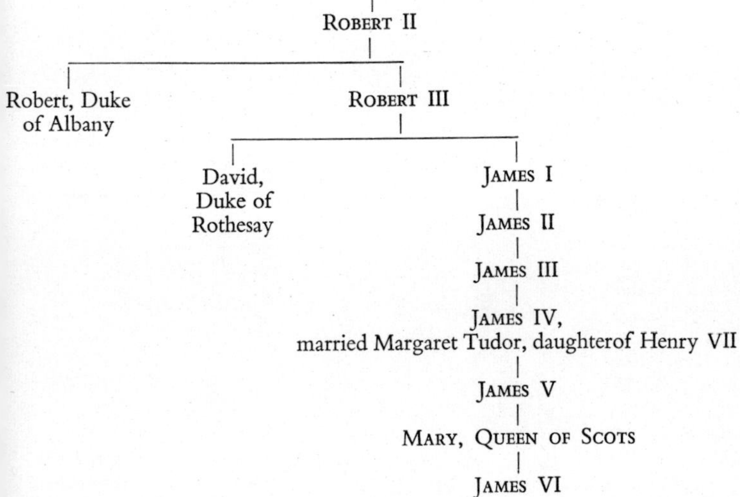

TABLE SHOWING HOW THE CROWNS OF SCOTLAND AND ENGLAND WERE UNITED

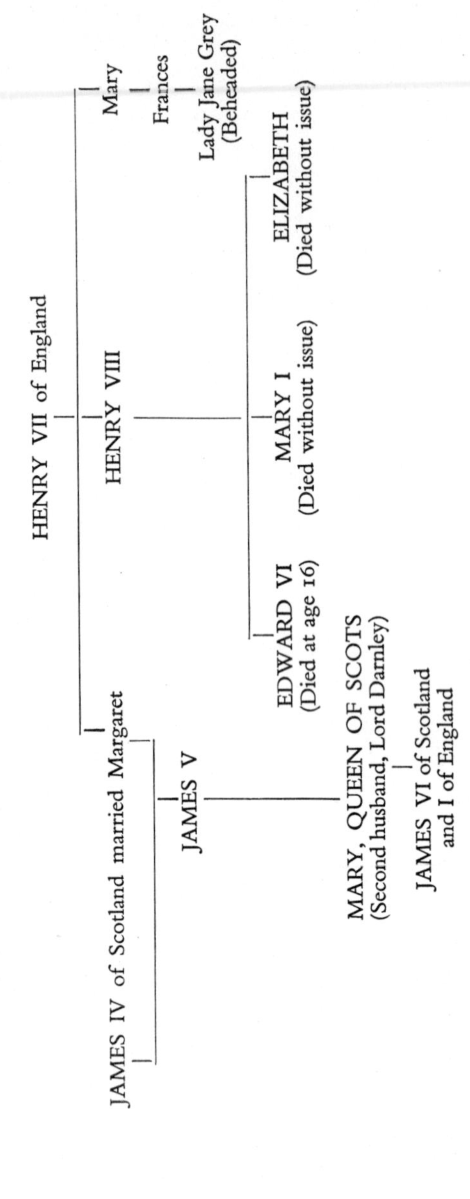

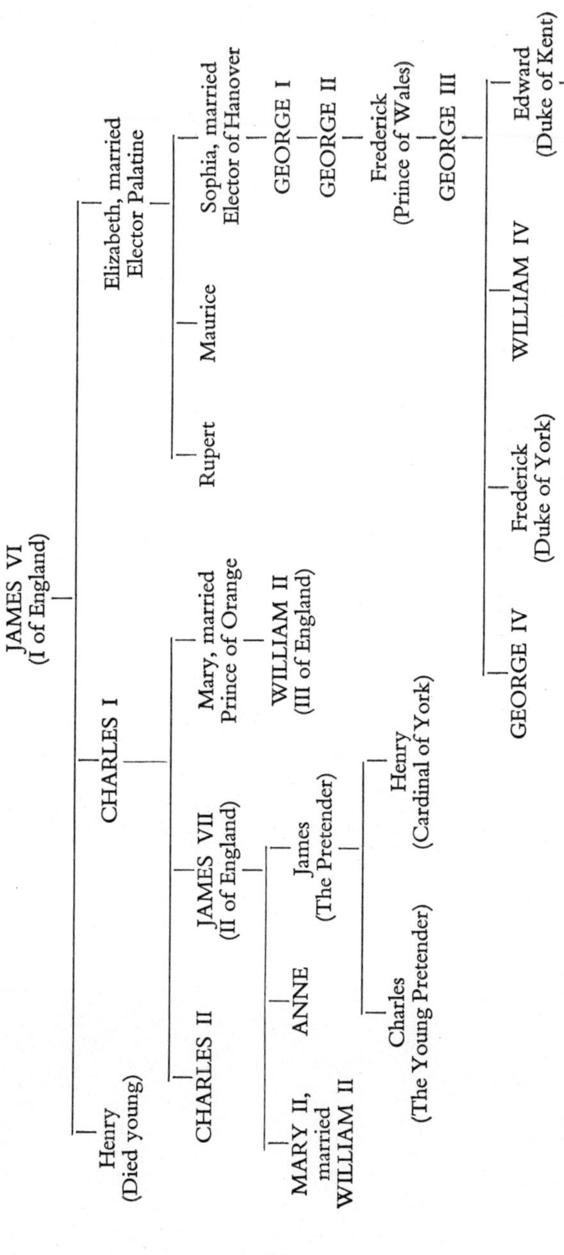
HOUSE OF STEWART AND HOUSE OF HANOVER
JAMES VI
(I of England)
Henry
(Died young)
CHARLES I
Elizabeth, married
Elector Palatine
CHARLES II
JAMES VII
(II of England)
Mary, married
Prince of Orange
Rupert
Maurice
Sophia, married
Elector of Hanover
MARY II,
married
WILLIAM II
ANNE
James
(The Pretender)
WILLIAM II
(III of England)
GEORGE I
GEORGE II
Charles
(The Young Pretender)
Henry
(Cardinal of York)
Frederick
(Prince of Wales)
GEORGE III
GEORGE IV
Frederick
(Duke of York)
WILLIAM IV
Edward
(Duke of Kent)
VICTORIA

INDEX

INDEX